Lucy Worsley

AGATHA CHRISTIE

A Very Elusive Woman

HODDER

First published in Great Britain in 2022 by Hodder & Stoughton
An Hachette UK company

This paperback edition published in 2023

2

A CIP catalogue record for this title is available from the British Library

Paperback ISBN 9781529303919
ebook ISBN 9781529303896

Typeset in Bembo MT by Hewer Text UK Ltd, Edinburgh
Printed and bound in Great Britain by Clays Ltd, Elcograf S.p.A.

Hodder & Stoughton policy is to use papers that are natural, renewable
and recyclable products and made from wood grown in sustainable
forests. The logging and manufacturing processes are expected to
conform to the environmental regulations of the country of origin.

Hodder & Stoughton Ltd
Carmelite House
50 Victoria Embankment
London EC4Y 0DZ

www.hodder.co.uk

This book is dedicated with gratitude
to the memory of Felicity Bryan

'Mrs Christie is a very elusive person. I cannot be bothered with her.'

Contents

Preface: Hiding in Plain Sight   xiii

PART ONE: VICTORIAN GIRL – 1890s

1. The House Where I Was Born   3
2. Insanity in the Family   8
3. The Thing in the House   13
4. Ruined   20

PART TWO: EDWARDIAN DEBUTANTE – 1900s

5. Waiting for The Man   29
6. Best Victorian Lavatory   33
7. The Gezireh Palace Hotel   36
8. Enter Archibald   42

PART THREE: WARTIME NURSE – 1914–18

9. Torquay Town Hall   51
10. Love and Death   60
11. Enter Poirot   67
12. The Moorland Hotel   73

PART FOUR: BRIGHT YOUNG AUTHOR – 1920s

13. Enter London 79
14. Enter Rosalind 84
15. The British Mission 88
16. Thrillers 95

PART FIVE – 1926

17. Sunningdale 107
18. The Mysterious Affair at Styles 114
19. Disappearance 123
20. The Harrogate Hydropathic Hotel 134
21. Reappearance 156

PART SIX: PLUTOCRATIC PERIOD – 1930s

22. Mesopotamia 173
23. Enter Max 182
24. I Think I Will Marry You 188
25. Eight Houses 197
26. The Golden Age 210

PART SEVEN: WARTIME WORKER – 1940s

27. Beneath the Bombs 221
28. A Daughter's a Daughter 232
29. Life Is Rather Complicated 243
30. By Mary Westmacott 253

PART EIGHT: TAKEN AT THE FLOOD – 1950s

31. A Big Expensive Dream   263
32. They Came to Baghdad   270
33. Christie-Land after the War   280
34. Second Row in the Stalls   289
35. A Charming Grandmother   297

PART NINE: NOT SWINGING – 1960s

36. The Mystery of the Christie Fortune   305
37. A Queer Lot   315
38. Lady Detectives   324
39. To Know When to Go   330

PART TEN: CURTAIN – 1970s

40. Winterbrook   337
41. After the Funeral   348

Sources   357
Acknowledgements   365
Notes   367
Index   399
Picture Acknowledgements   415

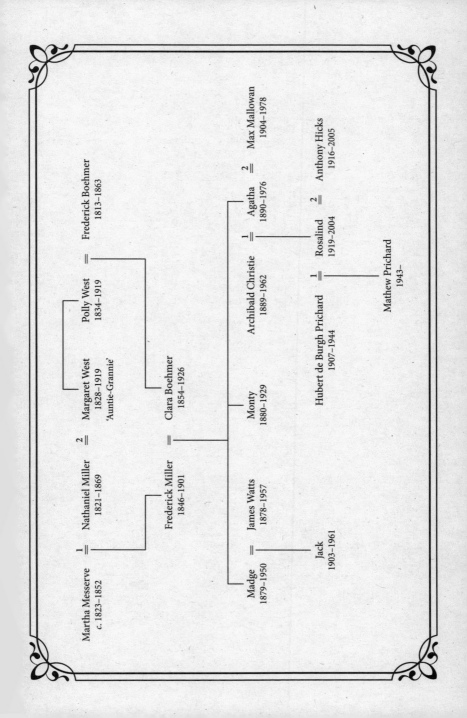

Preface: Hiding in Plain Sight

Agatha Christie was sitting quietly on the train when she overheard a stranger saying her name.

In the same carriage, she said, were 'two women discussing me, both with copies of my paperback editions on their knees.' The ladies had no idea of the identity of their matronly, middle-aged fellow passenger, and proceeded to discuss the most famous author in the world. 'I hear,' said one of the ladies, 'she drinks like a fish.'[1]

I love this story because it sums up so much about Agatha Christie's life.

Firstly, she told the anecdote in an interview published to celebrate her eightieth birthday in 1970. What a long and tumultuous life she'd had!

She was born into a luxurious, late-Victorian world: her family had inherited wealth, a house with a ballroom, and domestic staff galore. All this would be lost, leaving Agatha to earn her own living. Her eight decades also took her through two world wars, the decline of the British Empire, and nearly a century of violent social change. She'd chart all this in her eighty books. They're not just addictive entertainment, they're also a marvellous resource for the historian.

Secondly, there's the fact that *both* ladies on the train had Agatha Christie paperbacks. Of course they did. She was simply ubiquitous, especially in the post-war period when a 'Christie for Christmas' became an annual ritual. Christie is the best-selling author after Shakespeare and the Bible, so the cliché runs. What interests me, though, is the fact that not only does she hold that position, but holds it as *a woman*. And she wasn't just a novelist, either, she also remains history's most-performed female playwright. She was so successful people think of her as an institution, not as a breaker of new ground. But she was both.

Thirdly, the misconceptions. There are so many of them! To go back to the ladies on the train: far from drinking 'like a fish', Agatha was in fact teetotal. She didn't enjoy wine, and her favourite drink was a glass of neat cream. But the ladies assumed the writer must be addicted, damaged, unhappy.

And then, in the railway carriage, there's also the watchful presence of Agatha herself. Present but unnoticed, she was using life for her art. This particular incident, a novelist overhearing herself described as a drinker, made its way into Agatha's novel *Dead Man's Folly* when it happens to her fictional alter ego, the detective novelist Mrs Ariadne Oliver.

The scene also contains an essential truth about Agatha Christie as a person. Yes, she was easy to overlook, as is the case with nearly any woman past middle age. But Agatha deliberately played upon the fact that she seemed so ordinary. It was a public image she carefully crafted to conceal her real self.

If the two ladies on the train had asked her name, she wouldn't even have said 'Agatha Christie'. She'd have answered to 'Mrs Mallowan', the name she'd taken from the archaeologist, fourteen years younger than herself, to whom she'd made an impetuous marriage.

If asked her profession, she'd have said she had none. When an official form required her to put down what she did, the woman who's estimated to have sold two billion copies always wrote 'housewife'. And despite her gigantic success, she retained her perspective as an outsider and onlooker. She sidestepped a world that tried to define her.

In this book, I'd like to explore why Agatha Christie spent her life pretending to be ordinary, when in fact she was breaking boundaries. 'Nobody in the world,' she once said, 'was more inadequate to act the heroine than I was.'[2] Her view was partly her own extreme modesty. But it also had much to do with the world into which she was born, with its imperatives about what women could and couldn't do. This is a biography with a historical bent, the life of a woman whose story intertwines with that of the twentieth century.

When I told people I was writing about Agatha Christie, their first questions were often about the eleven dramatic days in 1926 when she 'disappeared', causing a nationwide hunt for her corpse. It's often been claimed she went into hiding in order to frame her husband for her murder. Was this true?

It's frequently said that Agatha remained silent about this notorious incident for the rest of her life. But that's incorrect. I've pieced together the surprising number of statements she *did* in fact make about it. And looking at them carefully, I believe much of the so-called mystery melts away.

Agatha shattered the twentieth century's rules for women. Females of her generation and social class were supposed to be slender, earn nothing, blindly adore their numerous children and constantly give themselves to others.

The only one of these Agatha completely fulfilled is the last. She did give the best of herself – her industry, her creativity, her occasional genius – to her readers. No wonder they still love her for it.

These days we don't need to put women on pedestals. And that means we have to face the fact that somewhere in the mass of contradictions making up Agatha Christie was a very dark heart. It's not just that she could dream up stories in which even children can kill. It's also that her work contains views on race and class that are unacceptable today.

But that doesn't mean we should tut-tut and look away. This matters, because Agatha Christie's writing has become a sort of shorthand for a typically English view of the world. The prejudices of her class and time, often revealed in her fiction, are part of the history of twentieth-century Britain.

And despite the surface conservativism of her work, I *also* believe that Agatha was quietly changing her readers' perceptions of the world in a positive way. Her stories show that a short, effeminate 'foreigner' with a funny name can beat evil, using brains not brawn. That even a fluttery old lady can bring nemesis to the wrongdoer. And that childless singletons – both Hercule Poirot and Miss Marple are unmarried – don't need a conventional family round them to thrive.[3]

Finally, I want to make it clear that Christie to her first readers wasn't 'nostalgic' or anything to do with 'heritage.' In my childhood, I used to watch cosy, cleaned-up versions of her stories on television. But the original novels were a product of a twentieth century that had broken with the past. Christie herself lived a 'modern' life: she went surfing in Hawaii; she loved fast cars; she was intrigued by the new science of psychology. And when her novels were published, they were thrillingly, scintillatingly 'modern' too.

In this book we're going to meet one of the great writers of the twentieth century, someone who's constantly disparaged and consistently misunderstood, whose towering achievements are almost hidden in plain sight.

But first let's go back to the beginning, to meet a little girl with flaxen hair.

❖ PART ONE ❖

Victorian Girl – 1890s

I

The House Where I Was Born

Agatha Miller grew up in a special place. Her childhood home stood on a hill above the seaside resort of Torquay in the south of Devon.

Ashfield, as the house was called, was a substantial Victorian villa set in a garden full of numerous, numinous trees. Agatha loved these great trees of the earliest garden she could remember: 'the big beech-tree, the Wellingtonia, the pines, the elms' and 'the green grass fairy ring by a monkey puzzle' where she played with her hoop.

The garden is gone, and Ashfield itself has long since been demolished. But if you walk between the blocks of flats that now occupy its plot, one thing remains the same. There are still distant views of the sea, sometimes with great heaps of storm clouds piled up over Brixham across the bay.

Despite all the adventures that were to come, Agatha's family home would remain the most significant place in her life. As an old lady, she came to write the story of her life which was published as *An Autobiography*. She both begins and ends at Ashfield, and with an image of herself in its garden: a 'solemn little girl with pale flaxen sausage-curls.'

So it was appropriate that when Agatha, daughter of Frederick and Clara Miller, was born on 15 September 1890, the event took place at home.

The midwife delivered baby Agatha on a Monday afternoon. She was her 36-year-old mother's third child, and seems to have been a delightful afterthought. Clara (really Clarissa) already had a daughter and a son who were respectively eleven and ten.

Also present at the birth was Agatha's Great-Aunt Margaret. As well as being aunt to Agatha's mother, Margaret was also stepmother to her father, which is why the Millers called her 'Auntie-Grannie'. Yes, this was a complicated family. You have to concentrate to remember who's who, almost as if following the plot of a detective novel. The complicated families often found in Agatha's fiction began life close to home.

The Miller family were significant enough for Agatha's arrival to be reported in both the local paper and the London *Morning Post*.[1] Her father, Frederick Alvah Miller, had contributed money to the recent rebuilding of the 800-seat All Saints Church down the hill where Agatha was baptised. The parish register recorded his 'rank or profession' as 'gentleman'. There were an impressive array of sponsors round the font: the wife of the president of the local hospital, an Honourable, and a future viscount.

Perhaps because this third baby seemed to Clara like an unexpected gift, it was nearly two whole months before she hired the usual nurse to help her look after the child.[2] Her baby was a beauty. Agatha's eyes are sometimes described as grey, sometimes blue, sometimes green.[3] In photographs, she is swaddled almost to immobility in the stiff white cotton frills and bonnets of the genteel late-Victorian baby.

Little Agatha seems to have wanted for nothing that an overstuffed, overfurnished, overconfident high-Victorian household could offer. Photographed as a tiny child, she stares haughtily from her miniature upholstered chaise longue; from between the protective knees of her solid-looking father; through a curtain of verdant leaves in the luscious Ashfield garden.[4]

Agatha also possessed something else that doesn't come across in the stiff genre of Victorian photography. It was *joie de vivre*. She was good at living in the present and was proud of her ability 'to make the best of everything'.[5] Her own grandson, to whom she was very close, says she had a peculiar 'gift for happiness'.[6] There was nothing prim or stereotypically Victorian about this particular Victorian girl.

As she grew, Agatha relished everyday pleasures: her piano lessons, her food, especially cakes and cream, although she utterly hated both the taste and smell of hot milk. She was full of high spirits. At seven, she described her greatest dislike as 'bedtime when you are wide awake', and her 'present state of mind' as 'excited'.[7] She was 'wildly untidy', and left possessions, notes, toys behind her in a trail as she moved through the house.[8]

And she was loved. It was both a blessing and a curse. Could anyone in later life ever encircle Agatha with affection as completely as her parents did, in this comfortable world of Ashfield and its gardens?

The other girls of Torquay, neighbours, or the pupils from her dancing class, remembered Agatha's physical ease and beauty. This might surprise people who can only picture her in her stately later condition when that love of cream was beginning to tell. 'I remember you,' recalled one fellow dancer, 'in a lovely accordion pleated silk dress, & laughing . . . you were like the sea nymph Thetis with your flowing golden hair.'[9]

Yet still you get no sense of this energy from the poses the young Agatha strikes for her photo-mad parents as the years roll on. Girlish Agatha proudly uses a watering can while wearing high boots; she sports tiny mutton-chop sleeves on a sailor-suit coat. As she grows older, her fine hair is corkscrewed with tongs, a sense of solemn mystery descends over her face. She sits impassively amid a pile of sticks with her dog George Washington. She is self-contained.

We know from her autobiography, which details the games she played in her garden, that those sticks must represent some imaginary world now lost. Agatha was happy alone, making up stories, inventing pretend friends. Although relaxed with her family, she would remain tongue-tied with strangers. 'Inarticulate I shall always be,' she explains, 'it is one of the causes that have made me a writer.'

This autobiography I've mentioned is the source that best reveals how Ashfield was the place – and her mother the person – most vital to Agatha's life. At a first reading, the autobiography tells a story of growth and what the author appears to feel is unexpected and undeserved happiness and success: 'just to *be* alive is a grand thing.'[10] Some readers have been disappointed by its shallow, sunny tone: chatty tales, curious characters, changing social customs, but little searching of the soul.

Yet there's a shadow story lurking there too. Like everything connected with Agatha Christie, the autobiography's glossy surface hides more difficult truths beneath. Her life would also include periods of great unhappiness.

Agatha believed that Ashfield was really her mother's house; that Clara Miller had bought it for herself, unexpectedly, at a time when Agatha's father Frederick was out of the country. Agatha tells the story at the start of her autobiography:

> 'But why did you do that?' he asked.
> 'Because I liked it,' explained my mother.

Agatha suggests that her mother believed it was natural, almost inevitable, that a woman should casually buy a house, just because she liked it.

But look: we've hardly started and already we're on shifting sands.

While Clara and Agatha may have *believed* the story, that's not how it really happened. In fact, Clara could not legally have bought Ashfield. A woman in her position was a *feme covert*: the law treated a married couple as one person, and that person was always the male. Clara did have some money of her own, a legacy, but it was tied up in a trust, and she had to persuade others to allow her to access it. And indeed, Ashfield wasn't really for sale; it was only a leasehold property.[11] In telling the story, though, it isn't as if Agatha is setting out to deceive. It's more that her dreams, memories and storytelling are more important to her than the cold hard facts.

But this story about her mother casually buying a house *does* reveal a deep truth about Agatha's life. Her mother was a controlling presence, and Clara had a sense of destiny and intuition about what was right and what was wrong.

Agatha was observing her mother's impulsive behaviour. She would copy Clara in becoming a nester, a hoarder, and a compulsive purchaser of houses of her own, at one stage owning as many as eight.

And Agatha kept returning to the idea of owning a house as the perfection of happiness. Even in childhood, she wrote stories to entertain herself and her family, and the earliest of them all was about 'the bloody Lady Agatha', and 'a plot that involved the inheritance of a castle'. In another early story, the narrator dreams of a house:

> A very beautiful House . . . I stood and looked at it . . . it doesn't sound much, but it has haunted me all day. The wonder of it, the perfect absolute happiness.[12]

In one of the last really good books Agatha wrote, late in life, a house is once again the centre of an obsession, 'the thing that mattered most to me.'[13]

But life at her beloved home at Ashfield, with her father and mother, could not always remain the paradise it seemed in Agatha's early years.

2

Insanity in the Family

The author Agatha Christie would be marketed by her publishers as a quintessentially English lady, a lover of cream teas, who was rooted in the rich red soil of Devon. In reality, though, she came from a family of globetrotters. Right from the start she had an outsider's perspective on Britain and the British.

Her father Frederick was born in New York City to American parents, while her mother Clara's place of birth was Dublin. Clara's father came from a German family, and her English mother had travelled the world as an army wife.

The founder of Agatha's family fortune was her American paternal grandfather, the self-made businessman Nathaniel Alvah Miller, of Massachusetts. Nathaniel had started out as a salesman, hawking cutlery from door to door, before becoming a clerk. His wife, alternately named as Martha or Minerva, was a butcher's daughter, and they lived in a boarding house on the Lower East Side. But Nathaniel had a gift for making money. He rose up from his position as a lowly clerk to become a partner in the wholesale firm of Claflin, Mellon & Company (Agatha often misspelt it as 'Chaflin'). This was a vibrant business based on Broadway.

The Millers' son Frederick was born on 31 October 1846. When Frederick was only five, though, his mother died of consumption. After this Nathaniel grew increasingly European. He sent Frederick to Switzerland to be educated, a sophisticated choice, and often made the eight-day steamship journey to Manchester to source the sewing machines he sent back to be sold in America. In 1861 Claflin, Mellon & Company opened a new flagship store in Manhattan with 700 counter assistants. When Nathaniel applied to become a natu-ralised citizen of Great Britain, the friends he listed as his supporters were merchants and bankers.[1]

In England, Nathaniel married a second wife: Margaret West. This was Auntie-Grannie, Frederick's new stepmother, who brought her niece Clara along with her into the Miller family.

Frederick and Clara were much thrown together as they grew up, and it was characteristic that when it came to marriage, Frederick wouldn't bother to look far for a wife. 'A very agreeable man,' was how his daughter described him, but he was also undeniably lazy. 'By modern standards,' Agatha admits, her father 'would probably not be approved of . . . if you had an independent income you didn't work. You weren't expected to. I strongly suspect that my father would not have been particularly good at working anyway.'

Frederick was terribly addicted to shopping, although, in his own words, his absolute favourite occupation was 'doing nothing'. It was one of the answers he gave in a book of printed questionnaires the whole family enjoyed filling in from time to time. Frederick reserved his longest and most excited response for the question about his favourite food: 'Beefsteak, Chops, Apple Fritters, Peaches, Apples. All kinds of nuts. More peaches. More nuts, Irish stew. Roly Poly Pudding.'

An agreeable man, a lazy man, Frederick breezed into marriage at the age of thirty-one, in April 1878, at a church in Notting Hill. His 24-year-old bride Clara, much less lazy and rather less agreeable than her husband too, was buttoned into a stiff cream damask gown with a tight, pearl-encrusted belt.[2]

Although Frederick and Clara were to live mainly in England, Frederick still paid frequent visits back to America. He was listed in the New York Social Register, one of its few members from new money. Despite his father's career, his friends were quick to explain, Frederick himself was 'never in business' and he was 'received by every one in New York society.'[3]

But Frederick and Clara decided to take a house in the comfortable, sociable English seaside resort of Torquay. Always a lover of joining societies, Frederick belonged to the Yacht Club, and kept score for the Torquay Cricket Club. ('I was extremely proud of being allowed to help,' Agatha recalled, 'and took it very seriously.')[4]

In the 1890s, Torquay was known chiefly as a good place to pass a mild winter. Frederick and Clara's first child was born in a rented house there on 9 January 1879. Naturally, the baby was named Margaret after Auntie-Grannie. But Agatha's elder sister would generally be known as Madge.

In June of the following year, Clara's son Louis Montant, or Monty, was born during a visit to America. The family decided to settle in America permanently, and came back to Torquay to wind up their affairs. Frederick had returned to New York by himself when the villa called Ashfield caught Clara's eye. It had six bedrooms and a connection to Torquay's drains, but the real attraction was that garden, with its 'large greenhouse, orchidhouse, fernery, large well-stocked fruit garden, choice lawn and vegetable garden'.[5]

And so Clara decreed that the move to America would not happen. She wasn't a woman whose mind could easily be changed. Her dress was theatrical: she had 'elegance and dignity . . . in a long black coat of flowing marocain . . . she used to walk into the house with her head held high.'[6] She had highbrow tastes: she admired Tennyson, Landseer, Mendelssohn and 'Miss Nightingale'. But Clara was only human. She also admitted a weakness for 'ice-cream' and 'American soda cooler.'[7]

Despite having strong passions, what Clara Margaret Boehmer really craved was stability. She was the daughter of army officer Friedrich Boehmer, born in Martinique to a German father, and his English wife Polly. The couple had five children, four boys and Clara herself, who was born while Friedrich was serving in Dublin.[8]

When Friedrich retired from the army, he took his family to Jersey, where he died. According to Agatha, it was a fall from a horse that killed him. According to the more prosaic evidence of the local parish register, he died of bronchitis.

This left Polly to bring up five children on an army pension, and her offspring were in danger of losing their weak grip on middle-class status. So she sent the nine-year-old Clara to live with her sister Margaret ('Auntie-Grannie'), who was on the point of marrying her rich American businessman. Clara would never quite be able to forget that her birth mother had given her away. She remained needy and clingy, prone to 'work herself into terrific states'. Agatha thought her mother 'shy and miserably diffident about herself'.

Clara's life as the Millers' 'poor relation' gave her this sense of insecurity, but new research shows there was also a tendency to mental illness throughout her family.[9] Clara's elder brother Frederick shot himself; a first cousin named Amy Boehmer drowned herself, as did a second cousin too. Clara's great-uncle died in an insane asylum, and her great-aunt likewise spent a spell in an asylum in 1850. Her first cousin once removed died of 'mania' in an asylum in 1880, while this cousin's sister was confined in a mental hospital in 1891. Another first cousin once removed was a convicted wife-beater and alcoholic.

Whether or not all these things were connected didn't matter. These were the sort of stories that made a Victorian family feel fear and shame. The insanity – as people called it then – in her mother's family would come to haunt Agatha's writing. The heroine of her early story about the beautiful house has a mother who died in an asylum:

> They've got insanity in the family, you know. The grandfather shot himself, and a sister . . . flung herself out of the window . . . and Allegra's mother has been in this home for some years. She wasn't just – peculiar, you know, she was quite – quite raving mad! It's a dreadful thing, insanity.[10]

But although troubles would come, there is not a flicker of discontent in all the evidence that survives from Clara's long and happy marriage to Frederick. From the age of ten she never even looked at another man. Yet it's also fair to say that Clara's worship of her husband was built into the Victorian marriage contract.

Clara herself was Agatha's first role model as a writer, for she produced both stories and poems. It's Clara's private poetry, written out in her own hand, that casts a particularly Victorian light on the way that she and Frederick saw their marriage. Clara viewed herself as essentially inferior:

> God in Heaven listen to me,
> Listen to my whisper'd prayer
> Make me worthy, though so lowly
> All his love and life to share.

Frederick in his answering poem reveals a view of his wife as 'the Angel in the House', that classic Victorian conception of a woman who was restful, chaste, domestic: the moral centre of the home.

> But my heart is all true & tender
> Full of love for my darling wife
> For she is my white-souled angel
> Dearer to me than life
> She alone has the power to guide me
> From darkness into light.[11]

These two with their unshakeable relationship would make Agatha feel deeply loved for the first decade of her life. With Clara in particular she shared a special language of thought, 'an intuitive understanding of situations hidden from normal mortals'.[12]

And yet, at some point, Agatha would have to leave Ashfield behind, and face a twentieth century where women could no longer afford to be 'white-souled angels', where they had to deal with indignity, work, and not enough money.

3

The Thing in the House

S trolling round his garden on New Year's Eve, 1892, Frederick Miller noticed the hot-water pipes in the hothouse felt cold. Strange. The surprise sent him in search of his 'painstaking and industrious' gardener of three years, William Henry Callicott.

Callicott was not easily to be found. Frederick continued to hunt, and finally he opened the door to the disused stable.

There was the missing man, dead, his lifeless body hanging from a rope.

Because Ashfield had a telephone, Frederick could call the police at once. It emerged that Callicott had failed to attend the Ashfield Christmas party with the other servants, citing the illness of his little girl. But in truth the gardener had been worried he had heart disease, and his fear was suspected as his reason for taking his own life.[1]

The clue of the cold pipes and the discovery of the corpse sounds like the opening of an Agatha Christie mystery. In fact, the incident appears in one of her non-mystery novels, the semi-autobiographical *Unfinished Portrait*. It's just one of ever so many of Agatha's books featuring a home as both a marvellous and a sinister place.

During her childhood, Agatha absorbed the very Victorian feeling that home was the epicentre of life.

She wrote later of the rich, intense sensations she experienced in Ashfield's enclosed world, where Jane Rowe, the cook, was a powerful figure. Agatha loved Jane's kitchen. The food at Ashfield could never be too plentiful or too rich, and Agatha was a self-professed 'greedy girl', whose 'favourite thing has been, is, and probably always will be, *cream.*' The words 'add half a pint of cream' appear over and over again in a handwritten book of recipes collected by Clara for her daughter's future use, in dishes ranging from chicken in sauce to 'Chinese rice'.[2]

The census of 1891 reveals the names of the rest of Agatha's constant companions in girlhood: the staff. She described them intimately in her autobiography seventy years later: not only Jane Rowe, but also parlourmaid Jane Ratcliffe, housemaid Charlotte Froude and, all importantly, Agatha's nurse, Susan Lewis. Agatha came from a class that could not imagine living without servants. She was once overheard talking to Susan: 'When I grow up, nanny, we'll build a little cottage inside Ashfield gardens and you and I will live there for *always.*'[3]

As well as providing abundant food and deep female relationships, Ashfield was an overwhelming visual experience. Photographs show it was over-full, almost bursting, with possessions. Many of these items would, in due course, make their way to Agatha's later home, the mansion called Greenway in Devon. There, a first-floor bedroom was converted in the 1990s into a bathroom. In its linen cupboard, carefully catalogued, lie stacked solander boxes full of packed papers containing the evidence of Frederick's compulsive shopping habits.

Opening the boxes reveals bills for a pair of Wedgewood medallions, '2 Oriental Bowls' and '8 Soapstone Figures on a Stand'. Frederick could not resist a shop dealing in 'objects of art, rare porcelain, antique bronzes and all articles of vertu'. For himself and Clara he bought an amethyst ring, an umbrella stand, a pair of cut-glass decanters, 5 fine mahogany Chippendale chairs in needlework, and 18 pairs of silver and mother-of-pearl dessert forks in a case.[4] Frederick had to extend the house to make room for all this, adding a ballroom 'capable of accommodating 120 dancers'.[5] He also loved to crowd oil paintings as closely as possible onto the walls.

Agatha copied her father in becoming a homemaker too, on a tiny scale. She used her pocket money to buy furniture for a beloved doll's house:

> There were dressing tables with mirrors, round polished dining-tables, and a hideous orange brocade dining-room suite . . . soon my doll's house looked more like a furniture storehouse.

In old age, she realised the seeds of a lifelong passion had been sown. 'I have continued to play houses ever since,' she wrote,

> I have gone over innumerable houses, bought houses, exchanged them for other houses, furnished houses, decorated houses, made structural alterations to houses. Houses! God bless houses!

Agatha saw more of the dark, intoxicating interiors of her grandparents' generation when she went to stay with Auntie-Grannie at her home in Ealing. Nine Craven Gardens was a house in a row of stout, uniform villas, convenient for Ealing railway station.

Auntie-Grannie was a central presence in Agatha's childhood, with her strongly held views and weakness for 'cherry brandy'. She claimed to have a 'quick perception of human character', and Agatha would put something of the penetrating, understanding gleam of Auntie-Grannie's eye into Miss Marple's.[6]

Auntie-Grannie had a shrewd knowledge of what people, especially men, 'really' wanted. One imagines Agatha thinking of her when Miss Marple discreetly dispenses whisky with the murmur that gentlemen 'want something stronger than tea'.[7] Auntie-Grannie also thought that 'every woman should always have fifty pounds in five pound notes with her in case of what she called emergencies,' words given to an aunt in a Christie novel as late as 1968.[8]

On visits to this stately mid-Victorian world, the young Agatha was amazed by her Auntie-Grannie's magnificent toilet with its 'splendidly large mahogany lavatory seat . . . one felt exactly like a Queen on her throne.' In the dimly lit drawing room,

Auntie-Grannie lived a stationary life, moving only to unlock her store-cupboard and dole out 'French plums, cherries, angelica, packets of raisins and currants, pounds of butter and sacks of sugar.' As she grew older, she became even more of a hoarder. Gradually Agatha came to see the aging Margaret Miller not so much as beloved and all-powerful, but as beloved and vulnerable. Not even her splendid store-cupboard could save Auntie-Grannie from the approach of death.

Life at both Ashfield and Craven Gardens depended on the labour of the domestic staff. Rereading her early novels in the 1960s, Agatha was astonished by 'the number of servants drifting about.'[9] As a child she took it all for granted, but in time she would come to explore and probe this business of domestic service. The women of her family, Agatha thought, 'worked their servants to the bone but took a lot of care of them when they were ill. If a girl had a rather disorganised baby, granny would go and speak to the young man: "Well, are you going to do the right thing by Harriet?"'[10] She thought both sides were invested in this relationship: a servant's status was raised by having a place with a 'good' mistress.

But this is only one side of the story. Agatha had no real insight into the indignity also experienced by those working in the homes of others, and one of the points often made 'against' her as a writer is her lack of humanity towards domestic employees. This can be seen in novels like *Evil under the Sun*, where the staff of a hotel are freed from suspicion entirely on the basis of class. But she also plays with prejudice, and woe betide the reader who assumes that a servant in a Christie story 'couldn't have done it'. Agatha the writer doesn't despise servants. She's interested in them and their changing status, and there are some points in some stories when she pauses to explore their lives.

Although life in Ealing was largely sedentary, Agatha's childhood in Torquay was full of good health and a surprising amount of physical exercise. She was a frequent and confident swimmer. There was roller-skating to be enjoyed on the pier and riding ponies to be hired; Torquay had many attractions for the young. Since the 1860s, the resort town had boasted the Imperial Hotel – the first five-star hotel outside London – which would appear in Agatha's novels *Peril at End House* (1932) and *The Body in the Library* (1942). Meanwhile, the Grand Hotel was built in the 1880s to cater for the visitors now arriving at the nearby station of the Great Western Railway.

But despite Agatha's easy life in a town devoted to pleasure, there was something unexpectedly dark about her view of the world.

In the early story we've already encountered, 'The House of Beauty', there's the germ of an idea that would be threaded right through Agatha's fiction: that evil lurks within the home. In a weird, intense atmosphere, the narrator imagines he has encountered the perfect house, before realising that something evil lives there:

> Never in all his dreams, had the House appeared fairer or more exquisite than on this night [. . .] someone was coming to the window . . .
>
> He was awake! Still quivering with the horror, the unutterable loathing of the <u>Thing</u> . . . the Thing that had come to the window and looked out at him malevolently . . . for it was a Thing utterly and wholly horrible, a Thing so vile and loathsome that the mere remembrance of it made him feel sick.

Here it is already: Agatha's belief that even at the heart of a happy home, a canker of evil might exist.

It's an idea that will appear over and over again, even in the very last published Miss Marple novel, in which a character named Gwenda discovers a lost door. 'Quite suddenly,' Gwenda 'felt a tiny shiver of uneasiness.' This was because the finding of the mysterious door would lead to the return of a suppressed childhood memory of witnessing a murder. Suddenly, Gwenda discovered that her home was unsafe: 'the house frightened her'.[11]

The idea that a house, a person even, could suddenly flip from familiar and friendly to evil and wicked was all too familiar to Agatha, for it emerges in her childhood nightmare of the Gunman or Gun Man.

The Gun Man was a vital and terrifying imaginary figure. Agatha described him in her autobiography and also in her autobiographical novel, *Unfinished Portrait*, the book in which, according to someone close to Agatha, 'we see many intimate flashes from earliest childhood till the beginnings of middle age.'[12] Sometimes wearing an eighteenth-century coat, sometimes missing an arm, the Gun Man would suddenly appear from nowhere in the middle of an ordinary day. Sometimes he would even occupy the body of someone else.

> You looked up in Mummy's face – of course it was Mummy – and then you saw the light steely-blue eyes – and from the sleeve of Mummy's dress – oh horror! – that horrible stump. It wasn't Mummy – it was the Gun Man . . .[13]

There were other ways in which horror could come knocking on the nursery door. Agatha's sister Madge was a talented actress. At Agatha's request, she would sometimes adopt her terrifying alter ego, the 'Elder Sister'. Looking exactly like Madge, the 'Elder Sister' had a different, frightening, 'oily' voice, and she'd say, 'You know who I am, don't you, dear? I'm your sister Madge. You don't think I'm anyone else, do you?'

In the 'Gun Man' and the 'Elder Sister,' Agatha imagined her own mother and sister becoming strange and horrible. They are important, these childhood fantasies, because they illustrate something that would be particularly modern about Agatha's detective fiction. In Sherlock Holmes, for example, the criminal is often far outside the social circle of the victim. And yet, in Agatha Christie, the murderer was often a trusted family member.[14]

Agatha was certain that Madge really was Madge, and yet still doubt would enter her mind: 'that voice – those crafty sideways glancing eyes . . . I used to feel indescribable terror.' And you can see her using her own fear to craft an incident in 'The House of Beauty'. A female character was:

huddled up on the sofa in a strange attitude [. . .] Slowly she raised her head, she was looking at him . . . He stopped, paralysed. For in her eyes was a look he knew.
It was the look of the Thing in the House.[15]

But the real dirty secret at Ashfield, the 'Thing in the House' lurking behind the prosperous life of the Millers, was that the family were running out of money.

4

Ruined

A gatha was hardly old enough to understand what was happening when the Millers' financial troubles began.

Towards the end of the 1890s, she overheard her parents discussing the declining rate of income from the family's investments. To Agatha it all sounded very familiar: this frequently happened to the families in the stories she read. She confidently told her governess that the Millers were ruined. Retribution was swift. 'Really Agatha,' said her mother, cross about both the indiscretion and the inaccuracy. '"We are *not* ruined. We are just badly off for the time being and will have to economise."

"*Not* ruined?" I said, deeply chagrined.

"Not ruined," said my mother firmly.'[1]

But the Millers would not have to wait long before the word 'ruined' could quite legitimately be applied to their status.

Agatha's grandfather Nathaniel had grown rich through Claflin, Mellon & Company, later H.B. Claflin. He'd invested his fortune partly in the company, and partly in property. With the passing of time, though, Frederick found his income inexplicably diminishing. In 1901 one of the trustees of the family's fund went to a hotel room and attempted to kill himself with a pistol. To the Millers, it looked like a guilty conscience about financial mismanagement.[2] Certainly Agatha's imagination in later years would run away with the idea of a crooked trustee to create Andrew Pennington, embezzler of a young lady's fortune in *Death on the Nile*.

And yet it wasn't in Frederick's nature to stint or save. Five years earlier, he'd launched his elder daughter Madge into society with the greatest of fanfare, taking her to New York for her debut at the tail end of the city's Gilded Age. On Madge's seventeenth birthday, Frederick accompanied her into the ballroom of the Waldorf Hotel on Fifth Avenue. Here, along with 600 other guests, she was received by the queen of society, Caroline Astor.[3]

After four months in New York, Frederick and Madge sailed home with thirteen trunks of luggage. But Frederick failed to make any link between jaunts like this and his declining fortunes. He was 'bewildered and depressed,' Agatha wrote, 'but not being a businesslike man he did not know what to do about it.' Eventually Frederick was forced to do something drastic. He rented Ashfield to tenants, and took his family to live in a succession of hotels in France. They spent a year wandering from Pau in the south to Paris, to Dinard in the north, and finally to the island of Guernsey. Agatha's memory placed this journey in her sixth year; in fact she was nine.[4]

But even then Frederick and Clara did not truly embrace the spirit of economy. Agatha described the palaver of the packing: her mother's 'solid leather topped trunks, a Gladstone bag or two a valise, two immense hat boxes large square affairs, jewel cases, travelling bags, dressing cases. Nothing was ever overcrowded, or squeezed, plenty of tissue paper.' All these trunks ran up huge bills for excess luggage. 'Really,' Frederick would say, 'the charges on these French railways are iniquitous.' 'And we've taken so little,' Clara would sigh.[5]

Once they were back in Torquay, funds were low enough for Frederick actually to consider taking a job – not that he was qualified for one. And, worse still, the stress began to make him ill. Even though her parents tried to shield her from the truth, Agatha understood that his worries were affecting her father's health.

After her spectacular New York debut, Madge was enjoying an energetic social life. But another weight on Frederick's mind was Monty. His father's favourite, Monty was similarly leisurely and

lazy. His favourite occupation was 'flirting', while his chief characteristic was 'talking slang & getting into tempers.'[6] 'I hate work
of any kind,' Monty insisted.[7] He had rather disappeared from
Agatha's life after going to Harrow. But even Harrow, not known
for its high intellectual standards, had kicked Monty out. His only
real passion was messing about in boats, so his parents found him
work in a shipyard. When the Boer War broke out, it seemed at
last to offer Monty some direction in life. In 1900, he signed up to
the army.

The following year Frederick began to worry even more seriously about his health. He suffered from what seemed to be a series
of heart attacks, twenty-eight of them by September. 'Short sharp
attack', 'bad attack' and 'very bad attack' read the notes on his list.
He also made a serious effort to lose weight, tracking his progress
from fourteen stones down to thirteen. But the pace of the attacks
seemed to be stepping up.

A visit to a specialist in London eased Frederick's mind. 'My
darling Clara,' he began a letter home, telling her the doctor had
recommended 'plenty of fresh air, distilled water, milk after meals . . .
he says most positively my heart is not dilated.' Relieved and happy,
Frederick couldn't wait to see his wife. 'I have felt wonderfully
better,' he wrote,

> scarcely any breathlessness & splendid nights. I don't know whether
> this is owing to a prescription of Taylor's with digitalin in it or to my
> doing much less walking . . . I have decided to return on Wednesday
> 30th if all goes well.

Until then, he was planning to stay with Auntie-Grannie in Ealing,
and admitted to Clara that 'I should much prefer – between
ourselves, coming down now but Mother is so kind and good that
I cannot bear to disappoint her.'[8]

But fresh air and milk after meals were not enough to prevent
Frederick's decline. In November he was back in London, looking
for a job, when he once again fell ill. On 2 November, his daily

diary recording his small personal expenses – haircut, cocktail, papers, cab – came to an end. Sick and lonely, he was desperate to get back to his family. 'I am so sorry you are still ill,' ran a letter from his little daughter, 'Jane let me make cakes in the kitchen . . . I had Devonshire cream for tea! . . . your loving Agatha.'9

Now severely ill with pneumonia, Frederick must have hardly been able to bear thinking about how his daughter's happy life might soon be disrupted. He had a premonition about what was coming. He penned one last letter to Clara, which can scarcely be read without a lump in the throat. 'You have made all the difference in my life,' he told her.

> No man ever had a wife like you. Every year I have been married to you I love you more. I thank you for your affection and love and sympathy. God bless you, my dearest, we shall soon be together again.

On 26 November 1901, he died. Agatha was just eleven. Not only was the family ruined, but her jovial, reassuring father was also gone for ever.

The blow nearly broke Clara. She would always keep and treasure the printed card from Frederick's funeral, a pressed rose from Ealing Cemetery where he was buried, and his 'last letter'. She stored them in a little embroidered case she'd made for him, years before, with the horribly prescient quotation on it: 'To Frederick from Clarissa [. . .] love is strong as death.'10

Life at Ashfield without Frederick continued in a minor key. Madge finally married and left home. Feckless Monty did not come to his father's funeral, nor even answer the telegram announcing the death.11 He remained in Africa after the Boer War, working as a game hunter, and being tried (and cleared) on the charge of illegally shooting fifteen elephants. He was heard boasting he'd 'broken the law of a lot of countries. Got a nice little hoard of illicit ivory tucked away.'12

While Monty remained absent, financial ruin was staring his mother and younger sister in the face. Clara would continue to get £300 a year from the wreckage of Frederick's affairs. All Agatha personally had was '£100 a year' from her grandfather's will.

Given that the average annual income per Briton in 1901 was only £42, and given that the average salary of a housemaid was £16, Clara and Agatha Miller were clearly well off.[13] But they aspired to the life of gentlefolk, and this did not *feel* like wealth. They'd also lost a niche in society. They were no longer a family, just a widow and daughter, looked after by the remnants of Ashfield's staff.

Young Agatha tried her hardest to console her mother, telling her that 'Father is at peace now. He is happy. You wouldn't want him back, would you?'

Agatha knew she was supposed to say things like this. It was the sort of thing, as she put it, that many children 'have been *told* is right, and what they *know* is right, but which they feel may, somehow or other, for a reason that they don't know, be *wrong*.'

And wrong it certainly was. Clara almost snarled at Agatha. She:

reared up in bed, with a violent gesture that started me into jumping back. 'Yes, I would,' she cried in a low voice. 'Yes, I would. I would do anything in the world to have him back – anything, anything at all.'[14]

Her mother had become a stranger. It was as if the Gun Man had dared to penetrate even the familiar surroundings of Clara's own bedroom.

Agatha shrank away, terrified. The strength of her mother's feelings appalled her.

She began to fear losing her mother too. 'I used to wake up at night,' she explains, 'my heart beating, sure that my mother was dead.' She would creep along the corridor to Clara's room, and listen at the door for the sound of breathing within. Their grief bound Agatha and the strange, passionate Clara ever closer together.

Agatha's life, which had begun so well, had taken a terrible turn. How could this lonely, anxious girl ever survive the loss of both a fortune and a father? How could she ever regain the security she'd known as she played so happily in the fairy ring near the monkey puzzle in Ashfield's garden?

⚜ PART TWO ⚜

Edwardian Debutante – 1900s

5

Waiting for The Man

O ne of the twentieth century's most popular authors describes an upper-middle-class girl's coming of age in the early 1900s:

> We were fenced round with narrow restrictive social customs, nurtured on snobbery and isolated from any contact with, or knowledge of, people outside our own accepted class.[1]

That was actually Barbara Cartland, who, just like Agatha, lost a fortune and a father in her youth. In Agatha's case, these 'restrictive social customs' were even trickier to negotiate because although the Millers were losing caste, Clara still wanted an upward trajectory for her younger daughter. Agatha must still marry into a class slightly higher than her own.

Agatha's mother believed this was more likely to happen if she failed to educate her daughter. The 'best way to bring up girls,' Clara thought, was 'to give them good food, fresh air, and not to force their minds in any way.'

There was no question of Agatha learning the skills to earn a living: that was the business of her future husband. A census from 1901, the first year of the Edwardian era, reveals that only 31.6 per cent of females in Britain were in employment, mostly in domestic service or textile manufacturing.[2] Agatha described the philosophy with which she was brought up: put simply, 'you were waiting for The Man, and when the man came, he would change your entire life.'

Of course this didn't apply to boys, and Monty had gone to public school. Rather more interestingly, so had Agatha's older sister Madge.

More dynamic than dreamy Agatha, Madge had attended the boarding school in Brighton that would become known as Roedean. Along with Cheltenham Ladies' College, Madge's school was at the forefront of education for girls, preparing them to enter Girton and Newnham, the new ladies' colleges in Cambridge. At school Madge was moulded into the new kind of woman who was emerging in middle-class feminist circles in the early twentieth century, known literally as the 'New Woman'.

Agatha was full of admiration for her pretty, witty sister. Madge's most characteristic quality was 'impatience' and her motto was 'go ahead'.[3] But she always made time for Agatha. 'I hope you are conducting yourself in a highly respectable way,' ran one of her letters from boarding school, '& not forgetting me.'[4] Madge was one of those people who can do almost anything they put their mind to, Agatha thought. When Madge turned her hand to writing stories, they were published in *Vanity Fair*.

But when Madge came home from school, her parents were displeased. She was heard expressing the view that wicked people had more fun than good ones. Agatha noticed her sister had also begun to exude 'a great deal of sexual magnetism'. This was worrying. When the time came, her parents decided Madge should not go to Girton. Instead, she should enter the marriage market. Once there, Madge did predictably well. But Margaret Frary Miller, with the right sort of encouragement, could clearly have done something much more extraordinary with her life.

After the unsatisfactory experiment with Madge, Clara reverted to a more traditional education for Agatha, with an emphasis on music, French, conversation and 'character'. Clara wasn't unusual: many people in the 1890s believed that overeducating girls overstrained their health. An 1895 book on child development argued that if a girl overused her brain, it would damage her reproductive powers. 'The New Woman,' this doctor concluded, 'is only possible in a novel, not in Nature.'[5]

As a result of Clara's change of heart, Agatha would lifelong express an aversion to the values of the 'New Woman', always speaking against careers for women, or financial independence, or anything like equality with men. But she would also be endlessly interested by the idea of the 'New Woman'. Countless dynamic and attractive heroines (with Madge's panache) would appear in Agatha's books.

Agatha's sketchy education left her with plenty of time, and it was in order to entertain herself that she learned to read. 'Of course, a lot of the time I was fearfully bored,' she recollected.[6] So she became a bookworm, devouring everything she could get her hands on, educating herself where the adults had not.

Looking at her life ahead, the one thing that would have really helped Agatha was a financial education. But the Millers didn't talk about money. Before Frederick had died, he'd given Agatha lessons in arithmetic on the dining room table, and she'd enjoyed them. Had she gone to a proper school, Agatha thought later, she would have loved to have studied mathematics properly, as she'd always found it fascinating.

She did go for a couple of days a week to Miss Mary Guyer, whose private 'ladies' school' in Torquay was named after the infamous Girton Hall. But for the rest of the time, Agatha wallowed in books. 'I was brought up on Dickens,' she says, 'I love Jane Austen, too – who doesn't?'[7]

Agatha's lack of formal learning would leave her with an unconventional freshness of mind. Later on, though, as she encountered educated people, she'd also feel a sense of inferiority. When she'd outgrown some of the Millers' hang-ups about 'New Women', she would even use the resentment felt by the undereducated as a motive for murder. 'I always had brains, even as a girl!' says one of her murderesses, 'but they wouldn't let me do anything . . . I had to stay at home – doing nothing.'[8] And eventually she is driven by frustration to kill.

But even if Agatha's education omitted maths and science, it was more rigorous than meets the eye, because of the care put into her piano-playing and singing. As with anything she cared about deeply, Agatha applied herself intensely to her musical training. In consequence, she reached almost professional standard.

When Agatha was fifteen, Clara sent her off to a succession of small French finishing schools, where music was a priority. Elegant in her stiff collar, cravat, and little tipped-down pancake hat, a nearly grown-up Agatha in the family photo album smiles from a hotel balcony overlooking a wintery Parisian boulevard. Part of the motivation was once again to save money: with Agatha and Clara away, Ashfield could be shut up.

Despite the dedication Agatha showed in her music lessons, her teachers in Paris concluded she lacked the showmanship to be a real performer. Despite her talent, music turned out to be a dead end. Clara also thought it was unsuitable that Agatha should follow another plan she'd proposed, that of becoming a nurse.

Practical, precise, interested in problem-solving, Agatha could, in a later age, have become a scientist. But naturally her mother intended her second daughter to follow her first into a successful marriage.

6

Best Victorian Lavatory

In the Millers' photographs, the teenage Agatha has a challenging, cool, mysterious gaze. She grows tall and athletic. She lounges on a yacht, roller-skates, plays tennis, all in the gigantic hats and wasp-waists of her Edwardian adolescence. Agatha described the physical pain caused by fashion: the 'agony of small spirals of wire holding up the net collar of one's blouse . . . one's afternoon or party shoes of patent leather with highish heels . . . the discomfort was extreme.'[1]

Agatha had to walk to parties in heels because the Millers' finances did not now stretch to a carriage or taxi. But she could still experience luxury on visits to Madge. She'd be a welcome guest at Madge's husband's family home, the resplendent Abney Hall in Cheadle. Here she learned how to live in a country house, and how to get along with wealthy people.

Madge's marriage at twenty-three, within months of Frederick's death, must have been made in a moment of uncharacteristic self-doubt. Her father hadn't particularly approved of James Watts as a suitor. But once Frederick was gone, Clara, anxious about Madge's future, was 'urgent that the marriage should take place'. Even Agatha's French governess had a view. James, the governess thought, would be good for Madge: 'it will suit her well to have a quiet and steady husband, and he will appreciate her because she is so different.'

So they were hustled off towards the altar. Madge was twenty-three, and James was twenty-four, and eleven-year-old Agatha enjoyed 'the importance of being first bridesmaid'. James or Jimmy, fresh from Oxford, was destined for the family textile firm. He was a sensible chap, and Agatha always liked him. His 'favourite virtue' was 'reliability'.[2]

Madge would now live with reliable James at the substantial Manor Lodge, Cheadle, waiting to inherit the big house at Abney Hall.

The Watts family had acquired Abney two generations previously. When Agatha began to visit in 1902, its occupants were Madge's parents-in-law, their cook, two waitresses, kitchen- and sewing-maids, four housemaids and a nurse. In the park lived the Watts's gardeners, bailiff, farmer and cowman, while the park lodge housed the dressmaker.[3] Agatha came at first for Christmases and holidays. From 1926 onwards, once Madge herself was the chatelaine, she'd always be welcome.

Abney, wrote Agatha, had 'passages, unexpected steps, back staircases, front staircases, alcoves, niches – everything in the world that a child could want . . . all it lacked was the light of day; it was remarkably dark.' An architectural historian has described the hall as 'Puginesque Gothic at its most sumptuous and hence its most oppressive.'[4] There were 300 oil paintings, and a stuffed lion.[5]

Agatha was too young to appreciate Abney's gloomy, glinting interiors, which by 1902 had fallen out of fashion. With the same interior designer as London's Palace of Westminster, A.W.N. Pugin, the Hall was a high-Victorian gem, glowing with ultramarine, vermilion and rich red. But Agatha described its style as 'best Victorian lavatory'.

Jimmy Watts's grandfather Sir James Watts was the man responsible. He'd started out as a weaver before building up a drapery business grand enough to acquire a warehouse in the form of a Venetian palazzo, and had served as Mayor of Manchester.

His Victorian palace would stimulate Agatha's imagination many times in fiction to come. Its splendours would be reborn in her Enderby Hall, where the Abernethie family gather in *After the Funeral*. (Their wealth had come from making corn plasters.) In

They Do It with Mirrors, Abney becomes Stoneygates, housing an institution for troubled children. And in *4.50 from Paddington,* a railway borders the park of Rutherford Hall, just as the park at Abney was bounded by the lines to Manchester and Stockport.

Equally important to Agatha were her new and irrepressible family-by-marriage. James had five younger siblings. The youngest, Nan, was particularly cheeky and outrageous; she 'fired off *damns* and *blasts*', and once painted the family's piglets green.[6] Nan would become Agatha's lifelong friend.

Agatha particularly liked the fact that the Watts family were enthusiastic theatregoers and performers; indeed, one of Madge's brothers-in-law actually ran a theatre professionally. The Wattses in return found quiet Agatha a little fey: they called her 'dream-child' or else 'Starry Eyes'. But like many shy people, Agatha could transform herself on stage. She could entertain her relatives with improvised pantomimes. 'I was fondest of the part of principal boy,' Agatha tells us, for which she'd borrow her sister's stockings.

In these early days, Abney for Agatha represented feasting and fun. Only the most discerning of observers might have wondered if being the hall's chatelaine could fully occupy the time and talents of the remarkable Madge Watts.

And it was pretty obvious to everyone around her that Agatha should follow in her sister's footsteps and get herself married.

7

The Gezireh Palace Hotel

M any people think of Agatha Christie as the elderly 'Duchess of Death', intimidating in her cat's-eye spectacles, and fail to realise what a total man-magnet she was in her youth.

'I was good-looking,' she tells us in her candid way, 'my family, of course, laugh uproariously whenever I say I was a lovely girl.' But it was true. And Agatha had always been at ease with men. Although she disavowed the values of the 'New Woman', she'd silently absorbed at least some of them: she would always be frank and unstuffy about sexual relationships.

As Agatha came to maturity, money prevented her from having an epic coming-out like Madge's. Clara came up with a face-saving alternative. She pretended her health required a trip to the warm climate of Egypt. The real reason was that Cairo had its own expatriate social season, and there Agatha could be launched into society at a bargain price.

Even so, Cairo was a significant investment, for three months in Egypt could not be accomplished for much less than £500. And Agatha and Clara's income combined amounted to only £400 a year. Clara must have been digging into capital for this trip, which shows how much it mattered for Agatha to meet the right sort of man.

They set off together for the first three months of 1908.[1] Agatha at seventeen was thrilled by the adventure. They sailed on the SS *Heliopolis* from London, via Marseilles and Naples, which took four days, then took the train inland to Cairo.

Here, for European incomers, taxes were low and domestic labour was cheap. The French had left Egypt in 1901, and an uneasy country now lay under British control. Beyond Cairo's cosmopolitan commercial district was a Muslim city where Agatha and her kind never went.[2]

Clara and Agatha stayed at the Gezireh Palace Hotel on its island in the middle of the Nile. Built in the style of a chateau in the 1860s, it offered a telegraph office, a daily concert, and an electric tram service directly to the Pyramids.[3]

But Agatha hadn't come to see the sights. In E.M. Forster's *A Room with a View*, published that same year, the heroine visits Florence without meeting anyone she couldn't have met in Surrey, and thus it was for Agatha in Egypt too. The photos Agatha and Clara took show a succession of captains, majors, a general, a baronet, and even one lonely duke. Egyptians appear in their album only as a conjuror, and a nameless dragoman. The Sphinx is the single antiquity to merit a snap. Agatha's camera preferred a picnic, a polo match, tea on the terrace.[4]

For three months, she went to five dances a week in the grand hotels of Cairo, mingling with the young men of the British regiments stationed in the city, and finding herself 'somewhat plagued by a young Austrian count of excessive solemnity'. She preferred subalterns.

Entering the ballroom each evening, Agatha was enviably slim, tall (five feet seven inches[5]) and golden-haired. Yet she had a teenager's anxieties about her appearance. 'Bosoms were very much in fashion,' she wrote, 'how long should I have to wait until I, too, could have that splendid development?'

Agatha later luxuriated in the memory of her debutante gowns. A 'most beautiful yellow satin' remained lodged in her mind, 'it did not quite "stand by itself" supreme phrase – but very nearly – yards and yards of it with a long train . . . five years that frock was with me, always giving me confidence in myself (badly needed – for I was a shy girl).'[6] In *Dead Man's Folly* (1956) she gives some of the same recollections to a former lady's maid. 'Proper stuff the ladies wore,' sighs Mrs Tucker, 'no gaudy colours and all this nylon and rayon; real good silk. Why, some of their taffeta dresses would have stood up by themselves.'[7]

Agatha diligently danced through fifty or sixty balls. These occasions had strict rules. 'You did not go to a dance with a young man,' Agatha explains, 'either your mother sat there, or some other bored dowager.' But later on, having danced with propriety, 'you then strolled out in the moonlight or wandered into the conservatory, and charming *têtes à têtes* [sic] could take place.'

The discipline of the nightly dances slowly taught Agatha how to make conversation. 'I was always so bad at that,' she remembered.[8] One partner returned her to her mother with the words 'Here's your daughter. She has learnt to dance. In fact she dances beautifully. You had better try to teach her to talk.'

Agatha left Egypt at the end of three months with her first proposal in the bag, although she didn't even know it. Clara, who'd received it, had turned it down flat without even consulting her daughter. Agatha was annoyed when she found out. But a much more valuable legacy from her time in Egypt would be her first full-length novel: *Snow upon The Desert*.

Agatha had in mind something more ambitious than the short stories she'd so far completed. Her novel was an extended satire about the Britishers abroad to whom Cairo seemed like Cheltenham. Writing was a welcome break from socialising. 'I had formed a habit of writing stories,' she explains. It 'took the place, shall we say, of embroidering cushion covers or pictures taken from Dresden china flower-painting. If anyone thinks this is putting creative writing too low in the scale, I cannot agree.'

This notion that writing was just one of a string of hobbies or accomplishments was more widespread than you might think. Madge sent her stories to *Vanity Fair* for pin money. Agatha's grandmother Polly, skilled at embroidery, used her needle to support her family. In each case, what was considered a harmless pastime led to cash. Nothing could be further from the Romantic idea of the artist: a starving, struggling figure in his garret, hurling his genius at his lonely task. But then female writers have always fitted their work in around the edges of ordinary life. 'How much more interesting it would be if I could say that I always longed to be a writer,' Agatha confessed, later, but 'such an idea never came into my head.'

Agatha would freely acknowledge her good fortune in having the leisure in which to write a whole novel before she was twenty. It was quite different for her almost exact contemporary, the poet Ethel Carnie. The so-called 'mill girl poet', born into a family of cotton-spinners, Ethel was working full-time in a mill at thirteen; she had her first poem published in the *Blackburn Times* at eighteen. 'We think we have found a new singer,' wrote a critic, 'what might such a singer accomplish if she had more leisure than hard factory work affords?'[9] In 1913 Ethel went on to write a novel, *Miss Nobody*, thought to be the first published in Britain by a working-class woman. Had Agatha likewise needed to earn a living, she may well have remained a Miss Nobody too.

The Gezireh Palace appears, lightly disguised, in Agatha's *Snow upon The Desert*, and its European guests are treated in the same vein as the uptight English ladies in *A Room with a View*. Two characters encounter difficulty in boarding a Cairo omnibus:

'I hope that wasn't swearing,' said Miss King as she safely ensconced herself inside.

'I think it was only Arabic,' answered Melancy gravely.

Snow upon The Desert contained the seeds of so much that was to follow in Agatha's work: well-heeled characters, thrown together in what Europeans thought of as an 'exotic' location, a feather-light touch in the description and dialogue, and a great dash of sex appeal in the male lead, who had 'a bad face, and bad eyes – but powerful –'. Even the title marked the start of a long career of picking just the right quotation: in this case from a Victorian translation of Omar Khayyám.

But the real pleasure of reading the novel today is imagining the young Agatha putting herself into her heroine, lolling in bed, looking forward to a day with her current young man.

It seemed to her that never had she been so happy. She was drifting on the high tide of expectation out to sea – a calm blue sea, under a cloudless sky. She was enjoying that supreme moment of anticipation which is the best gift the gods have to give.

Melancy lay quite happily beneath the mosquito net, watching the little dancing shadows on the wall. In a few minutes she would go and pull up the blind and look across the Nile.[10]

The voice is that of a writer we'll meet again, later, a writer called Mary Westmacott, whose name Agatha would use when she wasn't writing crime fiction. It's when Agatha was speaking with this voice that we get the deepest insights into a novelist who's much more autobiographical than most readers think.

Back in Torquay, her novel complete, Agatha took the next step on the journey towards becoming an author. She sought professional help.

Clara suggested that Agatha should consult their neighbour, the writer Eden Phillpotts. Phillpotts sounds like a jolly man, a friend of Arnold Bennett, hugely and commercially popular in his time, if largely forgotten now. He's remembered by history not least because of the generosity he'd show to his young mentee.

Phillpotts could see potential in the work before him. 'Some of these things that you have written are capital,' he now told her. 'You have a great feeling for dialogue.'

Encouraged, Agatha sent *Snow Upon the Desert* off to more than one publisher. But back it came, rejected. The problem wasn't the characterisation, or the dialogue. It was the ridiculous plot, in which the heroine loses her hearing.

Eden Phillpotts did his best, introducing Agatha to his own literary agent: 'we'll see if you can publish it. A little print is very encouraging I know.' But again, she was turned down. Refusing to be discouraged, though, she sent Phillpotts another story. Although he liked it, he was perceptive enough to see that she had little incentive to take writing seriously.

'All is going exceedingly well with your work,' he wrote,

& should life so fall out for you that it has room for art & you can face the up-hill fight to take your place & win it, you have the gifts sufficient ... however life knocks the art out of a good many people."

And he would seem to have been correct. For Agatha on her return from Egypt was almost inundated with offers of marriage.

8

Enter Archibald

While the suffragettes were planting bombs and the Balkans were ablaze, Clara was sending Agatha to house parties all over England in the hope of meeting The Man. As her confidence grew, Agatha became adept at passing as someone much richer. She once descended from a train wearing a velvet toque of such smartness the stationmaster assumed she must have a lady's maid travelling with her. Of course her budget did not extend that far.

Someone who knew Agatha at this time described her slightly reserved charm: 'tall, very pretty, Scandinavian colouring and a lovely complexion. There was always a quiet shyness about her.'[1] Yet she was devastatingly attractive. Her autobiography mentions or hints at no fewer than nine different men who proposed marriage, and indeed two actual engagements. Agatha is joyfully matter-of-fact when talking about her suitors, describing one of the rejections she made. 'We have only known each other ten days,' she told this particular man, 'it's really an awfully silly thing to go and propose to a girl like that.'

Clara was closely watching every turn of events. She was still clinging to the model of a marriage like her own in which men and women were expected to behave differently. She thought one of Agatha's suitors highly acceptable, despite his being fifteen years older and having had a good many affairs. 'That my mother did not really mind,' Agatha explained, for 'it was an accepted principle that men sowed their wild oats before marriage.' Or even afterwards.

Agatha would give her mother's generation's views to the formidable Lady Tressilian in *Towards Zero* (1944): 'men had their affairs, naturally, but they were not allowed to break up married life.' But Agatha and her contemporaries were hoping marriage would be something different, companionate, more of a partnership, less of a hierarchy. More *fun*.

Other pieces among Agatha's unpublished early writing reveal further thoughts on marriage. As well as stories, she wrote plays that weigh up matrimony. She positively undermines it in *Eugenia and Eugenics*, for example: the heroine takes the view that men and women should have equal access to divorce. But the heroine's maid has a more practical outlook: 'it seems to me M'am, what with the gentleman being as difficult and scarce to get hold of as they are, that it's a pity to ask too much of 'em.'[2]

Agatha's potential husbands came from the upper-middle class, and she had a sense of inverted snobbery towards the aristocracy. The titled, she thought, just weren't *sensible*: she'd once have a character define an aristocrat as fearless and truthful but 'extraordinarily foolish.'[3] Unlike her fellow novelists Dorothy L. Sayers or Margery Allingham, who loved toffs, Agatha would often make an aristocrat a baddie. For example, her shady Lord Edgware had a 'queer secretive' look, while a 'weak but obstinate' duke resembled 'a weedy young haberdasher'.[4]

Upper-middle class, for Agatha, was perfectly fine. Colonel Arbuthnot defines Agatha's social circle in *Murder on the Orient Express*:

'About Miss Debenham,' he said rather awkwardly. 'You can take it from me that she's all right. She's a *pukka sahib*.'

Flushing a little, he withdrew.

'What,' asked Dr Constantine with interest, 'does a *pukka sahib* mean?'

'It means,' said Poirot, 'that Miss Debenham's father and brothers were at the same kind of school as Colonel Arbuthnot.'[5]

In 1912, the ninth of Agatha's rather desultory courtships was under-way, and this time she was actually engaged to an army officer named Reggie Lucy. But eventually Agatha walked into the ballroom where she met the tenth man, the one who seemed to hold out the promise of a marriage of equals, of shared values, and of adventure.

Archibald Christie was twenty-three years old, and the ball at Ugbrooke House in Devon was on 12 October 1912. Agatha was now a bewitching twenty-two. A friend had tipped her off that this Christie was a good dancer, and the two were introduced.

Physically, he was her own mirror image: 'a tall, fair young man'. It was only when I examined his photograph in the Christie Archives that an essential fact about Archibald Christie struck me that I hadn't gained from anything else I'd read. He was incredibly hot.

And, excitingly, he was a pilot. He'd qualified just four months earlier in one of the flimsy-looking Bristol biplanes. The previous year Agatha had flown in an aeroplane herself, and she'd loved it. With her mother's rather courageous permission, she'd paid £5 at an air show to receive in return five minutes of ecstasy.

Archie understood that feeling. Agatha was also immediately attracted to his 'crisp curly hair, a rather interesting nose, turned up not down, and a great air of careless confidence.' He also rode a motorcycle.

Shy, sensible Agatha was turned completely upside down. But Archie's attraction was not just that he was handsome and capable. He would also prove himself to be elusively, attractively, unreadable.

Archie's commanding officer described him as 'a good steady type, very popular, and one of the better types in a small elite corps.'[6] He'd been born on 30 September 1889 in Peshawar, then in Bengal, India, now in Pakistan. Archie's father, Archibald Christie senior, had worked in the Indian Civil Service, as either a barrister accord-ing to some sources, or as a judge according to others. His mother, Ellen Ruth Coates, known as 'Peg', was born one of twelve in Galway, Ireland. Peg had presumably gone out to India in the hope of bettering herself, and of meeting and marrying a husband.

But tragedy came when Archie was seven. The family returned

to England, and Archibald Christie senior was committed to an asylum. The records of Brookwood Mental Institution give the cause of his 'insanity' as 'Alcohol'. Four years later, in another institution, Holloway Sanitorium, Archie's father died of 'General Paralysis of the Insane'.[7]

This was modified in the family's own account of itself into a fall from a horse that 'affected his brain'. People did not then generally realise the cause of Christie senior's condition wasn't really alcohol, but untreated syphilis. They were, however, beginning to work out that it more often affected men than women, and that when women were affected, they were often sex workers. So 'general paralysis of the insane' was beginning to be associated with degeneracy, as well as with drink. It would have been surely a terrible source of shame to Peg. On top of this, Archie's brother would go on to suffer from mental illness as well.

With secrets like this in his family closet, it's no wonder Archie could come across as uncommunicative. To a genteel young lady of Torquay, though, it was devastatingly attractive. He was different to the usual ballroom-creepers she met: tougher, more practical. He was from a lower social class: his family worked, hers did not. They were 'poles apart . . . it is the old excitement of "the stranger".'

The death of Archie's father had left Peg a widow with two children in a country in which she'd only lived for four years. Not surprisingly, she quickly remarried. Her second husband, William Helmsley, was a teacher at Clifton College in Bristol. Agatha was suspicious of Archie's mother, when she met her, and described her as 'charming in a rather excessive Irish style'. Knowing the precariousness of Peg's life story, one understands her reliance upon charm.

Archie was educated at his stepfather's place of work. A public school, but not exactly Eton, Clifton aimed to turn middle-class boys into scientists or Empire-builders. Archie next went to the Royal Military Academy at Woolwich, then spent three years in the Royal Field Artillery. In July 1912 he paid £75 to learn to fly, and a month later he was considered qualified.[8] Archie hoped to enter the recently established Royal Flying Corps.

And so, stationed near Exeter, Archie found himself attending the dance where he met Agatha. In his own handwritten summary of his life, this was the first social event he ever mentioned; everything else was to do with the army or his training.

While we do have Agatha's first impression of Archie, his own terse recollections say nothing about her. Nor do they mention the visits he started to make, on his motorbike, to Ashfield. This was much to Clara's amusement. It was obvious what was going on: this new young man had fallen in love so badly he looked like 'a sick sheep'. We also hear nothing from him when, on 31 December 1912, Agatha invited him to dance again, at the South Devon Hunt ball.[9] But on 4 January 1913, Archie's journal springs back into life, as it does only on the most important of occasions. It tells us he 'went to Ashfield Torquay and concert at the Pavilion'.[10]

This was the 'Grand Wagner Concert' at the Torquay Pavilion Theatre, a fanciful many-domed construction down by the sea. The programme featured Madame Blanche Marchesi ('the Famous Prima Donna, from Covent Garden') and the Municipal Orchestra.[11] Sitting there in the dark beside Archie, Agatha was making what would become a lifelong association between Wagner and deep emotion, for somewhere deep inside, she 'already knew' what was about to happen.

Back at Ashfield after the concert, Archie could contain himself no longer. He

spoke to me almost desperately. He was leaving in two days' time, he said: he was going to Salisbury Plain, to start his Flying Corps training. Then he said fiercely, 'You've got to marry me, you've *got* to marry me.'

But there was a significant problem. Agatha, after all, was engaged to someone else.

She now wrote to Reggie, whose sisters were her good friends. Reggie, who was kind, respectable and in every way suitable, would have been the sensible choice. He was a known quantity, and Agatha might even have trumped Madge as chatelaine of his family's home, the immensely grand Charlecote House in Warwickshire.

Now though, Agatha simply broke it off without a second thought.

This was despite the fact that neither the Millers nor the Christies were thrilled by the new engagement. Archie's mother Peg thought him too young, and Clara was perturbed as well. 'Of course,' she'd say, 'I can't think *any* man would be good enough' for Agatha. But Archie didn't care. His determination to have Agatha seemed thrilling, compelling. His mind, she explained, 'was always entirely bent on what *he* wanted himself.' It was thunderously exciting to Agatha that what Archie now wanted was her. And in April 1913, he also got his wish of becoming a Flying Officer.[12]

Yet Archie and Agatha were so different from each other, and knew each other so little. There would be many ups and downs before they got anywhere near marriage. One of these was a further financial disaster. In June 1914, Claflin's in New York finally went bust, making the Millers' finances rockier than ever. Archie had a little income of his own, Agatha considerably more, but now Clara's income was deeply uncertain. How would they ever manage for money?

And then, of course, in August, came something equally unimaginable as the family firm going bust. War.

✣ PART THREE ✣

Wartime Nurse – 1914–18

9

Torquay Town Hall

In the summer of 1914, Agatha thought she knew what her future held. She was properly in love at last. She would follow her sister into marriage and motherhood.

She'd no idea that the coming war would both derail her life, and make her into an artist.

Her friends in Torquay were oblivious to what was going on in Europe. 'It was all rumours,' she explains, 'and then suddenly one morning *it had happened*.'

Agatha was affected shockingly soon. Archie had spent the summer at the Royal Flying Corps camp at Netheravon in Wiltshire. On a bleak expanse of Salisbury Plain near Stonehenge, the training centre was a miserable 'collection of weather board huts on a windswept hill'.[1] From here, he wrote Agatha lovelorn letters: 'nothing seems quite right. My one ambition now is to be with you always . . . nothing else matters.'[2]

Perhaps he should have focussed his mind more firmly on his training. The approach of war meant the RFC were no longer just boys playing with toys. But in Archie's letters at least, becoming an airman was a terrific lark. He reassures Agatha that he has acquired a revolver, 'just to please you . . . I may hit a large German if I see one which is unlikely.'[3] He performs acrobatics at the dangerously low height of 1,000 feet. He toughs it out when a colleague is killed: the 'Cody biplane is very unstable'. 'It does make one morbid reading about these accidents,' he admitted, 'still more seeing them – but confidence soon returns.'[4]

Archie did not tell Agatha what his logbook reveals: frequent mishaps such as 'engine running irregularly,' 'bad landing' and 'goggles stuck'.[5] But a whole generation of the so-called Officer Class had secrets like this to keep. In the main, Archie stuck to its creed of the stiff upper lip: 'you will be very brave won't you Angel. It will be very hard to sit at home and do nothing, and I am afraid you will have money troubles too, but it must all come right if we are steadfast.'[6]

Occasionally, though, he had dark nights when he considered breaking off their engagement. 'The reason I was unwell last week,' he revealed, 'was because I thought that it would be best for you if I never saw you again . . . I was only doing in a clumsy way what I thought would be best for you, wondering all the time what was going to happen to me.'[7]

A handsome aviator sounds terribly glamorous, and that's how Archie Christie is usually depicted. It hasn't been previously understood, though, that he wasn't exactly a flying ace. Archie said he was 'enjoying flying as much as ever.'[8] But by the time Germany invaded Belgium, he was a pilot no longer. His sinuses gave him trouble when he was aloft, there was a shortage of planes, and his service record notes that he wasn't a gifted flyer: he could 'fly safe machines' but not dangerous or difficult ones.[9]

So Archie was given alternative duties, as the Third Squadron's Transport Officer and then Equipment Officer, ordering spare parts.[10] It was in this capacity that he got ready to serve in France. If he was disappointed, it was something else of which he didn't speak.

It's not really surprising that Archie's short-lived career as a pilot overshadows the reality of his wartime service. It's part of a pattern in which the pilots of the Great War, those 'knights of the air', capture our imagination at the expense of those behind the scenes. Gallant pilots seem to stand for the individual in a war that was really characterised by death on an industrial scale.[11]

And so, it was with typewriter and telephone that Archie stood by, waiting for war. 'This waiting is rather hard,' he admitted, 'but all is ready.'[12] He was mobilised by 2 August, two days before Britain declared hostilities upon Germany. Just beforehand, he got himself to Salisbury for a little leave. Agatha in Torquay received a heart-stopping telegram with the news that she must come immediately to say goodbye.

Agatha ran for a train, taking Clara with her. The only money they had on them was a five-pound note, too large an amount for anyone to be able to give them change. 'All over southern England,' Agatha remembered, in a tragicomic retelling of the story, 'our names and addresses were taken by infinite numbers of ticket collectors. The trains were delayed.'

Eventually she and Archie managed to meet, for just half an hour, in a Salisbury hotel. It was tense: 'he was sure, as indeed all the Flying Corps was, that he would be killed, and that he would never see me again.' Later, in an autobiographical novel, she described his manner: 'very jerky and flippant, with haunted eyes. No one knows about this new kind of war – it's the kind of war where *no one might come back . . .*'[13] Agatha went to bed that night crying as if she would never stop.

On 5 August 1914, Archie left for Southampton, there to set sail for France. He gave Agatha a photograph of himself, looking impossibly handsome in his uniform, eyes lifted towards a distant horizon.

'No evil happen unto thee,' Agatha pencilled on the back, 'for he shall give his angels charge over thee . . . I am with him in trouble, I will deliver him, & bring him to honour.'[14]

Back in Torquay, fearful, underoccupied, Agatha felt desperate to do something. She volunteered for war service. Between October 1914 and December 1916, a pink record card shows she performed 3,400 hours of unpaid hospital work as a Red Cross volunteer (a Voluntary Aid Detachment or VAD).

Torquay's town hall had become a fifty-bed auxiliary hospital, and here Agatha began her new and more serious life. It was a steep climb downhill from Ashfield, and it can't have been pleasant walking back up after an evening shift. But a bigger challenge was the work itself. Agatha had to begin at the bottom: as a cleaner.

She wrote about her experience, firstly in the town hall field hospital, then later on in Torbay Hospital proper, several times. There's her humorous account in her autobiography. The same events appear in her autobiographical novel *Giant's Bread*, and there's also a comedic treatment in her 'thriller', *The Secret Adversary*. Here the heroine also starts hospital life by washing up 648 plates every day, progressing to waiting on the head nurses at their meals, and finally graduating to sweeping an actual ward.

With her level-headed approach, Agatha manages to make the horrors she witnessed in the hospital seem rather jolly. But appearances are deceptive.

Agatha's first task was to wash floors as a ward-maid, before being allowed to use her limited Red Cross training upon real patients. It was rather a shock. Like lady volunteers all over Britain, her eyes were being opened to the reality of work. This comes up in *Giant's Bread*:

I do sympathise with servants now. One always thinks they mind so much about their food – and here we are getting just the same. It's having nothing else to look forward to.[15]

Once promoted to working with patients, Agatha found some parts of it distressing. In common with her fellow VADs, she found that a little voluntary training was no real preparation.

Attending an operation for the first time nearly made her faint. 'I began to shake all over,' she said, at the sight of the patient's open stomach. She had to take an amputated leg down to the hospital furnace to be burned. She was given charge of a patient who died of tetanus after three days of her personal care.[16] Although conditions were nothing nearly as challenging as in the field hospitals of Flanders, all the south coast hospitals experienced surges of patients after a battle, when the numbers of wounded exceeded the resources to care for them.

But there were also parts of nursing that Agatha enjoyed. It gave her sensations of camaraderie and competence. Had she gone on to train properly, she thought, she'd have 'been very good at it'.[17]

How typical was Agatha's experience? Her statements about nursing echo those of many other VADs. Firstly, there was intense commitment: 'I felt,' she explained, 'mixed up in it completely and wanted to have a part in it.'[18] At the same time, nurse Vera Brittain, at a different hospital, discovered 'every task, from the dressing of a dangerous wound to the scrubbing of a bed-mackintosh, had for us in those early days a sacred glamour.'[19] Like Agatha, Brittain had to get used to dressing lacerated limbs, 'a gangrenous leg wound, slimy and green and scarlet, with the bone laid bare.'[20]

But Agatha's recollections are mainly about the characters of the hospital, especially the professional nurses who directed the VADs. As historian Christine Hallett puts it, the 'tension between trained, professional nurses and VADs is one of the strongest themes to emerge from women's wartime writings.' The VADs were closely observing their superiors, 'frequently with scorn for their excessive attention to hospital etiquette and discipline.'[21] Hospital ceremony insisted, for example, that Agatha could not hand an instrument directly to a doctor. She records being chastised for trying it:

'Really, Nurse, pushing yourself forward in that way. Actually handing the forceps to Doctor *yourself*!'

She was supposed to have handed the instrument to a more senior nurse, who would pass it on, rather like the rituals of an ancient court. What was *really* happening here, though, was that the professional nurses, who'd fought hard to get their status recognised, feared losing the gains they'd made if these volunteers were treated as equals. After all, many VADs, Agatha included, had hardly even been to school.[22]

And women like Agatha weren't at all used to being told what to do. Not only by the nurses, but also by the doctors with whom, outside the hospital, they'd have been social equals. Agatha says she learned 'to stand, a human towel-rail, waiting meekly while the doctor bathed his hands, wiped them on the towel, and, not bothering to return it to me, flung it scornfully on the floor.'

It was disrespectful to be treated like this. Agatha's experience, as a well-off woman entering the workplace, helps explain why the Great War marked the beginning of the end for a deferential society. She had one of her fictional nurses actually put it into words. 'I shall never feel the same about doctors again,' this nurse says. 'We shan't be able to grow out of it afterward.'[23] And thus it was for Agatha too: in her writing, doctors would become 'statistically the most homicidal profession'.[24]

When it came to the patients, though, Agatha began to wield a new kind of power over men. Helpless, suffering from trauma, they needed her. When they tried to trick her by insisting that the doctor had ordered them to drink wine, or that they needed to visit a shop that was conveniently adjacent to a pub, she saw through their ruses. When the illiterate wanted to write to family members, Agatha became the scribe. She controlled their very words.

Had it not been for the war, Agatha would certainly have spent these years from twenty-four to twenty-eight married, running a home, having children. Instead, she was getting an entirely unexpected glimpse into a world of work, where she experienced achievement and success.

From 1917, she even began to earn money: £16 a year.[25] It was the war, and only the war, that made this acceptable. 'It is a general opinion and especially, perhaps, among persons of the middle class,' wrote the author of a 1915 book, 'that the working for money of married women is to be deplored.'[26] Agatha had been brought up to believe this. But her hospital service led her into the labour market through the back door.

Agatha's family couldn't understand why she had to work on Sundays: 'some arrangement should be made.' But there was an even more important job that she and her fellow nurses also performed.

This was to witness the trauma that lay within the wards, to process it, and to give no testimony of it to the town outside.

We hear a lot more about this from men in the services, who were more readily expected to bear witness to horror. One soldier, Thomas Baker, tried to explain war to civilians. 'Impossible,' he said,

> to tell them really just how it was . . . people didn't seem to realise, you know, what a terrible thing war was, they didn't. You couldn't convey the awful state of things where you lived like animals.[27]

Female nurses had the same challenge of explaining the incomprehensible, but for them it was difficult in a different way. There was at least a label for the trauma some soldiers suffered: shell shock. For nurses, their unease had no name. This was storing up trouble for their future mental health.

And I also believe that nursing would be vital for Agatha as a writer of fiction. It gave her a desire to keep up an act, to go home to Ashfield and *not to tell* her mother that she had incinerated limbs, wiped up blood, and – shockingly for a young lady – witnessed the male body naked and soiled. This need to keep up a façade was something that Agatha's fictional characters felt all too strongly.

Agatha eventually made the decision – fateful for her future – to leave the wards to train to work instead in the hospital pharmacy. This had interesting challenges and better hours.

'I mastered the simpler facts,' she wrote, of her new job, 'and after we had blown up our Cona coffee machine in the process of practising Marsh's test for arsenic our progress was well on the way.' She also had to deal with creepy co-workers. A commercial chemist in Torquay gave her some extra coaching. But 'Mr P.', as Agatha names him, mistakenly mixed a set of suppositories with a highly dangerous drug. It was unthinkable to mention his error, but neither could she let the suppositories be used. So she knocked them onto the floor, and trod on them.

'That's all right, little girl,' he said. 'Don't worry too much,' and patted me tenderly on the shoulders. He was too much given to that kind of thing.

Urgh.

Agatha's allies against the stiff sisters and the snooty doctors were her fellow volunteers, who became friends. They showed they realised just how much they were going against their upbringing when they gave their group a name. They called themselves the 'Queer Women'.

Everyone in the hospital was desperate for fun, because as Agatha explains, 'they didn't like talking about the war.'[28] So, she and the other 'Queer Women' produced an amusing spoof hospital magazine. It includes watercolour portraits of them all, including Agatha herself (hair up, white jacket), and adverts for hospital fashion: an overall, for example, 'adorned with Futurist' designs. From the security of her magazine, Agatha counselled the nurses to resist the rudeness of the male bosses: 'We advise you (however much it may be against the grain) to assert yourself a little more.'[29]

It's noticeable that Agatha would live mainly among women for near to her first thirty years. At Ashfield, she and Clara lived with two female servants. Auntie-Grannie had come to live there as well, and now she had the intense female friendships of the hospital.

'Amazing Women!' begins a poem in the magazine, called a 'Dream of Queer Women', 'one by one they rise, And slowly pass before my startled eyes.'[30] Foremost among them was another dispenser, Eileen Morris, 'rather plain' but with 'a remarkable mind'. Agatha called her 'the first person I had come across with whom I could discuss *ideas*.' Eileen lived an apparently sexless life with her schoolteacher brother and five maiden aunts, and served for nearly 9,000 hours during the war as a dispensing and laboratory assistant.[31]

But clever female company wasn't the only bonus Agatha found in the dispensary. Her work also stimulated her imagination about the possible uses of poison. Her magazine contained an item of

'Police Court News' about an investigation into the death of a patient. The witnesses include the nurse and the lady dispensers. And the mysterious death had taken place 'suddenly, immediately after swallowing a dose of medicine.'[32]

Poison was suspected.

It was during the course of her work with the drugs in the dispensary that Agatha first had the idea of writing a detective story.

10

Love and Death

A gatha was an exceptional woman. But during the four years she was separated from Archie, she was part of an all too familiar story: young lovers parted by conflict.

A man of strong feelings he struggled to express, Archie in his correspondence reveals little of what he must have experienced in France. Agatha kept and treasured his letters. In their simplicity and certainty, they are a moving record of love in a time when death lay all around.

Archie and his colleagues were dumped at Boulogne by their transport ship on 13 August 1914 and spent the night 'on the quai'.[1] Meanwhile, two of the squadron's pilots who'd travelled by air were killed in a crash before they'd even landed.

During August and September, Archie was constantly on the move round north-eastern France. He was part of the retreat after the British defeat at Le Cateau, which saw a casualty rate of nearly 20 per cent. The British Army eventually ground to a halt and dug itself in, and trench warfare began.

The RFC set up its headquarters at the aerodrome of Saint-Omer, inland from Calais. Archie arrived on 12 October, and by the 19th he had already been mentioned in dispatches for his bravery in enduring 'great strain . . . almost every hour of the day and night.'[2] Later his squadron moved to Hinges, a village that had to be entirely rebuilt after the war because of the damage it suffered.

Archie's commander was the forceful and grumpy Hugh Trenchard, the man often given credit as the father of what would become the Royal Air Force. These were desperate times. The RFC had sixty-five aeroplanes, used mainly to spy out the location of the enemy's ground troops. They were intended to 'lift the roof off the battlefield, allowing commanders to peer into the enemy's intentions,' as aviation historian Patrick Bishop puts it.[3] As the war progressed, though, there were also hostile planes to deal with, as both sides became more adept at using guns in the air. The British had inferior machines and training, and were losing four times as many planes as the Germans. Pilots arrived in France with fewer and fewer hours of experience. One newcomer to Archie's base was asked how much time he'd logged.

'Fourteen hours.'
   'Fourteen! It's absolutely disgraceful to send pilots overseas with so little flying. You don't stand a chance . . . Another fifty hours and you might be quite decent; but fourteen! My God, it's murder!'[4]

Archie's job included tasks like arranging for a signalling lamp to be tested to see if it was suitable for him to order for his pilots.[5] And his efforts to keep his pilots aloft in their unreliable planes were rated highly by his colleagues. By November, he'd been promoted to temporary captain.

By December 1914, it was a different young man who went on leave to London to meet his fiancée. In one 1920s Christie mystery, the murder weapon is a paperknife fashioned from the wires of an aircraft wing, a souvenir brought home by a pilot. It sounds like a detail plucked from life, something Archie might have given Agatha.[6] Even bringing gifts, though, she found him uncommunicative, and was hurt by his 'flippancy – almost gaiety'. He gave her a thoughtless Christmas present of a dressing case. She hated it. It was off-key, too frivolous, too expensive. The engagement seemed to be cancelled. RFC ethos was that officers shouldn't marry. 'You stop one, you've had it,' Archie would say, 'and you've left behind a young widow, perhaps a child coming – it's selfish and wrong.'

Archie's diary of his first leave tells us blandly that it began on 21 December, and continued '24th to Bristol later Torquay. 26th Back to London. 30th Went to 1st Wing Headquarters.'[7]

But this dry record conceals an utter bombshell. On the evening of 23 December, having taken Agatha to stay with his mother in Bristol, Archie changed his mind. He insisted that they must marry. At once.

Tired, confused, Agatha fell in with his desires. As she put it in a piece of autobiographical fiction: 'lots of girls were doing it – flinging up everything, marrying the man they cared for . . . behind it lay that awful secret fear that you never took out and looked at properly. The nearest you got to it was saying defiantly: "And no matter *what* happens, we'll have had *something*."'[8]

No bureaucratic obstacle was too great for Archie, that able administrator, to overcome. Christmas Eve must be his wedding day. So off they went to hustle for a licence. The local registry office informed them that either an expensive special licence or fourteen days' notice were required, fourteen days that Archie did not have. Time was ticking away.

Only when a different and more helpful registrar came back from his elevenses was a solution found. Archie might be said to live at his stepfather's address in Bristol – 'you keep some of your effects here, don't you?' – meaning that the wedding could go ahead that same afternoon. In 1915, it would be officially confirmed that soldiers could marry from a parent's address, and also that a woman could register notice of a marriage by herself if her fiancé was overseas. This would make it easier and less expensive for the many soldiers who wanted a quick wedding during leave.[9]

The vicar was available at the Emmanuel Church, Bristol, and so Agatha Mary Clarissa Miller (24) made a hasty wartime marriage to Archibald Christie (25). 'No bride could have taken less trouble about her appearance,' she wrote, 'I wore an ordinary coat and skirt.' She hadn't even had time to wash her hands.

Archie's mother greeted the news with hysterics and a retreat to a darkened room. Feeling unwelcome in Bristol, the newly-weds travelled that night to Torquay, getting to the Grand Hotel at midnight, and spent Christmas Day with Clara. But Agatha's family too were disappointed by the secrecy and the speed.

'Everybody we were most fond of was annoyed with us,' wrote Agatha. 'I felt this but don't think Archie did.' There was just one thing on Archie's mind: he got out and proffered, once again, the dressing case. And this time it was received with graceful thanks. This business of the unwanted dressing case would come to stand for the balance of power within their marriage. He was the one to take the initiative, she was the one to accept.

But that is to skip ahead. As she settled into it, Agatha's new life as a married woman was delightful, blissful, companionate in the modern style. It was marred only by her husband's impending return to war. At the New Year she wrote a verse called 'The A.A. Alphabet for 1915,' a play on their initials:

A is for <u>Angel</u>, by nature (?) and name
And also for <u>Archibald</u>, spouse of the same.[10]

She was weaving Archie into the playful, creative world of the 'Queer Women'. The poem tells the story of an enjoyable country walk. But seeded throughout are references to boots for the trenches, the 'Huns', Archie's stores of spare wings in France and a part of their route that looked like no-man's-land. It was her usual trick of making difficult things fun.

And did Archie reciprocate this arch and playful way of love? He certainly tried. A note survives from July 1916, sent from his depot in France, and scribbled in pencil on a scrap of paper with a red SECRET stamp. It's poignant to imagine him turning away from his order book to think instead of the unusual, ardent young woman, loving him so much from so far away, and trying to raise himself to her level.

'A kindly and affectionate disposition,' he began, in a jokey summary of her character, fond of animals except worms and cockchafers; fond of human beings except husbands (on principle). Normally lazy but can develop and maintain great energy. Sound in limb and eye, wind not good up hill. Full of intelligence and artistic taste. Unconventional and inquisitive. Face good especially hair; figure good and skin excellent. Can wheedle well. Wild but if once captured would make a loving and affectionate wife.[11]

Archie sees so much of Agatha's true self here. But it's telling that his 'character' was still addressed to 'Miss A.M.C. Miller', as if she remained unmarried. 'Wild,' not 'captured'. They were both aware their marriage was not a real, solid thing. How could it be? It had been a succession of passionate encounters, keeping them in a suspended state, keeping them from maturity.

What isn't in doubt, though, was their sexual compatibility. Girls like Agatha were kept in a state of ignorance about sex.[12] Agatha did know of a girl who was made pregnant by another girl's father, but generally her kind were sheltered.

Which makes it all the more unusual that Agatha herself, lifelong, was generally so comfortable with the idea of sexual pleasure. It was never a source of shame or guilt. 'Passion can be taken for granted,' she says, discussing a good marriage, whereas tenderness and respect are rarer flowers, the more in need of nurture. A thought given later to Jane Marple may also illustrate Agatha's attitude. ' "Sex" as a word had not been much mentioned in Miss Marple's younger days,' she tells us, 'but there had been plenty of it – not talked about so much – but enjoyed far more.'[13]

The sense of shame attached to sex by the more conventional members of Agatha's generation began to diminish a little from 1918 onward with the publication of *Married Love*, by Marie Stopes. Stopes argued that sex (albeit within marriage) was natural and even enjoyable. Her own marriage had broken down when she and her husband found consummation impossible, and Stopes's lifelong journey to educate people about sex began. She found it extremely hard to locate a publisher. 'There are few enough men for girls to marry,' explained one who turned it down, 'and I think this would frighten off the few.'[14]

Stopes wanted women to enjoy sex, but her most important lesson was that men should be gentle. If a man 'plays the part of a tender wooer,' Stopes explains, 'a woman can generally be stirred so fundamentally as to give a passionate return.'[15] And it seems that Archie led, and Agatha willingly followed. 'You were really rather a dear last year,' he wrote in a first-anniversary letter, 'in trusting yourself boldly to me.'[16]

But Stopes has also left a darker legacy. Her preferred method of contraception was a sponge soaked in olive oil, and she believed that birth control was important for improving the 'purity' of the race. It was better for families tainted by syphilis or insanity not to reproduce. So contraception also had chilling overtones, and eugenics was becoming an obsession in British society. These concerns about the hereditary nature of illness would lie heavy on Archie and Agatha's shoulders, with so-called insanity in both their families.

Over the next three and a half years, Mr and Mrs Christie would only be together for the briefest of leaves. When they were finally able to cohabit, late in 1918, Agatha was pregnant within two months. The timing makes it seem likely that – either through olive oil or abstinence – they carefully avoided a pregnancy while the conflict kept them apart. 'Blast the war which keeps me here,' Archie complained from France.[17]

After one of his leaves, Archie returned to duty tired and lonely. 'Darling Angel,' he began another of his flimsy scribbles, 'the train journey was alright I lay dazed in my corner.' He crossed the Channel in a boat accompanied by two destroyers, was picked up by a car at Boulogne and taken back to his base, feeling 'weak as a kitten [. . .] I would have loved to have found a letter here from you tonight.'[18]

In 1916 he became a temporary major, with a pay rise to £700 a year, and the next year he was promoted to temporary lieutenant colonel, commanding a whole depot.[19] He became responsible for punishing rule-breakers: 'I sentenced a man to 28 days of . . . being tied to a tree and undergoing other punishment and fatigues because he refused to work.' Even though he was behind the lines, life was still challenging: 'I was glued to a telephone till 11 pm last night . . . I love you for yourself and I love you for your character. No one else would be the same to me.'[20]

This kind of language gives us a glimpse into a marriage quite different to that of Agatha's parents. This wasn't the love of a man for an idealised woman. No, he loved *her, for herself, for her character*. As Archie put it, *no one else would be the same to me*. This was bliss. 'When people loved each other,' thinks one of Agatha's most autobiographical heroines, 'they were happy. Unhappy marriages, and of course she knew there were many such, were because people didn't love each other.'[21]

But these high standards of loving and living would also make it impossible for Agatha, if the situation ever rose, to turn a blind Victorian eye to an affair.

That eventuality, though, would never arise. Of course not.

11

Enter Poirot

While Archie in France dashed off letters between telephone calls, Agatha's life at the hospital also provided the odd quiet moment for writing.

Work in the dispensary came in rushes. Once the prescriptions were filled, Agatha simply had to sit around until the next lot came in. One day she used the time to write a poem.

'In a Dispensary' shows how she found inspiration in her surroundings, however humdrum they might be. This would be a gift she shared with some of the most popular writers of the twentieth century. 'I don't want to transcend the commonplace,' wrote Philip Larkin. 'I love the commonplace. Everyday things are lovely to me.'[1] To Agatha even medicine bottles could contain romance:

> And high on the wall, beneath lock and key
> the powers of the Quick and the Dead!
> Little low bottles of blue and green
> *each with a legend red*
> In the depths beneath their slender necks,
> there is Romance, and to spare!
> *Oh! who shall say where Romance is?*
> *if Romance is not here?*[2]

The notebooks Agatha used to study for the Apothecaries Hall Assistants' Exam, still surviving in her family's care, show that in her breaks she revelled in all sorts of wordplay. 'Archibald Christie,' she wrote in pencil at the back of one of them, alongside her own name, before crossing out the letters in common to see how closely they matched. But flick to the front of the same book and you'll find a list of poisons: 'Alkaloid obtained from Belladonna ... Hyoscine Hydro-Bromide ... Alkaloid obtained from (Henbane).'[3]

When Agatha began to think about getting down to a second novel, it was obvious what her subject should be: a poisoning. This was the start of a career in toxicity. Of the sixty-six detective novels she'd write, forty-one feature a murder, attempted murder or suicide achieved through poison.[4] If you read through historian Kathryn Harkup's excellent seventeen-page table of Christie's means of death, 'fell off a cliff', 'electrocuted' and 'throat cut' stand out as the exceptions among the poisonings by strychnine, arsenic, morphine and atrophine. Cyanide would become a particular favourite: Agatha would use it to bump off no fewer than eighteen characters over the course of ten novels and four short stories.[5]

Agatha now began to create a character who was also a lady dispenser: the young and gorgeous Cynthia, who would appear in *The Mysterious Affair at Styles* (1921).

Perhaps the only surprise about Agatha's decision to write a murder mystery was the fact that it had taken so long. She'd devoured Sherlock Holmes, along with Anna Katharine Green's classic detective novel, *The Leavenworth Case*, and Gaston Leroux's *The Mystery of the Yellow Room*. These were stories she'd discussed with her sister, and they'd argued over whether Agatha could write something similar herself.

'I don't think you could do it,' said Madge. 'They are very difficult to do. I've thought about it.'

'I should like to try.'

'Well, I bet you couldn't,' said Madge.

There the matter rested ... but the words had been said ... the idea had been planted: *some day I would write a detective story.*[6]

By 1916, everything had come together for the creation of something surprising: a really excellent first detective novel, light as a feather, yet so well constructed it still reads addictively a century later.

Why is this book, *The Mysterious Affair at Styles*, so good?[7] To start, Agatha is writing about a world she knew well. Her characters were family, friends and servants, living in a country house, Styles Court, where tea is served on the lawn. These were her own people. Multiple courtships are in progress, and the 'upstairs' characters live off unearned income.

Yet the residents of Styles have been forced to adapt to wartime life, working in the garden themselves, and (this will be an important clue) recycling paper. Captain Hastings, the book's narrator, has been invalided home from the Front. One character works in a hospital, and the case will be solved by a Belgian refugee.

But the fictional mansion isn't just a shadow of its former self in terms of comfort. It's worse than that. It's also a place that's morally corrupt. No one is what he or she seems. The elderly woman who heads the household is a bully, the young marrieds seem intent upon adultery, and even the narrator, Hastings, is flirting when he should really have been fighting.

Although she painted it in dark colours, Agatha had created a fictional world that had much in common with her own. Even the novel's murder speaks directly to her own family situation. The victim, Mrs Inglethorp, is a matriarch: a powerful, older woman, along the lines of Auntie-Grannie, or even Clara, to whom the book was dedicated. This is a major difference between Agatha and her most obvious role model, Sir Arthur Conan Doyle. Right from the start, Agatha places the lives of women centre stage.

Styles tells the story of a battle to the death between Mrs Inglethorp and her companion, Evelyn. The men of the house are a fairly hopeless lot, and the same might be said of Agatha's own family. She'd watched her lazy father and useless brother waste the family fortune, while her mother and sister had given her stability and strength. Agatha's books would appeal to an important market of interwar readers. In them, women could see themselves.

But *Styles* also shines a troubling light on the remnants of the Miller family at Ashfield. Most people, perhaps women in particular, spend their lives pretending to be something that they're not: agreeable, biddable, conscientious. Yet the shadow side of the feminine, as Jung might have put it, was strong at Ashfield. Agatha's fiction shows she looked at her very feminine family and saw darkness there. We can intuit that while she loved her mother, she also feared Clara's power, and her clinginess.

At some level, Clara was holding Agatha back, preventing her from becoming an adult. Agatha was grown-up, married, experienced by her nursing in ways that Clara could not imagine. Yet here she still was, living pretty much the same life as she'd done for the previous twenty-five years.

Like Styles Court, Ashfield had become a place of stagnation. In a fictional account of her own life, Agatha describes her mother's love with that darker filter in place: it was, she says, 'a dangerous intensity of affection'.[8]

There were also reasons rooted in the recent history of Britain that made poisoning the perfect place for Agatha's mystery career to begin.

Auntie-Grannie's generation had believed there was an epidemic of poisoning in Victorian society. The nineteenth century was an age which prized domestic life more highly than ever before. Appropriately, poison was a weapon that could be wielded only *within* a household. It had to be administered by a doctor, a maid, a family member: someone you trusted.

The genre of detective fiction had taken off when the Industrial Revolution changed the lives of many Britons from rural to urban. Rising living standards, of course, were generally a 'good thing'. But a respite from the battle against nature opened up space in Victorian minds to accommodate new and specifically modern fears and neuroses. A nineteenth-century person could afford to worry less than her Georgian forebear about death by famine or disease. But that left room for other, less tangible, fears.

Once, you'd have known everyone who lived in your village. As a Victorian, you were much more likely to live in a town, with a stranger next door. Once, you'd have married someone introduced to you by your parents. But what did you really know about your new husband? Or maid? Or doctor? The new genre of crime fiction took these fears out of the closet at the back of people's minds, burnished them, and finally showed them being vanquished by that nineteenth-century invention: the fictional detective. The murderer is caught, order is restored, the uneasy can once again sleep at night.

Agatha decided that like Conan Doyle she needed a detective of her own. But she turned the idea of the well-connected and heroic Sherlock Holmes on its head.

The egg-headed Hercule Poirot with his ridiculous moustache, first introduced in *Styles*, was to be a new thing: a detective whom it was dangerously easy to underestimate. Agatha's choice of Belgian as his nationality was inspired by the growing number of refugees who'd started to appear in wartime Torquay.

More than a million Belgians had recently fled from a war-torn country where, as Rupert Brooke claimed, 'three civilians have been killed to every one soldier'. He described the people he'd seen fleeing Antwerp, their goods in perambulators, 'two unending lines of them, the old men mostly weeping, the women with hard white drawn faces.'[9] About a quarter of a million of them came to Britain.

By choosing to make Hercule Poirot a foreigner, and a refugee as well, Agatha created the perfect detective for an age when everyone was growing surfeited with soldiers and action heroes. He's so physically unimpressive that no one expects Poirot to steal the show.

Rather like a stereotypical woman, Poirot cannot rely upon brawn to solve problems, for he has none. He has to use brains instead. 'There is no need of *physical* effort,' he explains, 'one needs only – to think.'[10] There's even a joke in his name: Hercules, of course, is a muscular classical hero. But 'Hercule' Poirot has a name like himself: diminutive, fussy, camp.

And Agatha would show Poirot working in a different way to Holmes. In Sherlock's first fictional appearance, *A Study in Scarlet*, the great detective lies down flat on the floor to gather up 'a little pile of grey dust'.[11] It was cigar ash, and from his encyclopaedic knowledge of the different kinds of ash made by different kinds of cigar, he could deduce which brand the murderer had been smoking.

But Agatha deliberately parodies the scene in an early appearance of Poirot's. Unlike Holmes, he utterly refuses to lie down to examine a crime scene – the grass is damp! – and completely fails to 'scoop up cigarette ash when I do not know one kind from the other'.[12] Poirot will not stoop to 'gather clues'. He needs only his little grey cells.

Brainy, physically awkward, and unexpectedly brilliant, Poirot is liked by many. But by readers who are themselves a bit geeky, though, he's utterly beloved. Like Sherlock Holmes, he's an oddball and a loner. Yet unlike Holmes, with his ennui and his drug addiction, Poirot's completely happy with himself. He has *joie de vivre*. You can imagine him as an honorary member of the 'Queer Women'.

As she allowed him to exercise his talents in his first mysterious affair, though, Agatha can have had no idea she'd be living with Poirot for the next sixty years.

12

The Moorland Hotel

O n her days off from the hospital, Agatha got on with her book. She'd write out each chapter in longhand before inexpertly typing it up. She used three fingers of each hand, proudly joking that 'most amateur typists can only use two'.[1]

Even so, at the halfway point, she simply ran out of steam. 'I got very tired,' Agatha recalled, 'and I also got cross.'

It was Clara who suggested she should take a holiday on Dartmoor, and devote herself to finishing the story. Off Agatha went, by train and then coach. She stayed for two weeks at the remote Moorland Hotel, alone but not lonely, busy with her writing. The hotel advertised itself as the 'perfect Health Resort'.[2] A solitary visit to a health resort is not a common holiday choice for a 25-year-old. But Agatha was completely comfortable: 'the reason I began to write . . . was in order to avoid having to talk to people.'[3]

The grey stone hotel still stands on the edge of the moor to this day: a lovely location from which to walk across the green-bronze moorland, perhaps ascending to Haytor Rocks half an hour away. In that same year, 1916, Agatha's mentor Eden Phillpotts dipped his pen in purple to describe the scenery: 'the wilderness lifts up her head in peaks of granite, or rolls along in huge, hog-backed hills that swell to the sky-line.'[4] But Agatha would ignore all this, writing hard each morning. During an afternoon walk, she'd plan the next scene.

And so, gradually, the story unfolded.

Agatha would later claim her success happened almost by accident. 'I personally had no ambition,' she wrote. But this was really the powerful code of Edwardian ladyhood talking. Her actions belie her words, and here at the Moorland Hotel we catch her taking herself seriously. Lifelong she'd go on these occasional writing binges. They were memorable, powerfully felt times for her, times during which she'd feel close to God.

Agatha would eventually settle down to a preferred novelette length of 60,000 words. *Styles* is not yet fine-tuned. It's longer than her classic books, at 74,000 words, and it's a little dense with clues.

And even the writing retreat did not quite see the work finished. The story originally ended with a denouement in court, with Poirot explaining everything from the witness box. The problem was that witnesses simply aren't allowed to do this sort of thing. Agatha would learn, in time, to consult professionals: 'you ask any barrister and he will tell you with tears in his eyes what you can and can't do.'[5] The ending would eventually be rewritten, on a publisher's advice, creating the first of Agatha's famous 'drawing room scenes' where all is revealed.

What were the twists of the tale that Agatha refined during her moorland tramps? In this book, I'm occasionally going to take you behind the scenes to reveal some characteristic 'Christie tricks'.

A classic 'Christie trick' – and there's a brilliant example in *Styles* – is the hiding of an object in plain sight. Poirot, a neat-freak, notices the objects on a mantlepiece are out of line. That's because the murderer has hidden a key document by rolling it up into a spill for lighting a fire and has placed it, slightly clumsily, in a jar above the fireplace. This planting of a clue is doubly lovely because it's also a nod from Agatha to the history of her genre. It was in fact borrowed from one of her own favourite detective stories: *The Leavenworth Case* (1878), where Anna Katharine Green's detective discovers a vital letter 'torn lengthwise into strips, and twisted up into lighters'. Green herself, in a kind of passing of the torch between authors over the years, was paying homage to Edgar Allan Poe's argument 'that the best way to hide a document is to change its appearance and then place it on full view.'[6]

Styles also contains another marvellous 'Christie trick': the 'hidden couple'. These are two people who seem actively to dislike each other. Unbeknown to anybody, the husband of the wealthy Mrs Inglethorp, and Mrs Inglethorp's female companion Evelyn, are in fact secretly a pair of murderous adulterers.

We fail to detect their relationship because Hastings, our narrator, through whose eyes we see them, finds them so sexually unattractive that he cannot conceive of them as sexual beings at all. He looks at tweed-wearing, hearty Evelyn with her 'large sensible square body, with feet to match,' and sees a person who's barely feminine. And when it comes to Alfred Inglethorp, Evelyn's partner in crime, Agatha double-bluffs us by making him both unattractive in appearance and furtive in behaviour. She even gives him that clear marker of dodginess in the 1910s: a beard. And we think, no, that's too easy, the murderer can't possibly be him.[7]

It's not just Alfred and Evelyn in *Styles* who are pretending to be something they aren't. Practically all the characters are keeping up a pretence of one kind or another. Agatha was very familiar with this: after all, she was *pretending* to be married, *pretending* the work in the hospital wasn't awful. So many of her killers likewise try to pass for normal in the world of her books.

And so eventually *Styles* was finished, or at least, as finished as Agatha could manage. 'It could be much better, I saw that,' she wrote, 'but I didn't see just how *I* could make it better, so I had to leave it as it was.'

She sent her typescript to the publisher Hodder & Stoughton. But back it came with a rejection, 'a plain refusal, with no frills on it'.

That seemed to be the end of the story. Agatha did try other publishers, equally unsuccessfully, but then events overtook her. Something occurred that was much more important than a highly speculative project done purely for pleasure.

Real life began in earnest, for Archie came back from the war.

❖ PART FOUR ❖

Bright Young Author – 1920s

13

Enter London

In 1918, with the end of the war drawing near, Archie was posted back to London. He was to provide technical advice to what was now the Royal Air Force from the new Air Ministry in Covent Garden. He'd been mentioned in dispatches five times, and the *London Gazette* would shortly announce that Lieutenant Colonel Christie was to receive the Distinguished Service Order. He was coming home a hero.

In September 1918, Agatha came to London to join him. Although they'd been married for nearly four years, they'd never lived together. In practical terms, this was the start of Agatha's life as a wife.

Their first home was a cheap flat, two rooms in a house in St John's Wood. Five Northwick Terrace had come down in the world. Originally home to a household of thirteen, by 1918 it had been subdivided. Agatha and Archie's flatlet, furnished rather shabbily, came complete with a Mrs Woods, who occupied the basement and who 'did' for the young couple.

Agatha started a course in typing and bookkeeping. The Christies' finances were precarious, and it was at least possible she might have to earn some money. But she threw herself with greater zeal into the role of the housewife.

As the Great War drew to an end, most Britons wanted to turn back the clock and return women from the workplace to their homes. But everyone was having to work out anew what these dreamed-of homes might look like.[1] *The Times* even carried adverts for training courses in 'household accomplishments' for married women, like Agatha, who'd not yet had the chance to live with their husbands.[2] To make Archie one of the homes 'Fit For Heroes' that Lloyd George had promised to the returning soldiers was now Agatha's priority. After all, she and Archie were among the lucky ones. Thirty per cent of Archie's generation of males had lost their lives.

And it turned out that Agatha loved being a homemaker. For a start, she had few London friends, and it filled the time. The housing shortage meant it took a lot of energy to find and decorate Northwick Terrace and their two subsequent London flats, and she spills a lot of ink about it in her autobiography. To read of her problems with lumpy beds and being diddled by the fishmonger, running a two-room flat sounds like as much work as running Ashfield. This was despite the fact she had the help not only of Mrs Woods, but also of Archie's former batman, Bartlett.

Agatha wasn't the only middle-class woman struggling to reconstruct the solid comforts of an Edwardian youth. One of the most attractive things about Agatha, though, is her practicality. She simply persevered at tasks until she'd mastered them. She even fantasised about becoming a parlourmaid herself: 'I am sure I was well enough qualified.' She would probably have found it harder than expected, as the labour really required to run a home was practically invisible to middle-class eyes. Unlike many others of her sort, though, Agatha could at least imagine the possibility. Her fantasy life as a servant would emerge in the formidable Lucy Eyelesbarrow, who combines housekeeping with detection in *4.50 from Paddington*.

It's noticeable that Agatha's new life lacked that lynchpin of Ashfield: the live-in cook. During the war, even the well-off had had to get used to doing without, and as a result the status of cooking started to change.

In her tiny kitchenette, Agatha began to experiment with cooking herself, starting with light, luxurious dishes – cheese soufflé, for example – while Mrs Woods still produced the rest. Historian Nicola Humble explains that 'cooking was now sold as a high-status leisure activity,' something 'too interesting to be left to servants, even if there were any to be had.'[3] Even the famously impractical Virginia Woolf took a course of cooking lessons, during which she managed to bake her wedding ring into a suet pudding.[4]

The next upheaval for the Christies came with the Armistice in November. Agatha thought Londoners indulged in 'a sort of wild orgy of pleasure: an almost brutal enjoyment'. The drinking and dancing were disorientating. Another woman, Elizabeth Plunkett, found the Armistice equally strange. 'We seemed drained of all feeling. One felt nothing. We took up our lives again or tried to take them up . . . we sat at table and there were absent faces.'[5]

The disorientation increased when Archie suddenly revealed he was planning to leave his steady RAF job. He wanted instead to hunt for well-paid employment in the City. But he'd said nothing until he'd made up his mind, and the unexpected announcement left Agatha dumbfounded. Just as Archie had pursued her relentlessly after that first dance, here he was again revealing his decisive, almost ruthless, manner of living.

Many City firms were keen to help demobilised young officers, and Archie soon found a job. It was at a financial services company called the Imperial and Foreign Investment Corporation. His boss was Jewish, and both Agatha and Archie referred to him according to the nasty 1920s British convention as 'fat' and 'yellow.' Mr 'Goldstein', as Agatha called him, not having bothered to learn his real name, paid generously.

The Christies' annual income included Archie's army pension of £50, £50 from his personal investments, Agatha's inheritance of £100, and now Archie's salary of £500. £700 a year was twice the sum earned by a senior railway clerk, or a middle-aged civil servant. Even so, the young couple *felt* hard up. Everyone did: clothing, for example, was three times more expensive in 1920 than it had been in 1914.[6]

George Orwell, writing about 1920s Britain, considered that £1,000 a year was the amount you needed to live like a 'gentleman'. On the other hand, to live with aspirations to gentility on £400 a year:

was a queer business, for it meant that your gentility was almost purely theoretical. You lived, so to speak, at two levels simultane-ously. Theoretically you knew all about servants and how to tip them, although in practice you had one, at most, two resident serv-ants. Theoretically you knew how to wear your clothes and how to order a dinner, although in practice you could never afford to go to a decent tailor or a decent restaurant.[7]

Agatha and Archie were only just above this 'queer' level in society, which forced them to become adept at keeping up appearances. When Agatha's characters were to do this in her fiction, she could use personal knowledge to describe it.

In December 1918 came an election, the first in which some selected women were allowed to vote. It's often believed this was a thank-you for the work women had done during the war. But even war workers like Agatha were still excluded from the franchise. She didn't meet the criteria for eligibility: she wasn't over thirty, she wasn't a householder, nor a university graduate. And in fact, widen-ing the franchise had nothing to do with gratitude. Instead, as histo-rian Janet Howarth explains, it was a response to an expansion in the definition of citizenship. If women had contributed to the war effort, then they must be citizens. Citizenship, rather than manhood, was beginning to be taken as the basis for the vote.[8] But not too many women could be admitted to citizenship at once, or else – horrors! – they would outnumber men among the electorate.

The result of this, then, was that Agatha didn't seem to be a full citizen, and that formal politics and politicians didn't have much to offer her. Women like her were overlooked by a Labour Party that was really only interested in working males. Even the Conservatives would have more female MPs.[9] All this helps explain why Agatha would remain disengaged from politics, lifelong, although the Conservatives would be her natural political party.

But life in London must have been exciting. Archie and Agatha were to be companions, as well as spouses. They wanted travel and leisure. They expected children, but didn't think them vital. 'Married life to them was a game,' as Agatha says of another young couple in an autobiographical novel, 'they played at it enthusiastically.'[10]

The 1920s were just round the corner. Yet the thing that's often missing from our popular image of a decade of fun is the shadow left by the war. The twenties would witness, for example, a huge rise in the number of people committing suicide. Meanwhile – and Agatha would often write about this – other people were giving up on the Church and turning to spiritualism to contact loved ones lost between 1914 and 1918.[11]

If the war was over, surely the Christies should be having a good time? Sometimes it seemed surprisingly difficult. Even as Agatha did her best at cooking, Archie rejected her efforts, finding the meat 'uninteresting', the soufflés indigestible. Stress acted upon his stomach. He suffered from 'nervous dyspepsia', or indigestion without an obvious cause, and Agatha explains that on many evenings he was 'unable to eat anything at all'. 'Slightly lonely,' was how she described her new life.

Yet the valiant tone of her autobiography shows Agatha trying hard to be happy. And soon there was another reason for the Christie marriage to be considered a roaring success.

14

Enter Rosalind

The Christies were visiting Clara in Torquay when Agatha was laid low with 'tummy sickness'. It took her a while to work out what this meant, but she was thrilled when she realised she was pregnant.

Agatha had always wanted children; her dearest wish was to be 'surrounded by babies'.[1] It was her destiny, she thought, as did Poirot: 'to marry and have children, that is the common lot of women. Only one woman in a hundred – more, in a thousand, can make for herself a name and a position.'[2]

But Agatha was unprepared for the morning sickness that persisted for the whole of her pregnancy. She was frightened by the coming ordeal, and knew she might possibly die. This was a time when most people still had personal knowledge of a mother who hadn't survived childbirth.

Archie's reaction was conflicted too. Agatha described him as 'unexpectedly kind', for she knew he found it hard to cope with illness. When the time came, Agatha retreated to Ashfield to give birth with the help of a professional nurse, and, of course, of Clara.

In Agatha's most autobiographical novel, the heroine's strongest feelings remain, even after marriage, for her mother. She's happiest on visits to her childhood home. She

loved that feeling of stepping back into her old life. To feel that happy tide of reassurance sweeping over her – the feeling of being loved – of being *adequate*.[3]

Archie came to Ashfield as well, but Clara and the professional nurse had taken control of all the arrangements. When her daughter Rosalind was finally born, on 5 August 1919, Agatha's first reaction was not so much conventional joy, as relief: 'I don't feel sick any more. How wonderful!'

Right from the start, Agatha thought of Rosalind not so much as an extension of herself, but as a separate person. The new baby was, to her, already a personality: 'both gay and determined'. Rather than seeing her child as the most important thing in the world, as Clara saw Agatha, Agatha was different. She observed her daughter, respectfully, from a distance. And she'd never see motherhood itself through conventional eyes.

Auntie-Grannie wasn't there to witness the birth, for she'd died just three months before. And this year of change would be completed by the death in December of Agatha's maternal grandmother Polly as well. The older generation faded as the new one arrived, leaving Clara as the pin holding the family together; Clara, upon whom Agatha could depend. Strikingly soon after the birth, Agatha left Ashfield, leaving her baby with her mother. The nurse was kept on for two extra weeks so Agatha could go to London.

From the perspective of today's attachment parenting, this decision, to leave a days-old baby, seems odd. From a contemporary perspective, it was much more normal. But both Agatha and Archie were daunted by their new role as parents, 'a little timid, rather nervous, like two children who were not sure they were wanted.'

Agatha doesn't say much about Rosalind's birth in her autobiography, devoting many more words to the hiring of her nurse. But in her autobiographical novel, she describes the heroine's difficulties in coming to terms with her new role. She 'was now definitely playing the part of the Young Mother. But she did not feel at all like a wife or a mother. She felt like a little girl come home after an exciting but tiring party.'[4]

In her fiction, Agatha would even delve into the possibilities of mothers who resent, dislike or damage their offspring. 'Lots of mothers don't like their children,' she'd write in The Moving Finger.[5]

It's not at all that Agatha herself disliked kids. She just didn't feel obliged to treat them in the syrupy terms society preferred. When a musician Agatha knew gave up playing to prioritise motherhood, saying 'I do not mind – I find a baby more interesting,' Agatha found it 'extraordinary'.[6]

Her purpose in returning so soon to London was to look for a bigger flat, a live-in nurse and a housemaid. Archie's salary would not stretch to the regular purchase of new clothes, but even so they thought they needed these two staff members, 'essentials of life in those days'.

The new flat in which they eventually settled with Rosalind was in Addison Mansions, a giant red-brick block of six storeys, built in the 1880s near the Olympia exhibition halls. Agatha chose the furniture from Heal's. Archie was out at work, and with Lucy the maid and Jessie the nurse, the household was complete. 'We never had such a happy time,' Agatha wrote.

But it was also a time of shifting power relationships. Agatha enjoyed the autonomy Archie gave her over their home, but she now had to learn to manage staff. She was rejected as an employer by various nannies who were used to more lavish households. Even Miss Marple has a way of speaking that makes liberals uncomfortable: 'the accustomed tone of command of somebody whose business it was to give orders'.[7] Agatha's generation were growing less able to summon up that forceful voice.

And so we come onto the vexed question of what domestic service would mean in Agatha's life, and in her novels. The answer is that in the 1920s she, and her peers, were working it out. Nobody really knew what a servant was any more: the status had become ambivalent. 'Dear old Dorcas!' thinks the unobservant Hastings, in *The Mysterious Affair at Styles*. 'What a fine specimen she was of the old-fashioned servant that is so fast dying out.' This is often quoted as an example of class blindness. But then, of course, Agatha's characters are not always mouthpieces for her own views. Hastings does not really 'see' Dorcas, and Agatha is deliberately obscuring her by showing her only through Hastings' limited vision.

Yet this excuse doesn't hold in Agatha's own autobiography, where her employees are treated as music-hall turns, their irritating quirks laid out for the reader's entertainment. It was all too easy for employers to slip into a sense of martyrdom. One article of 1920 set out their complaints: 'unwilling service, ill performed, higher wages demanded than can be paid, principles of cleanliness and orderliness violated, appearances having to be kept up and rigid rules adhered to for fear "the girl will give notice". It is tyranny.'[8] Agatha was completely typical in her middle-class anxieties about domestic staff. It jars today, but these were vital concerns to women like her.

When Archie came in from work, he was at first happy to spend the evening with his daughter and wife. But he was used to the excitement and camaraderie of military service. Gradually he grew hungry for life outside the home, and started spending his weekends playing golf. Men like Archie, in Siegfried Sassoon's words, were 'everlastingly differentiated from everyone except his fellow soldiers'.[9] A journalist tried to sum up this generation in 1920, describing how 'something was wrong . . . something had altered in them. They were subject to queer moods, queer temper, fits of profound depression alternating with a restless desire for pleasure.'[10]

Archie 'never mentioned the war,' Agatha tells us, 'his one idea in those days was to forget such things.' 'Unemotional' was how she described him, accepting everything 'without surprise'. Archie's fictional counterpart, Dermot, in her most autobiographical novel, was like this too: 'when he did break through his reserve and say something,' his wife 'treasured it up as something to remember. It was so obviously difficult for him.'[11]

'There was no reason,' wrote Agatha, 'why we shouldn't live happily ever after' at Addison Mansions. But there was a reason – a large reason – sitting right there in her drawing room.

'I rather wish,' said Archie, 'I could make a change.'

15

The British Mission

C hange was indeed coming, in a surprising way.

Shortly after Rosalind's birth in 1919, around her twenty-ninth birthday, Agatha received a letter. To her astonishment, it was from the eminent publisher, John Lane, inviting her to call upon him in his office.

Agatha had given up hope of becoming a novelist. She'd practically forgotten about *Styles* after it had been rejected by no fewer than six publishers. Her life had changed, its path narrowing to that of a wife and mother. She accepted it. She'd never make a heroine; she'd never be the Lady Agatha of her childhood fantasy. For one thing, she was getting older. 'Make the heroine a little younger,' Eden Phillpotts had advised her. 'Thirty-one is rather too old – don't you think?'[1]

But now this unexpected invitation to adventure arrived in the post. Surely Mr Lane wouldn't have asked her to his office only to reject her? Full of excitement, Agatha set off to find out.

Born, like Agatha, in Devon, Lane was now sixty-five. As he sat waiting for her in his cluttered office, he looked 'like an old-fashioned Sea Captain, with his small grey beard and twinkling blue eyes'.[2] Lane had a nose for fresh, cheap, eye-catching writers. They'd helped him build up his publishing business, The Bodley Head.[3]

'Agatha,' Lane mused about this potential new author, 'is an unusual name which remains in people's memories.' And he knew that when it came to Mrs Christie's work he was in a strong position. He'd commissioned some expert readers to review the manuscript. *Styles* would 'very likely sell,' read one of them, 'the story holds the reader.' A second reader thought that although the author's gender had not been revealed, something about the writing 'makes me suspect the hand of a woman'.[4] Both readers agreed, though, that the trial scene at the end was implausible and needed revision.

John Lane shrewdly noted both this and Agatha's inexperience, and decided to milk the situation to his advantage. Sitting her down, he gave Agatha a talking-to about the necessary rewriting, and how little money he was likely to make on a novice.

But his negotiating tactics weren't needed. Agatha was thrilled. By the time he whisked a contract out of his desk, she didn't even read it with the care it deserved: 'he would publish my book . . . I would have signed anything.'

She was embarking in an amateurish way upon what would turn out to be a career. As one of what Virginia Woolf described as 'the daughters of educated men', Agatha belonged to the group in society least expected to have to think about money. Signing this contract would take her into a more rackety world. She was the only one, for example, of the main four writers of the Golden Age of Detective Fiction – Dorothy L. Sayers, Margery Allingham and Ngaio Marsh being the others – to give birth to a child within wedlock. Agatha took this first step enthusiastically, but blindly, not realising where it would lead.

An agent, had she had one, would have advised Agatha against signing. Lane's contract committed the inexperienced author to stingy royalties. Flatteringly, he was already talking about her next book. But he was also quietly locking her into a restrictive five-book deal.

Even so, Archie took Agatha out to celebrate at the Hammersmith Palais, a venue that could take 6,000 dancers. No drinks stronger than tea were served, but life was intoxicating. Agatha was to be published. And when *Styles* came out, it was a significant success.

In the meantime, Agatha got to work on a follow-up.[5] It was clear that with this first taste of accomplishment, Addison Mansions now contained two people who were no longer quite as content with life as they had been. In another book of the 1920s Agatha would describe the dreary women who talked for hours of nothing but 'themselves and their children and of the difficulties of getting good milk . . . they *were* stupid.'[6] She, meanwhile, was enjoying her work. In a newspaper interview, she made her priorities clear. 'Even my little two-year-old daughter does not deter me,' she said, from her pursuit of crime. 'When once you adopt crime it's difficult to give it up, I know I can never do so.'[7]

That interview, playing down her role as a mother, and playing up her role as an author, was significant. As was the fact that she was *being* interviewed: she was becoming a public figure. The 1920s saw the creation of something like a modern celebrity culture, with people looking for distraction in commercial fiction and newspaper articles about famous people.[8] Agatha was entering into a pact with the press that would turn out to be both wonderful and terrible.

Archie was proud of his clever wife, keen on the money she was beginning to earn. But one cannot help suspecting that Agatha's unexpected success unsettled him even further. And then he was offered an extraordinary chance to get out of the rut.

A massive exhibition was being planned, to take place at Wembley in 1924, to promote trade and showcase the products of the British Empire. As the British began to think about withdrawing from the administrative rule of places like India, they were looking for new ways – like this one – to keep the Empire alive. The manager of the project was a teacher from Archie's school, one Major Ernest Belcher. He was going to lead a mission round the world to drum up support for the exhibition, and invited Archie to go with him as his financial officer.

Major Belcher, unmarried, egocentric, some twenty years older than Archie and Agatha, was a slightly comedic figure. During the war he'd occupied the position of controller of the nation's potato supply. Agatha was snide about his achievements. 'We never had them,' she said, of potatoes, 'whether the shortage was entirely due to Belcher's control of them I don't know, but I should not be surprised to hear it.'

But Belcher at first seemed harmless enough. And the Christies decided that not only should Archie take the job, but that Agatha should go too, while Rosalind would stay behind with Madge. It was a risk, for Archie would have to leave his employment. Yet the chance was irresistible. To circumnavigate the whole world would be rather like an aristocratic Grand Tour of old, at a bargain price. The adventure was part of a wider travel boom following the war, for many naval ships were being repurposed into ocean liners. The dominions Agatha would now visit were becoming seen by British middle-class people as destinations not so much for work as for holidays.[9] Agatha had always loved motion: 'your travel life,' she wrote, 'has the essence of a dream . . . you are yourself, but a different self.' Archie did not really like the man he'd become at Addison Mansions. Perhaps he'd find a more satisfactory version of himself at sea.

The day the mission set off from London was also the day Agatha's second book, *The Secret Adversary*, was published. The departure was considered important enough for a photograph in *The Times*, which shows Agatha laiden with flowers, like a celebrity. But at this stage, still a newcomer as a novelist, she was misidentified in the caption as the daughter of the mission's agricultural advisor, a potato magnate named Mr F. Hiam.[10]

Their route took them via Madeira to South Africa, then Australia and New Zealand. Agatha and Archie next planned a holiday in Hawaii, before rejoining the mission for Canada. They were following in the footsteps of the Prince of Wales, who'd made a similar round-the-globe trip a couple of years previously to try to keep the dominions engaged. But Belcher's mission seemed a little quixotic even to those most closely involved. On the voyage, Agatha wrote home, 'we have trained the Chief Engineer, at whose table we sit, to drink "Success to the Mission" every night, which he does, murmuring "But I'm still not sure what kind of mission it is. They say it's not religious."'[11]

Their boat to South Africa was the *Kildonan Castle*, which becomes the *Kilmorden Castle* when the heroine travels to the same country in Agatha's novel *The Man in the Brown Suit*.[12] As would be the case for the rest of her life, everything Agatha experienced became copy. She spent her time mainly among British expatriates, and her glance at them was sidelong. Everywhere she found irony, something to laugh at, something to cut down to size. Even the cultivation of pineapples was amusing: she'd imagined them to grow gracefully from a tree, and was disappointed to find them planted in a field, like cabbages.

This note of mockery would be the mode in which, more or less, Agatha would lifelong discuss the British Empire. She wasn't there to bang the drum for it. She was there for the fun both of seeing it, and of making fun of it.

The photographs from the voyage show them having a wonderful time: Agatha lounges against the rail of a liner; she swims in a pool, she poses with a surfboard – a new sporting accomplishment for the girl who'd always loved swimming – on a South African beach. She surfs in a pearl necklace and a bathing cap decorated with petals. Garlanded with flowers in Hawaii, she steps out of a bungalow hidden in a banana grove.

But the longer it lasted, the more tiring the mission became. Like a royal tour in miniature, Belcher and his minions were meeting new people and admiring fruit farms: 'a long weary day . . . civic reception, factory inspections, lunches and dinners with speeches etc.' Belcher was revealing himself to be a petty tyrant, less and less pleasant as the months progressed. 'Wild Man worse than ever this morning,' Agatha reported, 'he is in his room darkened like a primeval cave, eating bread and milk, and growling at everyone.'[13]

There was another notable downside to the journey: the absence of Rosalind, left behind in her aunt's care. Clara had completely supported Agatha's decision to accompany her husband, fearing that a man left alone would stray: 'if you're not with your husband, if you leave him too much, *you'll lose him.*' Madge, though, taking Rosalind and her nurse into her own household, had been less enthusiastic. She pointed out that their brother had come home from Africa unwell, and needed his sisters' support. But Agatha had chosen to go.

A psychologist today would probably tell you that to leave a two-year-old for nine months simply cannot be done without creating lasting fears of abandonment. Yet Agatha wanted to be different to Clara, to give Rosalind space to grow. Any child, says Agatha, in the closest she got to a statement of her child-rearing philosophy, 'is mysteriously a stranger . . . you will be allowed to have charge of it for a period: after that it will leave you and blossom out into its own free life.' And Rosalind remained a little mysterious to her. Archie loved his daughter in a more simple, straightforward way that suited them both: 'they understood each other,' thought Agatha, 'better than Rosalind and I did.'

Even so, Agatha certainly felt conflicted. 'I think about you such a lot, my own baby,' she wrote in a letter intended to be read aloud to Rosalind. As she admitted to Clara, she felt guilty: 'I feel rather awful being away enjoying myself.'[14]

It was the same guilt that was always there when Rosalind interrupted her writing time, her nurse calling out, 'We mustn't disturb Mummy, must we little dear?' Agatha was unusually honest about her resentment of the need to look after a child: 'you had either to converse with Rosalind and play with her, or see she was suitably occupied in playing with somebody else.'

Agatha tried to put her guilt aside as the holiday part of the trip began: a blessedly Belcher-free month in Honolulu. The surfing was wonderful, 'one of the most perfect physical pleasures I have known.' But the strong waves were dangerous, and both Archie and Agatha were badly burned by the sun.

On the final leg of the tour in Canada, the fun definitely ran out. So too did their money, and Agatha found herself reduced to having meat extract in hot water for dinner. Archie's sinuses were inflamed; Agatha had a shoulder condition, neuritis, perhaps brought on by all the surfing. She was 'longing to get home'.[15] Finally, nine months after leaving, they were on the boat home. Two years later, the exhibition itself would attract 27 million visitors, leaving a lasting legacy in the shape of Wembley Stadium.

While Agatha had been away, the press cuttings sent on to her convinced her that her second book, *The Secret Adversary*, was going to be a success too. Money was coming in from things like the sale of Swedish rights. And in autumn 1922, before Agatha had even reached home, plans were made for the serialisation of her third book, *The Murder on the Links*.

Now that she was three books in, Agatha was looking back upon that first meeting with John Lane, so exciting at the time, with mixed feelings.

He'd stared at her so sharply with his 'shrewd blue eyes'. His gaze ought to have warned her, perhaps, 'he was the kind of man to drive a hard bargain'. Little did Lane know that when The Bodley Head's hottest new author returned to London, she was making plans to escape from him.

16

Thrillers

Although she seems the most English of authors, Agatha Christie was an international success from the start. *The Mysterious Affair at Styles*, for example, came out in America first, in October 1920, even before its British publication.

The reason was that in Britain the story was serialised in *The Times*, albeit in a special weekly edition of the paper mainly read by expatriates. This took five months, and meant the novel didn't appear as a single volume until 21 January 1921. Agatha was a magazine writer before she was a novelist.

She was also a more versatile writer than many people give her credit for, and would write in other genres than crime. But her career in detective fiction had started fantastically well. Despite the frustrating wait to see it between hard covers, *Styles* was a critical success. *The Sunday Times* found it 'very well contrived' and *The Times* 'brilliant'.[1] *The Times Literary Supplement* had only one criticism: 'it is almost too ingenious.' Agatha proudly clipped that review out of the paper, and saved it.[2]

One interesting review came from the *Pharmaceutical Journal*, which praised the 'knowledgeable' way Agatha had dealt with poisons.[3] A set of agreed 'rules' for detective stories was emerging, including the notion that the author must 'play fair' by the reader, giving her at least a chance of guessing the identity of the criminal. 'Mysterious poisons unknown to science' were among the tricks considered to be unsporting, and Agatha would be pretty good at avoiding them for her whole career. In just one late novel – *The Mirror Crack'd from Side to Side* – would she fall back upon an imaginary barbiturate she called 'Calmo'.[4]

But although readers liked *Styles*, it was much more profitable for its publisher than its author. As time went on, Agatha grew suspicious that John Lane was not playing fair. She became good friends with his nephew, Allen. 'I used to say suddenly: "Allen, isn't it about a *year* since I've had any royalties from you?"' she recalled. 'I wondered whether you'd noticed,' he'd reply.[5]

In her autobiography, Agatha tells us *Styles* had given such a poor financial return she decided not to write anything else. What changed her mind? What motivated her decision to write a second book, which would establish her in a career, rather than leave her as a lucky dilettante?

The official explanation she gives in her autobiography was the deteriorating situation at Ashfield. In 1919, when Auntie-Grannie died, her little stream of income had dried up too. The big old house was becoming too expensive to maintain. It would have to be sold.

But with so much of herself invested in Ashfield and its gardens, Agatha was heartbroken by the prospect: 'it's – it's – it means everything.' So, practical Archie, she tells us, came up with a practical solution. Why didn't she write another book, in the hope of making some money to save her mother's house?

This, though, was a fairy-tale version of events, conforming to the old idea that a woman should only write for money in cases of dire necessity or to help her family. It's belied by evidence from 1920. Before *Styles* had even come out, Agatha was writing to The Bodley Head to tell them she'd already 'nearly finished a second one'.[6] She was eager to get cracking on a career.

And Agatha confirmed she was already a career author in an interview she gave in 1922. 'Crime is like drugs,' she told a journalist. 'Once a writer of detective stories . . . you inevitably return – the public expect it of you!' She had 'a public', she had a product, she was under pressure to produce.[7]

If you look at Agatha's publishing record over the twenties, it's obvious there was strategy behind her growing success. The years 1921–1931 would see her write eleven books, but only five were in the classic detective format. One was a book of poetry, one a straight novel, and five were what Agatha called 'thrillers'. She was experimenting with genre, finding out what would sell best. 'One is a tradesman,' she explained, 'in a good honest trade . . . you must submit to the discipline of form.'

Agatha's idea of herself as a craftsperson writing for the market would exclude her from the roster of the interwar period's 'great writers': the Bloomsbury group, Eliot, Forster, Joyce, Auden, Lawrence, Orwell, Waugh. In the 1920s, the *avant-garde* writers of the Modern Movement were bothered by the way that mass-market forms of culture such as newspaper-writing were gaining currency.[8] Setting out a defence of 'high culture', they began what became known as 'The Battle of the Brows'.

The year 1922 – the year in which T.S. Eliot published *The Waste Land*, James Joyce *Ulysses*, and Agatha Christie her 'thriller' *The Secret Adversary* – does as well as any other as the date for the Modern Movement's start. The term would first be used in a book of 1927.[9]

But what exactly is modernism? Agatha's character Leonard in *The Murder at the Vicarage* (1930) thought he knew. Poems with 'no capital letters in them,' he says, with more than a hint of snark, are the 'essence of modernity.'[10]

Essentially, modernism was something experimental, different from what had gone before. And it was not universally welcomed. Writers like Agatha, using traditional narrative, began to define themselves almost in opposition to the highbrows, defiantly calling themselves middle- or even 'lowbrow'. Agatha would respond to career successes with the feeling that 'it's one up to the Low Brows!!'[11]

The Battle of the Brows aroused powerful feelings. If you want to know how strongly the highbrows felt middlebrow culture was second-rate and distressingly commercial, let Virginia Woolf step forth. 'If any man, woman, dog, cat, or half-crushed worm dares call me "middlebrow",' she wrote, 'I will take my pen and stab him dead.'[12] This blast appeared in a letter Woolf wrote to the editor of the *New Statesman*.

Yet things are never as straightforward as they seem. This celebrated letter actually remained unsent. Perhaps Woolf had scruples about her occasional work as a contributor to *Vogue* and *Good Housekeeping*, or perhaps she felt genuine support for other professional female writers, who were, by and large, as middlebrow as Agatha herself. As the literary historian Maroula Joannou puts it, the letter may never have been posted because Woolf was all too aware 'of the contradictions of her own position'.[13]

And here's another twist in the tale. What if the middlebrow and the modernist could actually be the same thing? A more inclusive definition of modernism might mean that you can also find it in works that don't necessarily bludgeon you in the face with the shock of the new in the manner of *Ulysses*. And so we find the literary critic Alison Light debunking the very idea that 'modernist' *has* to mean 'highbrow'. Light puts the case that Agatha Christie was in fact an unrecognised modernist herself.

This is perhaps most clearly revealed in the 1920s books Christie called her 'thrillers'. Much less well known than her detective stories, they are arch, glamorous, implausible and pacey. They have a modernist concern with symbolism, with people and places sketched in with the lightest of touches.

These stories mark the entrance into Agatha's writing of Tommy and Tuppence, a former soldier and hospital nurse, who first appear in *The Secret Adversary*. Agatha describes them as an 'essentially modern-looking couple'. Down on their luck but hopeful for the future, the intrepid pair have recently been released from wartime service. Desperately short of funds, they decide to set up an investigation agency. Tommy is a poor man's Sherlock Holmes, with hardly enough money even for tea and buns. He and Tuppence each pay their own way in a Lyons Corner House, showing they're happy to ignore the rule that the man should foot the bill.[14] Bright Young Things on a budget, they aspire to a 1920s version of hedonism: eating 'Lobster *à l'américane*, Chicken Newberg and Pêche Melba';

being on first-name terms with the head waiter at the Ritz; having a ride in a new Rolls-Royce. And who does a former soldier married to a former nurse remind you of, if not Archie and Agatha?

But after her excursion into her first thriller, Agatha went back to detection once more, building on *Styles* and some subsequent short stories by reintroducing Poirot in *The Murder on the Links*. Agatha could already see, though, that Hastings was becoming a bit of a bore, and she decided to get rid of him: 'I might be stuck with Poirot, but no need to be stuck with Hastings too.'

Captain Hastings only looms so large in people's minds today because of his prominence in the 1980s and 1990s TV adaptations of the Poirot stories. Agatha found it hard to think of plots where Hastings could be physically present to witness and narrate a whole book's worth of action.[15] And he was a bit dull anyway. So Agatha concluded *The Murder on the Links* by getting Hastings married, and sending him to live in Argentina.

The Bodley Head were pleased with Agatha, but she was less pleased with them. As the 1920s progressed, she began to develop a healthy sense of what her work was worth. After all, she was now a star. In 1923 a flattering, soft-focus photograph of her and Rosalind appeared in the centre of a picture page in the *Daily Mail*, surrounded by other, lesser mortals: an actress, the female Conservative candidate for Berwick, and the Prince of Wales.[16]

Agatha's letters to her publishers, sometimes using Archie as her secretary, began to contain complaints: about typos, about promised but unsent accounts of her sales, about the 'crude and amateurish' design of her books' covers.[17]

Despite her increasing professionalism, Agatha went on telling herself that writing wasn't really work. When an inspector from the tax office enquired how much she'd earned, she was 'astonished. I had never considered my literary earnings as income.' But the Inland Revenue thought differently. This was the beginning of a toxic relationship between Agatha and the taxman. Shaken by the realisation that she hadn't kept proper records, she once again approached the literary agency to whom Eden Phillpotts had introduced her years before, the firm of Hughes Massie. This time, an agent named Edmund Cork agreed to represent her.

Agatha's new agent, highly discreet, with his posh English voice and slight stammer, would help her square this circle of being an unprofessional professional. He decided at once to get her something better than her exploitative contract with The Bodley Head. Cork used to enjoy telling the story of what happened. He went to Lane with the proposition that Agatha should get an advance of £250 for each book. But Lane said he wasn't used 'to being talked to by an agent in this way and sent him away.'[18] On 27 January 1924, therefore, Agatha signed a new contract with a different publisher, William Collins, Sons, led at that time by Godfrey Collins. This was the first of ever so many more that would be negotiated for Agatha by Cork.

Yet escaping from The Bodley Head would turn out to be harder than expected, especially now feelings had been hurt. Agatha's old publishers began haggling about terms. Her contract said she owed them her first six books. They questioned whether *Poirot Investigates*, a collection of short stories, should count as one of the six. But Agatha pointed out she'd offered them as a third book a novel called *Vision* – which wasn't about crime – and they'd turned it down. Their loss, she argued; it still counted.[19]

This argument over the short stories confirms that novels weren't the only strand of her career. In the 1920s, Agatha was just as much a journalist, writing to short order.[20] In 1921 *The Sketch* commissioned those Poirot stories that might or might not have been a book. Magazines like *Grand Magazine*, *Flynn's Weekly*, *Royal Magazine*, *Novel Magazine* and *Story-Teller* all began to want her work.

And the *Evening News* offered Agatha the seemingly enormous sum, £500, for the serial rights of her next thriller, *The Man in the Brown Suit*. She could hardly believe it. Magazines, particularly American magazines, would always provide a surprisingly large proportion of the income of someone who was never comfortable in claiming herself to be a novelist anyway. All this has helped conspire to prevent her from being taken as seriously as novelists often demand.

Agatha spent her £500 on the 1920s luxury of a little Morris Cowley car. For a girl whose movements had been restricted to the distance she could walk in heels, this was magnificently modern. She was also able to contribute to the running of Ashfield and have a book of poetry published at her own expense. She was beginning to act as if she were well able to buy her own buns and tea. Some historians have speculated that Archie did not like this.[21] There is no evidence for it; indeed Agatha goes out of her way to say he actively supported her career.

But even if it went unsaid, a bit of resentment wouldn't have been surprising. Another novelist, Daphne du Maurier, believed 'it's people like me who have careers who really have bitched up the old relationship between men and women. Women ought to be soft and gentle and dependent.'[22] Agatha thought she and Archie were a team like Tuppence and Tommy. Yet when he struggled to find a job after the world tour, he grew depressed. Getting on badly, the couple even discussed living apart. But Agatha refused to go either to Ashfield or Abney. She insisted on staying in London, and getting on with her work.

When, in January 1924, Agatha signed her new contract with Collins, she still owed The Bodley Head one final book. *The Secret of Chimneys*, another thriller, was published in the frothy wake of P.G. Wodehouse's *The Inimitable Jeeves*, and takes place in a similar country-house world.

Containing some great 'Christie tricks', it also introduces one of the sprightly, go-ahead young women who represent Agatha's most likeable heroines. The 'New Woman' of Agatha's youth had made way for the 'Bright Young Thing' in the 1920s. Call her what you will, Agatha has fun with her. In *Chimneys*, the fascinating Virginia Revel has a peer for a father, and a fabulously understated wardrobe of mannish 1920s sportswear. *Chimneys* is also worth a look to see how Agatha approaches a country house. Unlike her fellow writers Dorothy L. Sayers and Margery Allingham, with their aristocratic detectives, Agatha never took the upper classes very seriously. Take the passage describing the house called Chimneys itself. You might assume Agatha would give us some atmospheric description of ancient brickwork, turrets, maybe stained glass. But she doesn't bother, merely enumerating the facts that the mansion has a Holbein, a priest's hole and a secret passage. They exist, but they're unimportant: 'I believe I've been shown them once,' says Virginia, 'but I can't remember much about them now.'[23] It's a neat solution to a Christie problem: 'I don't like describing people or places,' she once admitted, 'I just want to get on with the dialogue.'[24]

Another 'Christie trick' in *Chimneys* is the use of clothing to force us into making assumptions about a person. When Virginia first meets the hero, she writes him off with a casual snobbery that would not appear to reflect well on her. Anthony has presented himself as a hard-up ex-serviceman, and at first Virginia assesses him merely as 'a more pleasing specimen than usual of London's unemployed'.[25] Virginia will grow as a person as she learns who he really is.

And the unfortunate truth is that leaping to conclusions from people's appearance is human nature. When another of Agatha's jolly heroines, Frankie Derwent, says that 'nobody looks at a chauffeur in the way they look at a *person*', she's saying something that's still true: we see the uniform, not the individual.[26] It worked even better in the 1920s when class could be more easily read from clothes. Christie's readers were used to being served, and to taking those who served them for granted.

But there's a final thing about *Chimneys* that modern readers find even more troubling. Because people think of Agatha as a timeless writer, they're sometimes surprised to find that the politics of her novels haven't always aged well. The baddies of the 1920s thrillers are typical of that decade: vague, global conspiracies, sometimes communist, sometimes criminal. And another feature of this world is that both the authorial viewpoint and that of the characters is repellently anti-Semitic. Herman Isaacstein in *Chimneys*, for example, has a 'fat yellow face, and black eyes, as impenetrable as those of a cobra. There was a generous curve to the big nose and power in the square lines of the vast jaw.' It's an unimaginative cliché, almost identical to Dorothy L. Sayers' description of a Jewish character of her own in 1923. In Sayers' version, 'the features were thick, fleshy and strongly marked, with prominent dark eyes, and a long nose curving down to a heavy chin.'[27]

Anti-Semitism was something Agatha would never entirely grow out of. But it did perhaps subtly change after her first encounter with a member, in the 1930s, of the Nazi Party. Someone mentioned the word 'Jews', and his face 'changed in an extraordinary way . . . he said: "You do not understand . . . They are a danger. They should be exterminated." . . . There are things in life that make one truly sad.' Even so, it is not true to say, as critic Robert Barnard does, that from this point in time onwards Agatha's 'offensive references to Jews cease.'[28] Prejudice towards Jewish characters would still remain.

As the 1920s progressed, though, Agatha would cut down on her thrillers. She was becoming best known as a writer of detective stories. This was not least because immediately after *Chimneys* she published her acknowledged masterpiece, Poirot's mystery, *The Murder of Roger Ackroyd*.

But that was to be published in what would prove to be the most difficult year of her life so far: 1926.

❖ PART FIVE ❖

1926

17

Sunningdale

The new edition of *The Sketch* treated readers to pictures of the celebrated author Agatha Christie, photographed at home. In her crowded, colourful living room, china plates are mounted on the walls.[1] A wooden giraffe purchased in Africa is squeezed with other ornaments onto a side table.

By the start of 1926, the Christies had settled into yet another new home, this time in Sunningdale, Berkshire. It was a much grander flat than Addison Mansions, occupying the upper floors of an 1890s mansion with a sweeping gravel drive. It provided the perfect setting for the middlebrow lady novelist as subscribers to *The Sketch* wanted to see her: in all the glory of her middlebrow home.

The successful authoress was now well into her thirties, and looked it. As a teenager Agatha had longed for a chest, failing to predict she'd find herself 'at thirty-five with a round womanly bosom well-developed'. Alas, fashion had changed, and everyone else was 'going about with chests as flat as boards.' In photos, Agatha is matronly, stately, still somehow Edwardian.

Anyone reading *The Sketch* must have thought Mrs Christie's life was going remarkably well. She'd had a new novel and two short-story collections published that year; Rosalind was growing up. Archie had eventually found work in the City, at the Austral Trust Ltd, and began to take on extra responsibilities such as being a direc- tor of a rubber company.

This growing prosperity explains why the Christies moved out of London. Sunningdale offered an easy commute to the City. Then, as now, it was a low-key but luxurious place to live. Today, exiting the railway station, you encounter a Waitrose, adverts for 'Ascot Wealth Management' and a Rolls-Royce showroom. Archie had also wanted to live near Sunningdale golf course to indulge his new-found passion for the game. Its fifth hole, according to a guide of 1924, gave a 'rich, sensuous satisfaction as the ball soars and swoops'.[2] Sunningdale was situated in Berkshire, but only just: the border with Surrey was nearby. The position of that county boundary would turn out to have an unexpected significance.

But Sunningdale suited Archie better than it did Agatha. Although she liked golf, she didn't love it, and she found it hard to make local friends. Another golf widow had nothing good to say about either golf clubs or Sunningdale itself: 'very rich people . . . horrid furniture and pictures, ugly faces and dull minds.'[3] In Agatha's short story 'The Sunningdale Mystery', it was on Sunningdale golf course's seventh tee that the victim was found stabbed to death.

Agatha could not accept dinner invitations, because Archie was too tired to go out in the evenings. People in the City, thought one of Agatha's characters, were like mice in a treadwheel: 'however rich you are, you always catch the 9.17.'[4] Neither did the Christies have quite enough money to enter the local 'Smart Set', even if Agatha could now observe it at close quarters. And this was important because the leisured ladies of Sunningdale were in fact her readers. The 'Smart Set', according to a book of 1928,

plays a little tennis, dances a good deal, keeps the most fashionable kind of dog . . . This public reads a large number of novels. It only glances at the papers; its interest in home politics is, for the most part, confined to thinking how wicked the working-man is to want the money and material comforts which it regards as all-important.[5]

In May 1926 Archie would himself drive a lorry in the hope of helping to break the General Strike. This was a conservative society in which it was each-for-his-own.

But Archie didn't seem to notice his wife's failure to thrive. Slowly, imperceptibly, the companions – Tommy and Tuppence – were growing apart. During the week Archie was absent, and in his leisure time he was tired. All Agatha had wanted was the closeness of their early married life:

> D. Their <u>Desire</u> to go walking together
> For better, for worse, and in all kinds of weather.[6]

But Archie at the weekend didn't want to walk, or to talk, he wanted only to play golf. There was Rosalind, of course, but Rosalind was a much-loved mystery. Taking after her father, she was growing up to be practical, cool and self-contained.

To pull the focus back, momentarily, from Archie and Agatha in Sunningdale, many other British couples were feeling an unexpected discontentment. Ten years after the Great War, its shadow still fell. And people were beginning to talk about it in a way that hadn't previously felt possible. Memoirs of the war were starting to be published. The records of the pensions paid to Agatha's fellow nurses show claims being made, throughout this period, for help in facing mental disorders, like the condition known in the 1920s as neurasthenia. This was a more technical word medics preferred to use instead of 'shell shock.'[7] There'd been a great silence about the Great War, and an eagerness to embrace life in its wake. But it would not be possible forever to put it so firmly out of mind.

At least Agatha got on reasonably well with Archie's mother, who now lived an hour's drive away in Dorking. And Madge came on visits. Rosalind could sense that her 'Auntie Punkie' was special: 'more entertaining than my mother. She was great fun. Slightly buried in Manchester.'[8] Agatha too suspected that Madge found day-to-day life unfulfilling: 'Sisters are very queer – and how they think they know!!! But they are an unhappy lot at Abney, I think.'[9]

Now, though, brilliant Madge had at last been allowed a bit of success of her own. Without much apparent effort, she'd written a play that was being performed on the West End stage.

Of course, Madge had always been a writer, published in magazines in her teens. Agatha had wondered if Madge would have gone on writing if she hadn't married. Well, here was the answer: at forty-five, Madge's script for *The Claimant* had caught the eye of a producer.

Perhaps it seems surprising a new writer could break into the West End. But Madge's producer had enjoyed a hit with the female playwright Clemence Dane and might have had an eye out for a similar writer. Madge, however, chose to call herself by the male-sounding name of 'M.F. Watts'. She believed the producer harboured 'a lurking doubt if I (or some unknown man) had <u>really</u> written the play.' But she found herself enjoying giving her views at rehearsals: 'gives one a sheer sense of power . . . it's queer but they all think I matter.' Agatha observed all this perhaps with a tinge of jealousy. When busy, important Madge came to spend Sunday at Sunningdale, she was so tired that she 'kept dropping off to sleep'.[10]

But Madge's play was only moderately successful. Perhaps Agatha felt she could do better, and she certainly had a go. One of the major reassessments of her reputation in recent years has been an acknowledgement of her talent not just as a novelist but as a playwright too. While her plays from the 1920s are rarely performed, theatre historian Julius Green has pointed out that this neglected strand of her writing gives insight into her feelings, and in particular her feelings about marriage.

We already know Agatha admired companionate marriages of the kind her parents hadn't had. 'Marriage, the kind of marriage I mean, would be the biggest adventure of the lot,' says the scrumptious hero of *The Secret of Chimneys*. He's talking about marriage as a team effort, with constant growth, rather in the way that Tommy Beresford describes it as a 'damned good sport'.[11]

Yet two plays Agatha wrote in this period, *Ten Years* and *The Lie*, show women dissatisfied with marriages that had begun as companionate before tilting off balance. *Ten Years* is about a married couple who agree to rethink their relationship after a decade together, a milestone Agatha and Archie reached in 1924. Onstage, the wife longs for more. 'We women were slaves once and self sacrifice was expected of us as a matter of course,' she says, 'but now we're free to live our own lives . . . I'm still young . . . I want romance – passion – fire – the things we had once . . . I want to <u>live</u> – to live <u>my</u> life – not yours.'[12] She sounds like a woman, like Agatha was beginning to be, whose husband never seemed to talk to her any more.

The Lie deals with the same issue: a marriage in which the flame has died. Agatha would write a lot about her marriage and its troubles, in fiction and in her autobiography. But these works were written years later. It's tempting to think that her unpublished plays from the 1920s are dispatches from the front line of a marriage that was curdling.[13]

Meanwhile, life was complicated by yet another of Agatha's relations. To Archie, the Millers must have seemed to supply unending drama. Just before the Great War, Monty wasted a lot of money on a failed attempt to build a boat he planned to use to run a transport business on Lake Victoria. Then he served in the East Africa Transport Corps. But a wound left him dependent upon morphine for pain relief. Returning to England in 1922, he was in a bad way.

Monty went to live at Ashfield with Clara, accompanied by his Black servant Shebani, who must have had a horrible time in Torquay. 'What does he know about cleaning, I should like to know?' asks a cleaning lady in *The Sittaford Mystery* about a manservant, 'nasty black fellow.'[14] Stupid and bored, Monty would entertain himself by firing his revolver out of his bedroom window: 'some silly old spinster going down the drive with her behind wobbling. Couldn't resist it – I sent a shot or two right and left of her. My word, how she ran!' Inevitably, the police were called; inevitably, charming Monty persuaded them there was no need to worry, he was just an old Africa hand, keeping up his skills by shooting rabbits.

Monty, with his drugs and his gun, is made to sound funny in Agatha's autobiography, but he must have been a fearsome responsibility. Agatha and Madge between them raised £800 to take their unpredictable sibling off their mother's hands. Part of Monty's problem must surely have been the comparisons people made with his clever, capable sisters: 'why is it,' he asked, that 'a greater insight is given to the feminine sex . . . give me a little confidence.'[15]

His sisters fixed him up with a place to live, a 'small granite bungalow' on Dartmoor.[16] It was a quiet, remote place. Monty bought a motorbike to get about, before he either decided he didn't like it or was banned from riding it, for soon he was offering it for sale.[17]

And perhaps Monty's giving up of his motorbike was connected to the heart of his problems: those opiates he'd been given in Africa, and to which he was now addicted. As Agatha observed, 'he would find it difficult to break the habit.' Just like his sisters, Monty thought he too could write. In one of his unfinished stories, events take an autobiographical twist when an African servant offers a sick European 'a cup of steaming hot coffee and two little brown Tablets. What are they I asked? "Opium" was the answer, "do you good."'[18]

Agatha is surprisingly straightforward and shame-free in what she says about her brother's addiction. But drugs in the 1920s were widely available and not subject to the same stigma they carry today. During the Great War, for example, a chemist placed a completely legitimate advert in The Times suggesting that gelatine sheets containing morphine and cocaine would make excellent presents for 'friends at the front'.[19] The law on supplying morphine, cocaine and heroin was tightened up in 1920, but until then, you could even buy them – plus syringe – at Harrods.

And addicts would make frequent appearances in Agatha's fiction: Lady Horbury in Death in the Clouds (1935) carries cocaine in her dressing case; drug use is uncovered in Murder in Mesopotamia (1936); Poirot confronts dealers in The Labours of Hercules (1947). A soldier addicted to morphia also plays a walk-on part in Agatha's autobiographical novel Giant's Bread: 'The morphia – it's got hold of him,' says his wife, 'we're going to fight it together.'[20] Agatha and Madge now searched for the right housekeeper to help their brother 'fight' morphia. They located the widow of a doctor who'd been an addict, and who knew how to handle people like Monty.

In Monty's lonely bungalow, he produced sad little fragments of writing, terrible poems, unfinished stories. He often writes as if under the influence: 'surprise gentle unrest soft lingering pain again my heart again oh again savage dull longings.' But he also sounds like he wants to break his addiction: 'something quite wrong here, so wrong that it must be altered and tomorrow I begin.'

Ultimately, though, the plan for keeping Monty safe on Dartmoor failed. He dreamed of building a splendid new boat, but he secretly knew he would never manage it. 'Total Gloom, Total Despair,' he wrote, 'I say ahoy and then at last goodbye.'[21] In 1929, he'd go to live in the south of France, where, on 20 September, he died.

After his funeral, Agatha had the task of disposing of his bungalow and belongings. The advert she placed for the sale of Monty's goods ends – poignantly, in the light of their father's passion for the sport – with a 'Leather Cricket Bag'.[22]

Back on a Saturday in May 1897, when Monty was sixteen, the *Torquay Times* had reported on a cricket match at the town's ground within sight of the sea. His six-year-old sister Agatha might well have been present, as she often was, beneath the oak where she helped their father to keep score. At the game Monty, full of life and promise, 'did much towards trying to save his side from defeat'.[23]

In the end, though, Monty was defeated by morphia. And in Sunningdale, it would turn out, life would nearly defeat his sister too.

18

The Mysterious Affair at Styles

While Monty was suffering, Agatha was working. In the summer of 1926 came her greatest achievement yet. Her sixth published novel, *The Murder of Roger Ackroyd*, is not only one of her very best books – it's one of the greatest detective novels of all time.

She invested a lot of care in this book. In it, Poirot moves to an English village to spend a quiet retirement growing vegetable marrows. Instead, he's called upon to solve a fiendishly complex case. A notable character is the local doctor's sister, Caroline Sheppard, a sharp spinster who's extremely knowledgeable about village life in a way that foreshadows Miss Marple.

It's well known that *Roger Ackroyd* plays the most remarkable trick on the reader. The story's told by a narrator so unreliable that eventually, in a brilliant twist, he's revealed to be the killer himself. And this begs the question: is it fair?

The query only makes sense if you believe in those emerging 'rules' for detective fiction, which would not actually be codified until 1929. It was writer and priest Ronald Knox who then decreed that 'the stupid friend of the detective, the Watson, must not conceal any thoughts which pass through his mind.' In *Roger Ackroyd*, the story's 'Watson', Dr Sheppard, does not tell the reader everything he knows, and his skilfully placed silences create a false impression. This 'Christie trick' – the omission of tiny but key facts by someone we've come to trust – would be one she'd play again and again. If not a break of the 'rules', it was a bend.

Much has been made of the 'scandal' *Roger Ackroyd* caused. One review did indeed call it a 'tasteless and unfortunate let-down by a writer we had grown to admire'.[1] But Agatha thought she'd played completely fair: 'there's lack of explanation there, but no false statement'.[2] And Dorothy L. Sayers agreed, arguing that it's 'the reader's business to suspect *everybody*'.[3] Most readers agreed as well. The *Daily Mail* found it 'one of the most thrilling and well-told detective stories we have ever read'.[4] The only downside, in fact, of writing such a perfectly constructed piece of deception is that it added to Agatha's growing reputation for guile. As the events of 1926 unfolded, this would come to count against her.

Agatha may have given the book everything she'd got because it was her first with her new publisher, William Collins. Collins made *Roger Ackroyd* a success, and Agatha rewarded them with lasting loyalty. Amid all the excitement, the Christies also decided to move to a new home in Sunningdale, not a flat this time, but a whole house. It was a half-timbered, tall-chimneyed, rather gloomy place, and Archie and Agatha gave it a new name when they took over the lease in June 1926. They called it The Styles.

It takes a certain sangfroid to name your home after a crime scene, even a fictional one, and it all added to the sense of the sinister that would come to gather round the property. The Styles had lingered on the market for a long time, despite being advertised as 'particularly attractive' with its twelve bedrooms, three bathrooms and 'excellent garage accommodation with chauffeur's room'. Its owners had finally resorted to flogging it at auction.[5]

In her autobiography, Agatha could not resist describing The Styles in ominous tones, preparing us for bad things. Today the house lurks behind a high holly hedge. An unlucky house, Agatha called it, whose residents always 'came to grief in some way. The first man lost his money; the second his wife.' Other rumours included the claim that a woman had been murdered at the end of the garden. Inside, the house was unnecessarily lavish: 'a sort of millionaire-style Savoy suite transferred to the country,' Agatha thought. Her acquaintances round Sunningdale noticed she hadn't been able to settle. They recalled hearing her say, 'I cannot stand the house. It is getting on my nerves. The lane is terribly lonely.'[6]

When they moved in, though, The Styles must have seemed to the Christies to be a bold new beginning, perhaps a reboot of their marriage. They expanded their household to four servants, plus an important new employee. Agatha sometimes used the services of a typing agency to produce clean copies of her work. But she now decided to employ a live-in member of staff both to help her with secretarial services, and to look after her daughter.

Charlotte Fisher was a tall, bony woman, formidable in appearance, but with 'a nice-looking twinkle'. She also became a friend. Miss Fisher was known by Agatha as 'Carlotta', and then eventually 'Carlo'. In return, Agatha became 'Missus', and thus inscribed the copies of each of her books that she gave to Carlo on publication, and which Carlo kept for the rest of her life. Carlo was also, importantly, something of a second mother to Rosalind, who called her 'much more than a secretary, and I doubt if my mother could have managed without her.'[7] When Archie was too tired to go out in the evening, Carlo and Agatha would set out without him, to a class in Ascot where they were learning to dance the Charleston.[8]

The capable and likeable Charlotte Fisher was one of the so-called 'surplus women'. Born in 1895, she and her sister Mary were the daughters of an Edinburgh clergyman. She was among those who might have married had not the war killed so many potential husbands. She'd worked before as a nanny, but certainly found Agatha her most engaging employer. As she grew close to the Christies, though, Carlo's status became ambivalent. Did she resent being 'in' but not entirely 'of' the family? Her own name was reduced to a nickname, but in return she called her boss by a corruption of 'Mistress'. It was a joke, but we don't know how funny Carlo found it. She was utterly discreet. However, Carlo must have known that *Roger Ackroyd* would not have been the triumph it was without her own contribution, taking down dictation and typing up. 'In memory of commas, colons & full-stops!' Agatha wrote in the front of Carlo's copy. Grammar and punctuation were never Agatha's strong points, but with Carlo to help they became easier.[9]

But Carlo's job would call upon her courage more deeply than she could have expected. That was because in the summer of 1926, soon after moving into The Styles, Agatha's health took a turn for the worse.

The trouble had begun on 5 April 1926, when Clara Miller finally died of bronchitis, at seventy-two, while staying with Madge. Agatha was called to the bedside, but arrived too late. Such was the strength of her bond with her mother, though, she believed she'd felt the actual moment Clara passed away: 'I felt a *coldness* . . . and I thought: "*Mother is dead*".'

For Agatha, who'd remained exceptionally close to her surviving parent, it was devastating. But her grief was compounded by the weakness that would now be exposed in her marriage. Archie, it turned out, simply wasn't able to offer any support.

At the time of his mother-in-law's death, Archie was abroad for work, and didn't even return for the funeral. He preferred to avoid difficult situations. Agatha realised she'd always known about his 'violent dislike of illness, death, and trouble'. When Archie did get home, he was at first acutely embarrassed, which 'made him put on an appearance of jollity'. Nothing could have been less sympathetic to a woman facing the first real emotional trial of her life since losing her father at eleven.

Carlo was so much part of the family, now, that Agatha's little dog Peter slept on her bed. And it was obvious to her that Archie was letting Agatha down. It was partly a matter of temperament. But also, like many a survivor and witness of war, he 'could not stand tears and depression'.

The Styles could now no longer function without Miss Fisher. 'I tried to keep the house running smoothly for your sake,' she told Rosalind, later, of this trying period.[10] But then even Carlo's steadying presence was removed: her father was ill, she had to go to look after him.

Agatha decided she needed a break from both her husband and the lonely house. She intended to go with Rosalind to Ashfield, for the highly necessary task of clearing it out. It was both a practical and a spiritual labour. Ashfield was full of hoarded junk that needed disposal. And Agatha could not mourn her mother without being in her mother's house.

In her autobiographical novel, Agatha dramatises a conversation similar to the one she must now have had with Archie about her plans. She becomes 'Celia' and Archie 'Dermot' – a man insensitive enough to think his wife might actively enjoy clearing out her deceased mother's home.

> Dermot was so inadequate! He persistently ignored the significance
> of emotional stress. He shied away from it like a frightened horse.
>   Celia cried out – angry for once:
>   'You talk as though it was a holiday!'
>   He looked away from her.
>   'Well,' he said, 'so it will be in a way . . .'
>   How cold the world was – without her mother . . .

Dermot, based on Archie, had become a stranger.

During the six summer weeks Agatha spent at Ashfield, with only Rosalind for company, she began to feel awful: 'for the first time in my life I was really ill'. Her love of 'playing houses' became compulsive, irrational, as she sorted trunks of forgotten possessions for ten hours a day in rooms dripping with water from the holes in the roof. She described her tearfulness, her forgetfulness, as 'the beginning of a nervous breakdown', which would, tragically, play itself out for the rest of the awful year of 1926.

Previously so physically robust, Agatha began to suffer from insomnia. When she asked a chemist for a sleeping draught, he later recalled how the conversation had turned to suicide. 'I would not commit suicide by a violent method,' she'd supposedly told him, while poison was available.[11] Chance words, snippets of conversation, clues to Agatha's state of mind: all would become important in the light of what was to follow.

The chapter in Agatha's autobiography about the year of 1926 has been combed over carefully by historians seeking to understand what happened that summer.

And here we come to the central issue in trying to understand Agatha: can we believe her? What do her words really mean? Should they be taken literally? Agatha's first official biographer, Janet Morgan, was given access to some letters from Carlo that were most probably destroyed after Morgan read them.

So Morgan's reports of these letters – she did not quote verbatim – give us glimpses of an important lost source. And she notes inconsistencies in the timeline of this whole year between Agatha's and Carlo's accounts.[12] The matter has received close attention because of the persistent idea that maybe Agatha was only pretending to be ill. But the timeline of many parts of the autobiography is demonstrably wrong. Such details weren't important to Agatha. What mattered was emotional truth. And she did not *want* to remember this time anyway. She'd done her best to forget it.

Agatha was now famous enough for her illness to make the newspapers. A gossip columnist wrote in August that the novelist was unwell. He thought writing 'must be a terrible strain on the nerves', and particularly hard on a woman: 'I was not surprised to hear . . . that Agatha Christie, who writes detective yarns better than most men, has had a breakdown.'[13]

He also thought (wrongly) she had gone to the Pyrenees to rest. It was true that Archie and Agatha had planned to go abroad. But when he came down to Ashfield to visit, it turned out he hadn't booked the tickets after all. Why not? It was hard to tell. He seemed different. To Agatha, he was horribly like the Gun Man of her childhood nightmares. The closest she'd been to this feeling before, Agatha explains, was in 'that old nightmare of mine – the horror of sitting at a tea table, looking across at my best loved friend, and suddenly realising that the person sitting there *was a stranger.*'

She asked Archie what was wrong. Finally, reluctantly, he came out with it.

Archie blindsided his wife with the news that he was in love with someone else, a woman called Nancy Neele. And he wanted a divorce.

To add insult to injury, Agatha knew this woman well. Nancy was a friend of Major Belcher's. In 1925, when the British Empire Exhibition was running, the two women had sat together on a committee to create a children's area.[14] Nancy worked as a typist at the Imperial Continental Gas Association. She was an excellent golfer, and while playing at the Sunningdale course, she'd even come to stay at The Styles.

Nancy was lively, chatty, and — perhaps crucially for a man at midlife — young. Born in 1899, she was nearly a decade Agatha's junior. Her family lived near Rickmansworth, and her father had been chief electrical engineer for the Great Central Railway. Nancy had a trim figure, springy black curls, strong eyebrows and — killingly — a face more conventionally pretty than Agatha's own. When the newspapers became interested in Nancy, as they later would, they described her as 'bright', 'handsome' and 'popular', an 'open, frank, athletic girl'.[15]

The combination of Nancy's attractions, and Agatha's grief, had been too potent a combination for Archie to resist.

Agatha could see, with hindsight, what had happened. He'd often warned her, saying, 'I'm no good, remember, if things go wrong . . . I can't bear people to be unhappy or upset.' Archie confirms this in one of his surviving letters: 'I can't bear to think of you being ill or unhappy,' he wrote. At the time he probably meant it kindly, but in retrospect it reads another way as well.[16]

A wise friend would have warned Agatha that when a man tells you he cannot be relied upon, there's no reason not to believe him, and leave him. 'Evil people are those who will not or cannot grow up,' Agatha wrote.[17] 'A man who is a child,' says one of her characters, 'is the most frightening thing in the world.'[18] Archie, with what seemed to Agatha to be this fatal flaw, his lack of empathy, was a man who was a child.

But Agatha had believed him to be better. It would be this betrayal of her own ideal of her husband that would turn her into a truly Gothic writer. Gothic not in the sense of seances or the supernatural, but in the sense that evil can enter, *will* enter, even the snuggest of homes; the sense nowhere is safe.[19] From now on, Christie novels would firmly address dark, uncomfortable feelings. They address the darkness that can lurk within even normal, respectable people.

People like your own spouse.

When Agatha writes about this period in her autobiography, she takes care to depict Archie's good qualities. Yet with just one or two killer quotations from things Archie is supposed to have said, she leaves an overall impression that he was a nasty piece of work. No wonder, for Agatha was a writer who could skilfully, with a tiny number of brushstrokes, depict two completely contrasting sides to one single character. She did it all the time with her murderers. In her autobiography, she paints Archie as the murderer of her happiness.

This means Archie is generally known to history as a villain. It would be interesting to hear his own side of the story about the extraordinary wife he couldn't handle. But we never shall.

For the time being, though, Agatha refused to accept that the marriage was over. She simply denied it. She believed that ultimately Archie would return to her because of a trump card she held. Rosalind. She knew Archie loved Rosalind. Surely Nancy wouldn't expect him to leave his daughter.

So, as autumn arrived, Agatha and Rosalind returned to The Styles, and Carlo came back from her father's bedside as well. There was stalemate. Archie stayed some nights each week at his club in town. Carlo was convinced that although he was often physically present at The Styles, he was absent in spirit. Agatha told friends her life was becoming unendurable. 'If I do not leave Sunningdale,' she was heard to say, 'Sunningdale will be the end of me.'[20]

On Friday 3 December 1926, the sun rose at 7.47 a.m. A weather front was moving in from Iceland, ground frost was expected, and the outlook was 'rather unsettled'.[21] Archie caught the train to work, and planned to be away for the weekend. Agatha took Rosalind out to tea before coming home to dinner.

Carlo had an evening off. She went up to London for a night out dancing. It must have been a welcome relief from the tension.

But when Carlo returned, late that winter evening, she found Agatha had disappeared.

19

Disappearance

The week leading up to Agatha's mysterious disappearance on Friday 3 December had been a busy one. On the Monday, she'd gone shopping in London with her sister-in-law Nan. Her purchases included an 'elaborate white satin' nightgown, something she said she'd wanted for the weekend.[1] She was planning a few days in Yorkshire. The trip had taken on prominence in Agatha's mind as some sort of a turning point. Perhaps she was hoping Archie would come with her.

She'd take several other actions that seem irrational unless she was thinking of herself as a bride preparing for a new beginning. On the Wednesday, Agatha went to London again with a Sunningdale friend, Mrs Joyce da Silva. Agatha told Joyce she was hoping to let The Styles and take a house in London, in order to spend more time with her husband.[2] This was a marriage, in Agatha's mind, that was still very much alive.

Agatha stayed overnight that Wednesday at her club in London. As Joyce returned to Sunningdale, though, she was worried about her friend. Agatha had been unwell for months. It wasn't long since Joyce had seen her looking so ill she'd sent her straight to bed. Agatha's 'brilliant brain,' Joyce believed, was 'taxed to its limit to satisfy a never-ending demand of the public for the fancies it could weave.'[3] Joyce wasn't alone in believing that brainy women were somehow overtaxing the strength of their bodies. One physician, for example, thought pain was more deeply felt by women who 'carry hard mental work than in the case of the less intelligent persons who earn their living by manual labour.'[4]

On the Thursday, Agatha went to see her agent. Edmund Cork noticed 'nothing peculiar in her manner'. But he was eager for her unfinished follow-up to *Roger Ackroyd*.[5] 'They rather pressed her for it,' said someone close to Agatha, 'and also wanted to know something about two stories she had to write.'[6]

This was a crushing workload for someone in good health, which Agatha wasn't. Her success was running out of control. Ever greater demands were being heaped upon her at a time when she should have been mourning both her mother and her marriage.

Agatha had completed half of her new novel, *The Mystery of the Blue Train*, but she'd then got stuck. 'She has not written a word,' said Agatha's mother-in-law, Peg, in whom she'd confided 'her worry at not being able to complete her commissions'.[7] But Agatha still believed she had to keep her promises and deliver her work. As Joyce saw, 'it was clear that she suppressed her emotions rather than cause distress to anyone.'[8]

On Thursday afternoon, Agatha returned to Sunningdale, and that evening, she and Carlo went out to their dancing class as usual. And then came Friday 3 December 1926, the day it all happened.

That morning, nothing at The Styles seemed out of the ordinary, although the cook and the maid thought afterwards Agatha had been in an 'excited state'.[9] Archie left by train as usual at 9.15. In the afternoon, Agatha took Rosalind on a visit to Peg near Dorking. It was about an hour's drive in Agatha's beloved little Morris car.

During tea, though, Peg could see that something was wrong. Agatha was at first cheerful, and again spoke of going away to Yorkshire. Then Peg noticed Agatha wasn't wearing her wedding ring, and asked where it was. In response, her daughter-in-law 'sat perfectly still for some time, gazing into space, and giving a hysterical laugh, turned away'. When Agatha and Rosalind left, Peg watched them disappearing down the drive while 'waving farewell'.[10] Peg had no idea of the significance of that casual wave.

Now it's time to hear from Agatha herself. Her route to Peg's house that afternoon had taken her over the Surrey Hills past the elevated beauty spot of Newlands Corner. 'I was at this time in a very despondent state of mind,' she says. Her feelings were almost suicidal: 'I just wanted my life to end.' Passing by Newlands Corner, she saw a quarry. And, at the sight of it, 'there came into my mind the thought of driving into it. However, as my daughter was with me in the car, I dismissed the idea at once.'[11]

Agatha got Rosalind home at about six. Carlo, out dancing, was anxious enough about Agatha's state of mind to ring home to see if Missus was all right. Agatha could not bring herself to say out loud that anything was wrong. But – characteristically – she did instead write Carlo a letter. Agatha ate alone, for Archie hadn't come home. According to the staff at The Styles, it was during the course of this dark, solitary evening that Agatha 'found out' – whether by phone or a note – where Archie was, and what he was doing: 'her husband was spending the week-end with friends'.[12] Agatha was told, or worked out, who these 'friends' were.

She came to some kind of decision. Perhaps she guessed that this time he was really not coming back. And she could hardly bear to remain in the house a minute more. There were three people at The Styles: the cook, the parlourmaid, Lilly, and the cook's husband. Carlo was expected back later. So Rosalind had people – people better qualified and safer than Agatha – to look after her. Agatha felt she had to leave.

Where should she go? Well, she could decide as she drove. Perhaps she would go to Yorkshire after all. Or perhaps, as she'd thought earlier, she would end it all. Either way, she was clear, she 'could go on no longer'.[13]

Agatha was wearing a grey knitted skirt, a green jersey, a cardigan and a 'small velour hat'. She packed a fairly irrational selection of items into a suitcase: a frock, a jumper, two pairs of black shoes. She also took a fur coat and a small case containing papers including a driving licence.[14] She had a large sum of cash, about £60, to hand. She'd withdrawn it from the bank after other, earlier, thoughts of escape. She'd been toying with the idea of fleeing to South Africa – a place she'd loved, a place she'd been happy – with Rosalind. And finally, she took a photograph of Rosalind, with her nickname written upon it: Teddy.

Late that evening, Agatha's servants saw her 'go to her daughter's bedroom and kiss the child and come downstairs into the hall.' There she kissed her dog Peter too, before going out to her car.[15]

It's heart-wrenching to read about this taking leave of Rosalind. But surely Agatha did it for Rosalind's own safety. She'd had a suicidal thought with Rosalind in the car. Could she, Agatha must have been wondering, be trusted to look after her own daughter?

At nine forty-five, Agatha drove away into the darkness.

Nobody knew then – and nobody knows now – exactly where she went.

When Carlo returned, late in the evening, to find both Agatha and her car gone missing, she also found the cook and maid worried and confused.

And then she discovered that Agatha had left her a most distressing letter. Its contents remain unknown, but there would be many reports over the coming days of what this key document said. One report claimed it read, 'I shall not be home tonight. I will telephone directly I reach the place to which I am going.'[16] On a practical note, the letter asked Carlo to cancel the previous arrangements for Agatha to spend the weekend at a hotel in the Yorkshire town of Beverley. The more troubling phrases, though, were Agatha's reported need to 'get away from here', her feeling that she 'must leave this house', and that 'it just isn't fair'.[17] Another version included a chilling statement: 'my head is bursting.'[18]

This letter would be central to the case of the missing novelist. It would now be read in alternative ways: by Carlo, who felt it indicated that Agatha was in pain, but would come home when she was better. By Archie, who was chiefly concerned that it didn't make a specific complaint about him as an unfaithful husband. And, in due course, by a certain policeman named Superintendent Kenward, who was convinced, from the tone of it, that Agatha was dead: either through suicide, or possibly, through murder by her husband. What would happen next hung on these different readings of a woman's words.

Carlo could take no further action that night. The next morning, Agatha was still absent. As requested, Carlo sent a telegram to the Beverley hotel, cancelling the booking for Christie.[19] It seems that Rosalind was told, as was often the case, that her mother had gone away to write a book.

But then matters were taken out of Carlo's hands. The Styles telephone rang. It was the police. Agatha's empty car, damaged, apparently in a crash, had been discovered at a place called Albury Down, a steep hill just below Newlands Corner on the road across the Surrey Hills.

In the abandoned car were various clues: Agatha's driving licence, which was how the police had known her address, her fur coat, her suitcase and her attaché case.

This sounds, of course, like the set-up for a detective story. And some of the assumptions police and journalists alike would now make — that foul play must have taken place — were quite understandable. After all, Agatha was a detective novelist. Life and art were getting mixed up.

Carlo told the police she thought Agatha might have gone to Ashfield, that place of refuge in all kinds of trouble. But the Torquay police were sent to check it, and found no clue: 'leaves lie in the doorways, all the windows are fastened, and there are no signs of footmarks in the drive or on the garden paths.'[20]

It was the only place Agatha might plausibly have gone. If not Ashfield, then where?

It's time to reveal what really happened that night on the grassy slope of the hill rolling down from Newlands Corner. Agatha later felt forced to give her side of the story.

What she said has the unfortunate effect of sounding like one of her novels, in which the 'loss of memory' plot would feature time and time again. But we know that Agatha's writings about her life have had this novelising tendency all along. It doesn't mean she is lying.

'All that night I drove aimlessly about,' she explains.

> In my mind there was the vague idea of ending everything. I drove automatically down roads I knew . . . I believe I then drove out to Maidenhead, where I looked at the river. I thought about jumping in, but realised that I could swim too well to drown. I then drove back to London again, and then onto Sunningdale. From there I went to Newlands Corner.[21]

Throughout the whole distressing year of 1926, Agatha had developed this habit of driving about aimlessly to soothe herself. In the days immediately after Clara's death, for example, her dog Peter was hurt in a car accident. Agatha felt 'frantic with grief' and 'never quite knew how she got home . . . she drove in a frenzied condition for miles and did not know what roads she was taking.'[22]

Wherever she went that Friday night, Agatha ended up on the road towards Dorking she'd taken earlier to visit her mother-in-law.

She was driving her little Morris, a common make that constituted half the cars on the road. But these 1920s cars were not completely reliable. Driving in one today feels noisy and jerky, and the various knobs and levers require a surprising amount of physical force. In the darkness before dawn, somewhere near Newlands Corner, Agatha's car stalled, and she could not get it going again. In fact, she 'could never crank up a car if it had stopped'.[23]

One thing seems certain: she had been in the car all night. A witness later said he'd helped a woman start a stalled car near Newlands Corner at six twenty on the Saturday morning. Ernest Cross, a farm worker, told the *Daily Mail* he'd come across this woman 'in a frenzied condition . . . moaning and holding her hands to her head, and her teeth were chattering with cold.' He asked if he could help, and she said 'Oh! do try to start it up for me.' He thought

Agatha with her dog George Washington, whose name reminds you that her father was American. In her childhood garden Agatha played with imaginary friends beneath the monkey puzzle tree.

The villa named Ashfield in Torquay was central to Agatha's life. In it she was born, grew up, accepted two proposals of marriage, and gave birth to her daughter.

Agatha with her mother. A strange, passionate woman, Clara Miller loved her daughter with 'a dangerous intensity of affection'. Clara's death would send Agatha into a dangerous spell of depression.

Clara with Agatha's older sister Madge in Ashfield's conservatory. These two creative, strong-willed women, both writers, were vital forces in shaping Agatha's life.

Agatha's forceful Auntie-Grannie, who had something of Miss Marple about her, could read people's minds. She said every woman should carry fifty pounds with her in case of 'emergencies', and liked cherry brandy.

Agatha, back row, left, reached almost professional standard as a pianist and singer. The other girls of Torquay described her as looking like a 'sea nymph' with 'flowing golden hair'.

A shy seventeen-year-old, Agatha made her debut into society in Egypt. 'She dances beautifully,' one young man told her mother, but 'you had better try to teach her to talk.'

By twenty-two, Agatha had received nine proposals. 'We have only known each other ten days,' she told one suitor, 'it's really an awfully silly thing to go and propose to a girl like that.'

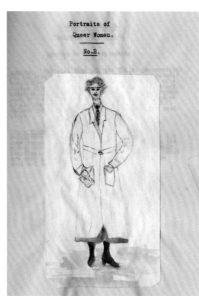

Portraits of
Queer Women.

No.2.

Working as nurses in Torquay during the Great War, Agatha and her friends created a 'hospital magazine' to keep up their spirits. They called themselves the 'Queer Women'.

What we did in the Great War.

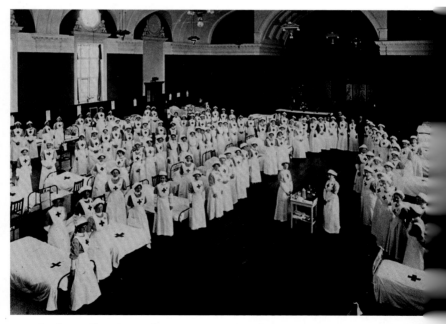

In the auxiliary hospital at Torquay Town Hall, Agatha began at the bottom, scrubbing floors as a ward-maid. When she first witnessed an operation, she 'began to shake all over'.

Pretty, witty Madge, Agatha's sister, had 'a great deal of sexual magnetism'. She seemed to write her stories and plays effortlessly, and married the heir to Abney Hall.

Agatha often visited the grand but gloomy Abney Hall, which she described as 'best Victorian lavatory' in style. It was here that the press besieged her in 1926.

Agatha's brother Monty liked flirting, 'talking slang' and 'getting into tempers'. He disliked any kind of work. In later life he behaved badly with firearms and became addicted to morphia.

This photo shows exactly why Agatha fell for the glamorous Archibald Christie, who qualified as a pilot in 1912. 'You've got to marry me, you've *got* to marry me,' he told Agatha, fiercely.

Agatha's daughter Rosalind was born in 1919. A child, Agatha thought, 'is mysteriously a stranger . . . it will leave you and blossom.'

A happy-looking Christie family: Archie, Rosalind and Agatha. As for many families in Britain, though the supposedly 'Roaring Twenties' would turn out to be deeply distressing for them.

Agatha surfing in Hawaii in 1922. A very modern young woman, she loved swimming, and fast cars, and was intrigued by the new science of psychology.

From right to left are Agatha, Archie and Major Belcher, in Canada to promote the British Empire Exhibition. Belcher was an egotist whom Agatha called the 'Wild Man' for his unpleasant behaviour.

Agatha enjoys breakfast in Honolulu in 1922. She loved life in motion. 'Your travel life,' she wrote, 'has the essence of a dream . . . you are yourself, but a different self.'

Agatha moved to The Styles in 1926. An unlucky house, she called it, where people always 'came to grief'. It was from here, on 3 December, that she 'disappeared'.

From left, Charlotte Fisher, Rosalind, and Charlotte's sister Mary. Also known as 'Carlo', the capable, likeable Miss Fisher gave Agatha secretarial help, childcare and friendship in difficult times.

Archie fell in love with Nancy Neele, a golf lover described as an 'open, frank, athletic girl'. She's seen here at Hurtmore Cottage, where they both were the night Agatha disappeared.

Agatha transports her surfboard in her beloved Morris. When in 1926 the car was found damaged and abandoned, its owner missing, it seemed exactly like a detective story.

it odd that she was out so early and dressed so inadequately. Cross managed to start the car and watched the woman drive away.

But different newspapers ran different stories. The local paper, the *Surrey Advertiser*, implied that Cross was some sort of lazy invention of the national newspapers, as its representatives had failed to trace him. Instead, the locals believed the man who'd found the woman and her car in the lane was actually Edward McAllister, a worker in the gravel pits nearby. 'Would you mind starting up my car for me, please?' she'd asked, according to McAllister, and he'd managed to get it going. He too said her manner was 'a little strange, which he put down to the worry of the car.' According to the *Advertiser* at least, 'the police accept his story that it was Mrs Christie he helped'.[24]

Perhaps the car stalled twice. Whoever got it going, Agatha did not drive far. Shortly after 6 a.m. on Saturday 4 December 1926, she made a half-hearted attempt to take her life.

It was still dark. A 1920s map shows the road down from Newlands Corner – now the swift A25 – was then a much narrower and more dangerous route, dropping steeply. Off to its right runs a track called Water Lane, stony, slippery, and descending to the village of Albury. And just a short roll down the hill, at a bend in the lane, was an old chalk pit – the 'quarry' Agatha had glimpsed earlier.

She was tired, she was in deep distress. She was cold, as she hadn't thought to put on her fur coat. Now, at last, she put into action a vague plan that had occupied her thoughts for the previous twenty-four hours.

When I reached a point in the road which I thought was near the quarry I had seen in the afternoon, I turned the car off the road down the hill towards it. I left the wheel and let the car run. The car struck something with a jerk and pulled up suddenly. I was flung against the steering wheel and my head hit something.[25]

After Agatha pointed her car towards the steep white lip of the quarry, it ran over the grass and down the slope. It was later found lodged in a hedge, its front wheels 'over the edge of the chalk pit.' Had it not been for the hedge, 'the car would have plunged over and been smashed to pieces.'[26]

When she heard about this, Peg was inclined to think her daughter-in-law had 'planned her end'.[27] But this was not a very determined or well-planned effort. And neither is the one made by Agatha's heroine in an autobiographical novel, who wanders at night in the rain:

> She *must* remember her own name . . .
> She stumbled over a ditch . . .
> The ditch was full of water . . .
> You could drown yourself in water . . .
> It would be better to drown yourself than to hang yourself. If you lay down in the water . . .
> Oh, how cold it was! – she couldn't – no, she couldn't . . .[28]

It seems that both the fictional Celia and the real-life Agatha shocked themselves into realising that whatever happened, life was worth living.

But now there was another problem. How could Agatha live with the shame of having tried – for however short a moment – to throw her life away? Yes, suicide was a sin, as powerfully expressed by Agatha's character Midge in *The Hollow*: 'the sin of despair, that priests talked of, was a cold sin, the sin of cutting oneself off from all warm and living human contacts.'[29]

Someone close to Agatha described her as having given way that night to 'blank despair', and this, for her, was a source of burning guilt.[30] It was wrong from the point of view of the law – suicide was a crime in 1926 – and it was wrong spiritually, too, to have committed the sin of despair. But neither could Agatha go on living as she was. It was time to become someone new.

Agatha's autobiography implies that what brought her back from the brink was the remembered voice of a woman. A teacher had once told her the essence of Christianity was the defeat of despair.

'Those few words,' Agatha wrote, 'remained with me [. . .] they were to come back to me and give me hope at a time when despair had me in its grip.'

And so Agatha, dazed, distressed, but alive, saw some kind of salvation ahead. She got out of her car. With injuries from the impact to her head and chest, she now walked through the wintery countryside in a dreamlike state. She was reborn. 'Up to this moment I was Mrs Christie,' she explains.[31] Now, she was Mrs Christie no longer. She had sloughed off the past like a dead skin. Only that way could she survive.

She abandoned her car. The lights were still on, the gearstick was in neutral, her driving licence, coat and possessions were inside. But she simply walked away, out of her old life.

This was the action that would leave her family, friends and the police absolutely flummoxed.

At 7 a.m. on Saturday 4 December, it was still dark on the Surrey Hills. A cowman going to work saw something odd: the 'dazzling headlights of a car against a bush'. He hurried on without investigating further. At 8 a.m., a boy of fifteen called Jack Best, in cap and gaiters, also saw the abandoned car. He went and told the Guildford police.[32]

When the police arrived, they found the car in a position that indicated 'some unusual proceeding had taken place'.[33] The man who ran the tea stall for sightseers at Newlands Corner helped to pull the vehicle back onto the carriageway.[34]

At Guildford's police station, Superintendent William Kenward of the Surrey Constabulary now swung into action. 'I immediately instituted inquiries,' he tells us, in an official account, 'and found that the lady had left her home in Sunningdale in the car, late the previous evening, under rather unusual circumstances.'[35]

Kenward, a portly, moon-faced man with a little moustache, was evidently a genial and committed officer. He was soft-hearted and compassionate, buying corn for the pigeons at Guildford police station, and starting a fund for widows and children.[36] Yet he had an unhelpful weakness for drama, and there was also a macho streak in his character. He was celebrated among his colleagues, for example, for having tackled 'an armed lunatic' by pretending to be a doctor and seizing his revolver.[37] Kenward now seemed almost determined to find evidence of foul play. He assumed that 'disaster' must have occurred, and felt it was his duty, 'from the point of view of humanity alone, to endeavour to find Mrs Christie if she was wandering about, out of her mind because of nervous collapse.'[38] On one level, three cheers for Kenward. On another, though, this single-minded pursuit of the most dramatic possible outcome would cause him to overlook vital evidence.

Kenward soon found Agatha's friends had a certain amount of support for his theory that something terrible had happened. 'It is my opinion,' said Peg, that Agatha 'wandered away . . . in a fit of depression.'[39]

It's striking the people who seemed to care most about Agatha's absence were not her blood relations. Peg, Agatha's friend Joyce and her assistant Carlo were the women who worried. Agatha had somehow assembled a second family for herself, a chosen family of friendship rather than blood. This was an important gift she'd possessed since the days of the 'Queer Women' of Torquay Hospital.

The police must have thought the most important evidence would be forthcoming from Mrs Christie's husband. But he was absent from his home. Where was he?

That Saturday morning, Archie had to be called back from the mystery location at which he'd planned to spend the weekend. This was Hurtmore Cottage, Godalming. It wasn't far from Newlands Corner, a fact that would lead to speculation it might have been Agatha's destination during her midnight drive.

Archie had gone to Hurtmore Cottage to stay with friends named Sam and Madge James. They weren't just any old friends. Madge James was a bosom buddy of Nancy Neele – they'd trained together as typists – and the fourth member of the quartet was Nancy herself. This was explosive information. If it got out, it could add a whole new dimension to Agatha's disappearance. Archie did not want the police to know about his adultery.

But now the geography of Sunningdale would come into play. The Styles was in Berkshire, which meant that the job of questioning its inhabitants would fall to the Berkshire police, under Superintendent Charles Goddard. Kenward, who was responsible for Newlands Corner as the scene of the possible crime, belonged to the Surrey Constabulary. Communication between the two forces was poor. And clearly everyone involved felt highly respectful of Archie. If this turned out to be murder, then he was obviously a suspect. And yet he was a gentleman, and a war hero. The police felt they'd have to tread carefully.

Social deference meant Archie's relationship with Nancy would be kept quiet for some time. But later on, crime reporter Ritchie Calder claimed Mr and Mrs James's servants had characterised that Friday night party at Hurtmore Cottage as a celebration: 'an "engagement" party for Colonel Christie and Miss Neele'.[40]

Some reports have Carlo phoning Hurtmore Cottage to tell Archie about his wife's absence on the Friday evening, others have her doing it on Saturday morning. Either way, the situation required him to come home. And there at The Styles on the hall table he found a letter from Agatha in a sealed envelope.[41] He read it, and then – causing much later speculation – he destroyed it.

He probably wouldn't have done so had he realised the importance it would take on as evidence for his wife's state of mind. And neither did Archie realise that his adultery was soon to become a very public matter.

20

The Harrogate Hydropathic Hotel

New York, 2008. A young teacher, Hannah Upp, completely disappeared from the lives of her family and friends.

They knew she wasn't dead because one day she was spotted browsing in the Apple Store. She left before anyone could challenge her. Hannah was finally identified after being fished out of the sea not far from the Statue of Liberty. She was alive, and moderately well, but she had absolutely no memory of the last three weeks.

Her first words were, 'Why am I wet?'

But many people simply couldn't believe that Hannah hadn't faked her condition. As she began to recover her memory, she started to feel terrible shame at the media reports she read about her ordeal. Journalists had written that she might merely have pretended to have lost her memory. They suggested she'd wasted police resources and public goodwill, and forfeited her family's love.

Yet psychiatrists believed Hannah had experienced a perfectly genuine medical condition called dissociative fugue, which takes its name from the Latin word for 'flight'. One psychiatrist told the *New Yorker* that dissociative fugue has been poorly studied partly because 'the phenomenon is so frightening. It's terrifying to think that we are all vulnerable to a lapse in selfhood.'[1] In fugue, a state brought on by trauma and stress, you literally forget who you are. Sometimes the memory comes back again afterwards, sometimes not.

For a long time, people investigating Agatha's 'disappearance' have tended towards one of two positions. One is that in the days following her car crash she was experiencing the specific condition of dissociative fugue, like Hannah Upp. The alternative position is that she was faking it.

While psychiatrists today broadly agree on what 'dissociative fugue' is, the language people had in the 1920s for talking about mental health was unhelpfully imprecise. 'Nervous breakdown' and 'loss of memory' (perhaps the closest correlation for the modern term 'dissociative fugue') were terms that had come to prominence after efforts to help soldiers traumatised in the Great War.

But these were blunt terms. And in fact, neither 'loss of memory' nor 'dissociative fugue' captures the range of symptoms that Agatha reported: exhaustion, muscular pain, insomnia, feelings of helplessness, withdrawal from social situations, difficulty in focussing her mind, loss of appetite and suicidal thoughts. Depression seems likely, with the addition of a period of fugue as well.

In Agatha's case, though, once the incident was labelled as 'loss of memory', the bar was set for a certain type of experience she did not exactly meet. Only one thing can be said for certain: on Saturday 4 December 1926, and for some days thereafter, Agatha experienced a distressing episode of mental illness, brought on by the trauma of the death of her mother and the breakdown of her marriage. Agatha's experience encompassed *more* than just the 'loss of her memory'. It was even more frightening and disorientating than that. She lost her way of life and her sense of self.

Doctors haven't much studied memory loss, because it's both rare and hard to treat. In the 1970s, though, the condition became topical when people started to come forward with claims of suppressed memories of being abused as children. When some of these cases were investigated and proved to stack up, memory loss started to be taken more seriously.[2]

When – that is – the victims were believed. The condition has always been accompanied by doubt: doubt on the part of the sufferer about what happened, doubt on the part of the onlooker that the sufferer might not be telling the truth.

And just like with Hannah Upp, Agatha's statements about her celebrated disappearance have been questioned and her story disbelieved right from the start. Part of this was doubtless to do with gender. If even today we are conditioned to doubt the truth of what women say, in the 1920s the situation was even worse. Agatha did have the huge advantage of her social class: some people would have believed her, simply because of that. But she also had a double disadvantage: the fact that she was a working woman, and the nature of her profession, both of which damaged her credibility.

Additionally, as we'll see, the matter was made much worse by her celebrity. She would now be subjected to a merciless trial by a media that reached a very different conclusion from mine about why she'd left home: that she was a jealous, manipulative, attention-seeking person, vengefully seeking to frame her husband for her murder.

The great injustice of Agatha Christie's life was not that her husband betrayed her while she was mourning her mother. Nor was it even the mental distress.

It was the fact that she was shamed for her illness in the nation's newspapers in such a public way that people ever since have suspected her of duplicity and lies.

Unfortunately for Agatha's lasting reputation, many of her biographers, notably her male biographers, have been as heavily invested in this narrative as the male police officers and journalists who made it into such a sensation at the time. 'She set out deliberately – the facts shout it – to throw murder suspicion' upon her husband, says one of these writers.[3]

And so the injustice has been perpetuated.

It's time to do something radical: to listen to what Agatha says, to understand she had a range of experiences unhelpfully labelled as 'loss of memory'; and perhaps most importantly: when she says she was suffering, to believe her.

So what should we believe? Agatha tells us that on the Saturday morning of 4 December, while the police were investigating her abandoned car, she had – in the slightly unhelpful language of the time – 'lost her memory'.

With the help of a psychotherapist, she would later begin to put together a narrative of the movements she'd blanked out. 'I remember arriving at a big railway station,' she recalled, eventually, 'and being surprised to learn it was Waterloo.'[4]

Many other people were also keen to work out where she might have been. According to investigators from the *Daily Mail*, following in her tracks, it was most likely she'd found her wandering way to Clandon station, about three miles from Newlands Corner. She took only her handbag, £60 in cash, and the photograph of Rosalind. From Clandon, trains to Waterloo left at 6.42, 7.22, 7.52, 8.22 and 8.56, and it seems likely that this was the way Agatha got herself to London.[5]

When she finally spoke about her experience, Agatha turned to the language she knew best, the language of her novels, in which 'loss of memory' repeatedly forms a plot point. It means she can't help sounding like Tuppence Beresford, out on a mission, which gives her words a sense of unreality when she describes her arrival at Waterloo. 'It is strange,' she says, that 'the railway authorities there did not recall me, as I was covered with mud and I had smeared blood on my face from a cut on my hand.'[6]

Even though she'd been suicidal just hours before, she'd now 'dissociated' herself from all that. Those thoughts had belonged to someone else. Agatha turned her attention to cleaning herself up. It seems likely she took a taxi to a department store; some reports claim Harrods, others Whiteleys. For a woman like Agatha, with £60 in her handbag (more than £2,000 in today's money) a big shop is a warm and welcoming place to be. There are indications she bought a hot-water bottle. Some accounts also say she lost a ring, others that she left one behind to be repaired.[7] Agatha would want that ring back again. It was part of her bridal daydream.

In London, Agatha also did something else of significance: she posted a letter. It was addressed to Archie's brother, Campbell Christie. She'd always been close to Campbell, who often helped her with her work. The letter was posted in the SW1 district of London, in which Harrods also lies, and got to the sorting office to be stamped there at 9.45 a.m.[8]

How could a woman who'd 'lost her memory' post a letter? This is where the limitations of the term begin to appear. But Agatha, in a fugue state, was acting irrationally. The night before, when she'd written to Carlo and Archie, it seems possible she'd also written, addressed and stamped this letter to Campbell, putting it in her bag to take to the post. The letter said she was leaving home for a while, to stay at a spa in Yorkshire. It was a backup plan. If she *didn't* end her life, then Agatha would, of course, want her family to know where she was. If she had found this letter in her bag, ready to go, it would have been natural to post it.

As she washed in the department store cloakroom, Agatha's mind now began to protect itself from further pain by inventing a new identity for herself as a completely different woman. 'I had now become in my mind Mrs Teresa Neele of South Africa,' she says.[9] Where did this persona come from? Someone who had the same surname as Archie's lover, someone who came from a place where she and Archie had been happy. These details came together to create a character she felt she could sustain. 'You can't write your fate,' Agatha would say, years later, but 'you can do what you like with the characters you create.'[10] So she created a new character for herself, a character in which she could do what she wanted. What she wanted most of all was to escape from the unbearable life of Mrs Christie.

After a restorative spell in the shop, 'Teresa Neele' went to King's Cross and bought a ticket for the spa resort of Harrogate. The town's famous Royal Baths were the pinnacle of perfection in healthcare. Agatha, later on, found nothing odd about her choice of destination: 'the motor accident brought on neuritis, and once before in my life I had thought of going to Harrogate to have treatment for this complaint.'[11] She'd experienced neuritis as pain in her shoulders while surfing during the Grand Tour, and hot water had relieved it.

This self-diagnosis of 'neuritis' is significant. In the 1920s, it would have been understood as a painful inflammation of the nerves with a physical or biological origin. Yet there was a similar condition, 'neurasthenia', which saw the same sort of pain as a response to emotional distress. It was hard to distinguish between neuritis and neurasthenia, and the treatment for both was a rest cure at a spa.[12] But there were also important class distinctions between the two terms. It was more likely middle-class people would lay claim to neuritis (biological) than neurasthenia (emotional). Agatha's choice of words acknowledges the scale of her problem, yet uses a social code that distances her from 'the mad'.[13]

Either way, heading for a spa was a sensible thing to do, and Agatha's actions make a kind of upside-down sense. She thought herself a danger to Rosalind. Rest was essential. What had Joyce said? That 'her doctor told her that she must have rest, and things would right themselves'.[14]

The winter light must have faded by the time her train arrived in Harrogate. She took a taxi to a hotel, apparently picked at random, called the Hydropathic.[15]

The Hydropathic, or the 'Hydro' as locals called it, had three storeys and a portico built of sooty-coloured stone. A rather grand establishment, it had been taken over by the Harrogate Hydropathic Company in 1878. Today it's called the Swan. Then, it had parking for twenty-six cars, five acres of gardens, and a ballroom. The Royal Baths were just a short walk away, as were other smart hotels such as the Majestic.[16]

The electric lights must have spilled out of the Hydro's windows to warm the December night; guests were coming and going. Like the department store, this was somewhere Agatha could feel safe. She'd always liked the anonymity of hotels, where she'd often stayed, alone, writing.

Agatha arrived with no suitcase, but explained she'd recently come from South Africa and had left her luggage with friends. She gave her name as Mrs Teresa Neele, of Cape Town, South Africa, signing the register in her usual handwriting.[17]

The surname obviously hints at some conflation between Agatha and Nancy Neele. But was the first name chosen for St Teresa of Avila, the literary saint whom Agatha admired? Or – in a twist that only the most dedicated of sleuths could unravel – was it an anagram of 'teaser'?[18] All that remains unknown. But Agatha, who had a passion for crossword puzzles, had a mind made for thinking up such fantastic things.

Mr W. Taylor, the hotel's manager, stated later that his new guest took a 'good room on the first floor, fitted with hot and cold water'. The price of seven guineas a week caused her no hesitation: 'she seemed to have as much money as she wanted'.[19] That £60 was coming in useful.

Agatha's room was serviced by a young, shingle-haired and pretty chambermaid named Rosie Asher, who seems to have kept a particularly close eye on her. Asher spotted that 'Mrs Neele' had brought hardly anything with her: just 'a comb, new hot-water bottle and a small photo of a little boy, across which was written "Teddy".'[20]

Agatha herself later remembered wondering why she had bruises. But 'Mrs Neele' was desperate for her life to unfold in an orderly fashion. So she went down for dinner, and even took part in the evening's dancing. Falling into conversation with her fellow guests, she gave out hints of tragedy. She told one her 'little girl had died and that she had come to Harrogate to recuperate'. The guests, who were also referred to as 'patients', embraced this single woman in their midst. 'I danced with Mrs Christie the evening she arrived,' one of them said later, 'she does the Charleston, but not very well.'[21]

Agatha danced – badly – in the skirt in which she'd spent the night. Clearly, she'd have to get hold of the correct costume for her new character. After she'd rested, and when the shops were open, she'd need clothes.[22] This was something that hadn't changed. Like Agatha Christie, daughter of Frederick Miller, it would turn out that Mrs Teresa Neele – whose life had begun in a department store – loved to shop.

*   *   *

Meanwhile, back in Surrey, Kenward spent the weekend with seven or eight policemen and some civilian volunteers, searching the countryside near Agatha's car.[23] It was a fruitless business, and he felt he should widen the investigation.

The police also put out a missing person statement, and the press quickly picked it up. Monday morning's papers contained its details. Missing from her home in Sunningdale was 'Mrs Agatha May Clarissa Christie, wife of Colonel Christie, aged 35 [actually she was thirty-six], height 5 ft. 7 in., hair, reddish and shingled, eyes grey, complexion fair, well built.'[24]

The description also noted she wasn't wearing her wedding ring, something she'd left behind at The Styles. Those in the know about the breakdown of the Christie marriage took this as a disturbing indication about her state of mind. Others took it as an equally disturbing symbol of Agatha's modernity.[25]

The press now painted Archie as a tragic hero. 'Here in Sunningdale,' reported the *Daily Mail*, 'the mystery of Mrs Christie's disappearance is the one topic . . . anxiety as to the fate of a brilliant woman is only equalled by the sympathy evoked by the pitiful figure of Colonel Christie.'[26]

But Kenward was growing suspicious of Colonel Christie. Having read Agatha's letter to Carlo, he believed there was a risk she'd committed suicide, or – although Kenward never quite spelt it out – been murdered. He didn't see his job as simply to find Agatha. Instead, he pontificated on the need to confirm this was 'not a matter of foul play'. In an exclusive interview with the *Surrey Advertiser*, Kenward would throw out dark hints that foul play had indeed been 'suggested very freely by people who knew her, includ-ing some of her own relations'.[27] It's worth saying that Carlo, however, with access to the same letter, 'could not believe' Agatha was dead.[28]

At the same time, Superintendent Goddard of Berkshire, whose force were responsible for interviewing the Christie servants, also believed Agatha was still alive. And Goddard of Berkshire was less addicted than Kenward of Surrey to talking to journalists. Crime reporter Ritchie Calder was covering the hunt. A socialist with no love for the upper-crust Christies, he was not an unbiased witness. But his memories do reveal his strong perception that the two police forces could not agree. 'The Berkshire and Surrey police were hardly on speaking terms,' he said.[29]

It was growing increasingly frustrating that Archie had destroyed his own letter from Agatha, and he was curiously cagey about its contents. He fenced around, saying it 'referred to a purely personal matter . . . I cannot discuss what that was.'[30] Archie was both covering himself and trying to protect Nancy, whose good name would be tarnished if she were dragged into this mess.

Kenward in Surrey forged ahead with his mission of finding a corpse. He made plans to drag a pond near Newlands Corner, which had the unfortunately melodramatic name of the Silent Pool. The prospect made journalists salivate. The *Daily Sketch* was almost beside itself: 'in local tradition there is a feeling that the pool has an irresistible fascination on those who are brought into close touch with it, as Mrs Christie was.'[31]

The press couldn't get enough of this sort of thing. The *Daily Mail* drafted in a retired policeman to provide expert comment. While he proved disappointingly dull on police procedure, he hit the nail on the head in another way. 'Mrs Christie,' he wrote, 'has, wittingly or unwittingly, in real life been the central figure in a mystery that surpasses anything in her clever novels.'[32]

Meanwhile, in Harrogate, Agatha was embracing her life in limbo. Her chambermaid noted that on Sunday, while Kenward was searching the downs, Agatha 'slept until 10 a.m., had breakfast in bed and then went out.'[33]

On Monday morning, Asher noticed Agatha had the 'London newspaper taken up with breakfast in bed'. It would have been hard to avoid the story about Mrs Christie's disappearance, which was now international news.[34] But Agatha somehow still managed to set the knowledge aside. She began to equip herself with a new wardrobe. Later that day, after a visit to the shops, packages began to be delivered to her room: 'new hat, coat, evening shoes, books and magazines, pencil and fruit and various toilet requisites.'

People at the hotel noticed that Agatha usually had a book in her hand. She'd been to the WHSmith Library in Parliament Street, where Miss Cowie, the librarian 'gathered from her selections that she had a taste for novels of sensation and mystery'.[35]

That evening, Agatha came down to dinner in a proper evening dress, with a new 'fancy scarf'. Hotel staff would report that in the drawing room and on the dance floor, 'she has made a number of friends'. She played billiards and even sang aloud for the other guests' pleasure.[36] Miss Corbett, the hotel's entertainment hostess, spotted that 'Mrs Neele' still had the price – 75 shillings – pinned to her new shawl. 'Is that all you are worth?' asked one of the guests. 'I think I am worth more than that,' was Agatha's answer.[37]

The following day, Agatha took delivery of another parcel. She'd written to ask if the ring left at the department store in London could be sent on to her. According to some reports, it was specifically a diamond ring. On Tuesday 7 December, it duly arrived at the Hydro.[38] Putting her ring on her finger was perhaps like filling in a final gap in her identity as a different, and better, wife.

On Tuesday 7 December, the stakes were rising in the hunt for Mrs Christie. The *Daily News* offered a reward of £100 to anyone able to give information leading to Agatha's discovery.[39]

But the continued absence of a corpse meant a new theory began to enter the press reports: the suggestion that Agatha might have lost her memory. 'The only explanation I can offer,' Archie said to one journalist, was that his wife was 'suffering from loss of memory.'[40] Agatha's friend Joyce was also sure that this was 'a case of absolute exhaustion – loss of memory or something like that.'[41]

The following day, Wednesday 8 December, the *Daily Mail* took up the loss of memory theory and ran with it. 'The subconscious mind takes charge,' one of its writers explained, 'and where that mind has been trained by the creative faculties of an artist in devising mysterious disappearances for works of fiction, it might plan an actual disappearance with great ingenuity.'[42]

A good number of Archie's generation, having come through the Great War, believed loss of memory to be a plausible reaction to trauma. In his chapter on 'Nervous Shock' in a book on war medicine, the doctor Wilfred Harris gives an account of memory loss that tallies perfectly with what Agatha would later report about her state of mind. A patient, says Harris, 'may present total loss of memory, and every fact of his life preceding the accident may be strange to him. He may not know his name, occupation, or where he lived.'[43] When details finally emerged of Agatha's car crash, the hitting of her head would be stressed. That was because it was commonly thought in the 1920s that people who'd 'lost their memories' had most often been triggered by concussion or a blow to the head during shelling.[44]

At the Hydro, though, people were beginning to suspect who 'Mrs Neele' really was. After all, on Tuesday 7 December, a portrait of Agatha had appeared on the *Daily Express*'s front page. The resemblance was unmissable.

'When she had been here about four days,' recalled the hotel's manager, 'my wife said to me: "I believe that lady is Mrs Christie!"'[45] Mr Taylor thought his wife was being 'absurd', but she wasn't the only one to have worked it out. 'Some of the servants here had said that there seemed to be a great resemblance between the woman and the pictures,' said Mrs Taylor, 'I told them to say nothing.'[46] The spas of Harrogate were patronised by the ill, the bored and the rich. These sorts of people expected publicity when it was desired, secrecy when it was not.

But the secret was bound eventually to spill. Miss Corbett, the entertainment hostess, later admitted the truth: 'we have all been saying it was Mrs Christie.'[47]

It must have grown harder for the hotel staff to follow their instructions to keep silent as they read in the papers on Wednesday 8

December about an even bigger search Kenward had organised in Surrey.

The *Westminster Gazette* reported that no fewer than 300 policemen and special constables had taken part and that 'tangled heaths were beaten down by men walking ten yards apart armed with long sticks . . . they could be heard calling to each other through the dank drifting hilltop mists, while overhead sounded the drone of the 'planes as they cruised to and fro.'[48]

Kenward was now pretty certain he was hunting for a corpse. 'The official view was freely expressed,' reported the *Telegraph*, 'that Mrs Christie would be found not far from the spot where her car was found.'[49]

After all, Kenward might well have read Agatha's story 'The Disappearance of Mr Davenheim'. In it, Poirot riffs about the possible meanings of an absence. 'You might lose your own memory,' the detective says, 'but someone would be sure to recognise you.' On the other hand, he continues, it's not possible that bodies can 'vanish into thin air. Sooner or later they turn up, concealed in lonely places, or in trunks. Murder will out.'[50]

Pictures of Kenward would now appear in the press, standing in commanding postures and directing his legions of searchers.[51] Persisting in his heroic search of the lonely, misty places of Surrey, he seemed convinced that indeed 'murder will out'.

But Kenward might better have spent his time investigating a new clue, which had emerged that Tuesday while he was busy searching Newlands Corner.

It finally came to light that Archie's brother Campbell had received that third letter from Agatha, posted in central London on the previous Saturday. He'd received and read the letter, but thought nothing of it until he heard she'd 'disappeared'.

When Campbell realised the letter could be important evidence, he couldn't find it, though he still had the envelope. He had to rely on his memory for its contents. The *Daily Mail* reported his statement that Agatha had said 'she was going to a Yorkshire spa to stay with friends and to recuperate'.[52]

One might expect, in the light of this, that the police search would be redirected towards Yorkshire. But Kenward reacted as many an investigator does when confronted with a piece that doesn't fit into the jigsaw he has in his head. He did his best to reason the letter away. After all, it wasn't necessarily evidence that Agatha had been alive on the Saturday. She need not have posted the letter herself, and may have 'made arrangements' for someone else to post it for her.[53]

The police made a perfunctory effort to bring Yorkshire into the sphere of their search. But *The Times* reported that Kenward's Guildford team were satisfied that 'Mrs Christie is not in that county'.[54] So the search continued locally, Kenward convinced that the Campbell Christie letter was some sort of a feint from a deceptive woman.

After all, the search was proving rather enjoyable. Two pilots had offered their services, circling 'many times around the spot where the car was found'.[55] The police had technology at their disposal: 'the wide network of telephones, and hundreds of motor-cars [. . .] and now diving apparatus is to be used.'[56]

It was a reporter from the *Daily Chronicle*, keen to break what was building to be the story of the week, if not the year, who carried out the fullest search of the hotels of Harrogate. He spent an entire day on the task, but he was unlucky, and found nothing.

All this time, though, Superintendent Goddard of the Berkshire police was following a different line of inquiry. His officers had interviewed Agatha's parlourmaid Lilly, who reported Agatha's words: 'I am going away for the week-end, probably to London first.'[57] Then the letter to Campbell Christie mentioning Yorkshire added to Goddard's firm impression that Agatha was still alive. Goddard thought that a wide campaign, using 'missing person' posters, and aimed at finding a living person, was better than a narrow campaign in the Surrey Hills to find a dead one.

The two different approaches appeared unhelpfully competitive. 'If a senior detective inspector from Scotland-yard were called in by either county,' complained the *Express*, 'the whole work would be under the single direction of a man trained to grapple with the most complex difficulties.'[58] Archie had indeed requested that Scotland Yard be consulted. But the local forces, each eager for glory, thought it wasn't necessary.

Goddard's 'missing person' search included working with the press. In its Thursday edition, the *Daily Mail* included a 'composite photograph' of Agatha, prepared by an artist with the advice of the Surrey police and input from Carlo. Agatha was shown wearing the cardigan she'd been wearing at the time of the disappearance. The picture in the newspaper was just a start: it was also to appear on posters.[59]

In Yorkshire, the Harrogate police also began to search the hotels, without success. But they did discover an unknown woman of Agatha's age with a 'very queer' manner had visited the Royal Baths.[60]

It was the Royal Baths, constructed in 1897, that had placed Harrogate in the 'forefront of European watering places'. Besides Turkish and Russian bathing, the establishment also offered massages, with 'thoroughly trained rubbers'.[61] Agatha tells us that in Harrogate she went to these baths 'regularly' to ease what she described as neuritis.[62] The police may have missed her, but the net was tightening. Officers instructed that 'a sharp look-out is to be kept at the ticket office in the baths in case the woman returns.'[63]

Agatha was oblivious, though, to the police being hot on her heels. Life was much better for her now. 'As Mrs Neele,' she said later, 'I was very happy and contented.'[64]

She was paying attention to her health; she was turning herself into someone new. Slowly, surely, she was becoming a well-dressed, sane and stylish young woman, someone much more like Nancy Neele than Mrs Christie had been.

At some point – surely? – Archie would see sense, and come back to her.

Yet real life was trying to force its way back into Agatha's attention. Thursday found her – according to Rosie Asher – 'very cheerful and bright'.[65] But this was a bad day, perhaps the worst day yet, for both Agatha and Archie.

In her newspaper Agatha must have read about the search for Mrs Christie. Some part of her subconscious must have begun to appreciate the scale of it, and to begin to anticipate the shame she'd experience if she ever reclaimed her true identity.

She seemed determined instead to work herself further into her role as Mrs Neele. Later that day, she placed an advert to appear in *The Times*. It read 'FRIENDS and RELATIVES of TERESA NEELE, late of South Africa, please COMMUNICATE. Write Box R.702.'[66]

It reads like a veiled plea for help to her husband. Archie knew Agatha well enough to understand the panic the press attention would cause her. 'I am sure she will not return until all is quiet,' he said, 'those who understand her shy and retiring nature know she will come back when all has settled down.'[67]

But even worse, this was also the day the real Nancy Neele first appeared in the press.

Nancy had gone to ground, sheltering anxiously with her parents in Rickmansworth. But now the *Westminster Gazette* reported that during Colonel Christie's stay with Mr and Mrs James, there'd also been present a 'Miss Nield [sic], a young woman friend of the family'. It was exciting to have a 'young woman' in the story. The paper's special correspondent also said the police had interviewed the staff at The Styles about the state of the Christie marriage: 'I understand that there is "no truth in the rumour",' ran his article, 'that there were "high words" between them at the breakfast table' the day Agatha disappeared.[68] But this left the very opposite impression.

This was a terrible turn of events for Agatha. If Nancy's name was known, she was on the brink of being outed as an abandoned wife. The kind of person who'd been left by her husband for a 'young woman friend'.

So she dug in ever deeper. 'At Harrogate,' she remembered later, 'I read every day about Mrs Christie's disappearance . . . I regarded her as having acted stupidly.'[69] A fellow guest at the hotel remembered her saying that 'Mrs Christie is a very elusive person. I cannot be bothered with her.'[70] Also, according to this witness, Agatha was beginning to show signs of inexplicable mental distress. She 'would press her hand to her forehead and say, "it is my head. I cannot remember."'[71]

Nancy's name getting into the papers was equally upsetting for Archie. This was what he'd been dreading, for as well as the social shame it would also provide him with an excellent motive for murder. Had a body been found in the Silent Pool, for example, claimed Ritchie Calder, 'I have no doubt from what I knew of the police attitude, that Colonel Christie would have been held.'[72]

Archie certainly believed that to be the case, and said as much to a colleague at his office in the City. The pair of them met in the lift. 'He was in a terribly nervous state,' this colleague testified, 'and told me the police had followed him up Broad street . . . "They think I've murdered my wife," he said.'[73]

That Thursday evening, Archie was called to the police station to be questioned, and a policeman would from now on be stationed outside The Styles. Archie claimed the guard was there 'at his request as he did not wish to be harassed' by reporters.[74]

But actually the policeman was posted to stop Archie, chief suspect, from disappearing too.

Friday 9 December dawned, and the end of the year was approaching. The 'Spirit of Christmas' appeared on the front page of the *Daily Mail*. It had been a whole week since Agatha had left The Styles. That Friday morning at the hotel, she 'seemed rather strange for a minute or so . . . went downstairs early and then to Leeds for shopping.'[75]

Meanwhile, it emerged that Archie, stressed and terrified – 'the suspense of the uncertainty is terrible' – had made an awful mistake. The previous evening, he'd given an ill-advised interview to the *Daily Mail*. Perhaps hoping to divert attention away from 'Miss

Nield', he introduced the idea that maybe his wife had *deliberately* disappeared.

'My wife,' he'd said to a reporter, 'had discussed the possibility of disappearing at will ... engineering a disappearance had been running through her mind, probably for the purpose of her work. Personally, I feel that is what happened.'

Archie had moved on from the theory of 'memory loss'. Like Carlo, he'd never had any time for the suicide theory. And he now defended himself against the charge he'd been a bad husband:

> It is absolutely untrue to suggest that there was anything in the nature of a row or a tiff between my wife and myself on Friday morning ... I strongly depreciate introducing any tittle-tattle into this matter ... My wife has never made the slightest objection to any of my friends.

Readers must have thought he protested far, far, too much.

And Archie then expanded upon how his wife might have pulled off her trick. 'She may have accumulated a considerable sum of money secretly,' he said, making Agatha sound avaricious and fraudulent. 'She was very clever . . . she was very clever at getting anything she wanted.'[76]

This long interview got summarised in a damning way in the special Atlantic edition of the *Mail*. 'Colonel Christie told me today,' ran this summary, 'that his wife, whose novels dealt with mysteries, had discussed the possibility of disappearing at will.'[77] And foreign papers compressed the story even more. The *Baltimore Sun*, by 12 December, baldly headlined a short article with: 'Police Believe Missing Woman Novelist Is Hiding. Work On Theory She Deliberately Staged Disappearance.'[78]

And so, foolishly, Archie gave readers all the ammunition they needed to think that Agatha had wilfully disappeared.

If this were true, though, the motive must have been the revenge of a wife betrayed, and this Archie could not admit. 'I left home on Friday to spend the weekend with friends,' he told the *Evening News*, whose reporter must have been all agog to know who Archie's friends were. But Archie refused to tell: 'I do not want my friends to be dragged into this.'[79] The police have often been condemned for their failure to find Agatha more quickly. But Archie, with his shifty statements, and yet his convincing tone of command, was a major obstacle in their way.

However, he wasn't clever enough to protect himself consistently. 'You must remember,' he said, in yet another interview published on Saturday 11 December, 'we have been married for some years and, like other married couples, led to a certain extent our own lives.' He had his business affairs, he explained, and his 'wife had her literary work'.[80]

He'd put a final nail into the coffin of the Christie marriage. Readers were left with an entirely negative picture of Agatha: an inadequate wife, overly absorbed in her work, neglectful and cold.

On Saturday morning, the day Archie's troubling statements were printed, Agatha's hotel chambermaid thought 'Mrs Neele' 'seemed agitated' by the newspaper.[81]

That same day, the *Telegraph* carried a big advert for a coming serialisation of *The Murder on the Links*. It was trumpeted as the work of an author called 'Agatha Christie The Missing Novelist'.[82] These were obviously the words of Agatha's publishers, not Agatha herself. But readers could be forgiven for thinking the author was somehow cashing in on her new notoriety.

The author herself had had enough of reading the papers. At the Hydro, on the Sunday, no newspaper was taken up to the bedroom.

On this day, Sunday 12 December, the Surrey police organised what would become known as the Great Search or Hunt for Agatha's body in the beautiful countryside of the Surrey hills: 'one of the greatest organised searches in the records of the police'.[83] *The Times* claimed 2,000 people turned up to help, and that 'the roads were blocked with traffic . . . parked cars covered the whole of the plateau where the abandoned motor car was found.'[84]

Kenward appeared to be enjoying himself a bit too much. 'I have handled many important cases,' he told the *Daily Mail*, 'but this is the most baffling mystery ever set me for solution.'[85]

It was a sodden day in Surrey. 'The mist-laden countryside was scoured by thousands of men and women on foot, and by scores on horseback,' wrote an excitable reporter in the *Daily Mail*. 'Six blood-hounds were used [. . .] the women were as thorough as the men. Caring nothing for sudden tumblings into concealed ditches and the wounds they received from thorns which drove through their gloves and stockings, they resolutely beat their way.'[86]

Agatha's fellow crime writers were also being irresistibly drawn into the mystery. The searchers that Sunday included Dorothy L. Sayers. Sir Arthur Conan Doyle, who had a longstanding interest in spiritualism, gave to a medium a glove that had belonged to Agatha. The medium, not knowing whose it was, nevertheless said at once that its owner 'is not dead as many think. She is alive. You will hear of her, I think, next Wednesday.' Conan Doyle passed this good news on to Archie.[87]

But nothing of note emerged all day. Kenward thought he hadn't looked hard enough, and began to think about yet another hunt.

Meanwhile, more sober heads had been doubtful all along that success would be found in the Surrey Hills. Kenward was losing the confidence of the pack of reporters, whose tone had changed. They were now more interested in 'the theory of deliberate disappearance'. The three letters, especially the one to Campbell Christie, the packing of the suitcase, the statement to the housemaid, might all indicate such a plan.

But even so, people were still looking in the wrong place: 'there is now a strong belief in official quarters that she may be found in London, disguised as a man.'[88]

Hundreds, possibly thousands, of police and volunteers had taken part in the Great Hunt. Shared memories of a huge endeavour, motivated by curiosity but also by kindness, were created that Sunday on the Surrey Hills. And many hopes were dashed when it bore no fruit.

The effort, the disappointment, would now become part of Britain's folk memory. And disappointment can quickly turn to anger.

Yet another crime writer, Edgar Wallace, was engaged by the *Daily Mail* to air his views. On 11 December his article struck a newly hostile note. Agatha's disappearance was probably voluntary, he said, and

> a typical case of 'mental reprisal' on someone who has hurt her. To put it vulgarly, her first intention seems to have been to 'spite' an unknown person who would be distressed by her disappearance . . . it is impossible to lose your memory and find your way to a determined destination. [89]

Wilfred Harris, that expert on wartime trauma, would have been all too familiar with this kind of reaction to 'memory loss.' 'Amnesia,' he'd written, 'is liable to be mistaken for malingering.'[90]

Kenward, however, remained against the idea of a deliberate disappearance and thought the suggestion 'cruel'.[91] He was far from callous, and Agatha's family and friends had convinced him her shyness would have made 'a stunt' the last thing she'd have done.[92] But in the absence of any other convincing explanation, the idea gained traction.

On Tuesday 14 December, the *Daily Mail* ran an editorial. If Agatha were alive, its writer argued, 'she must be ready to inflict intense anxiety on her relatives and heavy expenditure on the public' in 'a heartless practical joke'.[93]

And this kind of speculation has gone on ever since. There've been plenty of writers inclined to argue the case that Agatha did disappear deliberately. One of them was Gwen Robyns, whose 1978 biography the Christie family refused to authorise. Biographer Jared Cade in 1998 also believed Agatha 'deliberately staged her disappearance'.[94] 'The need to retaliate' had motivated her, argued Richard Hack in his own unauthorised biography in 2009. When it came to Agatha's desire to make Archie suffer, 'her plan was going well'.[95]

And from there, the respectable-looking, footnoted works of biographers, the idea has spread into popular culture: into films and novels. The milder have her down as a woman wronged, with an understandable desire for revenge. The more extreme – notably the feature film *Agatha*, made in 1979 – present her as the would-be murderer of Nancy Neele.

Of course, fiction and fact are different things. But, as we've seen many times, many people simply don't understand the difference.

Unknown to Kenward in Surrey, matters in Yorkshire were moving swiftly towards a denouement. That Sunday evening, two men went to Harrogate police station to report their suspicion that Mrs Christie was staying in the hotel where they worked.

Bob Tappin and Bob Lemming were musicians in a group called the Happy Hydro Boys, to whose music Agatha had danced. Another band member, Albert Whiteley, explained why it had taken them so long to come forward. 'The band leader didn't want to know,' he explained, 'if it turned out we were wrong he'd lose his job.'[96]

When she heard the police had been tipped off, Rosie Asher was unsurprised. She'd long ago recognised who 'Mrs Neele' really was, but 'it would have cost me my job to cause anyone any trouble, especially a guest.'[97] On Monday 13 December, the local police came to the hotel.

This fear for their jobs on the part of the hotel staff, and the respect shown towards the privacy of a paying guest, explains why, even now, the mystery was still allowed to drag on. It would not be until Tuesday 14 December that Carlo and Archie were finally informed of the strong suspicion that Agatha had been found.

Kenward wasn't really interested in what his colleagues in Yorkshire might have to say, because he was too busy. On Monday, eighty members of the Aldershot Motor Cycling Club had tendered him their services. He was also engaged in 'mapping out the whole area into sections, making a note of all the pools and ravines'.[98] He'd been offered divers, and 'two thousand motor coaches' for ferrying policemen about.[99]

But even while all this was happening, the afternoon edition of the *Evening Standard* came out. Published at 2.30 p.m. on Tuesday 14 December, it contained news of another, and more significant, development.

It had happened – as much of the evidence had suggested all along – in Harrogate.

21

Reappearance

On Tuesday 14 December, acting on information from the Harrogate police, the Surrey police finally rang up The Styles. They told Carlo that multiple people strongly suspected Agatha was alive, and well, and staying at the Hydropathic Hotel.

It had been eleven eventful days since she'd left home.

Carlo telephoned Archie at his office. He listened to the details provided, and decided it did indeed sound as if the person being described was his wife. He would go up to Yorkshire to see. Carlo couldn't go, because she needed to look after Rosalind.

Would the mystery finally be resolved?

Archie took the 1.40 train from King's Cross to Harrogate, arriving after sunset. Journalists reported a look of 'intense anxiety' on his face as he stepped down onto the platform.[1] He followed Agatha's trail over to the Hydro, where the manager showed him the visitors' book. And now Archie must have felt much more confident. Although Agatha hadn't signed in under her own name, he recognised her handwriting.[2]

The hotel's management must have been severely challenged by the twenty-five or so journalists swilling about their lobby and steps. But the police had a plan for Archie to set eyes on the woman in question without alarming her. They wanted to avoid 'frightening' a woman who might be in a parlous mental state. And not just any woman, a celebrity and a creative person too. It's rather fascinating to watch the police tiptoeing round the Christies, scared of doing the wrong thing.

Although Archie's nerves must have been pitched to the highest key, *The Times* reported how the meeting was managed in an unobtrusive manner. 'In company with Inspector MacDowell,' we hear, Archie 'took up a position in the lounge.' People came and went, the newfangled elevator sighed up and down, breathing out guests going into dinner. They waited half an hour. Then, at long last, the lady 'who was supposed to be the missing woman came down'.[3]

She was wearing a 'handsome mauve gown, with a pearl necklace, which she had bought in Harrogate', and reporters were struck by her 'beautiful fair hair'.[4]

But would Archie claim this lovely woman, looking better than he'd seen her for years, as his wife? What would he say, what would she do?

The manager of the hotel takes up the tale. Archie looked over at the police officer waiting with him and made the agreed signal: 'as she stepped out of the lift he nodded'.[5]

With that nod, Archie was a murder suspect no longer. His supposed victim was alive.

The police officers intercepted Agatha, and pointed out her husband. From the point of view of the journalists, it was a disappointingly undramatic reunion. One source records an 'affectionate greeting' between them, another said that 'Mrs Christie appeared perfectly composed at the sight of her husband and walked quietly into the lounge.' One report even claimed that 'Mrs Christie remarked on her husband looking nervous'.[6]

With incredible sangfroid, the Christies simply entered the dining room and had dinner, just as if nothing out of the ordinary had happened. The rules of hotel society held everyone to their appointed routines just as usual.

But it was clear that Agatha was still living some form of imaginary life: she introduced Archie to her acquaintances among the guests not as a husband but as her brother.[7] 'She came to me,' recalled one of them, 'saying "This is my brother, who has arrived unexpectedly." He was much more embarrassed than she was.'[8] For Agatha, her coping mechanism was still working. If she acted as normal, maybe real life would begin to match what was happening inside her head.

And it worked. Although he was embarrassed, even Archie fell into line.

Even if the guests weren't quite sure what had happened, there was a palpable sense of relief among the staff. The manager's wife, Mrs Taylor, was 'glad everything has turned out all right, because I took on a certain responsibility in not informing the police.'[9]

But Archie could not long hold at bay the wider world, which was waiting with bated breath outside the safety of the Hydro's illuminated dining room. What to do about all those reporters?

On the advice of the police, Archie spoke to one journalist from the pack, who passed the information on to the rest. Archie stated that yes,

It is my wife. She has suffered from the most complete loss of memory and I do not think she knows who she is . . . I am hoping to take her to London to-morrow to see a doctor.[10]

Even if he had harboured any doubts about the nature of Agatha's condition, this statement by Archie was irrevocable. Whether Agatha had 'lost her memory' or not, this was now the Christie family's official line, from which they could not deviate.

And so, the next day, everyone could read in every paper that the mystery was solved.

'Thank God for that!' was Carlo's reported reaction to the news that Agatha was safe. 'It is splendid. I felt that it must be so because I could not believe anything else.'

Superintendent Goddard now had a justifiable sneer at Kenward's expense. It was the missing person posters, he said, 'I think I may claim are responsible for the discovery of Mrs Christie.' Like Carlo, he'd always 'believed that she was alive and would be found if we made our search wide enough'.

Kenward was left licking his wounds. He harangued the *Daily Mail*'s crime reporter, insisting that he'd taken only the 'common-sense point of view'.[11] But Conan Doyle was happy, because his medium had been proved correct, and he concluded that the Christie case was an 'excellent example of the use of psychometry as an aid to the detective'.[12]

Archie had said he was taking Agatha to London. But that clearly wasn't practical with such a huge crowd of journalists following them. They needed a place of safety nearer by.

Help was at hand in the form of Agatha's sister. Abney Hall would provide a refuge, and Madge and her husband James came over to Harrogate to fetch the Christies.

Just before nine on the morning of Wednesday 15 December, the Hydro's coach drew up at the front door, apparently to take guests to the station, and two figures emerged to get into it. Among the pack of photographers waiting ravenously for images, 'a battery of cameras was raised hopefully'.[13]

But Archie was too clever to come out the front way. At that very moment, he and Agatha were attempting a discreet exit 'through a French window at the side of the building, where another car was waiting'. Unfortunately a photographer from the *Daily Mail* had guessed this might happen, and was lurking there to get the coveted first picture. As a result of Agatha's recent shopping spree, this picture would show her dressed up in the height of fashion, in a 'beige costume with a hat to match'. The outfit would prove unfortunate. A feeling was beginning to develop that if Agatha hadn't been murdered after all, then she should at least be repentant for the disappointment this caused. And certainly she shouldn't be so stylish.

The waiting car got Agatha, Madge and their husbands to the station. In their reserved first-class compartment on the train they pulled down the blinds, but not before reporters observed something else unseemly: Agatha had been 'smiling broadly'.[14] Looking lovely, enjoying herself: both were equally reprehensible. Agatha had caused anxiety. Agatha must be made to pay.

All along the line to London – Archie's stated destination – crowds had gathered in the hope of seeing the elusive woman, and 500 people had assembled on the platform at King's Cross. But when the train from Leeds finally pulled in, the train driver shouted out the disappointing news: 'we have not got her!'[15]

In fact, the party had outwitted many of their pursuers by changing trains at Leeds. They'd boarded a train for Manchester, heading for Abney Hall. Messages got to Manchester before the train did, and journalists gathered on the platform to see Agatha's 'long, beautifully cut coat'.[16] But as they pressed stiflingly close, a scuffle broke out. Archie seized a reporter 'by the shoulder and flung him half across the platform,' thundering: 'that lady is not to be spoken to! She is ill.'[17]

Agatha and Madge ran for the car that was waiting to take them to Abney. When it finally passed through the hall's gates, James Watts jumped out, and padlocked them. The Hall was now under siege.

The next afternoon, the gates were opened to admit two doctors. They issued a statement to the press: 'after a careful examination' of Mrs Christie, they had 'formed the opinion that she is suffering from an unquestionably genuine loss of memory.'[18]

But it would have been much more exciting if Agatha had *not* lost her memory, and if she'd disappeared of her own volition. The papers now sought opinions from other specialists with views more in tune with the sceptical public mood. The *New York Times* found one who was willing to say that a person with memory loss 'could not act in a normal manner nor mix with the public without arousing suspicions of insanity'.[19]

And now opinion would really turn against Agatha. The *Daily Mail* had published a letter from 'an ordinary woman', asking whether the elaborate search would have been made for anyone else. Would these extraordinary efforts have been made, for example, 'if I disappeared,' asked the writer, 'and if not, why?'[20] She had a good point. They would not have been.

The next day, another correspondent to the *Daily Mail* followed this up, complaining about the 'unjustifiable concentration of the police of two counties on the disappearance of Mrs Christie'.[21] And soon a third correspondent kicked off what would soon become the growing controversy of the cost of the search. Was Mrs Christie 'ready to pay the expenses incurred?' wrote this person. 'Many of us would like to know how the statement that she has lost her memory fits in with the fact that she has been staying in an hotel, paid her bills, danced and sung, and played billiards.'[22]

This kind of opinion emerged on both sides of the Atlantic. The *Washington Post* thought Agatha's press agent should pay the costs.[23] There was a persistent rumour that Surrey ratepayers would be charged extra to cover the police's expenses, and Kenward had to reassure reporters this was 'absolute nonsense'.[24] A notably venomous comment came from a less successful writer, one Mr Coulson Kernahan. 'The woman novelist,' he wrote, 'would be well advised to state publicly that no novel of hers will in future appear under her own name. That might prevent other persons "disappearing" for the sake of an advertisement.'[25]

Part of this negativity came from the timing. The post-war economic boom was over, and it was only months since the General Strike. There was understandable class resentment against this privileged woman and the treatment she'd received.

Questions even began to be raised in the House of Commons. A Labour MP asked how much the search had cost the government, demanding to know 'who is going to compensate the thousands of people who were deliberately misled by this cruel hoax?'[26] The official answer from an embarrassed Home Office was the implausibly low sum of £12 10s.[27] But the cost also included a huge deluge of negative publicity for Agatha.

Indeed, everyone involved was going to have to pay. Nancy's mother found it unpleasant for Nancy's name to be 'dragged through the mud', but the Neele family stuck to the (false) line that their daughter and Archie were no more than friends.[28] Nancy's father was indignant: 'I cannot hazard any theory why Mrs Christie should have used my family's name,' he spluttered. 'There is not the slightest reason for associating Nancy with the disappearance of Mrs Christie.'[29]

The Neeles thought it best that Nancy herself should disappear. She was packed off on a round-the-world cruise, only to return to her new love when things should have calmed down.

Back at Abney, the reporters remained outside the gates, almost baying for blood. Archie had to feed them something. On the 16th, he came out to make a statement. The journalists noticed his look of 'strain,' and the fact that he was wearing carpet slippers.[30] He begged them to leave and to 'drop the incident'. The doctors' report, he said, 'shows that it is no stunt to sell books.'[31]

Inside the Hall, Agatha was going through a painful period. She was forced to confront the reality she'd tried so hard to avoid. 'She now knows who I am,' Archie revealed, 'and has also realised that Mrs Watts is her sister . . . she does not know she has a daughter.'

Agatha was slow to return to her role as a mother. When she was shown a picture of Rosalind, 'she asked who the child was, "What is the child like?" and "How old is she?"'[32]

Soon Carlo brought Rosalind herself up to Abney. Although she was only seven at the time, Rosalind would retain lasting memories of the reunion with her mother. Distressingly, Agatha 'did not remember anything we had been doing together or even the stories she used to tell me.'[33] What a hideous experience for a child. Rosalind would face a lifetime of being asked about the events of 1926, and became skilled at deflecting questions.

But what's not generally realised is that 'loss of memory', bad though it was, wasn't the worst of the possible medical solutions to the mystery. It was a safer option than what in the 1920s was still called 'insanity'. Insanity had terrible implications for Rosalind in a decade where heredity, indeed eugenics, were taken with deadly seriousness. 'I am my father's son. Would anyone marry me, knowing that,' asks the son of a murderer in The Murder on the Links (1923). 'You are your father's son,' Poirot agrees, 'I believe in heredity.' An insane mother would spoil Rosalind's life and chances of getting married, especially as her grandfather had died of 'General Paralysis of the Insane'.

One of the physicians who'd examined Agatha was a special-ist from Manchester University, Dr Donald Elms Core. Author of a book on nervous disorders, Core had contributed to the important wartime debates about the nature of shell shock in the *Lancet*. In his book, Core acknowledged the terror many patients felt when they seemed able to find no physical cause for their pain: the 'fear is developed in them that they are becoming insane'.[34]

Core's proposals for treating someone in Agatha's state included a short-term prescription of drugs to provide sleep. Then came the therapy of sending a patient away from his or her home environ-ment. (This is exactly what Agatha had provided for herself, at least for eleven days.) After that came the hard work of psychotherapy and hypnosis, to explore the causes of the 'dread' that had worked such ill upon the individual.

But first, Agatha had to be willing. And her state of mind was lower than ever. As she lost her grip upon her dream life as 'Mrs Neele', depression came crashing back down. 'Many of my worries and anxieties returned,' she explained, and 'my old morbid tenden-cies.'[35] The public shame she'd experienced made it worse. 'I had always hated notoriety of any kind,' she said, and now she'd had such a giant dose of it that once again she felt suicidal: 'I felt I could hardly bear to go on living.'

When the doctors recommended that Agatha received psychiat-ric treatment, she resisted. But Madge insisted.

As well as having the benefit of reading a correspondence between Carlo and Rosalind, now believed destroyed, biographer Janet Morgan also had access to Rosalind herself, who witnessed these events. And Rosalind stated that under pressure from Madge, her mother had eventually agreed to treatment intended to 'restore her lost memories', or in other words, to seek a medical cure for her mental distress. Leaving Abney, Agatha went with Carlo and Rosalind to London. Here, she 'took a flat in Kensington High Street, from which she went to Harley Street for therapy.'[36] It's most likely she went to the practice of William Brown. Brown was one of just seven psychiatrists in Harley Street at the time. Experienced in war medicine and shell shock, he was particularly well-known for his work on cases of amnesia. He'd also treated many patients who'd experienced a fugue state.

As ever, we have to turn to Agatha's fiction for an account of what she might have experienced. In 1930 her non-detective novel *Giant's Bread* came out. Agatha used a pseudonym, for she did not want the inevitable speculation that would follow if she published a novel about memory loss.

In the story, a character named Vernon has a car accident, loses his memory, and eventually gets it back again after sessions with a physician who uses hypnotism, a 'man with eyes that seemed to see right into the centre of you and to read there things that you didn't even know about yourself'. Vernon painfully explores his lost past, as Agatha must now have done.

> Vernon cried out: 'Must we go over it again and again? It was all so horrible. I don't want to think of it any more.'
>
> And then the doctor explained, gravely and kindly, but very impressively. It was because of that desire not to 'think of it any more' that all this had come about. It must be faced.[37]

All this is consistent with William Brown's own book explaining how he treated amnesia. He would put patients under hypnosis, then ask them what had happened. Brown thought that a person with a 'lost' memory was fatigued and made ill by the effort of keeping it at bay. He insisted that the patient 'face the unpleasant memory fairly and squarely, and thus it becomes harmless once more.' Brown also believed in a talking cure: through conversation, a patient gains an 'objective view of the past course of his mental life. He learns to understand himself better . . . it is the knowledge that sets one free.' Agatha's seeking treatment like this was a slightly radical thing to do, because this wasn't mainstream medicine. Freud's work had indeed been known in the British medical community, even before wartime trauma made it doubly relevant. And it's true that books on the subject were growing more popular. The influential *Outwitting Our Nerves* (1922), for example, went through seven editions before the Second World War.[38]

But Freud's work was still controversial in Britain. Doctors didn't agree, for example, on what the subconscious and unconscious might be. And having therapy was still a source of shame. Many of the shell-shocked, for example, were not offered treatment until every other avenue – castigating them for their weakness, branding them as malingerers – had been exhausted. This society still attached terrible stigma to mental ill-health.

Agatha's choice of Harley Street, however, was a conventional marker of class. You needed money, and often social connections, to get onto the books of a doctor there.[39] Her treatment followed the textbook for the treatment of nervous shock as it had been developed for the wartime officer class. The wartime doctor Wilfred Harris quoted earlier claims a patient under hypnosis 'may in this state remember perfectly all the facts of his life which in his waking state are forgotten'.[40] This echoes Agatha's statement that her:

> memories were drawn from my subconscious mind slowly. First I recalled my childhood days and thought of relatives and friends as they were when children. By gradual steps I recalled later and later episodes in my life.[41]

But the process was still considered to hold risk. As Dr Harris tells us, hypnosis could have the reverse effect to what was intended. It might indeed unlock 'madness': 'the worst cases are those whose heredity is bad, with neurasthenia, epilepsy, and insanity in near relations.'[42] This was a bad outlook for Agatha and Rosalind, with their family history. And Agatha might well suffer again, her doctors warned: introspective patients were 'always liable to outbreaks of their original trouble'.[43]

But Agatha's treatment did not last long. On 22 January 1927, just as Dr Core had proposed, she went away on a recuperative trip to the Canary Islands. During the trip, however, and against the doctor's advice, she went back to her writing. This was because work, for Agatha, was both a curse and a relief. She justified the need to write as a fear about money; she might have to support Rosalind by herself. But it's also possible she found some solace in an imaginary world.

Returning from the sun, Agatha moved to Chelsea with Rosalind and Carlo, while Archie remained at The Styles and put it up for sale. Astonishingly, Agatha had still not entirely given up on him. Later in 1927, she saw Archie once more, to ask him if he would not stay for Rosalind's sake, saying 'how fond of him she was and how much she had been puzzled by his absence'. She also reported Rosalind's own devastatingly clear view of what had happened between her parents: 'I *know* Daddy likes *me*, and would like to be with me. It's *you* he doesn't seem to like.'

But Archie's mind was made up. Despite the enforced absence from Nancy, he and she still intended to marry. Eventually, in 1928, Agatha finally felt that she had to resign herself to a divorce.

And now the fallout from the 'disappearance' gave perhaps its cruellest twist yet. In a divorce, Agatha must secure custody of Rosalind. But her reputation had been so badly blemished. Perhaps the most pernicious of all the accusations in the media was the suggestion that she was a bad mother. Agatha had to say something to defend herself, to lay the ground for a divorce that would get her her daughter. 'I panic over Rosy,' she once said, 'and it infuriates me because I'm not really the panicky mother type – and yet I simply can't help it.'[44]

So in February, with her hearing coming up, Agatha felt forced to go public. She took legal action against the *London Express* for publishing a description of her as a woman who'd played 'some kind of foolish hoax on the police'.[45]

She also made the longest public statement of her lifetime on her disappearance, in an interview with the *Daily Mail* published on 16 February. Every word of it must have been painful. 'Many people still think I deliberately disappeared,' she said,

What actually happened was this. I left home that night in a state of high nervous strain with the intention of doing something desperate . . .[46]

Having been forced to reveal intensely private things, illness and suicidal thoughts, Agatha now needed to negotiate her divorce. Archie wanted her to instigate the process, something only possible because of a recent change to the law.

There were a great many dissatisfied wives in the 1920s, as hasty wartime marriages broke down. With the divorce rate four times higher than it had been in 1913, the process was made easier. The Matrimonial Causes Act of 1923 made it possible for a woman to gain a divorce on the grounds of her husband's adultery, something that until that point she'd simply been expected to endure. In 1923, 39 per cent of divorces were instigated by women. By 1925, this percentage had jumped to 63.[47]

Archie wanted Agatha to exercise her new right to divorce him. But neither did he want Nancy to be drawn in. So Agatha reluctantly agreed to take part in a new 1920s practice sometimes known as a collusive divorce, or 'Brighton Quickie'. Archie was to provide staged evidence, provided by accomplices, that he'd committed adultery with 'a woman unknown'. The seedy resort of Brighton specialised in providing the evidence needed for a collusive divorce, hence the name, though in Archie's case he went to the Grosvenor Hotel in Victoria. There he paid a solicitor's clerk and a waiter to agree to say they'd seen him with a woman in his bed.[48]

The case came to court on 20 April 1928, and Agatha had to steel herself to attend. The judge saw through the ruse, finding it 'difficult to believe that a gallant gentleman like Colonel Christie' would do anything so sordid.[49] But it worked. Agatha was awarded costs, and custody of Rosalind. She now just had to wait six months for the divorce to be finalised. During that time, in July 1928, the Representation of the People Act gave all females – not just the property-owning over-thirties – the vote. Emancipation was slowly coming not just to Agatha, but to all women.

If Celia, Agatha's fictional alter ego in her novel *Unfinished Portrait*, is to be believed, Agatha was disgusted by the charade of the collusive divorce. Celia might take another woman's husband, she admitted, but, she says, 'I'd do it *honestly*. I'd not skulk in the shadow and let someone else do the dirty work.'[50] Agatha had been drawn into a situation where 'dirty work' was done for money. On top of that, she'd committed perjury. The divorce required her falsely to swear that 'there is no collusion or connivance between me or my husband'.[51]

The 1920s had curdled, leaving the bright young author older and sadder. In the little case in which she kept and cherished Archie's love letters, she also stored some lines copied from Psalm 55:

> It is not an open enemy, that hath done me this dishonour . . . But it was even thou, my companion: my guide, and mine own familiar friend.[52]

Immediately after her divorce, Agatha must have only been able to see darkness. The whole business would leave her with her well-documented fear of opening up, either intimately, or to the press. After this, wrote someone who knew her well, 'she had a quality of elusiveness', a 'resistance to inquisitive probing, an inbuilt armour'.[53]

But what Agatha's publishers could see, even if she couldn't appreciate it herself, was that her public shaming had a financial benefit.

Agatha's 'disappearance' had the impact it did because of the 1920s context that saw a new kind of media celebrity being created. She wasn't alone in becoming an 'author-as-celebrity': others included J.B. Priestley and Arnold Bennett.[54] It was accidental, it was deeply unpleasant, but it would also become a central plank of her massive success.

Agatha's supporters sometimes argue that her disappearance certainly wasn't a stunt because she had 'no need of publicity', as her books were selling well.[55] That's true. But even so, the results of the incident were startling.

The Murder of Roger Ackroyd of 1926 had 5,500 copies printed in its first run, of which 4,000 sold within a year: good, but not sensational. But immediately after the disappearance, in 1927, a weak collection of stories, *The Big Four*, sold 8,500 copies. In 1928 *The Mystery of the Blue Train*, which Agatha called 'easily the worst book I ever wrote', sold 7,000. *The Seven Dials Mystery*, one of her rather tiresome thrillers, would shift 8,000 copies in 1929. In 1930, she'd sign a new six-book contract with Collins. The message is clear: it wasn't just quality that sold, but fame.[56]

This would create a terrible tension for Agatha between her life and her work. She could not speak of this link; it was humiliating. It left her with no explanation to offer for her success, beyond hard graft, and the belittling one of accident. How, otherwise, to unravel this deeply personal web of ambition, achievement, notoriety and pain?

The pain, though, would recede with time. Her mental illness of 1926 was nearly the breaking of Agatha Christie. But ultimately it was the making of her.

According to a friend, 1926 went so deep 'it left its traces all through her work. It also made her the great woman she became.'[57]

❖ PART SIX ❖

Plutocratic Period – 1930s

22

Mesopotamia

The divorce was finalised on 29 October 1928. Just a week later, at a register office in London, Archie married Nancy Neele. To Agatha it was another very public blow. A picture of Nancy, looking apprehensive but annoyingly pretty, made the cover of the *Daily Express*. In 1930, Archie and Nancy's son Beau would be born.

But Agatha sidestepped the whole experience of reading about her husband's wedding by leaving the country. Her marriage was over, Act One of her life was over. Even she had begun to see that within an ending may lie a new beginning. 'I am tired of the past,' she wrote,

> that clings around my feet,
> I am tired of the past that will not let life be sweet.
> I would cut it away with a knife and say
> Let me be myself – reborn – today.[1]

By the autumn of 1928, Agatha had sent Rosalind to a boarding school in Bexhill. Loyal Carlo was looking after the new home she'd bought in a Chelsea mews. And now she had all the time until the Christmas holidays to follow her passion for travel. Going abroad could serve several purposes: privacy, recuperation and inspiration.

She'd thought of going to the West Indies. But Agatha liked to tell the story of how she changed her mind after a chance encounter at a party with a naval officer and his wife who'd recently returned, utterly beguiled, from Baghdad. They'd spoken of the train journey across Europe, of Baghdad itself; the wonderful archaeological discoveries being made at the ancient city known as Ur . . . The following morning, Agatha changed her tickets. Five days later, she set off east. She would go to see Ur for herself, and travel by the fabled *Orient Express*.

The story of the journey makes one of the most exciting, glamorous passages in Agatha's autobiography. She tells the tale as a spontaneous act of reinvention: 'I was going *by myself*. I should find out now what kind of person I was.' And with freedom came a profound sense of self-reliance: 'never again, I decided, would I put myself at *anyone's* mercy.'

Among the things from which Agatha had become emancipated between 1926 and 1928 was worrying about her figure: 'I was a good weight – well over eleven stone.' The photos of the 1920s show Agatha trying to fit into a society-pages model of beauty: smiling, posing with dog or child, or else softly lit, dressed in evening wear, looking like a debutante. In her forties, though, she had to craft a new public image.

After 1930, she began to sit for simpler and more dramatically lit portraits. Photographer Lenare, for example, put her in a professional, powerful pose. No longer an ingenue, Agatha was growing into a more impressive physical presence. She was recreating herself, visually, as the 'Duchess of Death', a woman who, as journalists like to put it, 'made more money out of murder than Lucrezia Borgia'.

In private life, too, Agatha was feeling more comfortable in her own skin. 'Physical age,' she wrote, 'has very little to do with one's inside.'[2] She was just as addicted to swimming, eating, enjoying herself as ever. She was conscious that now she was divorced, men looked at her in a new way. She was surprised by the number of passes they made at her, and decided, on the whole, she was pleased.

So, in the autumn of 1928, after a whirlwind of preparation, her new life began at Victoria station:

Dear Victoria – gateway to the world beyond England – how I love
your continental platform. And how I love trains [. . .] a big snort-
ing, hurrying, companionable train, with its big puffing engine,
sending up clouds of steam, and seeming to say impatiently, 'I've got
to be off!'[3]

Iraq sounds a long way to go for a holiday, but it was increasingly
popular as a travel destination. Having crossed the Channel by sea,
British tourists would take the train from Paris, firstly to Istanbul
and then on to Damascus. The decades between the wars saw the
heyday of the service run by the Compagnie Internationale des
Wagons-Lits, and there were four trains a week.

As Agatha settled into her second-class compartment, she discovered a single female traveller is rarely short of friends. A missionary
lady tried to give her stomach medicine. In Istanbul, a charming
Dutch engineer subtly invited her to spend the night with him. He
was refused.

As the journey continued into Asia, Agatha was amazed by the
scenery. She was exhilarated by the sight of a beautiful sunset in the
pass through the Taurus Mountains, and found herself full of gratitude and joy for having made the decision to come. Arriving weary
at Damascus, she bought a chest of drawers inlaid with mother-of-
pearl that she'd keep in her bedroom until the end of her life. The
trip, the rebirth, was going well.

The next leg towards Ur, Damascus to Baghdad, was undertaken
in a bouncing six-wheeled desert minibus. Run by former members
of the British Army's transport corps, this motor link followed a
gash in the desert cut to guide planes to Baghdad after the British
had ousted the Turks from Iraq in 1917.[4] In the 1920s, the British
wanted to keep control of this area; Churchill's decision to change
over the Royal Navy's ships from coal to oil required it. But lacking
the resources to send in a traditional army, Britain relied instead on
the threat of aerial bombing. Iraq may have become a place for
tourism, but it was also still a place for the exercise of imperial
power.

The journey across the desert took all day and all evening, the darkest part of the night being passed in a desert fortress with armed guards. The next morning, at six, came a wonderful breakfast: tea and sausages, eaten in the sharp-toned air. 'What else could one ask of life?' Agatha asked.

But we need to examine the romance Agatha spins around her first trip to what Britons then called the 'Middle East'. At this point in her life, Agatha had nothing to do with archaeology. And she would never really be an archaeologist, in the sense that she was never paid for her work. Yet by the time she wrote her terrific passage about her crossing of the desert, as an old lady, Agatha had become an influencer and fundraiser for archaeology at the highest level. Her retrospective account of her trip on the *Orient Express* may reflect less her real experience in 1928 than the genre of archaeological writing which often begins with the 'epic journey'. The archaeologist narrating the story becomes the protagonist of an odyssey. Indeed, for popular archaeology, the fieldwork itself doesn't really matter. One notable archaeologist who always travels, and never actually arrives, is Indiana Jones.[5]

And although Agatha describes her choice of destination as a matter of chance, it was not as random as it may seem. Other British women were running away from their problems and finding new selves in ancient Asia: famous and less famous names like Gertrude Bell, Freya Stark and Katharine Woolley. Bell's lover died at Gallipoli, Stark wanted to escape a marriage, Woolley's husband had committed suicide. Agatha's decision fits into a pattern.

Agatha did not plan to spend long in Baghdad, especially not among its chattering colonial classes. She wrote it off as 'Mem-Sahib Land' and went quickly on to Ur. 'Ur of the Chaldeans', as it was known then, near modern-day Nasiriyah, was the site of an ancient city on the Euphrates. An archaeological investigation unfolding there had become almost as famous as the discovery of Tutankhamun six years earlier. British people in the 1920s were excited not least because they'd heard of Ur from the Bible: it was supposedly the birthplace of Abraham. Colonel Arbuthnot in Agatha's book *Murder on the Orient Express* thought his decision to take the land route back from India to England hardly needed an explanation: he wanted to see Ur.[6]

Many British people assumed that their contemporaries in West Asia were still somehow living the life that people had lived in Biblical times.[7] This intensely romantic view of Iraq explains something of the mess the British were making of governing the place. When British administrators took over Iraq in 1920 from the defeated Ottoman Empire, many were shocked to discover the locals didn't seem to want them either. An almost-immediate revolt ended with the British selecting a king, Faisel.

After concluding her long journey by train and then car, Agatha finally arrived at Ur. She was warmly welcomed, because the expedition leader's wife, Katharine Woolley, had recently enjoyed *Roger Ackroyd*. Agatha was given the signal honour not only of a tour of the site, but permission to stay.

This meant living in the expedition house. These archaeological facilities in Iraq and Syria, belonging to teams of different nationalities, were usually run up quickly and cheaply. They had rooms for processing finds, eating and studying as well as simple bedrooms. The industrious days of the archaeologists, seeking to do as much as possible before their money ran out or the weather changed, appealed to Agatha. So too did the convivial dinners.

The gigantic mound being investigated at Ur was a *tell*, a piling-up of ancient settlements one upon another, which rose 60 feet above the surrounding plain. One archaeologist described the mound as a 'great monster', 'teeming with antiquities, and swollen with subterranean buildings'.[8] It was a place where the ancient world seemed very close. 'I fell in love with Ur,' Agatha wrote,

> with its beauty in the evenings, the ziggurat standing up, faintly shadowed, and that wide sea of sand with its lovely pale colours of apricot, rose, blue and mauve changing every minute . . . the lure of the past came up to grab me.

But what Agatha really liked about archaeology was the glimpse it offered into a different daily life:

> here, picked up by me, this broken fragment of a clay pot, hand-made, with a design of dots and cross-hatching in black paint, is the forerunner of the Woolworth cup out of which this very morning I have drunk my tea.[9]

These two quotations show two distinct strands within Agatha's feelings about Iraq. On the one hand, the romance makes Iraq a place of release, and potentially of passion. This perspective on West Asia was epitomised by E.M. Hull's outrageous bestseller *The Sheik* (1919). It was innovative for its depiction of female desire, but as ancient as the hills in presenting Arab people as filthy and degener-ate. The book grew notorious for its fantasies of female submission. Agatha's character Bundle in *The Secret of Chimneys* gives an amus-ingly condensed version of its plot: 'Desert love. Throw her about, etc.' When Bundle's father reveals that he doesn't know what the book's about, Bundle gives him a look of 'commiserating pity'.[10]

On the other hand, though, by seeking out the equivalent of the Woolworth's cup, Agatha also imagined the ancient world being full of people just like herself.[11] We'll see more and more of this attitude in her writing about Iraq, which seeks to close the gap between East and West. She'd often give the literary equivalent of rolling her eyes at the full-on rhetoric of the British Empire. But to look for common ground and similarities between Iraqis and Europeans, as she did, was to remain equally blind to aspects of an extremely different culture.

Agatha's hosts at Ur would become good friends. Katharine Woolley, two years Agatha's senior, was eighteen months into an unconventional marriage. Her husband, Charles Leonard Woolley, was the titular leader of the expedition, although Katharine had the final word on hiring decisions, directed some of the labourers, and indeed received a salary. The Western archaeologists swarming into Asia in the twentieth century are at first glance a masculine lot. But historians are beginning to point out a hidden layer of female achievement below the surface. Some of these archaeologists are well known, like Dorothy Garrod, Oxbridge's first female professor, who excavated at Mount Carmel in Palestine with an all-female team. More typically, though, wives or female assistants did work as field archaeologists, cataloguers, photographers, illustrators, nurses and secretaries, which 'went unmentioned in excavation reports'.[12]

Katharine's husband Leonard, formerly of the Ashmolean Museum in Oxford, was 'something of a tyrant as all successful heads of expeditions have to be'.[13] He had a showman's gift for publicising his discoveries, which was important for raising funds. He was assisted by a key staff member, Hoja Hamoudi, who managed the local workers. Employed in large numbers, these labourers would crunch through the soil in a way that would be considered too careless today, but which produced lots of lovely finds that could be shown off to sponsors and published in the *Illustrated London News*.

Leonard Woolley had begun work at Ur in 1922, but it was his second season that saw the arrival of a young and attractive widow then called Katharine Keeling. Born Katharine Menke, to German parents, she met her first husband Bertram Keeling while working as a Red Cross nurse and married him in 1919. Within six months, Keeling had commited suicide in Egypt, using prussic acid.[14] Keeling's brother was an amateur archaeologist, working in Baghdad for the Turkish Petroleum Company, and it was probably through this connection that Katharine joined Woolley's dig. Petroleum and archaeology would be closely linked throughout the twentieth century. In the 1920s archaeology was an exercise in statecraft by the British, Germans and Americans in a part of the world they perceived as unstable. It was much more than the eccentric and mainly harmless activity it seems in most accounts of Agatha Christie's life.

Katharine's best known today, though, not for her archaeological work, but because Agatha made her the original of a captivating, troubling character in her novel *Murder in Mesopotamia*. 'Dangerous' was the word used for Katharine by Gertrude Bell; 'strange and possibly cruel . . . but quite irresistible' was Freya Stark's description. People began to find it odd that Katharine was out in the desert with Woolley's male team. The director of the American museum helping fund the excavation suggested that Katharine shouldn't be invited back to the next season of digging.

But Woolley wasn't having this. 'Mrs Keeling was at first very much hurt to think that her name could be so talked about,' he replied. 'Perhaps that is still the price which women may have to pay for cooperation in scientific work. Of course it's all wrong.'[15] He also described Katharine as 'nearly 40' and in possession of absolutely 'no intention of remarrying!'[16]

But with the funding of his dig in danger, Woolley decided to solve the problem. She'd have to be allowed to return if he married her. So he did.

From then on, Katharine and her supposedly demanding ways would become the stuff of archaeological gossip. 'Calculating, mischievous and self-interested,' is how Leonard Woolley's biographer saw her, with 'a very misleading sexuality.'[17] Agatha herself contributed to the impression that Katharine was as much a diva as an archaeologist, calling her friend 'temperamental', and describing her ability to make people nervous. An *allumeuse* – a creator of fire – is another word Agatha used. A lot of this was misogyny with the drama dialled up, but some of this mud would stick in a way that undermines Katharine's not inconsiderable work as a dig director.

But for Agatha, the archaeologists themselves were as interesting as the dig. Katharine and Leonard showed her a successful marriage that was deeply unconventional by the standards of Sunningdale. One archaeologist described Katharine as a woman 'not intended for the physical side of matrimony'. In 1928 Leonard actually consulted a lawyer because he claimed his wife had refused to consummate their marriage sexually, and he wanted to see if a threat of divorce would make any difference. There have been suggestions in recent years that Katharine may have been intersex, but with little evidence beyond an urge to explain a person with a powerful personality who seemed somehow less than feminine. Katharine would also soon begin to be troubled by multiple sclerosis, and the knowledge of that makes her seem less dangerous than vulnerable. When Agatha later drew an unflattering portrait of Katharine in her book, she was 'uncharacteristically nervous about any possible response'.[18]

But Katharine said nothing. Naturally, she had not recognised herself.

More positively, the Woolleys showed Agatha a model for a new kind of marriage: utterly companionate, based around work: a 'joint venture' of the kind she'd celebrated in her Tommy and Tuppence books. The Woolleys needed Agatha too, as a celebrity supporter for their dig. In addition, Katharine wanted to become a novelist herself, and in 1929 would publish *Adventure Calls*, about a female spy in Iraq who passes as a man.

All three of them wanted to see more of each other when Agatha returned home to Rosalind, Carlo and Christmas in England. And there would be many trips to West Asia to come.

23

Enter Max

In the spring of 1930, Agatha joined the Woolleys on a second trip to Ur.

And during this visit to Iraq she met a member of the team who'd been absent the previous year through illness. His name was Max Mallowan. A 'general field assistant' on £200 a year, the young Oxford graduate's duties included keeping records, administering the payroll, and giving tours.[1] He loved his work. Once, on the radio, he spoke in his calm, quiet, precise voice about the uncovering of the Royal Cemetery at Ur and its golden treasure:

> it was a marvellous moment when we entered these great shaft graves of the dead, and the entire soil was a whole carpet of gold, you know, from the golden beech leaves that decorated the women who had been put to death at the time of the king, that was a wonderful discovery.[2]

Photos show Max Edgar Lucien Mallowan as a small, neat person, with smooth dark hair and a moustache.[3] His wide Oxford bags give him what looks like a low centre of gravity. A 'thin, dark, young man,' was how Agatha saw him, and at first she found him 'very quiet – he seldom spoke, but was perceptive to everything that was required of him.' Agatha towered over him in height, and was more than a decade older. Their differences were legion.

After Agatha had spent a few days at Ur, Max was required by his bosses, the Woolleys, to escort the dig's distinguished guest on a tour of the other archaeological sites of Iraq.

This sightseeing journey involved long, difficult and sometimes dangerous drives. The unlikely pair, the famous novelist and the novice archaeologist, had to stay the night wherever they could: with acquaintances, with strangers, and once in a police station, where they discussed Shelley with their hosts. Agatha's account of the trip concentrates more on ancient than modern Iraq, although she does say that they visited the Shi'ite spiritual centre Najaf under police protection as Europeans were unwelcome.

She and her guide found themselves having rather a wonderful time. One day they swam together in a sparkling blue desert lake, Agatha in an improvised bathing costume of a pink silk vest and two pairs of knickers. After the swim, though, their car ran deeply into the sand. Stuck in the desert with no prospect of help, and a limited supply of water, Agatha nevertheless remained calm and even had a snooze. Max decided at that point she 'must be a remarkable woman'.[4]

Agatha was worried her chaperone had been forced to undertake an uncongenial duty. And while he was finding her pleasantly unpretentious, she in return was looking at him more closely. Max wasn't a beautiful giant like Archie, but he was indisputably handsome. He was better-looking, and of course fourteen years younger, than Agatha. But somehow he seemed the elder: he was in charge; he looked after her; he treated her 'with the air of an indulgent scholar looking kindly at a foolish but not unlikeable child'. He smiles less often than she does in the photos of the 1930s. In the pictures that show them together, though, she is often laughing.

Max was born in Battersea on 6 May 1904, but was much more cosmopolitan than that fact implies. His paternal background was Slav – a grandfather had lived in Syria – and his atheist father Frederick, a produce broker, was born near Vienna. His mother Marguerite was French, daughter of an opera singer.

Marguerite 'remained a Parisienne all her life', and she was no cold-blooded upper-class English mother.[5] Passionate and artistic, she remained close to her son. 'Good bye my dearest darling,' she'd end her letters to him, 'I send you my real & dearest love.'[6] Protected from the world by Marguerite's powerful affection, Max grew used to being cosseted, and also to pleasing. His parents had terrible rows: 'stormy scenes and the most violent quarrels'.[7] The point at issue was often Frederick's fidelity. Marguerite wrote of her jealousy at having been 'betrayed'. Her husband's behaviour 'depresses me terribly,' she wrote, '& it is all I could do to keep normal towards the boys.'[8] These upsets gave Max a lasting horror of shouting and confrontation.

When Max's brother was born, the family moved to Kensington. Max conducted his first dig in the new house's back garden, carefully photographing the Victorian pot shards he found. In 1918, at fourteen, Max was sent to Lancing College in Sussex, with its harsh regime of communal cold baths at 6.30 a.m. The school was close enough to the south coast for the boys to hear the guns in wartime France, and on Sundays the names of the Old Boys killed that week were read out after chapel. Max wrote in later life of his 'loneliness and difficulties in conforming' at school.[9] He felt accepted only by his mother. 'My Own Sweetest Darling Mamma,' he wrote in an eight-page letter from school, 'I keep thinking now, what I would have been doing at home . . . and I wonder what you are doing now too my pet!'[10] There was something of the mummy's boy, and the outsider, about the young man appointed to be Agatha's minder.

Max found New College, Oxford, much better than school, although friends, gambling and dining meant he only got a disappointing third-class degree. Part of the attraction was his best friend Esmé Howard, a Sebastian Flyte-ish character with aristocrats in his family, a Roman Catholic faith inherited from his Italian mother, and Hodgkin's disease, which would go on to kill him at twenty-five. Losing Esmé was the first serious setback in Max's life, and he suffered enormously. He'd even converted to Catholicism to please his friend. 'He loved you so!' Max's mother consoled him. Max's taking communion, she said, had given Esmé 'the greatest joy of his last weeks on earth'.[11] The rumours of homosexual attraction between the two young men, though, are based on nothing more than the similarity between real life and the plot of *Brideshead Revisited*.

Max's career in archaeology had fallen into place with little effort. He'd told one of his lecturers he wanted 'to go to the East and look for things there'.[12] An introduction to the Keeper of the Ashmolean led Max to discover that Leonard Woolley, whose work he'd read about in the *Illustrated London News*, needed an assistant. In no time at all, Max was off to an interview at the British Museum. He made a favourable impression, not only on Leonard, but on Katharine. Max believed the casting vote had been hers, and she'd liked him. The autumn after his final exams he was on his way out east. 'Provided one is born under a favourite star,' he concluded, 'opportunity comes to those who are ready for it.'

Tactful as he was, even Max found it hard to deal with Katharine. He was expected to massage her and apply leeches when she had headaches. She was 'opinionated . . . ultra-sensitive . . . entrancing,' in Max's opinion, 'to live with her was to walk on a tightrope.'[13] But he did a good enough job to be invited back. On the way out to his second season he visited Venice and decided he'd like to spend a honeymoon there. The breakdown of his parents' relationship had left him determined to make a success of marriage when his own turn came.

Max, who confessed to a fellow passenger that he had never yet 'consorted with a woman', was ready to meet someone.[14] What he valued was an absence of drama, just like Agatha herself. 'What a wonderful person,' she thought, 'so quiet, so sparing with words . . . he does just the things you want done and that consoles you more than everything else could.'

All this could make it seem possible that a relationship was on the horizon, but it never even crossed Agatha's mind. There was the age difference, although, as she told Max, she liked younger men: 'they have a finer vision and a bigger ideal of life'.[15]

Then there was the fact she'd known him for such a short time. And Max was Katharine's creature, naturally allowing her, for example, to have the first bath if only one was available. 'You know how much it is politic to humour the Queen!' he explained to Agatha.[16]

And then there was Agatha's own hard-won independence. She'd been turning down all sorts of offers: a marriage proposal from an old admirer; an invitation to a night of pleasure from an Italian (she got rid of him by telling him that as an Englishwoman, she was naturally frigid); a discussion with an Air Force friend as to whether she should take just the one, or several lovers. The world, it seemed, could not accept Agatha's decision that 'all men were out'.

But Max was 'not all men'. As he, Agatha and the Woolleys left Iraq and began their journey home, distressing news caught up with them at Athens. An accumulation of telegrams revealed that Rosalind was dangerously ill with pneumonia. She'd been taken from school and placed under Madge's care. Unlike Archie – who could not bear illness or difficulties – Max now came into his own. Rising to the challenge, he gave Agatha every assistance in making the journey home as quickly as possible, hiring an expensive car, bandaging her ankle when she sprained it, even getting his mother to lend Agatha some cash as they passed through Paris.

Back in England, the guilty mother found Rosalind recovered, although 'it wrung my heart to see her – skin & bones & pitifully weak.'[17] Agatha took Rosalind to Ashfield, and returned to work. Yet the thread spun between Max and herself did not break. He wrote from London, suggesting a trip to the British Museum, where he was now working on the finds from Ur. 'Can't you come down here some weekend, Max?' she replied. 'It would do me a lot of good to see you.'[18]

But their relationship in Iraq had taken place outside normal life. What would it be like to meet again in the cold light of an English day?

In the end, Agatha came up to London, and Max came to breakfast at her mews house in Chelsea. 'I was stricken with shyness,' Agatha admits, 'he too, I think, was shy. However, by the end of breakfast, which I cooked for him, we were back to our old terms.'

In April 1930, Max came down to stay at Ashfield. And it was there – in the house where Agatha had been born, accepted Archie, given birth and mourned her mother – that the next great event of her life happened.

On the last night of his visit, Max knocked on her bedroom door, came in, and asked her to marry him.

24

I Think I Will Marry You

'The whole thing had happened so insidiously,' Agatha explained. If she'd ever thought of Max as a possible husband, 'I should have been on my guard. I should never have slipped into this easy, happy relationship.'

That night, and for the weeks afterwards, she once again found herself in turmoil. 'I was such a calm comfortable spectator sitting in the stalls & looking at life,' she wrote to Max, yet he'd yanked her into 'living & feeling again'.[1] And she wasn't at all sure that was what she wanted.

Max, on the other hand, was quietly confident of success, from the moment he'd knocked on the bedroom door. 'I'm wise,' he replied, 'you have got far too much vitality to remain in the stalls.'[2] 'You are the most disarming devil that ever lived!!' Agatha admitted, 'And I think I will marry you after all because I foresee that you will always be able to manage me!!!'[3]

If a marriage were indeed to go ahead – which was by no means certain in Agatha's mind – it did have the potential to be quite different from the marriage Archie had wanted, with himself as its keystone. This might be a more truly companionate, compassionate arrangement: the kind of 'joint venture' Agatha had always dreamed of. 'Being with you,' she wrote to Max, 'is a kind of freedom . . . there is no feeling of restraint or captivity or being "tied down" – I would never have believed anything could be like it.'[4] In another letter, she put her finger upon the difference between Archie and

Max: 'you do seem to like everything about me – & that is so encouraging – I don't feel I have got to live up to some ideal.'[5]

By the 1930s, a companionate marriage was no longer such an outlandish desire as it had been when Agatha and her friends talked about it in the 1910s. It was as if the rest of the world was catching up with that vision of what a relationship should be.

Archie had wanted to leave his wife at home while he played golf, whereas Max wanted Agatha to read ancient Greek with him and go on adventures. It helped that she was already an independent, professional woman, and that they respected each other's accomplishments. Agatha found Max's work much more interesting than Archie's in the City. She and Max positioned themselves on opposite sides of the Battle of the Brows but could find common ground: 'I am a lowbrow and he a highbrow, yet we complement each other.'

And yet, despite all these advantages, there seemed to be an insuperable number of obstacles between Agatha, Max and the altar.

For a start, there was Agatha's fear of failing again. No, she wouldn't marry Max after all, she decided, for a simple reason: risk. 'I'm an awful coward and dreadfully afraid of being hurt.'[6] She gave her feelings to a character in *Murder in Mesopotamia*: 'lots of people have wanted to marry me, but I always refused. I'd had too bad a shock. I didn't feel I could ever *trust* anyone again.'[7]

The year 1930 is an exhilarating ride for readers of Agatha's correspondence, for she tried to clarify her feelings through constant letters to Max, expressing love, expressing doubt. She wrote from Ashfield, from Abney, from other places her work took her. Meanwhile Max was in London, employed at the British Museum, and living in Kensington with his father, who knew nothing about this secret semi-engagement. Characteristically, Agatha's letters are scrawled almost illegibly and mostly lack a date. Max's, on the other hand, reveal so much about what attracted her to him: neat, orderly, always dated, always reassuring: 'you must take tremendous care of yourself till I come to take care of you.'[8] But despite his calmness, Max must also have had serious doubts that the marriage was ever really going to happen. 'I am afraid,' he wrote, 'you may allow your-self to give way to fears and doubts.'[9]

One of the things they had in common was a belief in an afterlife. 'You have a much more <u>real</u> knowledge of spiritual things than I have,' Agatha told Max.[10] But there was also a problem here: his conversion to Roman Catholicism. She had a solution. 'I can be converted on my deathbed and die an R.C. and then you can repent of me,' she suggested, 'or shall we be heretically buried on a hillside in Greece?'[11] But Max now took the step of leaving the Catholic Church that wouldn't have recognised his marriage to a divorced woman. 'My love for you,' he told Agatha, 'is the perfect continua-tion of that friendship with Esmé that I thought I should never recover.'[12]

Sex could have been a problem, but it clearly wasn't. 'Agatha,' wrote Max, 'I don't love you merely with the glorious eyes of the blind, but I see you as you are and you are the more dear to me for that.'[13] She had plenty of sexual confidence and thought they could have a good physical relationship, despite the differences in their age and athleticism. She worried a little about her weight: 'Perhaps I am (little Piglet!) your favourite size!! Do say I am!'[14] 'Darling,' he replied, giving the perfect answer, 'you not only are my favourite size but always will be, expanding or contracting.'[15] He had the marvellous gift of giving her confidence: 'I know you are very beautiful.'[16]

But still she doubted. 'But you *mustn't* marry again,' I said to myself, 'You *mustn't* be such a *fool*.' And then Max failed to write for three whole days. 'You <u>are</u> a pig,' she wrote. 'Three days since you left – & not one word from you [. . .] No – I don't like you – it's <u>always</u> the little things that upset one & put one off [. . .] you can't really care.'[17]

It looked like everything was off. There were so many conven-tions to be broken here: his youth, his lack of money, his rackety parents. Max was of the same generation as Agatha's nephew Jack. When they attended a ball, Agatha was horrified at how much older she seemed than Max's friends. But then, it was understood between them that he was an old soul. 'You say I come at things like a child,' she wrote to him, 'I can see that in some ways that is so.' 'Like a child,' she concluded, 'I feel the world is frightening.'[18]

'That summer was one of the most difficult of my life,' Agatha remembered afterwards, as it became clear that 'one person after another' was against the marriage. When Max was with her, Agatha could feel comfortable. But when he left, doubts set in.

Perhaps most troubling of all, Agatha had an 'unhappy letter' from Madge, which took her 'a long time to answer.' Her sister was clearly anxious, and Agatha could not remain unaffected. 'A wave of reality comes over me,' she explained, 'and I say to myself "Idiot – haven't you any sense? What would you say to someone else who was doing this?"'[19] Madge must have been worried sick to learn that her sister was planning marriage, apparently on the rebound, to someone so much younger and so much poorer than herself.

Much later on, Max taunted Agatha for having listened to her sister's warnings. 'Do you remember how A.P. ['Auntie Punkie', ie Madge] tried to dissuade us and what a foolish thing that was to do.'[20] In later years, Agatha was more open in admitting what had happened: Madge had 'implored me not to marry Max'.[21]

And then there was the task of telling Rosalind, which Agatha shirked. 'Darling Max,' she wrote in late July, 'Rosie has GUESSED!! She will give her consent IF you send her by return 2 dozen Toffee Lollipops from Selfridges.'[22] Max dutifully exceeded the brief by sending twenty-six ('there were exactly twenty-six left' in the shop), and awkwardly supposed that his future stepdaughter 'will get accustomed to the idea little by little'.[23] And so Rosalind gave her cautious approval. In her mother's autobiography, though, Rosalind gets laughed at for her concerns:

'You know,' she said, 'when you are married to Max, you will have to sleep in the same bed as him?'

'I know,' I said.

'Well, yes, I supposed you did know, because after all you were married to Daddy, but I thought you might not have thought of it.'

It's hilarious for us, the readers, but I imagine Rosalind herself, reading this, may not have found it so. She also said, stiffly, she thought it 'rather a good thing having two sets of parents' and that 'Mummy will be much better with Max'. Again, Agatha thought it amusing, but the poor little thing had been left to work it out for herself. In her dry way, Rosalind was striving awfully hard to be pragmatic and grown-up.[24]

Even when Agatha felt she'd made up her mind in favour of marriage – Max never wavered – there was the judgement of the world to be endured. In May, Max insisted that they should steel themselves to tell Katharine Woolley, and they suspected she would not take it well. Leonard expressed only 'mild surprise', but Katharine, although she said generous things, was more negative, on the unexpected grounds that it would be detrimental to Max's character.[25] She thought he needed 'a little tribulation'.[26]

And the Woolleys had some power, in practical terms, to prevent events from unfolding smoothly. Leonard, as Max's boss, kept him hard at work throughout the summer when he would rather have been with Agatha. 'I hope that the agony will be over by Sunday,' Max wrote, amid the final push on recording the finds from Ur, which involved making nearly 400 tracings.[27] 'The devils are going to do their best not to make it easy for us,' he told Agatha. The emerging plan was to marry in September and then to take a honeymoon. But Leonard wanted Max back at his post in Iraq by 26 October.

There was no question, though, of Max doing anything other than pursuing his career, and in fact his investment in archaeology was one of the things Agatha most admired about him. When he told her about his work at the museum, his enthusiasm was infectious. He was cleaning the silver comb of a Sumerian lady: 'a wonderful feeling . . . it is five years since I began active work in archaeology but I still have the same thrill.'[28]

The only fear Max would openly admit to Agatha was about money: 'I may fail to bring you that material success that I feel is due to you.'[29] His salary would certainly not support Agatha's lifestyle, and his parents had financial problems too. Now having left Frederick, Marguerite was a terrible spendthrift. She told her son that having bought 'a woollen costume & a dress which I was badly wanting besides two hats,' she had plans for a flutter at baccarat to restore her finances. In the meantime, though, she confessed herself 'unable to pay the landlord'.[30]

During that difficult summer, Agatha talked herself into marriage, and out again, many times. 'One moment a bit of blind panic . . . I feel "I won't – I won't – I <u>won't</u> marry anybody. Never again."' Then, though, she'd think, 'but it's Max. It's being with Max and having him always – to hold on to when I feel unhappy.'[31] Carlo was also at hand to provide reassurance, once she was back from her annual holiday on a cruise.

Meanwhile Max was getting on with making plans, including characteristically geeky preparations for a honeymoon in what was then Yugoslavia and Greece: 'I've just bought a detailed map of the Peloponnese.'[32] He booked a train through to Venice, and then they'd travel by boat along the Dalmatian coast. 'I am having a white blazer made in anticipation of a warm séjour,' he wrote.[33] It seemed understood between them that Agatha was going to pay for everything, although he was to cover the registrar's fee himself: 'it's right that I should pay for all that.'[34] This kind of thing Agatha found rather sexy: 'If I marry a woman, I pay for the licence. You understand?' says one of her tougher characters.[35]

With Carlo's help, the marriage was to take place in Scotland in the hope of avoiding the press. Under Scottish law, this meant that Agatha had to live north of the border for two weeks beforehand. She went to Skye in August, spending her time 'lying in the heather and looking at the sea.'[36] She was accompanied by the intimates she called the 'Order of Faithful Dogs' – Rosalind, Carlo and her sister Mary – while Max went to visit Esmé's parents. Madge expressed her disapproval by staying away altogether.

During these final weeks before the wedding, the correspondence, which had been intense since May, stepped up to daily letters. 'You've got to write to me every day,' Agatha insisted from the remote Broadford Hotel in Skye. She was still worrying about exchanging peace of mind 'for great happiness but possible disaster'.[37] 'You're not panicking,' Max told her, firmly, 'the day will come when you'll laugh at yourself for ever having done so.'[38]

She was clearly in a tizz, filling in her passport application form wrongly, and repeatedly forgetting to tell Max, despite the frenzy of letters, the vital fact of which hotel she'd be staying in in Edinburgh.

And who knows what Agatha would have done without Max's daily letter? The envelope of his last missive to Skye before she travelled to Edinburgh for the wedding has been ripped open as if she couldn't wait to get her hands on what was inside.

The church, St Cuthbert's, in the shadow of the great rock of Edinburgh Castle, was chosen because Carlo's father was its associate minister. And there, finally, on 11 September 1930, 'Max Edgar Lucien Mallowan', aged thirty-one, and 'Agatha Mary Clarissa Miller or Christie', aged thirty-seven, were wed. The witnesses were Charlotte and Mary Fisher. Both bride and groom had given false ages to narrow the age gap. Max told Agatha he'd claim to be born 'whatever date you would like to make it – I don't suppose it matters much.'[39] In her passport she knocked off a year, taking 1891 as her birthdate. But their hopes of keeping the wedding, and their true ages, secret were both in vain. The next week the *Express* were on the case, reporting on the 'romantic' discreet marriage, at which 'Mr Mallowan is twenty-eight and his bride is thirty-nine.'[40] Even then the newspaper got it wrong: Max had added five years onto his age, and he was really only twenty-six.

Then, riding a great wave of relief, they were off to Venice and to five weeks travelling along the Dalmatian coast. They kept a joint diary of the trip, filling in alternate pages, in which Max recorded a 'luxuriant lobster' and 'the vision of a great torn sail silhouetted on the lagoon against a Venetian sun set sky.' Then Agatha chipped in: 'sad descent from romance – bitten by bugs.' After Venice, they spent their time sailing, sleeping, and swimming – once, at night, in the nude. 'Did the torch betray our guilty secret?' Agatha wondered, when someone spotted them. They had lovely times, 'a luscious pilaf at a particularly dirty cook shop' and a 'glorious walk through the olive woods'. But there were more painful bug bites, and the mix of travel and history was strenuous. 'He's too young for me!' Agatha sighed into the diary, after the wet day upon which Max had made her travel for fourteen hours by mule to see yet another ancient site, leaving her 'desperately weary'.

Finally arriving at a smart hotel in Athens, they found city life 'very queer – we no longer seem the same people. A *suite á deux lits* with bath makes us all shy & civilized. Gone are the happy lunatics of the last fortnight.' But they nevertheless went out to enjoy 'joyful eating of crevettes & langoustines'.[41] The shellfish turned out to be a terrible mistake, for Agatha was stricken with food poisoning so dramatic she needed medical treatment.

It was some days before she could face eating even plain macaroni, but Max had run out of time. He was expected in Iraq. Torn between conflicting duties to his employer and to his wife, he nevertheless felt compelled to get to Baghdad by the agreed date. This was considered to be monstrous by the Greek doctor treating Agatha: 'there is no doubt, from the coldness of his manner, that he regards you as a brutal and inhuman man.'[42]

The Woolleys had decided it would be inappropriate for Agatha to join her husband at Ur. But Max was no longer quite so reliant on his autocratic bosses, because he thought he had enough experience to find another job. 'I am beginning to feel a much greater confidence in my own powers than before,' he wrote. 'Archaeology is a great game. I think I have become keener on it every year and I can imagine no other profession.'[43]

Agatha gradually regained enough strength to travel home alone. From England, she wrote to Max that 'everyone has said I look very well and ten years younger and that being married to you suits me.' She was pleased to have lost weight during her illness. 'I have lost nearly a stone. Isn't it lovely? Married life has reduced me.'

Before taking the train to Devon, she sent him a final letter from London. 'Odd to be in the Paddington Hotel,' she began, the first time for several years that I have arrived in England without a feeling of sick misery – I always had it – as though I'd escaped from things by going abroad to sunshine – and then to come back to them – to memories shadowed and all the things I wanted to forget. But this time – no – Just 'Oh! London – rainy as usual – but rather a nice funny old place!!' My dear – you have lifted so much from my shoulders.[44]

Their letters before marriage had been devoid of any sort of sexual chit-chat, but now, with the deal sealed, they had clearly managed things well. 'Shut your eyes now and pretend you are in my arms and that I am returning your kisses,' Max would write from Iraq.[45] 'My sweet do you know what I miss most?' she replied. 'Being asleep with your arms round me.'[46] Agatha was now busy with work, family, and getting ready for Christmas, tiring days that meant she went 'to bed so sleepy I haven't even the energy for sensual thoughts! Oh! Max what fun it will be, to be with you again!'[47]

On Christmas Eve, 1930, she wrote him one of the final letters of a golden year for them both. 'It's my old wedding day to-day,' she confessed.

It's always been a sad day for me – but not this year. I feel so happy & safe and loved. Bless you, my darling, for all you have done & given back to me.[48]

25

Eight Houses

With the 1930s underway, Agatha's life seems to slow down and broaden out to fill a series of interlinking compartments: Ashfield, literary life in London, and travel to West Asia with Max. Her work was going well, money was pouring in, Agatha was happy.

But where did she live? It's not easy to say. People often assume that like Miss Marple, Agatha must have been rooted to a particular village. In reality, she was constantly on the move, perhaps most perfectly at home when travelling. Her books reflect this. Her signature character might well be a tenant, someone passing through. These agents of change might be rich, like the women who rent the big house in *The Sittaford Mystery*, or not: Poirot even takes part in 'The Adventure of the Cheap Flat'.[1]

Next to travelling, what Agatha liked best was moving into a new home. She called the 1930s her 'plutocratic period', and she bought numerous houses, throwing herself into the business of making each one comfortable. Homemaking was vital to her both in life, and art. 'You *have* to be concerned with a house. With where people *live*,' she once said about her novels.[2] She gives some of her own relish to the rich and independent Linnet in *Death on the Nile*. Linnet's house 'was *hers!*', she insisted, 'she had seen it, acquired it, rebuilt and re-dressed it, lavished money on it. It was her own possession – her kingdom.'[3]

Of course, there was a flipside to this. Agatha's fictional homes often represent the opposite of safety. Houses were the setting in which her nightmare of the silent, sinister Gun Man would appear. He'd slip into a domestic scene, 'sitting at the tea-table', or 'joining in the game', bringing with him that 'horrid feeling of fear'. Agatha's own experiences of mental distress had showed how easily you could slip from security into danger.

A hundred and fifty years before this, thrilling stories set in haunted castles or mansions had defined the detective story's precursor, the Gothic novel. Agatha's gift was to democratise the Gothic, making it appealing to the mass market.[4] In *The Secret Adversary,* for example, she turns a perfectly ordinary London flat into a place of horror. 'Little by little,' she tells us, 'the magic of the night began to gain a hold on them. There were sudden creaks of the furniture, imperceptible rustlings in the curtains.'[5] The middle-class home, as Agatha put it, could contain 'deep smouldering resentments that do not always come to the surface but which suddenly explode into violence.'[6]

The people who bought Agatha's books also loved thinking about houses and their meanings. Between 1920 and 1945, more than sixty new magazines aimed at middle-class female readers were launched, including *Good Housekeeping* and *Woman and Home*.[7] The home had been the whole world for women like Clara Miller. But for Agatha's generation, war, and the collapse of domestic service, meant that middle-class homes had to be reinvented. For Agatha's readers, the foundations of middle-class life were shifting, subsiding, declining.

This helps explain why Agatha specialised in a peculiarly homely brand of death, 'murders of quiet, domestic interest', as she once put it.[8] The critic Alison Light talks about a 'domestification of weaponry' in Agatha's novels. The poisons she chooses are often found round the house: arsenic used for the health of pets, cyanide for wasps, paint for a hat. She also employs the kitchen pestle, the meat skewer, the golf club, the paperweight, the tennis racket, and the steel ball from a bedstead as ways of killing.[9]

Agatha's interest in homes was a feminine concern, which in turn has made her work seem inherently inferior. She'd have agreed with this herself. Despite her publication record in the 1930s, she tells us that 'never, when I was filling in a form and came to the line asking for Occupation, would it have occurred to me to fill it in with anything but the time-honoured "Married woman".'

One of the ways she kept up this idea she wasn't what she called a '*bona fide* author' was by not having a dedicated writing room. She did her writing unostentatiously, round the edges of what she professed to think were the larger matters of life: shopping, eating, relaxing. 'I never know when you write your books,' Agatha's friends said to her, 'because I've never seen you writing.' Working in her bedroom, in odd corners, she was as unlike the conventional idea of the anguished author as possible. 'A marble-topped bedroom wash-stand table made a good place to write,' she tells us, as did 'the dining-room table between meals.'

And all this interest in domesticity helps explain why, in the 1930s, Agatha acquired property like a woman possessed, ending up with eight houses. These were relatively cheap buys, on the west side of London, for ease of access to Paddington and Torquay, and mostly they were let out to tenants. But she usually kept one house free for personal use.

By the time of her second marriage, she already owned 22 Cresswell Place, where she'd entertained Max to their reunion breakfast. It was part of a motley terrace of stables and servants' lodgings behind a row of grand houses. Today this is a wealthy, hedge-fund kind of neighbourhood, with Porches and Pilates instructors. In the 1930s, though, Agatha's little mews was a perch from which to take a sideways glance at what was then still the arty area of Chelsea. Journalists found it romantic, exactly the kind of place an independent, creative woman might live, its green paint-work making it like 'a radiantly green spring tree among grey roofs'.[10]

For her new marriage, Agatha went up in the world, purchasing 47–8 Campden Street in Kensington, near the Central Line for Max's commute to the British Museum. This was a proper house on a proper street, even if it was a narrow street with the underground railway at one end and a reservoir at the other. After the honeymoon, Agatha's letters to Max in Iraq show her exuberant homemaking in action. She describes, for example, 'a most exciting and reprehensible day – I have been to a SALE! & I have bought a walnut chest [. . .] Ah! It was lovely [. . .] buying things I don't need.'[11]

Her London social life included meetings of the Detection Club at the Café Royal. Open only to the published authors of detective fiction, it had the purpose, as Dorothy L. Sayers put it, 'of eating dinners together and of talking illimitable shop'.[12] But Agatha wasn't really clubbable. She contributed to some Club joint ventures, such as compendiums of stories, but soon decided it wasn't a good use of her time. Agatha was now the breadwinner not only for Rosalind, but for Max too, and would not sell herself short. She was also scarred by the experience in 1930 of a collaborative BBC radio series, written jointly with other detective writers. She found the project tedious and disorganised. Much more pleasurably, she discovered the same year that one of her plays – *Black Coffee* – was to be produced on stage. 'I wish you were here to share the fun,' she told Max in Iraq, 'I'm in the middle of rehearsals & meeting the broadcasting people & doing wild telephoning.'[13]

She reluctantly agreed to take part in a second radio series, but she'd been marked down by the BBC as 'difficult'. 'Will you explain to Mrs Mallowan, please,' wrote producer R.J. Ackerley to Carlo, 'the extreme difficulties her being unavailable has involved us in.'[14] Next time Ackerley got in touch with a proposal, he got short shrift. 'The truth of the matter,' Agatha explained, 'is I hate writing short things and they really are *not* profitable . . . the energy to devise a series is much better employed in writing a couple of books. So there it is! With apologies.'

This producer, Mr Ackerley, was rather stumped by an assertive woman. Trying to get Agatha on air, he was full of compliments: 'you read it most awfully well, and I am sure it will be the greatest success.' But behind her back he patronised her, saying she was 'surprisingly good-looking and extremely tiresome'. As a broad-caster, Ackerley said, he thought her 'a little on the feeble side'.

Then again, he admitted that anyone 'would have seemed feeble against the terrific vitality, bullying and bounce of that dreadful woman Dorothy L. Sayers'.[15] Sayers complained in turn to Agatha of 'great trouble with the BBC, who ring up every other day' about the collaborative radio series. She'd told them to 'go away & not keep on bothering!'[16] (I must admit that the thought of Dorothy L. Sayers bouncing on Mr Ackerley gives me a reprehensible thrill.)

While Agatha was motoring on with her career, Rosalind at boarding school found herself lower than she would have liked on her mother's priority list. 'What are you going to do?' she wrote plaintively, 'will you come home by America ... I suppose you know I am going in for the music exam.'[17] Agatha could tell herself that the self-possessed Rosalind was in perfectly good hands, first at a school called Caledonia in Bexhill, then at Benenden School in Kent. But her daughter was in fact failing to thrive. Rosalind's English was 'erratic', her History 'unsatisfactory' and her French 'uneven'. 'I have felt throughout her time here that she has only achieved mediocrity,' wrote her housemistress, 'I am sorry that she is leaving us before being in a position to develop a sense of responsibility.'[18]

Agatha had fallen into a pattern of spending part of every year with Max in West Asia. In 1931, he found a new boss, Reginald Campbell Thompson, who was excavating Nineveh near Mosul, the ancient capital of the Assyrian Empire. Unlike the Woolleys, Campbell Thompson agreed that Agatha could come along too, at her own expense. She also agreed not to publish anything about the site without discussion. Articles had value, both to the writer and as publicity for the dig itself. Max and Agatha were now a kind of two-for-one proposition. In 1930, she took an art course to learn to help with the archaeological drawing: 'I was very shy . . . I had that inferiority complex feeling.'[19] But she'd do virtually anything to please Max. 'I shall never get tired of your work,' she reassured him, 'Have drawn one super pot.'[20] She prioritised his activities, fitting her own work around his, not his around hers. For the expedition house at Nineveh, Agatha purchased a sturdy table upon which to finish her book *Lord Edgware Dies* (1933).

Agatha had made a start on the book during October 1931, when she stayed by herself for a few weeks in Rhodes on the way to Nineveh. Her letters reveal that she was missing Max physically: 'I want to lie on my face in the sun and have you kiss me all down my back.'[21] Sexual satisfaction made her possessive. 'As soon as one loves anyone one gets afraid,' she admitted, 'that is why dogs go about growling with a bone. They're convinced it will be taken from them by other dogs. Are there any other dogs at Mosul, darling? Perhaps you'd better not tell me if there are!'[22]

Her letters from Rhodes also make it clear they'd been hoping for a child, and the balance of evidence suggests that during this autumn Agatha was pregnant. Visiting a cathedral, she said a prayer to John the Baptist. 'Not perhaps a very good person to pray to for a son,' she admitted, but maybe 'after the wilderness & eating locusts so much he might be more disposed to be kindly to family life.'[23] Max was excited about the prospect, but also nervous: 'sweetheart, if we do have a son it will be a great joy, but if we don't we must accept that too joyfully . . . I would a thousand times rather forego a son than anything happening to you my darling . . . you are my lover and my first child.'[24]

And 1931 saw a disappointment: Agatha, now in her early forties, had a miscarriage. After that, Max and Agatha seem to have accepted that they would remain childless. He once wrote to her of some trees they'd planted together, those 'young oncoming trees that we planted with our own hands. These are our children, yours and mine.'[25]

In the wake of this bereavement, Agatha once again turned to her autobiographical fiction. Her second foray into non-detective fiction, *Unfinished Portrait*, published in 1934, helped her to process a chunk of her life that now lay in the past: her first marriage and its failure; her illness of 1926. She'd reached a new vantage point from which to look back.

And Max was maturing as well. He got the British Museum to sponsor his very first independent expedition. He and Agatha prepared to return to Iraq in 1933, the same year she bought their next house. Three storeys tall, with a grand stucco frontage, this was another definite step upwards. Agatha renamed 58 Sheffield Terrace in Kensington after her favourite colour, green, calling it 'Green Lodge'.[26] At the end of the road were the wooded grounds of Holland House.

Agatha had wanted this house as soon as she saw it. This was partly because of the big room on the top floor. She decided, contrary to all previous practice, it was going to be her workroom: 'everybody was surprised at this, since I had never thought of having such a thing before, but they all agreed that it was quite time for poor Missus to have a room of her own.' In it she had a piano, a big table, an upright chair for typing and an armchair for taking a rest. Here she would write at least parts of some of her greatest books, *Murder on the Orient Express*, *The ABC Murders* and *Death on the Nile*.

It's surprising to think that it was twelve years into her writing career before Agatha finally had 'a room of her own', Virginia Woolf's necessity for a writing life. But by this point, writes historian Gillian Gill, with a satisfying insight, 'Agatha Christie did not need a room of her own – she was used to having whole houses. She was one of those rare women who can buy property at will, and buy it with money earned by their own work.'[27]

Max's first autonomous dig, at Arpachiyah in Iraq, would cost £2,000, and tracing its funding takes you on an interesting journey. The British Museum contributed, the British School of Archaeology in Iraq gave £600, and the supervisory team partially volunteered their services.[28] Yet a shortfall remained. 'I hope Mallowan will stay in London for a bit,' wrote one of the Museum's curators, 'raising another thousand will require a lot of attention.'[29] Max managed to get £100 from the well-known donor to archaeology, Sir Charles Marston, and £100 was contributed by one Agatha Christie. But records at the British Museum show a significant gift of £500 from another anonymous contributor. This particular donor wanted the money back again if other funding towards the total came in (it didn't).[30] Who could this have been apart from Max's own wife?

Agatha was beginning what would be a long career as the funder of her husband's archaeological work.

Max also found his wife invaluable in winning coverage, and therefore money. 'Novelist on thrilling trip,' trilled a newspaper headline. 'Agatha Christie and a Lost People – Iraq Search.'[31] Max enjoyed working 'in the grand manner, on a grand scale', and in the 1930s funds allowed perhaps 200 labourers on site.[32] He and his peers carried out what would be considered today to be unduly destructive work. For the first few days at Arpachiyah, for example, Max simply had his labourers dig away randomly in order to practise. An excavation of 1976 revealed the mound was 'densely packed with structures' this approach missed or destroyed.[33]

In the desert, Agatha and Max emulated a European lifestyle: changing for dinner, and getting local cooks to recreate an approximation of European food. The utensils taken to Arpachiyah in 1933 included nineteen napkins, tablecloths, finger bowls and soup dishes.[34] The shopping list for a later dig included three bottles of gin, three of Châteauneuf-du-Pape, two tins of Danish butter, six of curry powder, two of 'Pate de Foie Gras' and twenty-four of 'Corned Beef'.[35] All this was driven to the site in Max's specially adapted lorry painted a lavender blue and known as 'Queen Mary'.

But Max's first independent dig in Iraq would also be his last. At the end of the season, it proved much harder than expected to remove antiquities from the country. Agatha's autobiography simply reports that they came home 'flushed with triumph', but the expedition had actually ended in what became known as the 'Arpachiyah Scandal'.

Iraq had just became independent, and growing nationalism meant the government decided to change the rules on the division of archaeological spoils. Previously finds had been split fifty-fifty between foreign teams and the Iraqi national museum. This process was administered by the museum's director, a German archaeologist, Dr Julius Jordan, who – in an extra twist in the tale – was also the head of Iraq's Nazi Party. But now the majority of the finds must stay. Max was not granted the expected permit for export.

A controversy sprang up, with Max and the international community of archaeologists complaining that the Iraqis were preventing important scientific work, while the British Foreign Office found itself caught in the middle. The archaeologists argued the new rules were conceived in a spirit 'of unintelligent nationalism', while the British diplomats thought in return that the archaeologists had an 'irritating and condescending attitude that they are, from purely altruistic motives, conferring a benefit to the country concerned'.[36]

In the end, the matter was put to the vote in the Iraqi cabinet. There, a majority of one single vote did finally allow Max to take finds home. He wanted to get on with writing up his discoveries, a task archaeologists are notoriously prone to putting off. From the perspective of the public, Max had an exemplary record in sharing his findings. In the 1930s, he produced many articles in the *Illustrated London News*. When pitching to editors, he was at pains to point out that 'in spite of their sensationalism all my facts are scientifically vouched for'.[37] From the perspective of his fellow archaeologists, though, Max's chatty style, perhaps influenced by his wife, didn't do justice to the material.

The 'Arpachiyah Scandal', which Max saw as an annoying bureaucratic delay, in fact saw the end of the assumption that Western archaeologists could help themselves to whatever they wanted from West Asia. The whole business meant Max decided not to dig again in Iraq for some time. But there were compensations, for in 1934 Agatha bought him his own house. The new property was a lovely Queen Anne house on the Thames not too far from London. Winterbrook, on the outskirts of Wallingford in Oxfordshire, would always be known by Agatha as 'Max's house'. A friend described it as 'a cosy, warm, hospitable, upper middle-class interior, with all the comforts and amenities, the pretty china and good furniture that Agatha's prosperity has bought'.[38]

In the later 1930s, Max moved his focus to Syria. Analysis of his financial records shows he paid the diggers a day rate, plus extra for finds. The reward for a good find had to be competitive with the black-market price for antiquities, to discourage the workers smuggling items offsite and selling them. It was a morally fraught business. Agatha helped police the system, as she slipped quietly round the site. Looking unbusinesslike and feminine, she was reporting any diggers who were idling or sleeping.[39]

A German archaeologist, Tom Stern, visited Syria in 1999 to try to discover how the people who lived there had viewed Agatha. He met two of Max's former diggers, who recalled 'a beautiful, strong woman. She supervised the workers. I remember her walking-stick. She could unfold it and sit down on it.' The description of a shooting stick rings true. Yet other local testimony shows the transitory nature of the Westerners' presence. An even older man refused to answer questions about Max's 1937 dig in Syria: 'I am not interested in any of that now. Only a hair's breadth separates me from death.'[40]

Agatha's attitude towards the people of the Middle East would develop over time. You can see a gradual liberalising of her views from the 1920s, when even a goodie in a novel says 'any name's good enough for a dago'.[41] She did not like to think of herself as demanding, dismissive and insular. When she kitted herself out for an expedition, struggling to find clothes to fit her girth, she laughed at herself for looking like an 'Empire Builder's Wife'.[42]

But even in her own and Max's published works there's always a shadow story going on in the background, hints of local discontent. There were conflicts among the labourers. 'We have a wild and woolly set of ruffians on the dig and it takes all the time to keep them in order,' Max admitted.[43] One season, two men were killed when a tunnel collapsed during an unauthorised search for treasure. And Agatha and Max would have to abandon one Syrian site, Tell Brak, because of what they saw as 'the blackmailing pressure' of locals who wanted higher wages.[44]

Meanwhile, being an archaeological wife remained a higher priority for Agatha than being a conventional mother. After school, Rosalind was packed off to Paris. 'I don't know what I shall do,' she wrote, 'I can't help feeling that it is an awful waste of money.'[45] Next she was sent to Munich, and complained of feeling neglected. 'Tell Mummy she really is a pig!!' Rosalind wrote to Max, 'it makes me absolutely miserable.'[46] Agatha sometimes simply failed to reply to letters. 'Would you mind telling me <u>when</u> you are coming home,' Rosalind ranted in one missive, 'you seem to tell Carlo and not me . . . I had another fit of depression.'[47]

After Munich, 1937 was to be Rosalind's season as a debutante, and Agatha did at least recognise the importance of the ritual: 'whether you enjoy it or not I think it will be an interesting experience'.[48] Rosalind had a proper London season, not a cut-price one like Agatha's own. The upside of having a distracted working mother was that the lost family fortune of the Millers was being restored. The downside was that Agatha, as a divorced woman, was ineligible to present her daughter at Buckingham Palace. Rosalind had to be taken by a friend instead.

Rosalind and her friend Susan North were thinking about careers, but modelling was the only thing that came to mind. Agatha didn't approve. Feeling at a loose end, Rosalind came out to join her mother and Max in Syria, and took over the drawing duties. Tensions ensued. Rosalind, a perfectionist, was not satisfied with her work, and wanted to start again.

'You are not to tear them up,' said Max.

'I shall tear them up,' said Rosalind.

They then had an enormous fight, Rosalind trembling with rage, Max also really angry.

Rosalind was now old enough to resist being made into copy. When Agatha came to write a book about life on the dig, *Come, Tell Me How You Live*, she had to promise her daughter, who loathed the very 'idea of this book(!) that <u>no</u> reference to her will be in it!!'[49]

Agatha was now a completely different person from the wreck of a woman of 1926. Perhaps her truest break with the past came at the end of the 1930s, when she decided – not without pain – to sell her family home.

Ashfield had been her country retreat for the last fifteen years. Cook Florence Potter had remained ever since Clara's death, producing enormous meals of up to seventeen courses for parties, including her celebrated 'Apple Hedgehog' (its prickles were almonds).[50] But visitors found the house gloomy and increasingly 'eerie' with its grandfather clock, marble effigies and stuffed animals.[51]

Agatha's decision to sell came in 1938, when an elegant, white-painted, Georgian mansion near Dartmouth named Greenway House came onto the market. Formerly owned by the MP of Torquay and perched high over a dramatic bend in the River Dart, this 'ideal Yachtsman's Residence' had seventeen bed, dressing and bathrooms, a billiard room, a library, and central heating.[52]

Country Life advertised it as 'suitable as a first-class hotel', and in 1938, most people were giving up on the country house as a private residence.[53] But not the Mallowans. The decision to go to see Greenway seemed almost to have Clara's blessing, for Agatha had once visited the house with her mother. It was Max who suggested Agatha should purchase it.

'Why don't you buy it?' asked Max.

I was so startled, this coming from Max, that it took my breath away.

'You've been getting worried about Ashfield, you know,'

I knew what he meant. Ashfield, my home, had changed.

Intruding into the view of the sea from Ashfield's garden was now a secondary school and a nursing home. But on top of that, Max had no emotional investment in the place. And so, to please him, Agatha came round to the idea of selling. Even using the proceeds of Ashfield, buying Greenway and its thirty-three acres for £5,690 was still a stretch.[54] Agatha then pulled down the Victorian wing at the back, thinking the 1790s house on its own would be 'a far better house, far lighter'. Later, she would wish she'd gone even further: 'I would have taken off *another* large chunk of the house: the vast larder, the great caverns in which you soaked pigs, the kindling store, the suite of sculleries.' In 1938, though, she had no notion that one day she might have to run the house without domestic help.

In 1939, even with war in the air, Agatha was acquiring more London properties, in Mayfair and St James's, her fanciest addresses yet. But this wonderful decade for Agatha and Max was drawing to a close. That year they left Beirut after what would prove to be a final archaeological season. World events meant they must have suspected they wouldn't be back for some time.

Agatha stood by the rail of the departing ship, looking back at the dim blue mountains of Lebanon as they receded into the distance. Max asked what was on her mind as nearly ten years of writing, travelling and digging together came to an end.

'I am thinking,' she said, 'that it was a very happy way to live.'[55]

26

The Golden Age

Agatha's happiness led her to create some of her best work ever. The decade drawing to a close in 1939 had been a golden age, both for detective fiction in general and for Agatha in particular. Marriage to Max had brought her ever-greater professional confidence. She was becoming the deft, demanding artist of her maturity, and her publishers, producers and business contacts were made to feel it. 'The world is very cruel to women,' as she once had a character say. 'They must do what they can for themselves.'[1]

Back in the 1920s, immediately after her disappearance, Agatha had for the first time experienced the feeling she *had* to go on working, despite the doctors' advice to rest: 'I had no money coming in now from anywhere except what I could make or had made myself.'

She later identified this as the moment she turned professional, which meant having to write 'even when you don't want to'. The book Agatha had to 'force' herself to finish when she was ill was published in 1928 as *The Mystery of the Blue Train*.[2] All the while Rosalind wanted her mother's attention, hovering round the typewriter: 'I can just stand here. I won't interrupt.' In consequence, the *Blue Train* became a painful memory: 'easily the worst book I ever wrote'.[3]

Because of the publicity of 1926, though, the *Blue Train* nevertheless sold an excellent 7,000 copies. In the 1930s, her sales sank back a little, then built again as Collins worked out how best to market her. By 1935, Agatha's *Three Act Tragedy* sold 10,000 copies in the first year, and by 1942, with *Five Little Pigs*, she was up to 20,000, and would never look back.[4]

To Agatha it felt like cash was plentiful, especially when her books were serialised in American magazines. This money, she explains, 'besides being far larger than anything I ever made from serial rights in Britain, was also at that time free of income tax. It was regarded as a capital payment.' This issue of tax in America, though, would come back to haunt her.

She was also opening up new income streams. In May 1928, a theatrical version of *The Murder of Roger Ackroyd* was staged. Entitled *Alibi*, and not adapted for the stage by Agatha herself, the *Observer* called it, rather charmingly, a new 'crook play'. Naturally it featured Poirot, although the doctor's middle-aged spinster sister Caroline in the book was changed to a sexy young thing called Caryl.[5] But Agatha thought she could do better, which led to her own Poirot play, *Black Coffee*, being staged in 1930. The experience of these two plays led her to feel that Poirot didn't work on stage: he was too flamboyant and hogged the audience's attention at the expense of the other characters.[6]

Agatha was increasingly interested by the stage, but she wasn't focussed upon it. She was just too busy. In the 1930s, the richest writing decade of her life, she produced twenty novels and five collections of short stories. 1934 alone saw her publishing two detective novels, two short story collections, and a non-detective novel as well. She was building not just a career but a brand. She developed new detectives: Mr Quin and Mr Satterthwaite, who were hardly even characters, more like modernist symbols who boot a plot into motion. And then there was Parker Pyne, who promised his clients not the solutions to mysteries, but the more elusive result of happiness.

Parker Pyne was a non-medical version of the sort of person Agatha herself had consulted in the late 1920s, and her experience of psychotherapy would enrich her work. She'd later explain how her first detective stories were 'a story with a moral; in fact it was the old Everyman Morality Tale.' After her divorce, though, the buried desires of the unconscious began to appear in Agatha's work much more often as a motivation for crime.

In the 1930s, Poirot would look less hard for physical clues, and rely more on what we today might call psychological profiling: 'the truer clues of the clash of personalities and the secrets of the heart'.[7] In *Cards on the Table* (1936), Agatha makes a rare author's statement. In this story, she says, the deduction is 'entirely *psychological*, but it is none the less interesting for that, because when all is said and done it is the *mind* of the murderer that is of supreme interest'.[8]

Agatha's own mind was a seemingly unending source of ideas. She'd spoof herself in her character of Mrs Ariadne Oliver, detective novelist. Mrs Oliver might be scatty, middle-aged and untidy, but she is almost absurdly well endowed with ideas. Here, in a mirroring of the way Agatha's own mind worked, she muses aloud about the possible motives for a murder. The victim:

> could have been murdered by someone who just likes murdering girls . . . or she might have known some secrets about somebody's love affairs, or she may have seen someone bury a body at night or she may have seen someone who was concealing his identity – or she may have known some secret about where some treasure was buried during the war.[9]

In 1930, Jane Marple would make her first appearance in a full-length novel, *The Murder at the Vicarage*, a book that's certainly among my top three favourite Christies. Agatha wrote it during the stressful run-up to marrying Max, and it was published during their honeymoon. It contained a wedding present to him in the form of an in-joke: one of the characters, posing as an eminent archaeologist, turns out to be a thief.

But Miss Marple did not, however, make her first entrance into fiction fully formed. Critic Peter Keating makes the convincing case that Miss Marple was Agatha's most treasured character, the one who stood for Agatha's own self, and that she could emerge only in tandem with Agatha Christie, the successful, professional, independent writer.

There'd been a proto-Miss Marple, the doctor's nosy sister, in *The Murder of Roger Ackroyd*, who could sniff out secrets without even needing to leave home. *Roger Ackroyd* was written in the final stages of Agatha's marriage to Archie, when she was beginning to grow away from him. Miss Marple proper appeared in two lots of stories published from December 1927, which must therefore have been conceived during the maelstrom of the disappearance.[10] And then Miss Marple made her first true novelistic appearance just as Agatha had met Max and the second act of her life was beginning.

Another prompt for Miss Marple to emerge was the more general prominence of the spinster across society in the period between the wars. Miss Marple herself was too old to have been among the 'surplus women', those two million unmarried young women who outnumbered the equivalent men in the census of 1921. But the 'surplus women' made spinsters more noticeable than they had been in previous generations.

Miss Marple also shared some attributes with interwar Britain's real-life female sleuths, or at least the ones with the desire to be interviewed in the newspapers. Annette Kerner, for example, started out in the detection business in 1915 and became known as 'Mrs Sherlock Holmes' from her agency's Baker Street address. A journalist was surprised to find her 'just a plump little woman . . . her silver-grey hair pinned into a bun.' 'Insignificant,' explained Mrs Kerner, 'that's how a detective should look.'[11] Just like Miss Marple.

The Murder at the Vicarage received tremendous reviews, but some people didn't 'get' the character of Miss Marple. The *New York Times* thought it contained too much about 'the local sisterhood of spinsters . . . the average reader is apt to grow weary of it all.'[12] In later years, Agatha would soften the edges of her Miss Marple, making her sweeter and with less bite. In *The Murder at the Vicarage*, though, she is described as a 'nasty old cat'. She doesn't even truly like gardening; she uses it as an excuse to hang around outside to watch who's coming and going. Early, acidic Miss Marple is actually the Miss Marple I prefer. But perhaps that's because I'm a nasty old cat myself.

The 1930s also saw some of Agatha's best-known books set in locations her British and American readers thought of as exotic. This was the influence of her travels with Max. These stories – *Murder on the Orient Express* and *Death on the Nile* – have traditionally been among the most popular of Agatha's books, not least because their locations have made them into the most visually arresting films.

Murder on the Orient Express was inspired by a return trip Agatha made from Nineveh in December 1931 when flooding held up the train for two days. Her letter to Max recounting the whole amusing adventure shows her novel contains many details adapted from real life. Her fellow passengers included a Greek with 'a <u>most</u> amusing wife of 70 with a hideous but very attractive face' (like Princess Dragomiroff), 'two Danish lady missionaries' (shades of the Swedish nurse, Greta Ohlsson), a 'large jocose Italian', like Antonio Foscarelli, and an American lady who kept up the continuous complaints of Mrs Hubbard.[13]

But the nugget of the plot was inspired by another 'Christie trick': the working in of details from a real-life crime she'd read about in the newspapers. In this case, it was the kidnapping and murder of the baby son of heroic aviator (and National Socialist sympathiser) Charles Lindbergh and his wife Anne, and the collective sympathy their horrible experience aroused.

In Agatha's book, the train itself was closely observed, and the timings she gives for its stops correlate with the published timetable for 1932.[14] In 1933, having finished the book, she made a second trip to verify various details. 'I had to see where all the switches were,' she explained. It was well worth doing, for one reader also made the journey himself to check.[15] There's evidence of other efforts Agatha made to research and solidify the situations she presented in her stories. But she wasn't always thorough enough. In *Death in the Clouds* (1935), she famously neglected to appreciate that a blowgun for the shooting of a poisoned dart must be at least forty-five centimetres long, and is often much longer. Much too long for it to be slipped, as Agatha described, down the side of an aeroplane seat.

In the December of 1933, Max and Agatha made a trip to Egypt, travelling along the Nile to the Cataract Hotel at Aswan, and *Death on the Nile* was born. This story is classic mid-period Poirot in that he does not play a significant part until well into the action. He is no longer needed as the story's stage manager, but Agatha didn't feel able to cut out her most popular character altogether.

Again *Death on the Nile* contains a dodgy archaeologist, and Agatha indulges herself in a discussion of the parallels between detection and digging.[16] Poirot describes his work as scraping away at the 'loose earth' until he – like Max – is left with 'the truth – the naked shining truth.'[17] Teasing Max became a theme throughout the 1930s: in *Death in the Clouds* a couple of gangsters turn out to be 'learned and distinguished archaeologists'.[18]

Max and his doings were even more central in 1936's *Murder in Mesopotamia*. Agatha's handwritten notes show it was based on the Woolleys and other real archaeologists. The narrator, Nurse Leatheran, has something of Agatha's sensible nature and outsider perspective, and, in a nod to Max, she's attracted to a quiet young archaeologist. 'I had taken rather a fancy' to him, she says.[19]

This story contains a beautiful example of the 'Christie trick' of the planting of a clue. We hear that 'Dr Leidner was bending over looking at a lot of stones and broken pottery that were laid out in rows. There were big things he called querns, and pestles and celts and stone axes, and more broken bits of pottery with queer patterns on them than I've ever seen all at once.'[20] The unfamiliar, unexpected word – quern – jumps out of the muddle of pottery and axes and broken bits, but then the narrator Nurse Leatheran moves on to something else, and all is forgotten. Unless, that is, the strange word has been registered by the vigilant reader, who might not then be surprised when the quern turns out to be the murder weapon. Critic J.C. Bernthal points out Christie clues are almost genius 'because in each case she almost says "ta da!" as she plants each one. "A quern?" you might ask yourself, on first reading the passage, what's that – oh, yes, it's something archaeological. And then later, you'll remember its existence.'[21]

Despite its setting, *Murder in Mesopotamia* was a much more traditional work than its predecessor, *The ABC Murders* of 1935. Here the 'Christie trick' is to imply that the thing linking the crimes is the alphabet. Wrong! What really forms the pattern is yet another dysfunctional family drama: 'the apparently public nature of the crimes has merely disguised a domestic murder after all'.[22] With this book, she'd also jumped head first into a new field, the nascent genre of the fictional serial killer.[23]

And then in 1939 came the brilliant book now known as *And Then There Were None*. Originally, and notoriously, it contained a racial slur in its very title. The title wasn't just lifted from a nursery rhyme: the 'N-word' was also the name of the island on which the story was set. Alison Light points out that this was a deliberate invocation of Africa, of the supposed 'dark continent' from which Monty had returned ill and addicted, where the normal controls on human behaviour didn't apply. The crime of killing one white person, in the book, is equated with the crime of killing twenty-one Africans. 'Natives don't mind dying, you know,' says murderer Philip Lombard, supposedly in his own defence.[24]

Part of the reason some of Christie's statements cause such pain today, I think, is because people think of her writing as somehow timeless. This itself was a consequence of the way it was cleaned up and televised in the 1980s and 90s. But it's also because her writing has such ease and clarity it doesn't immediately shout out about the particular year in which it was written. This in turn helps account for her widespread chronological and geographical popularity. But it also helps to disguise something that should be obvious: that each story is an artefact of its writer's class and time. Even if few of Agatha's middle-class British first readers would have taken the title amiss, it was different in a more racially sensitive America, where from the start it was published under the name *And Then There Were None*.

The *New York Times* loved the book, saying that 'the whole thing is utterly impossible and utterly fascinating'.[25] It marked a new level of achievement for Agatha as she becomes the supremely confident dispenser of death to those among the characters who deserve it. After Agatha's unsettled period of 1926–30 when psychology came to the fore, she was returning, in her prime, to a more straightforward position of black and white, of good and evil.

But an accident that happened during the publishing of *And Then There Were None* had an important and detrimental effect on Agatha's literary reputation. A story placed by her publisher in *Crime Club News* practically revealed the secret of the plot, which caused Agatha enormous annoyance. Her anger, as critic Merja Makinen has pointed out, led to her publishers becoming hyper-aware of spoilers. It's understandable, but the downside is the dampening effect it's had on critics' freedom to discuss and appreciate her work. The more you prioritise Agatha's plotting, or what's sometimes called the 'algebraic' quality of her writing, the less freedom you have to notice and enjoy the dialogue, the characters and the humour of her best books.

It's another of the things that's led Agatha Christie, so often, to be underestimated.

✣ PART SEVEN ✣

Wartime Worker – 1940s

27

Beneath the Bombs

In the autumn of 1941, Agatha was once again back at work in a wartime hospital pharmacy.

The tall, red-brick University College Hospital was in Gower Street. The library opposite had been bombed, and 100,000 books destroyed. 'Hospital still standing,' Agatha noted, 'though flattened buildings all around.'[1] 140 beds of the 500 in the hospital were kept free for air raid victims, such as the seventy who'd been admitted in a single April night.[2]

The worst months of the Blitz were now over, but Londoners still sometimes had to brace themselves for the air raid warning. And the USA had still not entered the war against Germany. Agatha's American publishers wanted photographs to publicise that autumn's novel. Images of the parlous state of the hospital might serve the purpose well, Agatha thought, both for publicity, and to make the case for supporting Britain: 'if they must have some kind of pictures, let them have that.'[3]

Leaving the hospital at the end of her shift, and walking uphill towards Hampstead Heath, Agatha would head home to begin what was now her second job as an author. She was also doing war work in her books. Her new novel *N or M?* featured spying, unpacked wartime paranoia, and – most famously – mocked the Nazis.

Agatha's current home, on the face of it, was an odd choice: the white-painted, startlingly modern-looking block called Lawn Road Flats in Belsize Park. It looked 'like a giant liner which ought to have had a couple of funnels'.[4] The other tenants found their matronly neighbour, just the wrong side of fifty, a little incongruous. One, a Hungarian architect, 'used to pass her in the corridor, a cuddly-looking, comfortable lady who one felt was much more likely to grow roses in her back garden than write detective novels.'[5]

Agatha was living here alone, separated from Carlo, from Rosalind, and – most importantly – from Max.

For the fêted, well-paid author of the 1930s, with her younger husband and glamorous second life in West Asia, the wartime world looked very different. Working harder than ever before, she was dangerously close to sinking into depression.

It was back in 1938 that the gilt had begun to come off Agatha's golden age. That year saw the death of Peter, the dog who'd comforted her in 1926, and who'd starred in her novel *Dumb Witness*. It was also the year she got a letter from Edmund Cork that at the time didn't seem too troubling. He informed her that the US tax authorities were asking about her earnings in America, money upon which she'd never been required to pay tax. Her American agent, Harold Ober, hired a lawyer to help answer queries.

It was as well for her peace of mind that Agatha had no idea how bad this business would get. A little later, the Federal High Court in the USA decided another British author would indeed have to pay American tax. Agatha's team would now argue that no tax had ever been requested of her and, in any case, how far back should this apply? She'd been published in the United States for some twenty years. The answer was worrying. 'The tax people here [. . .] are now demanding to see Agatha Christie's accounts from the very beginning,' explained Ober, 'I'm going to stall on this as long as possible.'[6]

And the news in the wider world was disturbing as well. On Sunday 3 September 1939, people all over Britain were listening to their radios when the prime minister announced that Britain was at war. Max and Agatha heard the broadcast in the kitchen at Greenway, where Agatha was making a salad. The parish register reveals the household at Greenway had grown quite substantial:

Agatha ('Authoress'), Max ('archaeologist'), Rosalind, and three domestic staff: Katherleen Kelly, Edith Perkins and Dorothy Mitchell. There was also Elizabeth Bastin, who lived at Ferry Cottage in the grounds. Max thought Mrs Bastin a 'silly' woman, and remembered how that Sunday lunchtime she 'wept into the vegetables'.[7] Yet Mrs Bastin was the more prescient. This wasn't just the end of a decade of peace. It was also the end of a lifestyle for Agatha and Max. Even setting aside the financial trouble brewing in America, their ambitious establishment at Greenway was about to become unaffordable.

Still, at Greenway they stayed, as the 'Phoney War' period seemed at first to offer little in the way of change. At the outbreak of the conflict, a million Britons immediately volunteered to help with the war effort, a third of them women. Combined with the response to later calls from the government, this would make Britain the combatant nation with the highest proportion of its civilian population stepping up. Agatha and Max would both want to play a part in this. But it took them time to find ways in which they could contribute.

Max, for one, was coming up against the suspicion of foreigners that was such an unattractive feature of the wartime years. His parents were an obstacle to his serving in the armed forces. Marguerite and Frederick Mallowan were classed as 'enemy aliens' because of their foreign places of birth, and had to go before a tribunal to see if they were to be interned.[8] These concerns work their way into Agatha's *N or M?*, where her hero and heroine Tommy and Tuppence question the general British enthusiasm for locking up refugees. Hating all Germans indiscriminately, Tuppence explains, 'is a war mask that you put on. It's a part of war – probably a necessary part – but it's ephemeral.'[9] Max could only hope that the authorities would set aside the 'war mask' and see that he had something to offer. At thirty-five, though, he was a bit too old for active duties. He did at least join Brixham Home Guard, where he found himself serving alongside a professor of ancient Greek: 'our experience in Hellenic warfare is second to none'.[10]

Graham Greene, working in the government's Ministry of Information, asked Agatha if she would join him there as a writer of propaganda. She refused, saying she didn't think she'd be any good at it. Yet propaganda is exactly what she produced – in her own way – in *N or M?*. In contrast to her earlier work, the story finally mentioned Jewish people in the context of victimhood. 'As far as I can see,' Agatha told Edmund Cork, 'if the Germans invade us successfully I shall be taken straight to a concentration camp for writing this!'[11] And as the war progressed, Agatha *would* sometimes write for the Ministry of Information. Once Britain and Russia were allies, for example, she produced an article on detective fiction for publication in the Soviet Union.[12]

The Phoney War, from autumn 1939 to summer 1940, proved a period of phenomenal output for Agatha. Anxious about her tax as well as world events, she wrote like a demon. The magnificent *Evil under the Sun* was a holiday story set in Devon that provided welcome distraction from the fall of France. She also pushed ahead with two more books, *Sleeping Murder* and *Curtain*. One featuring Miss Marple and the other the death of Hercule Poirot, these two were not to be published immediately, but stockpiled for the future. They were stored in a bank vault, insured against destruction, and given by deed of gift to Rosalind and Max. Agatha asked Cork to make sure her family would have money in the case of her 'sudden demise!'[13] Someone who'd been 'ruined' in her youth could never quite escape the fear of being in that position again. It caused her to overwork. 'I really do have too much to do,' she complained, 'my head gets addled.'[14]

In January 1940, Max finally found a voluntary post with a fund to help people affected by an earthquake in Turkey. And having taken the exam to join the 'Air Raid Precautions Auxiliary Reserve' of the St John Ambulance Brigade, Agatha went back to her old post in the dispensary of Torquay hospital. Her wartime identity card, much worn, shows her workaday appearance: serious, black-jacketed and double-chinned, but with her hair in scrumptious little pin-curls, and pearls firmly in place.[15] She also looked for canteen work, wanting manual labour to counterbalance the creative effort of writing. 'Sufficient activity for the physical side,' she explained, 'releases your mental side, allowing it to take off into space and make its own thoughts and inventions.'

Agatha's agent remonstrated with her, suggesting she should do something more 'important' than working in a hospital or canteen. But she gave Cork short shrift for his rather masculine hierarchy in which medicine or food were unimportant. 'It is all very well to say I "ought to be doing a more important job" . . . Now just tell me what your idea of an interesting important job is for me.'[16] I do rather like the idea of poor Mr Cork quaking in his shoes as he opened the letters of his most important client, who by now could definitely be described as formidable.

Gradually the conflict began to make itself felt even down in Devon. 'Bombs all round us whistling down!' Agatha wrote, 'I think they were going for a Hospital Ship moored near us in the Dart.'[17] Life was disrupted by Max's overeducated Home Guard colleagues getting in the way: 'we had a good invasion scare last week – house swarmed with Soldiers all so much dressed up they could hardly move!'[18] In London, Cork's work was also disrupted: 'the raid last night shook us up a bit – contract books thrown all over the office by the explosion.'[19]

The period just before Dunkirk found Agatha still hard at work, and increasingly irritable. She wrote again to Cork, having dealt with a request to change the ending of One, Two, Buckle My Shoe, a Poirot set around a dentist's practice. She signed off, 'yours in haste and rather a bad temper as the result of fiddling with this book.'[20] She was so focussed on her work it took her a long time to notice, during that spring of 1940, that Rosalind was on the telephone an awful lot.

The mystery would be solved in due course, but the family soon had to move out of Greenway. Agatha rented the house to a Mr and Mrs Arbuthnot, two nurses, and ten evacuees. The names of some of the children still survive in the haunting form of paper labels on the shelves of Greenway's linen press where their siren suits were stored: Maureen, Tina, Pamela, Beryl, Tommy, Raymond, Bill. 'On Sundays,' recalls evacuee Doreen Vautour, each lonely child's photo album was taken down from its storage place on a high cupboard, and 'we all got to look at the pictures of our parents and other relatives.'[21]

Meanwhile, from a rented cottage, Agatha was worried about her income: 'am I going to get some money from America soon? [. . .] good deal of red ink in my bank a/c.'[22] But the answer was negative. In August, the US authorities prevented her from taking money out of the country. Cork warned she might even have to pay $78,500 of American tax that had built up since 1930, plus possible 'penalties for non-filing of returns'.[23] On top of this, British taxes had risen too, to pay for the war. Agatha's fellow best-selling author Daphne du Maurier earned £25,000 in 1942, but paid 90 per cent of it as tax, 'enough to buy a Lancaster bomber!'[24] The British tax authorities wanted 80 per cent of Agatha's income, including the American money that she hadn't even received. She had to take out a loan to meet her tax bills, and even that was problematic. As Cork explained, 'she is a wealthy woman, and should have no difficulty in borrowing the amount, but war conditions have altered all this.' 'Mrs Christie would be the last person to evade improperly any taxation that was rightly due,' he concluded, but he was beginning to search around for some 'desperate expedient to enable the poor author to live'.[25]

Agatha's response to the situation was not particularly business-like. She simply settled down to write even more. 'Do you think you could get some typewriter ribbons sent down?' she asked Cork, 'this one is getting so pale I can hardly see it.'[26]

Amid this blizzard of writing, the Battle of Britain unfolded and the Blitz began. But it was only on 11 February 1941 that the Phoney War really came to an end for the Mallowans. That was the date upon which Max, having strenuously worked his contacts, finally got a commission in the R.A.F. This would be steady employment with a salary, of a type he hadn't had before. He realised that Agatha couldn't continue to pay for his career: 'we shall no longer be able to put up the money to indulge in digging and it is an uncertain profession.'[27]

Max's new job was in the administrative part of the RAF, and he obtained it through a friend from his British Museum days, the Egyptologist, Stephen Glanville. It was a bit non-U of Max to choose the RAF as opposed to the other services, but perhaps it was the most amenable to taking a nerdy-looking archaeologist. Agatha now had a second husband serving in the most junior – but most racy – branch of the armed forces.

So, in March 1941, in the seventh month of the Blitz, Max and Agatha moved to London, to live at Lawn Road Flats. Stephen Glanville would also live in the same block for a while. Stephen already worked in the RAF's Intelligence Branch in the Directorate of Allied and Foreign Liaison, and the two friends shared an office filled with pipe smoke.

Why did Agatha accompany Max to London? Perhaps she remembered what had happened when she'd left Archie alone to fall in love with golf and with Nancy. But the decision was not without its risks. The windows of Lawn Road Flats had been blown right out on just the second night of the Blitz, and between October 1940 and June 1941, thirty-eight bombs landed on the neighbourhood.[28] When Agatha and Max moved in, there were still two months of the Blitz proper to go. But they must have chosen Lawn Road at least in part because the building had a steel-framed, reinforced concrete structure, which was considered exceptionally safe during a raid.[29]

This wasn't everybody's idea of a homely place to live. In 1946, readers of the magazine *Horizon* would vote the Lawn Road Flats as the 'second most ugly building in England'.[30] Completed in 1934, the tenants included artists, socialists, at least four Soviet spies at different times, many immigrants and creative people of all kinds. Lawn Road Flats is also known today as the Isokon Building after the plywood furniture company that was another business venture of its builders, Molly and Jack Pritchard, left-leaning individuals with an open marriage.

The building's original prospectus promised flats for 'business men and women who have no time for domestic troubles'.[31] Agatha's home was designed for a new kind of person: an independent, hard-working professional. Most of the flats measured only 5.4 by 4.67 metres, with a sliding door to conceal the minuscule kitchen with its Belling oven and Electrolux refrigerator.[32] Tenants were really expected to eat in the building's restaurant, which was run by Philip Harben, often described as 'the first celebrity chef' for his appearances on television. Agatha liked the fact 'one can always go down in the evening and have a meal and talk to someone'.[33]

Given she'd once owned eight houses, Agatha had ended up at Lawn Road Flats because she was by now surprisingly short of homes. Greenway, Winterbrook and Cresswell Place were all let to tenants. Insurance against bomb damage was prohibitively expensive, so Agatha eventually sold her property in Campden Street. She couldn't use Sheffield Terrace because it had been devastated by a bomb on 10 November 1940. 'Front door & steps blown up,' Agatha noted, as were the roof and chimneys, while the 'houses next door & opposite more or less completely flattened.'[34] Agatha and Max felt lucky they hadn't been in the house at the time. Agatha had a fatalistic attitude towards raids and, she claims, 'never went down to any shelter'. She just stayed in bed. 'I hardly woke up,' she explains, 'I would think, half drowsily, that I heard the siren, or bombs not too far away . . . "Oh dear, there they are again!" I would mutter, and turn over.'

London beneath the bombs had become a different place. Graham Greene described its haunting, sometimes almost beautiful atmosphere during the Blitz: 'an empty, dark city, torn with great explosions, racked with ack-ack fire, lit with lurid flames, acrid smoke, its air full of the dust of fallen buildings.' A sight of 'monstrous loveliness' was how an American journalist described it, the city 'roofed over with a ceiling of pink that held bursting shells, balloons, flares and the grind of vicious engines. And in yourself the excitement and anticipation and wonder in your soul that this could be happening at all.'[35]

But it was for men-of-the-pen, not working women, to indulge in flights of fancy about the strange beauty of war. A reporter from the Mass Observation project noticed that 'this war has presented women immediately – and much earlier than in the 1914–18 struggle – with acute, far-reaching problems.' Women were made especially uneasy by the blackout. The 'woman in the street,' according to the report, 'is bearing the brunt of "this home-front war".'[36]

On top of her new job in the dispensary at University College Hospital, 1941 for Agatha was also filled with the physical labour of vacating, cleaning, and organising her too-many houses. In due course both Greenway and Winterbrook had to be packed up when they were taken over for military use. The servants of her youth were a distant memory. Even Carlo was now working in a munitions factory. Like most Britons, Agatha wasn't waxing lyrical about the colours of fire because she was exhausted.

Because the Lawn Road Flats were associated with socialists and spies, Agatha's residence there has led people to wonder whether she was a woman who perhaps knew too much. When her spy story *N or M?* came out in autumn 1941, it drew suspicion from the authorities for featuring a character called Major Bletchley. The top-secret work of breaking German codes had been going on since January 1940 at the Bedfordshire outstation of MI6 named Bletchley Park, and the name seemed a dangerously revealing coincidence. What alarmed MI5 even more was the fact that Bletchley codebreaker and classicist 'Dilly' Knox, who'd been involved in discovering the secrets of the Enigma machine, knew Agatha well.

Knox was now questioned about a possible security breach, and was told to ask Agatha to tea and to quiz her – without revealing his purpose – on how she'd come to select Major Bletchley's name. But Agatha told him the unexciting truth: she'd once been stuck on a delayed train at Bletchley station, a wait so boring it made her think 'Bletchley' suitable for a boring character.[37] So Bletchley Park's secrets were safe.

Agatha would continue to work at University College Hospital for three years, putting in two whole days and three half-days each week. 'Few people,' recalled a colleague, knew there was 'such a famous person dispensing in the out-patients' department.' Agatha liked chatting to patients through a pigeonhole that kept her safely invisible. On top of her regular hours, she'd telephone 'every morning to ask whether any of the staff were missing, in which case she would arrive post-haste from Hampstead to help'.[38]

Whenever she wasn't at the hospital, Agatha was writing. Another Mass Observation report found her consistently popular for air-raid reading: 'of detective authors mentioned, Agatha Christie certainly tops the poll at the moment.' One widowed lady of fifty explained the appeal: 'I like to have to concentrate. The suspects, and working it all out – you know – it soothes your nerves.'[39] Encouraging sales reports came in from America too. *Roger Ackroyd* was still selling 'at the rate of approximately 5,000 a month'.[40]

During this period, Agatha produced a whole run of brilliant books: *The Moving Finger*, *The Body in the Library*, *Towards Zero* and *Five Little Pigs*. The first two are classic detective stories, whereas the two latter introduce a more impressionistic tone, a move away from the 'rules' of the 'Golden Age'. In *Five Little Pigs,* the murder takes place in the distant past, and Poirot has to diagnose the nature of the relationships involved. It's the favourite Poirot story of many who prefer her in this looser, more 'psychological' mode. As we'll see, though, when Agatha was once again thinking and writing about psychology, it meant that not all was well in her own mind.

Of her wartime novels, only *N or M?* explicitly addresses the conflict: partly because of her publishers' requests for escapism, and partly because, for Agatha, subjects were best approached sideways on. *The Moving Finger*, for example, is a story where the war is present but offstage, as the action begins with a plane crash. While it's not spelt out, the Battle of Britain comes immediately to mind. The hero is forced to retreat from the masculine world to live with his sister in a small town with 'absolute rest and quiet'. Just what Blitzed Britain itself most desired.

J.C. Bernthal points out that Agatha's wartime oeuvre of novels included no fewer than fourteen female victims, in comparison to the three female victims in the whole of the 1920s. And the extreme femininity of some of these bodies is important too. The female body provides the key to the mystery in *Evil under the Sun*, where another woman impersonates the gorgeous suntanned actress, Arlena Stuart. And in *The Body in the Library* – 'the best opening I ever wrote,' Agatha thought – a chorus girl in a backless evening dress is discovered, dead, in Colonel and Mrs Bantry's library.[41] It's when Miss Marple notices the corpse's scruffy fingernails that she begins to realise the glamour girl is in fact a glammed-up Girl Guide.[42] Contriving a change of appearance was on many women's minds in a decade when drawing on the seam with a pencil became an alternative to wearing unobtainable silk stockings. Just as with the previous war, Agatha had returned, consciously or not, to what her readers required: a rest from violent masculinity.

But the critic Peter Keating finds it equally significant that the stresses of war emerged in Agatha's work through a fictional return to the analyst's couch. The wartime years saw the reappearance of Miss Marple, not only as a righter-of-wrongs, but also as a prober of the mind. *The Body in the Library* (1942) sees Miss Marple interpret a friend's dream to reveal her fears about her husband. She counsels the damaged hero in *The Moving Finger* (1943), just as a psychotherapist might, and she summons up the heroine's suppressed memories in *Sleeping Murder* (c. 1942) in order to heal.

Agatha Christie may have looked like she was long healed from the traumas of 1926. But this was not in fact completely true. The wartime years were in danger of bringing back her feelings of insecurity and depression.[43]

And Agatha was not only worried about herself, and about Max, but also – even particularly – about her daughter.

28

A Daughter's a Daughter

In the summer of 1940, as the fall of France drew near, Agatha was surprised when Rosalind suddenly announced that she'd changed her mind about a plan to join the Auxiliary Territorial Service or ATS.

'I've thought of something better to do,' the twenty-year-old mysteriously announced. The something, it turned out, was to get married. This explained the cigarette ends that had been mounting up by the telephone at Greenway during those long conversations.

Hubert de Burgh Prichard was a professional soldier in the Royal Welch Fusiliers. On 29 May 1940, many of his colleagues, though not Hubert's particular battalion, were involved in the evacuation from Dunkirk. On 11 June, in an atmosphere of desperate peril for Britain, Rosalind married him.

Thirty-three-year-old Hubert, tall, distinguished-looking, his dark hair brushed back, was a quiet man, the wearer of a monocle and a lover of greyhounds. In 1939 *Tatler* had published a poignant photo of him with the rest of his cricket team. All these young men were about to be called upon to serve.

Hubert, however, was used to it. He'd become a career soldier after Sandhurst, spending time in Gibraltar, Hong Kong, Lucknow and, most recently, Sudan.[1] Born at Pwllywrach, his family's manor house in Glamorgan, South Wales, the young Hubert's coming-of-age was celebrated with a dinner for ninety tenants and estate employees. Their gift to the young master was an inscribed gold watch.[2]

Rosalind met Hubert through her Aunt Madge at Abney. She was going up in the world. Her fiancé was more firmly a member of the landed gentry than any other member of the Miller or Christie clans. Nevertheless, Rosalind was rather unwilling to have even her mother present at the makeshift wartime wedding, with its shades of Agatha's own ill-fated first marriage. It was held in the registrar's office of Denbigh, North Wales, near Hubert's regiment's head-quarters at Wrexham.

Agatha wished she'd had 'a greater chance to know him better', for she suspected Hubert was a 'dear person', with 'a great vein, not exactly of poetry, but of something of that kind in him.' She worried, though, that he had some fatal flaw: 'not exactly melancholy, but that touch or look of someone who is not fated for long life.'

This wedding, about which all parties seemed just a little bit ambivalent, passed off like so many other weddings of 1940 with 'the minimum of *fuss!*' 'They wanted to keep it very quiet,' Agatha told Cork, 'I only hope he comes through safely.'[3] If she was pained by her daughter's swift and secret decision, the veteran of two swift and secret weddings of her own could hardly complain.

Yet the marriage is presented in Agatha's autobiography almost as a 'solution' to the 'problem' of what Rosalind was to do with her life. She had no real passion or plan. The picture Agatha paints of her daughter is funny, affectionate, but devastating. Rosalind is presented as a little machine, relentlessly secretive, humourless. Her daughter, Agatha says, has 'the valuable role in life of eternally trying to discourage me without success'.

It was hard to say exactly what motivated Rosalind. She herself described her chief characteristic as 'criticising others' and when asked who she'd rather be if not herself, she answered 'I don't care.'[4]

Poor Rosalind seems to have internalised the fact that she was less impressive, less important, than her mother. 'Has no personality,' her perceptive Benenden housemistress had written, 'appears to have no interests or enthusiasms at present beyond a mild wish to enjoy herself. I feel sure that with her brains she could develop something more than this.'[5] Agatha, who'd had such an informal education, had given her daughter something considerably better. But she'd failed to give Rosalind the space and stability in which to bloom into a separate individual. Rosalind was doomed to live in her mother's shadow.

When it came to work, Rosalind considered becoming a Land Girl, but made no decisions. Her friend Susan had taken what their parents considered a wrong turn, and was living with a married man. 'He is supposed to be divorcing his wife,' Agatha noted, 'she does all the housework & cooking etc.'[6] Yet Rosalind, drifting, was in no more satisfactory a situation. Historian Anne de Courcy points out that the debutantes of the late 1930s, like Rosalind, found 'the contrast between their peacetime lives and the war was sharper than for any other section of British society.'[7] Some found it liberating. But others found it overwhelming.

As Rosalind teetered on the threshold of adult life, she feared becoming her mother's stand-in for Carlo. 'Without Miss Fisher, I lose *everything!!*' Agatha complained. There was clearly a gap to be filled. 'I hope I shall have Ros to help me,' she wrote, when practical tasks needed completing at Greenway, 'run her down there by the scruff of the neck if necessary!'[8] But Rosalind instead spent her time 'roaming all over England leaving a trail of cigarette ash behind'.[9]

Many girls of Rosalind's class were brought up in material comfort but with a certain emotional chilliness. As the single child of a single mum, Rosalind definitely had a closer relationship with her mother than did many of her peers. Yet even Rosalind had been left behind, as a tiny child, while Agatha and Archie went away on their Grand Tour for nine months. On their return the little girl had treated her parents, as Agatha explains, 'as strangers with whom she was unacquainted. Giving us a cold look, she demanded: "Where's my Auntie Punkie?"'

Rosalind's 'secrecy', as Agatha describes it in her autobiography, also reads as defensiveness, a legitimate concern about being made fun of. In her book about archaeological life, Agatha describes saying goodbye to her fourteen-year-old: 'we climb into the Pullman, the train grunts and starts – we are OFF. For about forty-five seconds I feel terrible, and then as Victoria Station is left behind, exultation springs up once more.'[10]

Even though this is clearly Agatha's ironic take on life, perhaps Rosalind felt sad to read that her mother missed her so little. Rosalind's lack of candour in her surviving letters makes her seem defensive, someone who'd perhaps see marriage as a means of escape. After all, Max could see a certain pragmatism about his stepdaughter. 'She is more grown up than you isn't she?' he once wrote to Agatha.[11]

Would all this make Agatha that endlessly satisfying target to aim at, the 'bad mother'? Of course not, for there is no such thing as a 'bad mother'. There are just plain 'mothers', who sometimes have good days, and sometimes bad. But Agatha was an unusual mother, and it's one of the things that makes her interesting. She never felt she *had* to throw herself into mothering; she watched herself doing it, and wrote about it honestly, good and bad. Some of her most thoughtfully depicted relationships are those between mothers and daughters.

Yet her lack of conventional maternal qualities becomes one of the things that 'counts against' Agatha in the negative portrayals of her life. It was an issue at parties: 'I said something to her about my children, and you could tell she wasn't remotely interested,' said one person who met her, 'one of my friends even asked who the difficult woman was.'[12] Oh, the 'difficult woman'. How hard she tries to pass for normal, how severely she gets judged for her failures.

After her marriage, Rosalind had a new home with Hubert's mother and sister at the Prichards' seventeenth-century manor house. She still saw her mother on trips to London, and they spent time together lumping possessions from house to house.

From February 1942, Agatha had all the more time to fret about Rosalind, because another change was coming. Max volunteered to go abroad. He was to establish an outpost of the Directorate of Allied and Foreign Liaison in Cairo. During a cold spring, Agatha and Max spent his embarkation leave at Greenway, planting trees, Max recording in his notebook the late flowering of the camellias, magnolias and primroses.[13]

Agatha's autobiography, which paints even dark experiences in light colours, suggests that her upper lip remained stiff. But in her letters to her agent from 1942 onwards, and in her many, many letters to Max in Cairo and then other North African postings, she reveals terrible loneliness.

In years to come, Agatha would openly celebrate the post-menopausal state and how it renewed interest in the impersonal pleasures of life. From this, we can read that in the early 1940s she was probably experiencing not only war and isolation but also hormone changes. From the other side, she'd come to write of the 'second blooming that comes when you finish the life of the emotions and of personal relations: and suddenly find – at the age of fifty, say – that a whole new life has opened before you.'

But Agatha in 1942 wasn't quite there yet. Her letters to Max show her mental health was deteriorating without him by her side. She had dreams of abandonment: 'they told me that you no longer cared or wanted me and had gone away and I woke up in a panic.'[14] 'I have been sad tonight,' she'd write, 'and cried.'[15]

Yet, in a horrible way, the stress was good for her creatively. The middle years of the 1940s, such a trying time, would also see some of the most intense writing experiences of her life.

Meanwhile, what about Max's escape to the sunshine? He lived at first in the Continental Hotel in Cairo, with its famous rooftop restaurant. Cairo was now swollen by 35,000 British and Empire troops. Remote from the Blitz, it had something of a party atmosphere.[16]

Agatha longed for nothing more than to go to join her husband. She tried hard to find writing work that would take her to Egypt. She badgered Cork into getting the *Saturday Evening Post* to commission some articles, but in the end bureaucracy and her gender prevented her from going. Brendan Bracken, Minister of Information, had to pass on the disappointing news that the War Office's 'reluctance to accredit women correspondents remains unchanged'.[17]

All Agatha could do was read and reread Max's flimsy aerogram letters, and she began to worry that they might grow apart. 'I feel so afraid sometimes,' she wrote to him, 'write often, because I need cheering when there are no sunny days – Oh! To be in Egypt now that winter is here!'[18]

Her worries are understandable. Max was in a sunny city stuffed with British people without their families, facing danger, most of them under thirty, and so highly sociable that a middle-class white woman could dine out in restaurants with a different man paying the bill each evening for months. And Max wasn't always a diligent correspondent. 'I too miss you a lot but I have not had the time to mope,' he said, when he did deign to write, 'I have been too busy.'[19] At thirty-eight, after all, he was still right in the middle of what Agatha called the 'life of the emotions'.

One of the cleverest 'Christie tricks' is her manipulation of what we think about people by describing their appearances rather than their ages. This is obviously something Agatha thought about a good deal, having married a man many people would have considered inappropriately young.

In *Murder Is Easy* (1939), for example, the hero, a retired policeman, feels that he belongs to the generation of his 28-year-old girlfriend. It takes him some time to realise that the suspect, whom he sees as an 'old lady', is in fact more nearly his contemporary than his girlfriend, and that she too had once been considered attractive.

It would have been more conventional for Max in his late thirties to have been married not to Agatha, fourteen years older, but to Rosalind, fifteen years younger. If Agatha's life were one of her novels, then Max and Rosalind might well turn out to be a 'hidden couple'. Max's age meant that he and Rosalind's relationship was one of teasing equals, with occasionally fierce arguments. One of the things that Agatha recalled to the absent Max without fondness was 'you & Ros having rows'.[20]

Geographically separated, the three of them now had to re-estab-lish their relationship through the medium of letters: at least, when Max could be bothered. 'I am more really your friend than you might think,' he told Rosalind, 'from the little action I take to write to you.' He excused himself, rather unconvincingly, with the expla-nation that 'to those of whom I am really fond I find it difficult, really difficult to write.'[21]

On the other hand, he could also write surprisingly intimately to his stepdaughter: 'I have not changed towards you at all . . . long may I live to shake you, argue with you, criticise you, eat with you, quarrel with you, laugh with you, exchange ideas with you and find life more and more exciting because of you . . . I wonder if this embarrasses you at all.'[22] For my part, *I* wonder if Agatha ever read this particular letter from Max to her daughter, and I hope not.

One of the ways in which normal life seemed to recede ever further into the past was through losing Greenway. They had to face some 'unpleasant facts,' Agatha warned Max on 31 August 1942. 'The Admiralty are taking over Greenway . . . I hope they will let me keep two rooms (perhaps drawing room) to store furni-ture in.'[23] The task of packing stirred up old, dangerous memories of clearing out Ashfield. 'I am sick,' she wrote that autumn, 'of loading trunks and getting filthy with cobwebs etc & am generally fed up!'[24]

Around the time of giving up Greenway, Max wrote about money. 'How are your financial affairs,' he asked. 'You never speak of them . . . help yourself to anything in my bank if you need it.'[25] He was enjoying, for once, being the munificent one. Alone in Egypt, he was having to grow up. 'I know that I am doing a man's job,' he explained, 'it has been a leavening for my life, which always tends to take the easy path.'[26] It was Max's parents, though, rather than his wife, who were in most urgent need of his money. Max's father Frederick was charged in 1942 with trying to sell 1,224 tins of black-market canned plums.[27] Agatha tried to find work for Marguerite as a translator, but ended up simply giving her mother-in-law an allowance of £200 a year.

Because of the slow post, it was six months before Agatha received and replied to Max's question about her finances. By then her tax problems had escalated even further, with the British tax authorities wanting her to pay tax on the American earnings she hadn't even been able to take out of America. 'It is just like a nightmare,' wrote her British agent to her American one. 'I can quite understand your finding it hard to believe that Christie will have to find money for Income Tax on monies she has not received.'[28]

Yet Agatha shielded Max from reality. 'Worries, darling?' she replied to his query. 'As long as you are all right & happy I have no worries. My debts get more and more enormous but it doesn't seem to matter and I don't care. All worry of Greenway now off my hands – no bills, repairs, or gardeners!'[29]

But in this she was skating over a profound sadness about having to leave. She told Max how she'd taken a farewell look at the gardens:

> I walked up and sat on the seat overlooking the house and the river & made believe you were sitting beside me – it was very real – I felt we were there looking at the house together – it looked very white and lovely – serene & aloof as always. I felt a kind of pang over its beauty.[30]

Other members of the family were also experiencing the dislocations of war. Abney was likewise taken over by the military. 'Requisitioned!' Agatha told Max. '10 days notice! What a life!'[31] The Watts warehouse in Manchester was bombed, but its employees saved it from burning down by smothering the flames with the stored textiles it contained.

Madge, with the help of just a cook, now kept the fourteen-bedroom house going as an army billet. She would rise at five thirty and do the work that in Edwardian times had been done by sixteen servants: 'a kind of human dynamo' was how Agatha described her. According to family tradition, Madge would continue to indulge her theatrical instincts by dressing up and impersonating a maid to serve the officers living in her house. One morning, she found an unexploded bomb in the billiard room that had fallen through the roof in the night.

As the wartime years rolled past, Agatha's hoard of Max's tightly written airmail letters grew and grew. They were both aware that time was causing physical changes. 'I am still an awful gourmand-izer,' he admitted, describing an after-dinner snack of '<u>five</u> pancakes and a can of beer'.[32] In 1943, Max was posted to Libya, where he lived in a house with a garden of 'oleanders and bougainvillea'.[33] He was delighted to be near interesting ancient remains and wrote of plans to play hockey, although 'I expect I will be a bit short in the wind now'. But he also thought Agatha would be glad to hear he was 'getting much greyer'.[34]

Her main concern about their age difference, Agatha explained, had always been that it caused Max to miss out on experiences. When 'the wives of your friends were so young,' she told him, 'all with babies and young children and I minded − for *you* − that I should be so much older.'[35] When, on 6 May 1944, Max finally turned forty, Agatha was delighted: 'Darling! You are 40 today! Hurrah! At last! <u>Lots</u> of love to you − It makes a big difference to me − I feel it closes the gap a little − When you were in the thirties and I had reached the fifties it was pretty grim.'[36]

In May 1943, Max was still conducting his argument with Rosalind by infrequent letters. She'd failed to send him a birthday letter, he complained, but 'maybe I didn't deserve one . . . As a matter of fact I am still crackers about you and I think of you surpris-ingly often, just about every day! . . . I would like to come along and give you a good shaking.'[37] 'You have always meant a good deal to me and always will,' he promised, 'one of things I miss most in the war is the absence of beauty.'[38]

Max's letters verge on the inappropriate because he didn't really have the language for talking to anyone apart from male archaeolo-gists. But whatever the 23-year-old Rosalind may have made of her stepfather, she had other things to worry about. That same month, Agatha reported her daughter 'has unwillingly let slip the informa-tion that she is having a baby in Sept!! I am so happy about it . . .

secretive little devil – but I'm glad I didn't know before.' Rosalind had already had one miscarriage – just like Agatha herself. 'Do hope it will be all right this time,' Agatha prayed, 'she's well over the 3 month period.'[39]

In the late summer, as the Germans evacuated Sicily, and as the Allies bombed Italy, Rosalind retreated to Abney for the birth. 'Auntie Punkie' rather than her mother was the person who could be of the most practical help. 'I shall be so thankful when the baby has come,' wrote Agatha. She was hard at work in London where her stage play of *And Then There Were None* was about to open. Rosalind's pregnancy, Agatha said, was 'the one thing I want for her happiness . . . I know she'll be happy with a child – but if it should be stillborn or anything – I'm so afraid for her.'[40]

Rosalind's baby was late. After five days of waiting in a nursing home, she was discharged to sit it out at Abney, '& <u>was</u> she hopping mad!'[41] Despite all her fears, though, Agatha finally became a grandmother on 21 September 1943. Mathew Caradoc Thomas Prichard was 'a large boy . . . looking so like Hubert to my mind that all he needs is a monocle.' Agatha missed the first night of her play to rush north. Meanwhile Hubert, absent with his battalion in Northern Ireland, telephoned anxious questions. 'Does she like it?' Hubert asked. 'Tell him it's a monster,' said Ros. 'Far too big.' 'Is she getting cross again yet?' asked Hubert. 'I'll feel she's all right then!!' 'Oh darling Max – I am so happy.'[42]

'A boy too,' Max responded, 'really done the thing properly!'[43] He made a pompous effort to be amusing in his own letter of congratulation to Rosalind: 'the best news from home I have had in this war . . . don't bust the thing in the bath. I believe their arms are very fragile.'[44]

With her usual impassivity, Rosalind wrote back that 'I might make you a godfather but am not sure yet.'[45] So the triangular family developed a fourth corner – a baby who would in time bring them all closer together.

Yet Max in Africa, receiving his stream of loving letters from Agatha, did not perhaps quite realise that he himself was in some danger of being edged out. Just as when she'd been a divorcée in the 1920s, Agatha was now effectively a single woman in London. And she was still enormously attractive. To leave her unattended was to invite other suitors to gather.

29

Life Is Rather Complicated

Her new role of grandmother was one that Agatha embraced with joy. Her relationship with her daughter deepened now that Rosalind turned to her for childcare and practical help.

Rosalind and Mathew were due to go to live in Hubert's house in Wales, but while this was sorted out, mother and baby roosted in Agatha's property in Campden Street, London.

Agatha saw them every day. She slept at Carlo's nearby: her former employee had become a friend in need. Each morning Agatha would go over to Campden Street to do the work of the live-in maid and nanny who were no longer obtainable. She made breakfast and cleaned the bathroom, returning later to do dinner. 'My hands are like nutmeg graters from soda and soap,' she told Max, 'and my knees are sore.'[1]

When the sirens wailed, as they still often did, baby Mathew was put under the table. When he did finally acquire a professional nurse, Agatha still helped out. The new nurse saw the baby's grandmother not as a celebrated author, but as a domestic servant. When the nurse's family said they'd been to the theatre to see the massively popular *And Then There Were None* by one Agatha Christie, she responded: 'Ee, I know – she's our cook.'[2]

Despite Agatha's being helplessly in love with her grandson, war and work were beginning to tell. She suffered badly that winter of 1943 from flu. 'I don't know what is the matter with me,' she wrote, 'I'm so depressed – it is like a great black cloud . . . I just feel I don't want to go on – dread to-morrow coming. I have never felt it before.'[3] But she *had* felt it before, in that bad year of 1926. And the common factor was that then too she'd lacked the support of a spouse. This period of low spirits emerged in her fiction, when in *Sparkling Cyanide* Rosemary's 'depression after influenza' is taken as justification enough for her sudden and mysterious death.[4] 'It is not a real existence, somehow,' Agatha wrote of these later wartime years, 'as though I was "dimmed" like a headlight on a car.'[5]

Max, with his interesting work and Mediterranean lifestyle, was much better off. In Tripoli he'd become a political officer, helping with civilian 'food relief – the harvest, taxation, security, judicial, racial' as well as supporting the armed forces.[6]

Agatha had a long-running tease with Max about his 'girl-friends', who included her own friend Dorothy North, and she often nagged him to keep in touch with them. 'I must write to her and to all my girlfriends,' he dutifully agreed.[7] Agatha joked in 1943 that she could come out to Libya too, even 'if you've got wives living there'.[8] But the teasing stopped and she was genuinely hurt when Max failed to write for a whole month, and then went on a month's leave in Cairo. News of his leave gave her 'a terrible pang,' she complained, 'your leave ought to be with me.'[9] 'You are a dirty dog,' she wrote in another letter. 'I feel I am getting out of touch with you . . . the thought of another lonely winter ahead gets me down badly.'[10] 'Have a good time, darling,' she implored him, almost washing her hands of him, 'do <u>anything</u> that you want to and you need – just so long as I am held in your heart in deep friendship and affection and very close.'[11]

Agatha had to turn elsewhere for the conversation and support she required. And it was to a friend of Max's that she turned, as her separation from her husband dragged on into its second and then its third year.

Max's old friend Stephen Glanville was ten years younger than Agatha. He had an elfin face, large eyes and spectacles. A sensitive, articulate person, he suffered from migraines and enjoyed talking about relationships. Stephen's wife Ethel and their two children were safely in Canada. Left alone in London, Stephen acted rather like a single man about town, while continuing to serve in his Air Force role of liaising with Britain's allies. With his tact and eloquence, it's a job he did very well.

Stephen was another person to whom Agatha tried to get Max to write. He 'will be really hurt if you don't keep in touch,' she told her husband, 'he's a sensitive person and minds about things.'[12]

Stephen and Agatha were spending more and more time together. When she attended a public lecture he gave, she enjoyed it immensely: 'didn't realise what an attractive <u>voice</u> he has'. Typically, he said afterwards he'd been 'feeling very ill – that explained the gentle melancholy which I had thought such an artistic touch!'[13] Food was central to Stephen and Agatha's relationship:

> He would call for me at the Hospital and take me back to his house at Highgate to dine. We usually celebrated if one or other of us had received a food parcel.
>
> 'I've got some butter from America – can you bring a tin of soup?'
>
> 'I've been sent two tins of lobster, and a whole dozen eggs – *brown*.'

Agatha told Max about a meal she'd cooked for Stephen in her tiny kitchen at Lawn Road: 'a very good dinner, I thought (& he seemed to!) Some pâté (ersatz but I incorporated some truffles in it to create the right illusion), a lobster stewed cherries.'[14] Of course, all Londoners had been obsessed with food since rationing was introduced in January 1940. But this was Max's territory; eating and talking about food was also one of the things he and Agatha most enjoyed.

In May 1943, Ethel Glanville returned from Canada, and Agatha couldn't help feeling that 'it will cramp his style!!'[15] She was right: Stephen now wanted free of his marriage, and was not thrilled 'at the prospect of having his family home'.[16] After a painful period, he left them and moved into a flat at Lawn Road.

By November 1943, Stephen had almost become Agatha's squire, accompanying her to the first night of her play *And Then There Were None*. He wrote to her afterwards in intimate terms:

Agatha darling – Last night was <u>really</u> something to remember . . . best of all was the diverse experience of Agatha: Agatha really nervous (as she must be till the show is over) – not just shy – even in the midst of close friends: Agatha in the moment of triumph, quite radiant, but still asking only for her friends, & incredibly unegotistical; & last, and perhaps most precious, Agatha still quietly excited, but beautifully poised and content, balanced between the success of the immediate achievement and the purpose to achieve more . . . bless you & thank you, my dear, for a never-to-be-forgotten night.[17]

The attraction, perhaps the danger, that Stephen might have held is all laid out there in that letter: the close attention, the perceptive flattery. He could not even speak of his special relationship with Agatha to other people, Stephen claimed, because he had no way of describing 'the subtler delight of the talking that completed our evening'.[18]

Agatha was highly vulnerable to this sort of thing. She wanted and needed human contact. 'I want to talk to you so much sometimes that I could scream!' she told Max. 'I hate these November days.'[19] Max was himself worried. 'I think you will be wise to have people you can talk to available and not to live alone,' he counselled her.[20] But it's not clear whether he would have wanted her to lean quite so heavily on Stephen.

Stephen was also attractively generous with his knowledge about archaeology. In 1929, he'd delivered the Royal Institution's Christmas lectures for children on Ancient Egyptian daily life. In odd moments he was still maintaining progress on his catalogue of the papyri in the British Museum. And now he roped Agatha into his campaign to publicise Ancient Egypt.

Stephen suggested that Agatha should write a mystery novel set in Egypt, which ended up as *Death Comes as the End*. While it's not particularly well known among Agatha's works, it's immensely significant. Having already made an early addition to the serial killer genre in *The ABC Murders*, with this book she'd now invent the sprawling genre of crime set in the past.[21]

The story was loosely inspired by the Heqanakht Papyri, the letters of a priest living near Thebes, which had been discovered in a tomb in the 1920s. Agatha used them to spin a historical tale about the priest's taking a young new wife who upset his family. She also wove in various artefacts from the British Museum: a toy lion with opening jaws; a bracelet with golden beasts.[22] And Stephen was given something no one else had ever been allowed: a say over the plot. This made him the 'only man ever to have persuaded Agatha to alter the end of a book'.[23] Ultimately, Agatha regretted this. 'I am sorry to say that I gave in to him,' she wrote. 'I was always annoyed with myself for having done so.'

And Max did sense something worrying about Stephen and Agatha's joint project. He expressed some unrecorded concern about the book, and Stephen replied crisply: 'I am not clear whether you are afraid that the book will damage her reputation as a detective story writer, or whether you think that archaeology should not demean itself by masquerading in a novel.'[24] He did his best to put to rest Max's fears that Agatha would make herself ridiculous. Stephen claimed the book contained just the right amount of Egyptian colour, 'an extraordinarily difficult thing to do, and she's brought it off'.[25]

But Max's concerns were justified, for when it was published there was some gatekeeping by archaeologists unwilling to have novelists invading their patch. There was a negative review in a journal of Egyptology. Even the super-loyal Rosalind, who'd become the fiercest guardian of her mother's literary legacy, couldn't find much to praise. She called it 'a bold attempt to portray life in ancient Egypt, which, I must admit, does not really work.'[26] The critic Edmund Wilson, famously, found this particular book 'of a mawkishness and banality which seem to me literally impossible to read'.

Agatha gave in to Stephen over the ending partly because he'd done so much research for the book. And his friendship came at a price. It was time-consuming and could be intrusive: he had an impressive 'readiness to interfere in matrimonial troubles'.[27] But neither was his interest in Agatha permanent. Soon his intense conversations with her were less about Ethel or Agatha herself and more about his new mistress, Margaret.

Stephen's 'life is rather complicated at present,' Agatha wrote in 1944.[28] She didn't approve of Margaret, who was herself married and unlikely to stick around: 'I think myself she would only divorce her husband and remarry with money!'[29] But it was Stephen's abandoned wife, left to look after their two daughters, who became the object of Agatha's deepest pity: 'I keep thinking of the wretched Ethel – more or less thrown out after 19 years – it really is too cruel.'[30]

And what was the probability that Agatha and Stephen ever went beyond conversation, as some writers have suggested? Extramarital affairs were quite outside Agatha's experience. In her plots, she never punished a female character for being sexually active. But neither was she any good at writing a steamy scene. It was clear, as she said, that she found romance 'a terrible bore in detective stories'. What really interested her about Stephen, as he talked through the twists and turns of his love life, were changing ideas about modern marriage.

Agatha had been personally affected by the relaxing of the divorce laws in the 1920s, and more upheaval was coming in consequence of the war. Historian Claire Langhamer describes a change in the contemporary ideal of marriage as the conflict drew towards a close. Companionship, or a marriage of equals, had been the goal of the more radical among Agatha's generation. And that was exactly what she'd found with Max. But now romantic love, an undivided devotion to 'the one', began to be considered central to the marriage contract. This new 'cult of romance' would come to mean, ironically, that premarital sex in the 1940s was less frowned upon. If people were in love, they simply couldn't help themselves.[31]

Glanville's influence is obvious in *Death Comes as the End*, but it's also there, more subtly, in another novel. *Five Little Pigs* (1942), also dedicated to him, is a Poirot story that has at its heart a commentary on the changing nature of marriage.

'I loved him,' says home-wrecker Elsa Greer of her married lover, 'I would have made him happy.' She felt completely justified in trying to take him away from his wife. Her point of view was that if a marriage had broken down, and 'if two people weren't happy together, it was better to make a break.'[32] Other characters strongly disagree with Elsa. But she represents the future. By 1969, towards the end of Agatha's life, this cult of romance within marriage meant that 'irretrievable breakdown' – the failure of romantic love – would eventually become accepted as grounds for divorce.[33]

But the role Stephen really played for Agatha was in providing the companionship and conversation Max had withdrawn by going abroad. Max mattered most. 'Everything else comes and goes,' Agatha told him, 'against the background of you.'[34] 'Oh! Max, how I would like a good *laugh* with you,' she wrote. 'I use Stephen a good deal – but it's not quite the same thing.'[35] And she also still had a strong physical longing for him, 'a feeling like an ache in one's middle with a corkscrew,' she explained, 'I have had all sorts of dreams of you lately – really very erotic and rude ones!! Particularly after all the years we've been married, I wouldn't have believed it! Nice, except that it's annoying to wake up. I miss your nice coarse conversations too!'[36]

Agatha was pleased when Stephen, looking 'terribly thin and unhappy', finally decided to go back to Ethel and 'to try and keep things together for the children'.[37] That particular drama was over, but the year 1944 would prove the worst of the war so far.

London was now menaced by the terrifying V1 flying bombs, and Hubert was taking part in the Allied invasion of France. He'd joined a new battalion engaged upon the Battle of Normandy following the D-Day landings. 'A lot of his brother officers have been killed,' Agatha told Max. 'How I hope and pray nothing will happen to him.'[38]

Hubert's letters home, though, were reassuringly full of descriptions of high jinks: while shaving, he'd spotted and captured a couple of German soldiers, and he'd performed an act of gallantry in retrieving a bottle of whisky from a jeep under fire. And Agatha's anxiety was eased by her magnificent grandson. 'I have got much too fond of him,' she wrote, closely observing him while babysitting. Mathew too was becoming copy. A 'minute portion of custard pudding is inserted into M's mouth. He sits sampling it with the expression of some old man tasting some doubtful port – turns it over and over in his mouth and finally decides . . . "not at all a bad wine, Sir" and swallows it.'[39] In his turn, Mathew's earliest memories would include taking his soft-toy elephants into Agatha's room, and 'being told fantasies about their life in the jungle by Nima in her bed'.[40] 'Nima', yet another in the succession of Agatha's different names, was how Mathew always referred to his grandmother.

With Hubert away, Rosalind was becoming anxious and overburdened. Her new home in Wales was large and decrepit. When Agatha visited, she found that her daughter 'never sits down,' and 'is infuriated if anyone else does.' Rosalind was turning into practical, bustling Madge, saying things like 'mother, what are you doing just wandering about, <u>singing</u> too!? There's lots to be done – we must <u>get on!</u>'[41] 'How difficult everything is nowadays with no <u>servants</u>,' Agatha complained, 'I really wonder how Rosalind stands up to it all.'[42]

But those, it turned out, were the good times. In August, Rosalind learned that Hubert had been reported missing in action. 'Poor child,' wrote Agatha, 'I am going down there right away . . . I feel so sick.' She understood at once that no displays of emotion would be welcome: 'I must be very offhand and confident with Ros. The only way to help her.'[43]

'She is wonderful,' Agatha wrote to Max, as August wore on, and no further news of Hubert came, 'never turns a hair – carries on exactly as usual – with food, dogs, Mathew – we act as though nothing has happened . . . But I can't bear the unhappiness for her. If only he is not killed . . . and not knowing for months is dreadfully hard.'

Finally, in October, they learned the worst. Hubert wasn't a prisoner. He had died on 16 August at Les Loges-Saulces in Calvados. He'd been leading a forlorn-hope rescue expedition through gathering darkness to pick up some men who'd been ambushed. Before he could save them, though, his tank was blown up. 'A gallant but senseless act,' thought his colonel.[44] Agatha could imagine the scene: 'I can just see him rushing off on his tank – eager and reckless – like a little boy.'[45] 'No letters, please, to his wife,' ran the announcement his family placed in the newspaper. It hardly says much. But given Rosalind's general wordlessness, it reads as a terrible howl of pain.

The worst part for Agatha, who'd never had the chance to know Hubert well, was Rosalind's grief. 'The saddest thing in life,' she wrote, 'is the knowledge that there is someone you love very much whom you cannot save from suffering . . . I thought, I may have been wrong, that the best thing I could do to help Rosalind was to say as little as possible, to go on as usual.' Living and inwardly grieving with Rosalind in her overlarge house in Wales was more tiring than Agatha had thought possible: 'I do wish Rosalind had someone with her.' She found a potential live-in helper, but the woman left the next day: 'said house was too big'.[46]

After her bereavement, Rosalind 'let it make no difference to her – took Mathew out to tea with some people as arranged – eats her meals well and calmly makes arrangements about obituary notices, etc.' Agatha was deeply concerned: 'so much bottling up must be bad'.[47] When Rosalind wrote to Max, she sounds empty: 'I never think at all nowadays and never read a book . . . I do not think you would find me a very interesting companion.'[48]

And this wasn't just bereavement for Rosalind, it was also the end of her independence. The one unexpected action of her life – a sudden and secret marriage – had led to a dead end. She would now, in her mother's testimony, often become an opaque or a negative presence, sucking the joy out of life. 'Shall get a good blast of destructive criticism from Rosalind, I expect,' Agatha wrote, despondently, after completing a piece of writing. 'If she says "Not at all bad, Mother," I shall go up in the air.'[49]

At the end of October Agatha returned from Wales to the hospital in London, where 'everyone keeps saying I look ill and tired'.[50] War and bereavement were not her only troubles. Despite Cork's complaints to the US tax authorities that his client was having to pay 'vast sums' of interest on her bank loans, her tax case had been put on hold until the end of hostilities.[51] 'I am fed up with being an author in America,' Agatha groused, 'most unfair to the writer who has done the work & delivered the goods.' She thought she might simply 'take a comfortable place as a cook & stop writing'.[52] She was also selling jewellery, silver and furniture to reduce her overdraft. In December she was as low as she had ever been. 'Write me some words of faith and courage,' she commanded Max, 'so that I shall have them to read if another bad spell comes.'[53]

The worry of war, Max's absence, bereavement, even the withdrawal of Stephen's attention: all must have put Agatha in fear for the balance of her mind. Carlo provided some evidence of Agatha's seeking further professional help in the 1940s, probably from Robert Cecil Mortimer, an author and psychoanalyst.[54]

The ghost of Mrs Teresa Neele had not quite yet been laid to rest.

30

By Mary Westmacott

Agatha had predicted that if 'anything happened' to Rosalind or to Max she'd be 'quite paralysed'.[1] When Rosalind was widowed, Agatha's prophecy came true. She couldn't work: 'writing seems very futile'.[2]

But the words would return. Agatha had always had one reliable way of escaping from wartime London: through losing herself in her writing. And, ultimately, writing would save her once again.

It was only in retrospect she realised just how much she'd written in the wartime years: 'an *incredible* amount of stuff'. And looking back at the pattern of her life, difficult times personally were times of creativity for Agatha Christie the artist. She invented Poirot during the intensity of the First World War, produced *Roger Ackroyd* in the dog days of her marriage, invented Miss Marple in the aftermath of her mental illness.

'Writing during the war,' Agatha remembered afterwards, 'I cut myself off into a different compartment of my mind. I could live in the book.' In her Lawn Road flat, the trees outside tapping at the windows, the conditions for productivity were perfect. The flat was quiet, if cold. Agatha needed her hot-water bottle and warm clothes. 'I like to think of you with the thick woolly Jaeger's dressing gown I gave you,' wrote Max, 'my woolly bear!'[3]

'I am doing a lot of writing just now,' she told him in April 1943.[4] When she needed a break, she could flop into the distinctive bendy-looking plywood seat called the 'Isokon Long Chair'. One of these chairs, designed to provide 'scientific relaxation to every part of the body', was supplied to each flat in Lawn Road. Agatha told Max she'd sometimes 'lie back in that funny chair here which looks so peculiar and is really very comfortable', and imagine being with him in Greece.[5]

As well as detective novels, Agatha's work at Lawn Road included the strand of writing that perhaps mattered to her the most. It was a series of novels about which we've heard something so far, but not enough: novels published under the pseudonym Mary Westmacott. Mary was Agatha's own middle name, and 'Martin West' had been the pseudonym she'd originally wanted to use before her publishers talked her out of it; switch a few letters around and you have Mary Westmacott.

Agatha once explained why she used a different name for books that were neither detective stories nor thrillers. Of course, now that she was Agatha Mallowan, 'Agatha Christie' was itself a pen-name. But on top of that, she explained, it's 'better to keep the two sorts of books separate. I like keeping them to myself, too, so I can write exactly what I like.'

Part of Agatha's pleasure in publishing books anonymously was her feeling that 'you can write a bit of your own life into them'.[6] She was quite open about her use of real life as 'colour' even in her detective stories, putting the unpleasant Major Belcher, from the tour around the world, for example, into a story as the villain in *The Man in the Brown Suit*. But under the privacy of a pseudonym, she could go even further.

The main reason anyone reads Mary Westmacott today is for what she reveals about the life and opinions of Agatha Christie. *Unfinished Portrait* in particular records the experience of an upbringing and a marital breakdown similar to Agatha's own. In its heroine, Celia, Max thought, 'we have more nearly than anywhere else a portrait of Agatha'.[7]

The blurred line between fact and fiction in these novels is also a reminder that the autobiography itself is a compendium of a novelist's dramatised memories of people and places. There's an almost exact overlap between certain stories that appear in Agatha's autobiography, and scenes from the Westmacotts, particularly the earlier ones. For example, the character Nell's wartime work as a nurse in *Giant's Bread* is shot through with parallels to Agatha's own experience as recorded in her autobiography.

You can see the growing influence of 'Mary Westmacott' in even the Agatha Christie detective novels from 1930 onwards, as psychology came to intrigue her more than plot. With the passage of time, Agatha wrote in 1946, she'd become more interested 'in the preliminaries' of crime. The interplay of character on character, the deep smouldering resentments and dissatisfactions that do not always come to the surface.'[8] This is noticeable in her more character-driven detective novels, such as *Five Little Pigs*, or *The Hollow*. In the latter, for example, murderess Gerda is driven mad by her narrow life and her demanding, faithless husband: 'the whole world had shrunk to a leg of mutton getting cold on a dish'.[9] Agatha was really raring to write in the voice of Mary Westmacott and to drop the detective element altogether. She was dissatisfied with Poirot's presence in *The Hollow*, feeling – rightly – that he wasn't needed. 'Poirot is rather insufferable,' she complained. 'Most public men are who have lived too long. But none of them like retiring!'[10]

Agatha's flat at Lawn Road gave her not only time to write herself whole once again, but also the necessary solitude. And a period of solitude provided the hinge upon which her next Westmacott story would turn. Contrary to her detective novel practice, which involved a long period of plotting, she wrote it all in a rush. Indeed, she found herself growing obsessed. 'It's astonishing,' she wrote of non-detective fiction, 'how one always wants to do something that isn't quite one's work. Like papering walls – which one does exceedingly badly, but enjoys because it doesn't count as work.'[11]

Absent in the Spring is 50,000 words long, yet Agatha wrote it in just three days. On the third day, she even failed to go to her work at the hospital, 'because I did not dare leave my book . . . I had to go on until I had finished it.' She sat there writing, 'in a white heat', after which:

I don't think I have ever been so tired. When I finished, when I had seen that the chapter I had written earlier needed not a word changed, I fell on my bed, and as far as I remember slept more or less for twenty-four hours straight through. Then I got up and had an enormous dinner, and the following day I was able to go to the Hospital again.

I looked so peculiar that everyone was upset about me there. 'You must have been really ill,' they said, 'you have got the most enormous circles under your eyes.'[12]

Despite this, it had been an exhilarating experience. *Absent in the Spring*, to Agatha, was 'the one book that has satisfied me completely . . . the book that I had always wanted to write.'

To my mind, *Absent in the Spring* is one of the very best Westmacotts. The heroine, Joan, has something of Agatha's own duality: 'cheerful, confident, affectionate . . . bright and efficient and busy, so pleased and successful,' as her husband puts it. But he knows – and Joan comes to suspect – that beneath her shell she is lonely, and sometimes cold and hard and wrong. 'Hitler would never *dare* to go to war' is just one of her strongly worded, wrongheaded statements.[13] Living in the dark, deceiving herself, Joan is excluded from the grace of God. The flip-flopping between the two views of Joan is brilliantly done, an extended riff on the kind of contrasting views of the same character that form such an essential part of Agatha's murder mysteries. She wanted the story to develop 'lightly, colloquially, but with a growing feeling of tension, of uneasiness, the sort of feeling one has – everyone has, sometime, I think – of *who am I?*' In the story, Agatha's motif of the stranger, the Gun Man, once again appears. But this time, within the narrator's own heart.

Agatha's interest in psychology surfaces once more in my other favourite Westmacott, *A Daughter's a Daughter* (1952). In this story, a truth-telling character, Laura, is herself a psychologist. The plot features a mother who sacrifices an intimate relationship for her daughter's benefit, only to find that her daughter will never understand or repay the debt. It has a more satisfactory plot than some other Westmacotts because in its original form it was written *as a play* in the 1930s, which demanded pace and resolution. Theatre historian Julius Green argues that it should sit among Agatha's other, forgotten plays about the nature of marriage and the burdens it places upon women. Because of the tension in the plot between the mother and daughter, it's often been read as a commentary on the difficult relationship between Agatha and Rosalind. But that makes no sense once you understand it was written when Rosalind was still a small child.[14] It's less about Rosalind than about Agatha herself.

'What do you know of life?' asks the play's dark, damaged hero. 'Less than nothing. I can take you places, sordid horrible places, where you'll see life running fierce and dark, where you can feel – *feel* – till being alive is a dark ecstasy!'[15]

Archie Christie probably spoke less articulately, but no less convincingly, in a Torquay drawing room.

In *The Rose and the Yew Tree* of 1947, Agatha had set herself another difficult challenge: to show how potent erotic love could be. In this story, sexual desire has the power to change a bad man into a good one. Critic Martin Fido describes the book as 'a daring attempt to justify the miraculous ways of God to man in a rationalist materialist age'.[16] It was indeed daring, but ends up as unconvincing. Agatha's publisher, Collins, didn't like the novel either, on the grounds that it was a shame that the hero, who was standing as a candidate for the Conservatives, was such a nasty man. Agatha had some insight into a politician's life as her nephew, Jack, was involved in politics and would go on to become a Tory MP.

The Westmacotts are definitely uneven in quality, but their reception was also damaged by their female authorship and subject matter: 'somewhat juvenile romantic novels' was one conclusion by a male critic.[17] Yet they'll always have their supporters, especially among people who aren't ashamed to enjoy middlebrow mid-century writers like Monica Dickens or Dorothy Whipple. 'Mary Westmacott's work was mishandled,' thought American crime novelist Dorothy B. Hughes. 'There was always the addition of that disparaging throwaway line, "not very good, woman-type stuff". Woman-type indeed!'[18]

Rosalind, perceptively, claimed the Westmacotts 'have been described as romantic novels but I don't think it is really a fair assessment. They are not "love stories" in the general sense of the term, and they certainly have no happy endings. They are, I believe, about love in some of its most powerful and destructive forms.'[19]

But writing about love was not what was expected of Agatha Christie. After Collins' cool reception of *The Rose and the Yew Tree*, 'Mary Westmacott' parted ways with her publisher. 'Collins never have appreciated the lady,' Agatha complained to Edmund Cork, '*Do* let M.W. be published by someone else.'[20] So Westmacott moved to Heinemann.

Yet Agatha's career under her pen-name had a major setback in February 1949 when *The Sunday Times* revealed who Westmacott really was. Some people had known for a long time: Max had been let into the secret early on, and Agatha's sister-in-law Nan had simply guessed from the style of the writing. But *The Sunday Times* got onto the story via an American review of *Absent in the Spring* by a journalist who'd uncovered the secret from the records of the US Copyright Agency.

Agatha was devastated. It must have felt like the time she'd been exposed in the press before, when she'd 'felt like a fox, hunted'. 'I am sick of opening letters about it,' Agatha wrote, growing almost incoherent with annoyance: 'the people I really minded knowing about it were my friends (cramping to ones subject matter) its really all washed up.'[21]

After this incident, Agatha retreated further into privacy and secrecy about her work and her process. 'Jane Marple does not exist in the flesh,' she stoutly denied in later life, 'she is entirely a creation of the brain.'[22] This is simply not true: she'd earlier admitted that Miss Marple did contain snippets from her experience and memories of Auntie-Grannie. But in later life, she categorically refused to let other people into her mind.

Knowing her cover would no longer protect her, Agatha produced her last ever Westmacott title, *The Burden*. She wrote the book secretly, pleasurably, having 'knocked it off without saying a word to anyone,' according to Cork. But even he was lukewarm: 'it is not the major Westmacott which she has been thinking about for some time . . . the ending will pretty certainly be altered.'[23] After this Agatha retired her alter ego.

Agatha often and strongly claimed to be a craftsperson rather than an artist, and insisted that writing was a labour. But in unguarded moments, she did sometimes reveal it was also a labour of love. Nothing reveals this more clearly than those three burning wartime days in which she produced *Absent in the Spring*.[24]

'How sad it will be when I can't write any more,' she mused. She might well have been thinking of *Absent in the Spring*: 'written with integrity, with sincerity, it was written as I meant to write it, and that is the proudest joy an author can have . . . sometimes I think that is the moment one feels nearest to God, because you have been allowed to feel a little of the joy of pure creation.'

Perhaps the defining image of Agatha Christie should not be the one she presented to her neighbours at Lawn Road: that 'cuddly-looking, comfortable lady'. Behind the closed door of her modernist flat, bombs falling outside, Agatha was more like one of the most striking of her Mary Westmacott characters, Vernon of *Giant's Bread*.

Vernon is a passionate artist, intent upon creativity:

Vernon gave a sigh of relief.
There was nothing now to come between him and his work.
He bent over the table.[25]

❖ PART EIGHT ❖

Taken at the Flood – 1950s

31

A Big Expensive Dream

On 30 April 1945, Hitler committed suicide in Berlin. One chilly evening a few weeks later, Agatha was in her kitchen at Lawn Road when she heard a peculiar noise in the corridor outside. She looked up from the kippers she was frying, wondering what it could be. Opening the door, she found a figure burdened with luggage, 'clanking things hung all over him'. It was Max.

'What on earth are you eating?' asked Max.

'Kippers,' I said. 'You had better have one.' Then we looked at each other. 'Max!' I said. 'You are two stone heavier.'

'Just about. And you haven't lost any weight yourself,' he said.

But nothing else had changed. It was as if he hadn't been away. 'What a wonderful evening it was! We ate burnt kippers, and were happy.' It was just as Agatha had predicted in one of her letters: 'lovely times we shall have when we are together again – how we shall eat!! . . . chairs covered with books and a lot of laughing – And we will talk and talk and talk.'[1]

With the coming of peace, the Mallowans went 'gently' into the post-war world, 'thankful to be together, and tentatively trying out life, to see what we would be able to make of it.' At fifty-four, Agatha was ready to reinvent herself. She'd had enough of being a harried professional in a London flat, and Devon was calling her back home.

She once had a character say that women get better with age: 'a man of sixty is usually repeating himself like a gramophone record . . . a woman of sixty, if she's got any individuality at all – is an interesting person.'[2] After midlife, Agatha said, 'you are free again to look about you . . . as if a fresh sap of ideas and thoughts was rising in you . . . one's thankfulness for the gift of life is, I think, stronger and more vital during those years than it ever has been before. It has some of the reality and intensity of dreams.' More than forty years have passed since these words of Agatha's were published, but it's still unusual to read such an open celebration of a woman's life after menopause. And Agatha's actions mattered even more than her words. Her achievements in her own later life would put an indisputably older woman at the heart of popular culture.

But her next creative project wasn't a book. It was a house. On Christmas Day 1945, Greenway was derequisitioned. You can see the powerful pull of the place as Agatha slips it into her 1946 novel *The Hollow*: the 'white graceful house, the big magnolia drawing up to it, the whole set in an amphitheatre of wooded hills'.[3] The family who own the house in the story find it a potent influence in their lives.

Leaving Greenway and its gardens had been a poignant experience; so too was returning after the war. 'It was wild, wild as a beautiful jungle,' Agatha recalled, 'it was sad in many ways to see it like that, but its beauty was still there.' Now repairs were made and the gardens replanted. After the upheaval of the war, Greenway was the place where the family came to heal.

Agatha wasn't the only person in Britain turning with relief to domesticity. In 1943, 80 per cent of married women had been doing war work. By 1951, though, with the return of peace, only 34.7 per cent of *all* women were economically active. It's a figure that's astonishingly similar to the percentage of women who worked in 1931: 34.2 per cent.[4] In fact, a sociological study of women's lives published in 1956 begins with a bold statement. 'The cleavage between the two worlds of job and home,' the writers declare, is 'more complete today than it ever was in the past.'[5] Agatha *would* return to her work, but it slipped down her priority list. In the later 1940s, her most creative self was dedicated to making her house beautiful.

In general, the mansion had been well looked after by its American naval occupants. Fifty-one members of the US Coast Guard had slept three or four to a room. 'We were immensely impressed,' wrote one of them, 'by the huge mahogany <u>throne</u>', meaning the magnificent first-floor toilet.[6] Many of these sailors were from Louisiana, and referred to their absent hostess as 'Aunt Agatha'.[7] They'd been responsible for some of the boats taking infantry across the Channel on D-Day. Tessa Tattersall, a local child, remembers playing with the Americans, and enjoying their bounty: 'I recall being introduced to pineapple chunks, peach slices and halves and being given huge canisters of candies.'[8]

The Americans had used Greenway's library as a bar, and in it one of their number painted a frieze featuring a nude lady of the type also seen on the noses of wartime aeroplanes. On departing, they offered to paint it over. But Agatha asked them to leave it as a souvenir of their stay.

Because Greenway survives intact, because it is beautiful, and because the National Trust have lavished such care upon preserving it, people imagine that Agatha lived there for the rest of her life in ease and splendour.

In reality, though, this was only a holiday house, not used in winter. And it's hard to appreciate the number of wheels that had to be kept turning behind the scenes. Agatha could easily have gone somewhere smaller, and cheaper, and lived a leisurely life. Yet she loved being the hospitable country lady at Greenway so much that after a little break, she went back to producing the books to pay for it all.

Letters about what needed doing began to arrive with depressing regularity. There was a discouraging report concerning the water supply: 'cattle would appear to be drinking from it.'[9] It quickly became obvious that thirty-three acres of gardens would be costly to run for pleasure. Instead, Agatha tried to set up a market gardening business in the sunny walled kitchen garden. One Mrs MacPherson was employed to drive the produce to customers, to keep the accounts, and do 'practical work in greenhouses'. She was also given accommodation at Ferry Cottage.[10]

Cork tried to keep his distance from Greenway, but he was once forced to make an emergency visit when Agatha was away. He both understood what she was trying to do, and despaired at the scale of the task. 'I have never seen anything so lovely as Greenway,' he wrote,

> the freshness and the graciousness of everything was a dream; but it is a big expensive dream . . . the tax people are unconvinced that the present basis is a reasonable commercial one, and I am of the same opinion.[11]

Even though Cork was 'just' a literary agent, he found he was growing more and more engaged with Agatha's life. Her requests – for rare books, for maple sugar, for theatre tickets – became notorious among his staff. 'These chores for Agatha can be the devil,' one of them complained.[12]

And Cork became aware the employment of Mrs MacPherson had been disastrous. Unpaid bills for all sorts of items she'd ordered started to arrive at his office. Eventually, after she had run up £800 of debt in Agatha's name, it turned out the poor woman had a gambling problem, and attempted to commit suicide.

Cork also found fault with the enthusiastic but unbusinesslike head gardener, Bert Brisley. After the MacPherson affair, Brisley too got the sack, to be replaced by the highly skilled Frank Lavin. When Agatha won eighteen first prizes in the Brixham Horticultural Society Show, she was asked for the secret of her success. 'A first-class gardener,' she replied.[13]

The house at Greenway gradually filled up with the fruits of one of Agatha's main vices: shopping. Despite her tax problems, she simply could not restrain her magpie love of old furniture, ceramics and silver, modern art. The house became a treasure trove of quirky, pretty things, crammed together indiscriminately. A page chosen at random from one inventory reads: '12″ bronze bull on oak stand / China skull with frog lid / 2 Rockingham Cottage ornaments / Pair of Chinese brass hatchets decorated imitation rubies.'[14] Greenway was becoming more and more like Ashfield.

The food, some of it made by Agatha herself, also harked back to the Edwardian magnificence of the Millers. 'I like sauces,' she explained, 'it's nice to think up something with shellfish and avocado.'[15] 'How would it appeal to you to come about 8.30 and eat a *Great Deal* of Caviare?' ran one invitation to a friend.[16] But now Agatha was mainly glad to stay out of the kitchen. She was thrilled when she found a new cook: 'Her vol a vents!! Her Souffles!'[17] 'I ate too much,' she says, unrepentant, for 'what is life without an orgy now & then?!'[18]

Agatha now completely ignored any social pressure to watch her weight. A goddaughter, meeting her after a long absence, said 'with devastating frankness . . . You're *fat*. I remember you as thin!'[19] In the years of rationing, the height of luxury was rich food. A lunch in 1952 saw Agatha ordering lobster thermidor (lobster meat cooked in wine, mixed with a sauce made of Gruyère, egg yolk and brandy, placed back in the lobster's shell, and grilled) and Canapé Diane (buttered toast with bacon and chicken liver).[20]

Mathew recalled the afternoon ritual of the 1950s summers spent at Greenway: 'cream teas which Nima enjoyed even more than I did – she used to drink hers from a huge cup with *Don't be greedy* written on the outside; an injunction she never showed any sign of obeying.'[21] Agatha remained closely engaged in her grandson's fatherless life. Guests to Greenway were told the house rules: 'we do exactly what we like in this house. Most of us play cricket in the morning.' This was for Mathew's benefit, who grew better and better as the summers wore on, so much so that eventually he had to switch to playing left-handed with his grandmother and her friends.[22] ('Women don't play cricket,' says Inspector Kemp in *Sparkling Cyanide*. But Colonel Race replies, with a smile: 'Actually, a lot of them do.'[23])

In October 1949, Rosalind issued another unexpected invitation to her mother to attend a wedding. This second marriage of Rosalind's, at Kensington Register Office, was as quiet as her first.[24] She summoned her mother up to town for the occasion in her offhand way: 'it is a deep dark secret & no one is to know – I don't suppose anyone will enjoy it much but you have got to be there . . . you mustn't look too smart.'[25]

Rosalind's new husband was called Anthony Hicks. Trained as a barrister, though not active in his profession, Max thought him a man whose 'natural brilliance was unaccompanied by a particle of personal ambition'. He had a habit of twiddling his dark hair, which his new mother-in-law would use as a 'tell' for one character to recognise another, despite a transformation of appearance, in her play *The Mousetrap.* Max described Anthony as 'teeming with information of an unexpected kind,' about fine wines, Sanskrit, and a host of other arcane subjects.[26]

'I think you will find Mathew will be pleased,' Rosalind reassured her mother, 'he is always pressing him to stay a long time & I don't think really he will be jealous.'[27] He wasn't: Mathew describes his stepfather as 'quiet, witty, scholarly, devoted'.[28] He fitted perfectly into the family. Anthony was 'the kindest man I have ever known,' thought Max, and kindness was what lonely Rosalind needed.[29] In lieu of a career, Anthony would become drawn into Agatha's Greenway, as manager of the gardens, and supporter in all sorts of practical ways.

And, oh, how Agatha's ambitions for Greenway required manpower. Life there never went entirely smoothly or as planned. Novelist Edmund Crispin described his visit as:

> very informal. There was a massive dining room and you never knew what you were going to get. You might be eating off Georgian silver or something from Woolworth's. You might be pouring wine from an eighteenth-century port decanter or drinking from some cheap glasses Agatha had found when shopping. There were children and dogs and always amusing talk.[30]

Agatha knew she was storing up trouble in having this huge generous hospitable vision of a home. But she couldn't let it go. She once
argued with Rosalind about it and apologised. 'The truth is,' she
wrote, 'I've got a guilty conscience about Greenway ... I am a
bloody old Bitch.' She clung onto her house in defiance of econom-
ics 'because I love it so'.[31]

Summers at Greenway would become ever more important to
Agatha. That was because beyond the confines of its gardens, her
fame and her business affairs were piling on new and urgent
pressures.

32

They Came to Baghdad

Once Anthony Hicks had slotted into Agatha's court as Crown Prince, easing day-to-day pressures, she turned her attention once again to being an archaeological wife.

In 1947, having left the RAF, Max wanted to return to his career. Pre-war archaeology had suited Agatha and Max. It was, as Agatha put it, 'a private concern – and [we] are very private people.'[1] But post-war archaeology was different. It was becoming less of a private club and more of a public service.

The University of London's Institute of Archaeology, then located in a mansion in Regent's Park, had been kept going during the war by a temporary director, Kathleen Kenyon. Like many women, though, she was expected to step down again when the men came home. In 1946, the celebrated Australian Vere Gordon Childe took over the directorship, and he was prodded by friends into finding something for Max to do. He proposed a new chair in Western Asiatic archaeology, which would not be advertised, as 'we do not think that any good purpose would be served'.[2] And so Max become Professor Mallowan.

Max's new job came with a salary, and archaeological folklore claims that Agatha 'sponsored' his post.[3] There's no record of money going through the university's books, however, something that would have been damaging to masculine pride. The arrangement was an informal and direct top-up to his university income. 'It might be better,' Cork advised Agatha, looking to reduce her tax bill, 'for Max to draw his salary after April 5th of this year, as 49/50 has been a particularly rich year for you.'[4] Max also got work through Agatha from her good friend, publisher Allen Lane. Lane employed Max to edit archaeological books, and backed his digs both with cash and with enormous Stilton cheeses flown out into the field.

'I am very lucky to have hooked this job,' wrote Max, and he was all set up for just the kind of life he liked.[5] He went to work each day from a new London base at Swan Court, off the King's Road in Chelsea, then still an arty, creative area. Like Lawn Road, Swan Court was a convenient block of flats built in 1931, with sixteen well-lit 'studio flats for the artist' on the top floor.[6] Max and Agatha's flat was cluttered, comfortable and the opposite of grand: its notoriously ancient sofa had 'worn upholstery and seriously damaged springs'.[7]

Max also spent weekends at 'his' house in Wallingford, summer holidays at Greenway, and five months of each year digging in West Asia. At the Institute, he wrote, 'hundreds of persons, mostly women, prostrate themselves to the ground as I enter the building . . . I only wish to shut the door of my office and read my books.' Perhaps to his own surprise, though, he grew to like teaching, and 'to help others to think'.[8]

In his fieldwork, Max now set his sights upon the project that would make his name: the investigation of the ancient city known as Nimrud in Iraq, twenty miles south of Mosul. In ancient times the city was called Kalhu, and that's what archaeologists call it today, but to Max and his generation Nimrud was its name.

He was thinking big. He hoped to match the discoveries and prestige Sir Henry Layard had achieved there a century previously. Between 1845 and 1851, Layard had found the huge stone winged bulls that impress visitors to the British Museum to this day. But since then Nimrud had slept undisturbed.

Essential for Max's plans was the relatively welcoming political situation in Iraq. During the war, Britain had once again exerted control over the country, for reasons including access to oil. As historian Eleanor Robson explains, 'the monopolistic Iraq

Petroleum Company was Iraqi only in name. It was in fact registered in London and jointly owned by big Western companies
such as BP, Shell, and a consortium of American oil producers.'[9]
Max's expedition was effectively a tentacle of British soft power in
the region, and his work was intertwined with other British
concerns, industrial and military. His expedition reports show that
as well as the Iraq Petroleum Company lending a bulldozer, the
Imperial Chemical Industries provided materials, and the RAF
aerial photographs.[10]

Before travelling to Nimrud, though, Max's team set up a base in
Baghdad. This was a revived version of the British School of
Archaeology in Iraq, and Max was made its director. In October
1948, an archaeologist called Robert Hamilton was sent to Baghdad
to rent premises for the School. 'I have found just the house,' he
wrote, 'many rooms of various sizes.' He went 'whizzing around
Baghdad, buying aluminium saucepans, and doormats, and Harpic,
and sardines, and teacups.'[11]

Agatha arrived there with Max on 18 January 1949, and would
grow fond of this old house on the riverbank, with its cool court-
yard, and palm trees nodding by the outdoor balcony. While Max
was working, her own life was peaceful and creative: 'lovely to
crawl out into the sun on the terrace every day and look at the
Tigris. Rest – sit in the sun – think up a few juicy murders to
keep the home fires burning.'[12] There's a photo of Agatha break-
fasting on the balcony, in suit and pearls, reading a book, and
drinking tea out of a round brown teapot. After wartime England
this was bliss.

The school was run from day to day by another archaeologist
who enters our story as a bit-part player, but who will loom larger
in later years. Barbara Parker was officially the secretary/librarian,
although she did many other things as well. Tall and elegant, Barbara
had been a model for the fashion house of Worth before studying
Chinese art and then archaeology. Newly qualified, she went to dig
in what's now Israel, during which time a colleague was shot dead.
Back in London, during the Blitz, Barbara served in the fire brigade.

Agatha's intimate letters show the *joie de vivre* she hid in public. Here she tells Max her daughter Rosalind will consent to their marriage 'IF you send her by return 2 dozen Toffee Lollipops.'

The quiet, young archaeologist Max Mallowan was fourteen years Agatha's junior. At first completely ruling him out as a romantic partner, she was able to relax in his company.

Max took Agatha on yearly archaeological expeditions to Asia. In the 1930s photos of their travels, Max usually looks serious, but Agatha is very often laughing.

Adventures with Max provided the settings for many of Agatha's books, like *Death on the Nile*. In it, Poirot draws a parallel between detection and archaeology: both aim to excavate the truth.

With Agatha's financial backing Max began to lead expeditions of his own, such as this one to Chagar Bazar, Syria. Agatha would casually wander round, secretly checking that the diggers were working.

Living in the 'expedition house' with the archaeologists, Agatha would spend the morning writing fiction. She needed to earn the money to help fund the next season's dig.

Agatha was ambivalent about her fame and extraordinary professional success. In her passport she gives her profession not as 'author' but simply as 'married woman'.

Agatha has breakfast on the balcony of the British School of Archaeology, overlooking the Tigris in Baghdad. Sitting in the sun after the deprivation of wartime England was bliss.

In the 1950s, Max and Agatha excavated at the ancient site of Nimrud (or Kalhu) in Iraq. Agatha found the place 'peaceful, romantic, and impregnated with the past.'

'Plots come to me at such odd moments,' Agatha said, perhaps even during a family picnic. She planned books 'while lying in the bath and I eat apples'.

Greenway is an elegant Georgian house, 'very white and lovely,' high above the River Dart in Devon. Agatha and Max were delighted to return after it was derequisitioned in 1945.

Agatha's grandson Mathew never knew his soldier father, Hubert de Burgh Prichard, killed in Normandy in 1944. Agatha was closely involved in Mathew's life, and they had a special bond.

Widowed at twenty-five, Rosalind found a kind second husband in Anthony Hicks. This photo, taken during a happy family summer at Greenway, shows, from left, Anthony, Mathew, Agatha and Rosalind herself.

Again at Greenway, Agatha is seated to the left while Max stands behind the table. Next to Agatha is Barbara Parker, Max's saintly archaeological assistant, who would become his second wife.

The party celebrating the 2,239th performance of *The Mousetrap*. The hotel staff didn't recognise Agatha and refused her entry. Instead of announcing that she was the star guest, she shyly slunk away.

'I hope one day you will play my dear Miss Marple,' wrote Agatha in the 1950s to a young actress named Joan Hickson. Hickson did indeed become television's Miss Marple, from 1984 to 1992.

In 1974 the film *Murder on the Orient Express* became the most successful British film ever at the box office Albert Finney led a starry cast as Hercule Poirot.

Winterbrook, Wallingford, Oxfordshire, known as 'Max's house', where Agatha lived quietly as Mrs Mallowan. 'A delightful, small, Queen Anne house', it had 'meadows sweeping right down to the river.'

As Max and Agatha grew old together at Winterbrook, archaeology interested them much more than house maintenance. In 1971 Agatha complained that 'somewhere water is running or dripping'.

'What we have cannot perish,' wrote Max, 'for me you will remain beautiful and precious with the passing of years.' This picture, from Agatha's extreme old age, shows them still joking about.

Agatha grew very tiny after a heart attack shortly before her death. Asked how she would like to be remembered, she said simply, as 'a rather good writer of detective stories'.

Colleagues described Barbara Parker as 'disorganised', 'slap-dash', 'endearing' and 'extremely kind', qualities that led her to help other people and to neglect her own scholarly work as an epigraphist. But Hamilton described her more generously as 'faithful, ever-industrious and resourceful', noting how devotedly she helped Max to get things done, while in return he constantly made jokes about her.[13] One of Max's pupils described Barbara as his 'slave'.[14] Those around her liked to think of Barbara as one of those people who just can't help being taken advantage of, and Agatha called her 'Saint Barbara the Martyr'. While people may have laughed at her in the 1950s, though, she's now seen as one of the unshowy women throughout twentieth-century archaeology whose work lay behind the eye-catching books penned by their male bosses.

One of the books Agatha wrote in Iraq, *They Came to Baghdad* (1951), depicts the house used by the British School. Written chiefly so that she could classify her trip as a business expense, it was a 'thriller' rather than a detective story. Her publishers could tell it hadn't had her full attention. 'It is difficult to believe,' ran a reader's report at Collins, that 'Mrs Christie regards this as more than a joke.'[15]

But the interesting thing about *They Came to Baghdad* is its new awareness of the fragility of Britain's presence in Iraq. During the war, Max had resolved to change his ways when he returned to West Asia: 'we can no longer afford to stand aside and remain aloof from the native'.[16] For the first time in Agatha's work, the story contains significant Iraqi characters. The heroine Victoria is a tourist who becomes a spy, but only because the government organisation that recruits her hasn't been doing a very good job. Her predecessor, Carmichael, was an Eton-educated agent in the Edwardian mould. Victoria, a humble typist, nevertheless had an important quality seemingly lacking in Carmichael and the Establishment: common sense.[17]

But Baghdad was only a stop on the way to the excavations Max was to carry out between 1949 and 1958 at Nimrud, a mile distant from the great Tigris River. 'What a beautiful spot,' Agatha wrote, 'big stone Assyrian heads poked out of the soil. In one place there was the enormous wing of a great genie . . . peaceful, romantic, and impregnated with the past.' Here Max would investigate the home of King Ashurnasirpal II, a mighty monarch who once entertained 70,000 guests at a palace-warming party. Max's team would find wonders here. But it was after his time that the king's great golden treasure was discovered, by Max's Iraqi successor at the site, Muzahim Mahmoud Hussein.

As ever, the obstacles included not just digging in the right place, but managing what Max perceived as the discontented and disorderly local workmen. Some labourers had returned from his pre-war digs, and in consequence 'referred to Agatha as their aunt'.[18] Records were now kept in Arabic as well as English, and the diggers were paid a little more than previously.[19] But there were still arguments about pay, settled with 'maces and knives' and 'which resulted in a number of bruised and broken heads.'[20]

The discoveries at Nimrud included an almost incredible succession of marvellously carved pieces of ivory. According to a friend, archaeologist Joan Oates, Agatha's greatest contribution to archaeology:

> was her almost single-handed reconstruction of over thirty wood and ivory writing boards recovered from a well in 1953, in hundreds of very small and very similar fragments – just the sort of jigsaw puzzle she loved.[21]

Agatha herself was proud of her work:

> I had my own favourite tools . . . an orange stick, possibly a fine knitting needle – one season a dentist's tool which he lent – or rather gave me – and a jar of cosmetic cleansing cream for the face which I found more useful than anything else for gently coaxing the dirt out of the crevices . . . How thrilling it was; the patience, the care that was needed; the delicacy of touch.

She'd also take the necessary photographs, emerging 'perspiring from a morning's work in the small unventilated darkroom'.[22] As in her hospital days, she was supremely happy to be part of the busy team at Nimrud, surrounded by people she trusted.

Accounts of Agatha's time on the dig, like Oates's, usually play up the feminine nature of her work: the intricate labour, the delicate touch, the face cream. But this wasn't in fact her most significant contribution. It was just the most socially acceptable contribution for an archaeological wife to make.

Another of her jobs was to sit in the expedition house, handing their wages to the labourers through the little window in the wall. Sometimes tourists coming to see the site were overheard saying, 'Come and have a look at the men being paid and Agatha Christie paying them.'[23]

And indeed Agatha was paying them in more ways than one, because she'd contributed the money to make the dig possible in the first place. As well as underwriting individual expeditions, she also bankrolled the British School of Archaeology. In 1953, for example, she gifted the school the money from A Pocket Full of Rye, because, as her agent explained, 'the Metropolitan Museum in New York have discontinued their support . . . which means that Agatha's husband's life's work is threatened by lack of funds.'[24]

On the dig Agatha would, of course, act as if Max were in charge. Team members quickly learned they should treat the boss's wife as one of themselves. One archaeologist described her as 'inherently shy except with friends and members of the team who had learned not to discuss her writing'.[25] And yet, at the same time, everyone knew she wasn't just one of the gang. 'Max was very volatile,' explained Joan Oates, 'he used to flare up . . . all she ever did would be to say "Now Max," in a very quiet voice, and he would pause for a moment, and whatever he was raging about would drop.'[26] Dr Paul Collins, chair of the successor organisation to the British School in Iraq, says 'my sense is that she's a presence, making decisions'.[27]

According to the usual version of the story, one of the advantages of Agatha's life on the dig was that it kept her safe from her growing and increasingly importunate public. But this was not true either. Agatha's very presence at Nimrud was an attraction for sightseers. She was integral to the dig's sponsorship from the Iraqi Petroleum Company, writes Eleanor Robson: 'tea with Agatha was offered to IPC wives in exchange for the loan of heavy lifting and transport equipment.'[28] During one season, more than 1,500 visitors arrived to see both the site and Agatha, 'army officers on manoeuvres, children by the bus load, church dignitaries or even locals arriving on donkeys . . . Agatha sat at the head of the long table behind her tea or coffee pot dispensing hospitality to high and low.'[29]

Agatha kept up her end of the deal, but at some personal cost. Joan Oates remembered her as literally besieged:

this car was sighted coming, and Agatha always went into her own little room and locked the door. And there were two young men from Finland. They'd come to see Agatha Christie, and weren't going to be told no. They knew she was here, and they were going to see her . . . they actually went and banged on the door.[30]

The other way Agatha's presence was felt at Nimrud was through the food. British tax rules permitted an allowance that could be spent on business purposes, which she defined as getting 'local colour' for her books. It was therefore tax-efficient for Agatha to buy the expedition's food, and this, of course, was a source of enjoyment as well. She'd dispatch the cook to the shops with the words: 'and don't forget the cream.'[31] The archaeologists therefore enjoyed 'lashings of rich water buffalo cream on the hot chocolate soufflés miraculously baked by our Indian cook in a kerosene-heated box oven'.[32]

Even with all these activities unfolding, Agatha still had to produce the book that would help fund the next season's digging. So, in 1951, in another famous passage echoing Virginia Woolf, she explains that she had an extension added onto the dig house:

For £50, I built on a small, square, mud-brick room Donald Wiseman, one of our epigraphists, fixed the placard in cuneiform, which announces that this is the Beit Agatha – Agatha's House, and in Agatha's house I went every day to do a little of my own work.

This sign was quickly taken down again to make Agatha's hideaway harder for visitors to find. Her secret room looked towards the mountains of Kurdistan, and contained a home-made table, upon which stood 'her typewriter and a flurry of papers anchored down by some potsherds and a pile of paperback books'.[33] Here, says Max, Agatha spent part of each morning quickly typing her next book, 'more than half a dozen of them were written in this way, season after season'.[34]

But these annual expeditions would eventually come to an end. Tensions in Iraq were growing as the nation moved towards revolution in 1958, and Iraqi nationalism swelled once more. In 1955, the sixth season at Nimrud did not go smoothly. Agatha, now sixty-four, was ill with cystitis and had to be taken to hospital. In April, a hurricane nearly took off the dig house roof. Hamilton thought Max 'isn't coping with operations quite as successfully as usual'.[35]

And Max's preference for the old treasure-hunting type of archaeology was gradually being overshadowed by the 'scientific' approach of younger colleagues. Being one of his female students sounds particularly challenging. He thought he only began to make headway with a female pupil when he'd 'reduced her to tears', something he described as 'thoroughly wholesome'. Max was still publishing in the *Illustrated London News*, by now considered rather fuddy-duddy, and he openly regretted that his profession had been 'touched by the heavy hand of professionalism'.[36] The end was drawing near of those 'carefree days,' as one archaeologist put it, 'when Max and Agatha ran digs rather like private house-parties in exotic settings.'[37]

1957 was Max's last season as director, and on 14 July 1958 the Hashemite monarchy in Iraq fell to a new republican regime. But the real reason Max stopped digging was that Agatha, at sixty-seven, was no longer physically able to go too. His career in the field ended, as it had begun, with Agatha as his essential companion in a joint venture.

Back in England, Max worked away on his magnum opus: *Nimrud and Its Remains* (1966). Once again, it was his wife who made this possible, as Cork took on the project as a favour after it was rejected by Penguin. Harold Ober in the States was rather less enthusiastic, describing it as a book 'called *Nimrud* and something or other, I didn't get the rest of it, which I gather is on archaeology.'[38]

Although Max's name was on the cover, and Agatha's merely on the dedication page, it was really their joint achievement. And behind their names hover the ghosts of Barbara Parker, other assistants, and the hundreds of Iraqi workers who actually did the digging. In his choice of title, Max was positioning himself as the successor to the founding father of Iraqi archaeology, Sir Henry Layard. *Nimrud and Its Remains* echoed Layard's *Nineveh and Its Remains* of 1849.[39] Agatha also made the comparison in her autobiography, describing how the great ancient city of Kahlu or Calah

slept . . . Here came Layard to disturb its peace. And again Calah–Nimrud slept . . . Here came Max Mallowan and his wife. Now again Calah sleeps . . . Who shall disturb it next?

The answer to her question would be teams of Iraqi, Italian and Polish archaeologists. But their years of painstaking work were followed by a shocking and violent intervention. In 2015, militant forces of Islamic State (IS) apparently razed the remains of the ancient site to the ground. Their action was deemed by UNESCO to be a war crime, motivated by a determination 'to wipe out all traces of the history of Iraq's people'.[40] Agatha's writing room at Nimrud had fallen down through neglect in the early 2000s, but in 2015 the rest of the mud-brick expedition house had still survived. Its last moments of life are recorded in the video, posted on the internet, that IS made as they blew it sky-high with explosives.[41]

This event, the destruction of the site, seemed like the end of Nimrud's story. But Nimrud expert Eleanor Robson has visited since to assess the damage. She discovered the explosives were placed to create a good propaganda video, rather than completely to wreck the site. The ziggurat may have gone, but most of the rest of the site is intact. 'Messy, but not irreparable,' Robson says of the damage.[42] And one wall of Agatha and Max's house stands still. 'We will rebuild this legendary house,' said Kheiriddin Nasser, local archaeologist, in 2020, 'it has strong emotional value for us.'[43]

So Nimrud still remains, to sleep until the next generation comes along.

33

Christie-Land after the War

After the initial relief of returning to Greenway after the war, Agatha and indeed many other Britons found the peace a bit of a let-down.

'It's the aftermath war has left,' says one of Agatha's characters in *Taken at the Flood* (1948). 'Ill will. Ill feeling. It's everywhere. On railways and buses and in shops.' Many of the inhabitants of Christie-land in the later 1940s and 1950s were facing a slippage in the standards of middle-class living. They weren't seeking to better themselves, but simply to keep a grip on what they possessed. The new welfare state hadn't much to give them. Agatha thought it offered:

> freedom from fear, security, our daily bread and a little more than our daily bread and yet it seems to me that now, in this Welfare State, every year it becomes more difficult for anybody to look forward to the future.

Outside Christie-land, though, these sorts of concerns were beginning to seem parochial. In the 1950s Agatha would be ever more commercially successful, her sales roaring upwards, as she tapped into the imperial nostalgia and insecurity her readers felt. At the same time, though, her literary reputation would begin to fall. From now on, she'd be writing against the tide. Different people from different classes would lead the conversation: Kingsley Amis, John Fowles, Philip Larkin. In the 1920s and 30s, just as the modernists drew prestige away from the middlebrow, middle-class and often female authors who outsold them, the same thing would now happen with the Angry Young Men.

And even detective fiction had its angry men, although important voices among them like Dashiell Hammett weren't particularly young any more. The hard-boiled school of fiction, with its violence and misogyny, had begun to infiltrate Britain from America even before the war. Agatha didn't think much of the hard-boiled novel, and neither did Miss Marple. Jane Marple *has* heard of Mr Hammett, but puts him firmly in his place: 'I understand from my nephew Raymond that he is considered at the top of the tree in what is called the "tough" style of literature.'[1]

While Miss Marple might scoff at 'tough' literature, her creator's work was actually, in its own way, growing 'tougher' too. According to historian Nicola Humble, a new theme entered all British middle-brow novels after the war: a note of 'paranoid watchfulness'. Facing an existential threat to their way of life, the people in these novels turn inwards, upon themselves, with cruel 'exclusions and games of one-upmanship'.[2] As Miss Marple observed, the old rules of society no longer held: 'fifteen years ago one *knew* who everybody was.'

This loss of class confidence came about partly because of a squeeze on middle-class incomes. The theme of the struggle for a gracious life would dominate *A Murder Is Announced* (1950), where the local paper contains 'frenzied appeals for Domestic Help', and there are no servants to be found 'unless one has an old Nannie in the family'.

The lady of many a big house now had to get her hands dirty, even in families with old money like the Wattses at Abney. Agatha's sister Madge rose at five thirty to 'do' the house, she 'dusted it, tidied it, swept it, did the fires, cleaned brass, and polished furniture, and then started calling people with early tea.' Madge's method makes its way into *A Murder Is Announced* as the vicar's wife likewise gets up early to 'light the boiler and rush around like a steam engine, and by eight it's all done', all the while claiming valiantly that a big house is no harder to keep clean than a small one.

Loss of caste even emerges as a motivation for murder in Agatha's Miss Gilchrist, the villainess in *After the Funeral* (1953), who hates her demeaning work as a paid companion. She'd once run her own business, a tea shop, but had to close it during the war because she'd been unable to get eggs for her cakes. The other characters are amazed at the concept of a 'ladylike murderer', but a fall from independence and gentility was something that resonated for Agatha's readers in the 1950s.

Miss Gilchrist was a particularly savage murderer, chopping at her employer with a hatchet, and Agatha's post-war novels also got tougher about children. She had never been sentimental about the young: in *Murder Is Easy*, for example, a boy is killed off with distressingly little care from the author. But in *Crooked House* (1949) Agatha went so far as to write a murderous child. She was proud of her creation, later naming *Crooked House* as one of her favourites of her books.

But even if a new note of nostalgia came into Agatha's books, she didn't let it dominate. A little boy in *Ordeal by Innocence* (1958) is 'always talking and thinking about space ships', and Agatha still loved the future. In 1956, she gave an interview that nestled on the page between adverts for rayon and for General Electric televisions ('progress is our most important product'). She was 'enthusiastic about science-fiction,' she told the journalist, 'because of the wonderful new scope it offers in the realm of mysterious invention.'[3] One of Max's nephews, John Mallowan, spent school holidays with his uncle and Aunt Agatha. 'I used to feed her science fiction,' he says, 'she'd read absolutely anything.' He'd also egg Agatha on to drive her new Wolsey 1500 at its maximum velocity of 85 mph along the new-built M4 motorway.[4] She needed little encouragement, having retained her lifelong love of speed.

This is the constantly surprising thing about Agatha Christie, her passion for modern life. One 'Christie trick' was to use a contemporary news story in a plot. Her thriller, *Destination Unknown* (1954), has echoes of the spies Klaus Fuchs (unmasked 1950) and Bruno Pontecorvo (defected 1950), who'd worked at the Atomic Energy

Research Establishment at Harwell.[5] And her play *The Mousetrap* picked up on the real-life tragedy of foster-child Dennis O'Neill that emerged at the 1945 public inquiry into his death.

As well as real events, real places continued to tickle Agatha's mind. *Five Little Pigs* (1942) had made use of Greenway's gardens as a setting, and in *Dead Man's Folly* (1956) it was the turn of the boat-house to provide the scene of the crime. This use of an actual place to help make a mystery stand up is another 'Christie trick'. For *A Murder Is Announced*, Agatha persuaded neighbours to come into the drawing room and describe what they saw when the lights were suddenly switched off. 'What they do see and, even more interesting, what they don't see' becomes of vital importance in the finished book. When the novel was published, one of those involved realised he'd been in a novelist's field experiment.[6]

Agatha wasn't always even conscious she was incorporating life into art. In America, a junior agent, Dorothy Olding, was gradually taking over Agatha's affairs from Harold Ober. When Olding first read *The Mirror Crack'd from Side to Side* (1962), though, she became 'distinctly uneasy', rightly fearing Agatha was going to incorporate the effect of German measles on pregnancy.[7] The problem was the recent real-life case of the actress Gene Tierney. Like the film star in Agatha's story, she'd been infected by a fan, and in consequence had given birth to a disabled child. This looked like exploitation. *The Mirror Crack'd* did indeed produce numerous complaints: 'surely it is unnecessarily cruel to set forth Miss Tierney's problems and sorrows'.[8] Back in Britain, though, Cork defended his author robustly. This 'may sound incredible,' he admitted, but Agatha 'had no knowledge of the case.'[9]

Another way Agatha caused offence was through continuing to fail to see what was wrong with anti-Semitism. *A Murder Is Announced* introduces the unfortunate Mitzi, a refugee, who's treated as a figure of fun. Her fear of the police – 'you will send me away to a concentration camp' – is a joke that falls terribly flat.[10] 1947 and 1948 saw complaints escalating in America about *The Hollow* (1946). Readers argued that Agatha's reference to the 'raucous voice' of a 'vitriolic little Jewess' was an anti-Semitic stereotype. Eventually the matter was taken up by the Council Against Intolerance in America, who asked Agatha's publishers to eliminate the anti-Semitism from all new editions of Agatha's books, going right back to *The Mystery of the Blue Train*.[11] Agatha's team pussyfooted around the issue. 'Perhaps sometime when you are talking to her,' her American agent advised her British one, 'you might tell her that it might be wise in future to omit any references to Jews.'[12]

Of course, the views of an author and of her characters are two quite separate things. In *The Rose and the Yew Tree*, Agatha's often condemned for having one character criticise another for his so-called 'common' legs. It would indeed, if expressing Agatha's own views, be 'grotesque class prejudice'.[13] But in this case we are seeing the man's legs through the eyes of the slightly ridiculous narrator. Agatha had put into his mouth the words of a Torquay friend, Marguerite Lucy, who was roundly mocked for once having said of a man: 'it's a pity his legs are so common.'[14] It's possible, in different times, to miss the original irony.

But when Agatha gave individuals objectionable views in a way that did not reveal character or advance the plot, it was bound to offend. And Cork shirked the duty of addressing her on her anti-Semitism. In 1953, he did write unequivocally to her American publishers, instructing them simply 'to omit the word "Jew" when it refers to an unpleasant character in future books.'[15] In doing so, he tacitly admitted that Agatha could not be trusted to do so on her own.

Stereotypes in general were so integral to Agatha's work that she couldn't stop using them, even when she should have done. The 'foreigner' was a classic Christie misdirection. Poirot uses his nationality as a protective cloak: 'you unutterable little jackanapes of a foreigner!' cries the murderer, caught out in *The ABC Murders*. In *Ordeal by Innocence*, it's the other way round: the family's lawyer guides us away from suspecting the Swedish character, who *was* in fact guilty, because it would be all too obvious for the 'foreigner' to have done it. The problem with the 'vitriolic little Jewess' in *The*

Hollow was her religion was used simply to make her more dislikeable, and it's sad to see the decline in Agatha's subtlety. In *Hickory Dickory Dock* (1955), set in a hostel for students, Agatha attempted to engage with contemporary race relations, introducing the thinly characterised 'Gopal Ram' and 'Mr Akibombo'. It was poorly received. Francis Iles in *The Sunday Times* thought it weak: 'all foreigners are funny, but coloured foreigners are funnier', while Evelyn Waugh thought it 'twaddle'.[16] Agatha had once excelled at playing with stereotypes and readers' expectations, but as she grew older she found it harder.

In these post-war years, Agatha cut back on the productivity of the 1930s. To write too much, she felt, would mainly benefit the 'Inland Revenue, who would spend it mostly on idiotic things'.[17] But she still remained prolific. It became her pattern to work hard for six weeks to deliver a manuscript in March, for publication at Christmas. She would have a long summer holiday – 'delicious days of leisure and idleness' – before planning the next book.[18]

In a 1955 radio talk she played down her professionalism. 'The disappointing truth,' she claimed, 'is that I haven't much method. I type my own drafts on an ancient faithful machine.'[19] Yet even the 'ancient typewriter' was a prop for her scatty public image: she actually had the latest products with the highest specifications, such as the 'new noiseless Remington' her American agent sent over in 1949.[20] And Agatha had always had help with the typing anyway. Carlo's duties had included taking dictation, and from the 1950s, after she retired to Eastbourne, she was replaced by Stella Kirwan as secretary.

The writer John Curran is probably the person most familiar with Agatha's technique for developing plots, which involved making notes in exercise books. 'Plots come to me at such odd moments,' she claimed, 'walking along a street, or examining a hat-shop with particular interest . . . I jot down my splendid idea in an exercise book. So far so good – but what I inevitably do is lose the exercise book.' She also described dreaming up plots 'while lying in the bath and I eat apples and drink cups of tea and have bits of paper and pencils around.'

More than seventy of these intriguing notebooks still survive. They range from the cheap to the deluxe, with classy-sounding brand names like 'The Minerva', 'The Marvel' and 'The Mayfair'. One really ancient volume is inscribed 'Agatha Miller 31 Mai 1907', while another, from WHSmith, proudly announces that its PVC cover is – wonderful word! – 'spongeable'.

But opening up the notebooks is a tantalising experience, because much of what's in them simply doesn't make sense. More than anything else, the notebooks reveal Agatha's low-key approach to her work. Novels are plotted across multiple volumes, apparently according to whichever one happened to be to hand. Notebook 31, for example, has pages dated 1955, 1965, *then back to 1963*, then '1965 Cont' and then on to 1972. She didn't even bother to use the pages in the right order.[21] And the notebooks also reveal how work for Agatha was threaded right through life: alongside ideas for characters and plots are a list of furniture; a reminder to make a hair appointment; a note of the train times to Torquay.[22]

The closest she came to a 'method' was to list her scenes according to letters of the alphabet, and sometimes she'd rewrite a book to put them in a different order. Her notebooks reveal her iterative process particularly clearly in the case of *Crooked House*. She did not plan from the start to have the child as the killer, but considered three other characters before settling on the girl. 'She devised and developed; she selected and rejected; she sharpened and polished,' John Curran explains.[23] After years of study, he came to the conclusion that the 'very randomness' contained within the notebooks *was* Agatha's method: 'this is how she worked, how she created, how she wrote. She thrived mentally on chaos, it stimulated her more than neat order, rigidity stifled her creative process.'[24]

According to one of her friends, the part Agatha most enjoyed was the plotting, 'the one great pleasure she took in writing: all the rest was hard work'.[25] Still, she wasn't above recycling a good plot, and indeed it was one of her best 'Christie tricks'. The reader simply can't believe she might be playing the same game twice. Yet the unreliable narrator or witness, for example, debuts in *Roger Ackroyd*, appears again in *The Sittaford Mystery*, and returns once more in *Endless Night*.

Once the plotting was done, Agatha then had to put the words on paper. We have a clear picture of just how steadily and methodically she went about this, from letters she wrote to Max from a working 'holiday' in Rhodes. Staying by herself in a hotel, she told him:

> breakfast at 8 . . . meditation 'till 9. Violent hitting of the typewriter 'till 11.30 (or the end of the chapter – sometimes if it is a lovely day I cheat to make it a short one!) then to the beach and plunge into the sea . . . after tea some more work (sometimes no work but a sleep) 8.30 dinner – and afterwards work if I've slept.[26]

That was on 10 October. By 13 October, 'Lord Edgware is dead all right . . . Poirot is being most mysterious.' Six days later, 'the nephew who succeeds to the property is just talking to Poirot about his beautiful alibi!' and two weeks after that, 'I have got to Chapter XXI.' She was making good progress because she had no distractions: 'I should never have done that if you had been there!'[27]

Agatha's handwriting – in pencil, biro or ink – changed over the course of her lifetime. In her most creative period, before and during the war, it's almost illegible, as if the ideas come spilling out too fast to be captured in a way that would make sense to anyone else.[28] Its exuberance captures the joyful, lively Agatha who hid her joyful liveliness from people she didn't know well.

After the war, though, when the quality of the books was declining, the writing becomes bigger and more legible. Her later notebooks contain fewer jottings, and to produce the text she began to rely more on her Dictaphone. But the recording device had an unfortunate effect: it was almost *too* easy to use, and allowed Agatha to get long-winded.[29] 'Rewriting of first half,' runs a diary-like entry in one of her notebooks referring to *By the Pricking of My Thumbs* (1968), 'not so verbose.'[30]

During the Greenway years, a family ritual developed in which Agatha would read her latest book out loud. 'Nima read us a chapter or two of *A Pocket Full of Rye* after dinner each night,' says Agatha's grandson Mathew:

> It must have been 1953 . . . all the family sitting round the drawing-room at Greenway, coffee cups empty . . . Nima sat in a deep chair . . . after every session, except the first two or three, we were all invited to guess the identity of the murderer.[31]

It sounds like an important step in the process, a testing out of the plot. But the reading was done from proofs, far too late for Agatha to change anything significant.[32] She did it to entertain her family, rather than because she wanted to know what they thought.

After she'd corrected her proofs, woe betide a publisher who allowed any errors to remain. 'I am really <u>furious</u>,' she complained, when an American firm released an edition of *Five Little Pigs* omitting three words – 'with a crowbar' – from a character's statement about a murder. Readers know from other sources that this statement is untrue, and the words are included to show that the speaker is inaccurate and biased. Some unfortunate editor had unwittingly eliminated an important clue.[33] Agatha was particularly picky about blurbs, rejecting one simply with a scrawled capital '<u>NO</u>!'[34]

This professional self-confidence remained at odds with her public persona. 'Once I've been dead ten years,' she'd say, 'I'm sure nobody will ever have heard of me.'[35] Yet in August 1948 records were broken when 100,000 copies of ten of her titles – or a million novels – were all released by Penguin on the same day.

In 1950, a party was held to celebrate Agatha's fiftieth book. In a spirit of introspection, she began work on her autobiography, a task that would occupy her on and off for fifteen years. By the Fifties, despite her public statements, Agatha knew very well her life was worth recording.

34

Second Row in the Stalls

The evening of 13 April 1958 provided one of the defining
images of Agatha Christie's life.

What was described as London's 'biggest-ever theatrical shindig'
was staged that night at the Savoy Hotel.[1] Although Agatha's remembered today as a novelist, it was the crowning moment of the decade
in which she'd also become a world-famous dramatist. The previous
evening her play *The Mousetrap*, to the delight of its manager Peter
Saunders, had been performed for the 2,239th time.

The reason Saunders had dreamed up for the party was slightly
obscure. *The Mousetrap* was already the longest-running *play* in West
End history, and had been for six months. Now, in April 1958, *The
Mousetrap*'s run was overtaking the record of a hit musical from 1922,
making it the longest-running *theatrical production* of any kind
whatsoever.

But Saunders was brilliant at exploiting an opportunity. To
Agatha's mind, the occasion 'had everything that is most awful about
parties: masses of people, television, lights, photographers, reporters, speeches.' But she knew she'd have to go. She respected Saunders
deeply, she explained, 'for the things he has made me do that I said
I couldn't.'[2]

Saunders had invited a thousand guests, from Richard
Attenborough to Anna Neagle, but the most important was this
quiet woman with what the newspapers called 'a motherly smile'.[3]
Agatha prepared for her ordeal with a dark-coloured satin gown

with chiffon sleeves, white gloves and three strands of pearls. She did love actors and theatrical people, but too much of their rather demanding company tired her. 'Well – I must go and do my stuff,' she would say to Max before going out to face the thespians, 'Christian names and lots of "Darlings!"'[4]

Some thirty photographers were in attendance, and Agatha had been asked to arrive early at the Savoy to have some pictures taken. And here she tells the story of what happened next:

> I did as I was told, but was firmly rebuffed by the Savoy personnel –
> 'No admittance for another half-hour – you can't come in now.'
> Instead of being sensible, I couldn't utter a word, and just slunk away.

Eventually, Agatha Christie was discovered sitting by herself in the hotel's lounge by one of Saunders' team. 'Why didn't you say who you were?' she was asked, presumably with some exasperation. 'I just couldn't,' Agatha replied, 'I was paralysed.'[5]

When the time came, she made a perfectly acceptable speech. But it was the little cameo about her earlier humiliation that had diary-column currency. The *Daily Mail*'s journalist loved it. It captured Agatha as she now was at the age of sixty-seven: a deceptively ordinary-looking megastar.[6]

Agatha's reign in the West End is curiously overlooked today. But it was astonishing. In 1944, her play based on *And Then There Were None* was running at the same time both in London and on New York's Broadway. In 1954, she had three plays on simultaneously in the West End. It's almost even more impressive that two of the three are running in London theatres sixty-eight years later.

Despite this, though, Agatha's work as a playwright has a low critical standing. A dictionary of *British and Irish Dramatists Since World War II*, for example, has no entry for Agatha Christie at all. It has much more to say about Tom Stoppard's spoof of Agatha Christie's *The Mousetrap* than it does about *The Mousetrap* itself. She's only mentioned in a quotation from a male playwright, who gets sixteen pages, and who dismisses her as the author of 'the sort of plays one would never go to'.[7]

The historian of Agatha's theatrical career, Julius Green, explains some of the ways in which her reputation has become degraded. Christie plays particularly appeal to amateurs, for example: their casts are usually small and simple sets suffice. Licensing a play to amateurs meant a play could be commercially successful without a long professional run, so Agatha's management did not always prioritise the latter. And, again for commercial reasons, her name often appears on inferior adaptations of her stories done by other people.

It's also striking that Agatha's first wildly successful play was the first to be directed by a woman. Her reputation's also suffered through a campaign of denigration by male directors who weren't comfortable with an experienced writer making comments during rehearsals from her usual seat in the second row of the stalls. All this helped Green begin his magisterial reassessment of Christie's work for the stage with a striking statement:

> this is the story of the most successful female playwright of all time. She also wrote some books.[8]

But Agatha's success on the stage was a slow burn, and she had to work long and hard to achieve it. Her favourite occupation at the age of seven was 'reading a play', yet none of her works were staged until she was forty, and her career as a playwright only really took off in her sixties.[9]

The first play made from a Christie story was *Alibi*, the name given to a reworking by someone else of *The Murder of Roger Ackroyd*. It opened in April 1928, the month of Agatha's divorce hearing, at the Prince of Wales theatre in London. The *Daily Express* (inaccurately) described it as the work of 'the missing woman novelist', and said she 'was missing again at the end of last night, when they shouted "Author!" for she hid in a box.'[10]

Poirot in *Alibi* was played by a rather-too-charismatic Charles Laughton, whom Agatha admired but thought entirely unlike the character she'd written. It was an early experience of something she'd come to hate: having her novels dramatised by other people. In April 1941, therefore, she decided to accept a request to rewrite *And Then There Were None* for the stage herself. 'If anyone is going to dramatize it,' she told Cork, 'I'll have a shot at it myself first!'[11] She'd always loved writing plays, finding it 'much more fun than writing books . . . you must write pretty fast, keep in the mood and keep the talk flowing naturally.'[12] Of course, she'd never been known for describing places or people. Plays suited her because 'you are not hampered with all that description which clogs you so terribly in a book and stops you getting on with what's happening.'

There's something particularly stagey about Agatha's novels anyway, as critic Alison Light argues. Agatha was well aware that, in Noël Coward's words, life is 'a question of masks, really; brittle, painted masks. We all wear them as a form of protection; modern life forces us to.' In a decade as class-conscious as the 1950s still were, people were extremely sensitive to 'bearing, posture, appearance and the "proper" intonation of voice'.[13] Agatha's most successful plays have this idea at their heart.

But Cork struggled to find someone to stage Agatha's script, and the next year she decided to rewrite it, this time giving *And Then There Were None* a happy ending. Unlike the book, the play finishes with Vera and Lombard falling in love, and both of them are revealed to have been goodies after all: Lombard was 'really a hero who risked his life to save natives'.[14] Having apparently been shot dead, he gets up from the floor and says: 'Thank God women can't shoot straight.' The cheery finale, much less chilling than the novel's, was far more palatable in wartime London.[15]

And eventually Irene Hentschel, the first female director to have worked at the Shakespeare Memorial Theatre, agreed to direct. Agatha's first-night nerves were soothed by Stephen Glanville and a dinner at Prunier's.[16] But she'd had no need to worry: soon the play was touring Britain before opening in New York. In 1945, it became a film, in 1947 it was adapted for radio, and in 1949 it was remade for television. This made it the first of Agatha's stories to appear in book, stage, cinema, radio and television forms.[17]

Replicating this success, though, proved difficult. 'The notices had been pretty bad,' she admitted of 1945's *Appointment with Death*. This production was notable for introducing Agatha to a young actress with whom she'd have friendly lunches and correspondence. 'I hope one day you will play my dear Miss Marple,' ran one of Agatha's letters, and the woman who received it was named Joan Hickson.[18] Hickson would indeed become television's best-known Miss Marple, between 1984 and 1992.

It would be Peter Saunders who quite literally put Agatha Christie's name up in lights. Her plays were often ensemble pieces, rather than star vehicles, which seemed to present a problem. But Saunders thought laterally. She 'has a vast following from her books,' he mused, 'why can't we make *her* the star?'[19] This novel approach caused Agatha to agree to his selection as producer of her next play, *The Hollow*.

But the director the young and ambitious Saunders chose for *The Hollow* was the similarly inexperienced Hubert Gregg. In years to come, Gregg would denigrate Agatha in a particularly public and unattractive way. When he was given the script of *The Hollow*, he wrote in his memoirs, he thought it 'abysmal. The dialogue was unspeakable . . . the characters were caricatures . . . how amenable is the old bird to a bit of rewriting?'

In Gregg's hateful book, he not only claims to have rewritten *The Hollow*, he also said Agatha lied about her age, had a 'Gargantuan appetite' and loved publicity. His book includes a horrible photo of Agatha captioned 'as I remember her', and he also had an unpleasant habit of referring to his writer as 'a mean old bitch'.[20] There, staring us in the face, is the reason for Agatha's continued reluctance to perform the public role people expected.

Despite Gregg, *The Hollow* did quite well in 1951. But the best was yet to come. The story of Agatha's most famous play, *The Mousetrap*, started back in 1946. The BBC asked Queen Mary to select a gift for her eightieth birthday, and she requested a new

Agatha Christie play. The half-hour play, then called *Three Blind Mice*, was broadcast on radio on 30 May 1947. Agatha donated her writer's fee to a charity for children, an appropriate gesture because the plot was inspired by the true story of a boy, Dennis O'Neill, who died after terrible abuse by his foster-parents.

Made longer for the stage, and renamed *The Mousetrap*, the story has a specifically post-war setting of dislocation and bad food. In the guest house where the action unfolds, coke for the boiler is running low; dinner is tinned 'mince beef and cereal'; the pipes freeze. And British society, Agatha argues in the play, was failing its young. One character is a magistrate who'd sent children into the hands of abusers, another a schoolteacher who'd failed to answer their pleas for help. The tale would have tapped into the anxieties of the many parents who'd placed their own children into the care of strangers during wartime evacuation. The stage play opened on 25 November 1952. Although there were forty-three other London theatres offering rival performances that day, *The Mousetrap* would outlive them all.[21]

Agatha's second best-known play, *Witness for the Prosecution*, with its extraordinary double-twist ending, also had a long gestation. The plot was recycled from a story she'd published back in 1925. Agatha completed its dramatisation in one of her obsessional writing binges during a stay in Iraq in 1953. Suddenly, she explained, she was enjoying working on her play, 'that wonderful moment in writing which does not usually last long, but which carries one on with a terrific verve as a large wave carries you to shore . . . I think it only took me two or three weeks.'

This was a big, expensive, risky production. The only theatre available was a massive one, with 1,640 seats. There was a challenging scene-change halfway through, when the courtroom appeared onstage.[22] The anxiety was enormous, and tension mounted. 'Saunders,' Agatha admitted privately, 'seems to be rushing upon his doom!'[23]

But the first night, in December 1953, defied all expectation. 'They cheered, they stamped, they shouted "Author!", reported the

Daily Express. 'All thirty of the cast bowed solemnly to a stage-box. But Agatha Christie, 62, sat alone in the dark, looking like Queen Victoria, smiling.'[24]

Saunders also waxed lyrical about that night:

> I shall never forget it as long as I live . . . the cast turned to the upper box where Agatha was sitting, and the entire company bowed. There was pandemonium in the theatre. Not only clapping and shouting, but people standing and waving.[25]

In *Witness* the heroine, a foreigner, understands that prejudice among members of the jury means that what she says won't be believed. So when she wants to lie, she simply tells the truth. It's classic Agatha Christie in that it's hugely entertaining, but it also draws attention to the assumptions made by the British justice system.[26]

And yet Christie plays have never had the undivided respect of the theatrical community. Michael Billington, drama critic for the *Guardian,* thought Agatha 'a lousy dramatist'. 'I can still hear,' he said, 'from the days when I worked in rep, the agonising groans that used to go up from actors when forced to animate the walking dead in yet another revival of *Peril at End House.*' Maybe so, but as Green points out, Agatha didn't write *Peril at End House.* Another, lesser, playwright adapted it from her novel.

Peter Cotes, one of the directors involved in *The Mousetrap*, took the opposite view of Agatha from Hubert Gregg. He thought she showed extreme professionalism and 'a degree of receptivity not always to be found in highly successful writers.' Perhaps Gregg's real beef was that Agatha didn't feel a strong need to be liked: as Cotes admitted, 'she wished at all times to relieve herself of spare talk and theatrical chitter-chatter.'[27] In private, Agatha could be quite steely about her theatrical colleagues: she *had* to attend rehearsals, she said, 'if one doesn't go to them frightful things happen and actors write in lines for themselves which make complete confusion of the play!'[28]

In 1962 there was another *Mousetrap* party, this time for its tenth anniversary, and Agatha was forced to make a (rather confused) speech. 'Sometimes I really can't believe it's me,' she said,

> I mean, it's not at all the sort of thing that would happen to me. I mean, if I were writing a book, it wouldn't be a person like me who had written a play that runs for ten years.[29]

'You ought to have taken more trouble, Mother,' said Rosalind, 'and prepared something properly beforehand.'

But Agatha's reign as Queen of the West End would not last forever. Before it passes its zenith, though, let's revel in her own reminiscences about that epic opening night of *Witness for the Prosecution* in 1953. 'I was happy, radiantly happy,' she says,

> my self-consciousness and nervousness, just for once, were not with me. Yes, it was a memorable evening. I am proud of it still.

35

A Charming Grandmother

Once the wartime years came to an end, Agatha had less need to put her intimate thoughts down on paper. The feverish letter-writing to Max came to an end, for she was with him constantly. And when it came to her public persona, walls were going up. The myth was taking over from the real woman.

It's been rightly said the greatest character Agatha Christie ever invented . . . was 'Agatha Christie'. An interviewer for an American magazine in 1957 found her

> a smiling, gray-eyed charming grandmother who collects pretty papier-mâché trays like royalty, she gives the impression of being very vague on just the subjects a person would expect her to know most about. Agatha Christie, a queen with millions of subjects (her total sales are roughly estimated at 50 million), says in a puzzled tone, 'I don't know why people should want to write about me.'[1]

And yet in 1950 she became a Fellow of the Royal Society of Literature, in 1956 she became a Commander of the Order of the British Empire and, in 1961, the girl who hadn't really been to school was given an honorary Doctorate of Letters by Exeter University.

Some of the myths about her proved impossible to overturn. They ranged from the major – that she'd 'disappeared' to get her revenge on Archie – to the minor. Many people insisted on crediting Agatha with the statement that 'an archaeologist is the best husband a woman could have, as the older she gets, the more interested he is in her.' 'Agatha did not in fact say this,' Cork would explain, endlessly, 'and nothing infuriates her more than to have it attributed to her.'[2] Curiously, the first printed attribution of the phrase to Agatha appears in the *Gothenburg Trade and Shipping Journal* in 1952.

Reminders of the disappearance continued to cause her pain. In 1957, Cork complained vociferously to the *Daily Mail* because it had used the term 'doing an Agatha Christie' to describe someone who'd gone missing.[3] Agatha remained quite happy to pass up every opportunity of promoting herself. 'I suspect one of your talented staff can forge my autograph?' she asked Cork, hopefully, when signings were demanded.[4] 'Get me out of this nicely,' ran a typical letter to her agent, 'you know the things to say.'[5]

The image of the kindly grandmother, rooted in the Devon countryside, was created in cooperation with the select band of journalists who were allowed to interview her. But it would also be burnished brightly in the autobiography Agatha was writing in a leisurely manner throughout the 1950s and 60s. The book would only be published after her death, but Philip Ziegler, the editor at Collins responsible for the project, remembers that all the major decisions had been made by Agatha herself.[6] She'd begun the work for fun – 'I've been rather enjoying jotting down silly little things that happened' – but also as a tactic to put off other people from writing about her life.[7] Would-be biographers were dismissed with a curt letter from Agatha's agent: their efforts were unwelcome because 'she is writing her own full-length biography, which is in fact practically finished'.[8]

When it was finally published, Ziegler recalls being 'mildly disappointed it didn't get wider and more respectful treatment' by reviewers.[9] Readers expecting juicy revelations would be disappointed. 'To those interested in Victorian customs,' was one reviewer's verdict, it makes 'tolerable reading', but to others it was 'wearisome and disappointing'.[10] The real problem was that gap that existed between

Agatha's view of herself, and that unjust but persistent image the world still had: that she was a secretive and tricksy woman.

To people who knew her in real life, though, the autobiography made perfect sense. The archaeologist Sir Mortimer Wheeler thought the 'quality of reserve' Agatha possessed in person to be equally much 'an integral quality of her writing'.[11] Only to a trusted few did she open up. 'I believe what I really love in you,' she once wrote to Max, 'is your inwardly wild spirit – we're both alike in that. Outside we're quite well tamed & well behaved but inside we've got a <u>free</u> feeling.'[12]

Agatha's distaste for fame seemed increasingly out of step with the times. But it did remain completely typical of a middle- or upper-class woman born in 1890. Many of her novelist contemporaries likewise 'hid almost obsessively from press and public,' notes Gillian Gill. 'Margery Allingham, Josephine Tey, Ngaio-Marsh, Georgette Heyer and Dorothy L. Sayers were similarly determined to keep their lives private.'[13] The reason Agatha stands out as an unusually publicity-shy celebrity in the 1950s and 60s was partly because she was still producing new work while her peers faded away.

As she entered her sixties, Agatha was ever more reluctant to be photographed. She described herself as 'thirteen stone of solid flesh and what could only be described as "a kind face".' Advising Rosalind over an issue of health insurance, Edmund Cork privately gave her a warning: 'Between you and me, the Medical Superintendent is concerned about Agatha's weight.'[14]

Agatha strongly disliked the photographs taken for her sixtieth birthday. Their publication 'saddens me a good deal,' she said, '& deepens my inferiority complex about my appearance.'[15] 'Look here, Edmund,' she wrote to her agent after another unsuccessful photo-shoot, 'have I got to stand for this? I don't see why I should be constantly humiliated and made to suffer.'[16]

But apart from the misery of being watched and judged, there was a kind of freedom in not being thin. Agatha's appearance in later life became ever more distinctive: a dress in a bold print, cat's-eye spectacles, pearls, a long coat, a velvet toque or a big shady hat. Many people found her intimidating. 'She reminded me tremendously of Queen Mary,' wrote someone who met her in 1957,

a large bosom . . . lots of beads hanging round it and a big brooch. She looked enormous to me but . . . I think because I was very much in awe of her she was probably blown up to an enormous size in my mind.[17]

Agatha knew exactly what she liked to wear and stuck to it, and Misses Olive and Gwen Robinson of Dartmouth made many of her clothes.[18] In 1966, on a trip to America, her agent warned an American colleague that a shopping trip would be required. 'Be warned Dorothy dear!' Cork wrote. 'Agatha told me yesterday that the real object of her visit to America is to pick up some outsize knickers . . . she recalled your prowess with the swim-suit, and I am awfully afraid sweetie you are for it.'[19]

Max once described his wife as combining 'outer diffidence with a massive inner confidence', and there are sometimes hints that her public 'shyness' was less a genuine character trait than a weapon. Certainly this was a view held by male associates who found her less tractable than expected. People found her lack of small talk formidable: 'silences in which one was aware that she took in everything about one and saw right through one.'[20] Actor Geoffrey Colville, who appeared in *The Mousetrap*, claimed he 'couldn't quite believe she was as shy as everyone said. Perhaps she just didn't want to be bothered.'[21] Hubert Gregg likewise thought her cold: 'shrewd and a trifle ruthless. Insensible, a touch vain – and contained. She was very contained.'[22]

Understandably, Agatha parted ways with Gregg for her next play, *Spider's Web*. It was written to provide a part for the film actress Margaret Lockwood, with whom she got on well. Lockwood admired Agatha in return. 'Agatha has the gift of doing what all women want to do,' she explained. 'She achieves something . . . In her heart every woman . . . would like to do these things. But all we can do is dream.' 'It's a man's world,' Lockwood concluded, 'the only consolation I get is that Agatha kills off a few of you.'[23]

But *Spider's Web* was to be the last of Agatha's big theatrical successes. The later 1950s shaded into a darker, sadder time. Madge had died of a heart condition at seventy-one. In 1958, her son Jack sold Abney Hall and moved to London, ending a century of ownership by the Watts family. Agatha had tempted her sister-in-law Nan to come and live in Paignton, handy for Greenway. But Nan would die the following year, leaving Agatha devastated: 'the last of my friends – the one remaining person with whom I could talk and laugh about the old days.'[24] It was also in 1958 that Nancy Neele died. Agatha steeled herself to write to Archie expressing regret, the first letter in many, many years. He replied saying he was 'much touched'.[25]

One of the most depressing things about the year 1958, though, was that Agatha's new play, *Verdict*, completely flopped. 'GALLERY BOOS CHRISTIE PLAY – A MELANCHOLY OCCASION', ran a headline in the *Daily Telegraph*. It's interesting to put *Verdict* alongside that year's great hit: Shelagh Delaney's *A Taste of Honey*. Written by a working-class nineteen-year-old, this extraordinary play, set mainly in a bedsit, centres on a single mother and her daughter, with Black and homosexual characters as well. Astonishing to audiences unused to seeing working-class women's lives on stage, it achieved something of the status of *Look Back in Anger*. In a notorious interview of 1959, though, Delaney found herself being told by a snooty man that her play covered 'sordid' subject matter. She was asked what help she'd had in writing it, and was forced to deny rumours that she was about to get married. Delaney did not give another interview for fourteen years.[26]

Although Shelagh Delaney and Agatha Christie were extremely different in their subject matter, as female playwrights they shared some common experiences. The 1950s, the decade of Agatha's greatest successes so far, had also brought her cruel criticism. Far better to retreat to the fantasy world of Greenway.

❧ PART NINE ❧

Not Swinging – 1960s

36

The Mystery of the Christie Fortune

I n the 1940s Agatha was best known as a novelist, while in the 1950s her plays came to the fore. But the 1960s were the decade in which her work would reach more people than ever, through the medium of film.

Agatha's plots had in fact appeared in cinemas for decades. Her story 'The Passing of Mr Quin' was filmed in 1928, followed the next year by *The Secret Adversary*. At this stage, though, her authorship wasn't particularly important, to either the films' makers or viewers. The nascent movie business was desperate for material; almost any old story would do. Film historian Mark Aldridge, in his definitive study of Agatha Christie on film, notes her first production was a 'quota quickie'. This was a cheap project responding to an Act of Parliament that decreed British cinemas had to show a certain number of films with British writers. It was supposed to be a fightback against the dominance of Hollywood, but it didn't lead to quality film-making. The first Christie drama seen on screen was described by *Variety* as containing 'one of the most unconvincing scenes ever watched in any film'.[1]

Other feature films followed in the 1940s, but the only one anyone's likely to watch today is 1945's stylish Hollywood version of *And Then There Were None*. After the war, though, Edmund Cork had to manage an exploding market in the field of film. With their limited locations and casts, her short stories were perfect for the shorter episodes required by television. Ronald Reagan appeared in one made for CBS in 1950, and Gracie Fields in another for NBC in 1956.[2] But it became clear that cinema was where the big money lay, and Cork came to prioritise the sale of film rights over television.

Cork had been on quite a journey with his biggest client since starting out in the gentlemanly circles of London publishing in the 1920s. Inevitably, mistakes were made. 'I have never known such hell!' he wrote, after one particularly tricky deal.[3] He maintained his longtime collaboration with his American counterpart, Harold Ober, even though a third party described Ober as 'slow, old-fashioned and thinks $100,000 is a lot of money.' This was in fact borne out when Ober made a film deal for $325,000, but the purchaser of the rights immediately flipped them onto someone else for $435,000.[4]

In 1960, Cork decided to change tack, and to sell the rights to forty of Agatha's stories to Metro-Goldwyn-Mayer Pictures on a profit-sharing agreement. Agatha had some reservations about the ambition of the arrrangment. 'I hope there won't be "broken hearts",' she wrote, 'what one loses in cash one may gain in absence of worry.'[5] The press reported the deal's value as one million pounds, though Cork said the true figure was 'considerably less'.[6] 'The MGM deal has almost destroyed me,' he admitted, 'its fluctuations have been too numerous and violent to be believed.'[7]

MGM was one of the oldest companies in the business. In the 1950s, though, the studio had suffered from a drift of audiences over to television. So there was a lot at stake. The producer Larry Bachmann and his wife came to stay at Greenway to build a relationship with their new writer. At first everything went well: 'fortunately,' Agatha explained, they 'liked dogs.'[8]

In 1961, the first of these MGM films was finished. Agatha's book *4.50 from Paddington* was renamed as *Murder She Said*, and Miss Marple was played by Margaret Rutherford. She and Agatha, almost exact contemporaries, admired each other, and it was rather wonderful to have such an old lady carrying a film. Rutherford would celebrate her seventieth birthday on set, and Cork thought her 'a lot more like Marple than some of the sophisticated American minxes that were proposed.'[9]

Yet on 17 September 1961, Agatha acknowledged that *Murder She Said* was a disappointment. She took her family to see it at the Paignton Picture House. 'Frankly, it's pretty poor!' she wrote, 'as my eldest nephew said to me in a sad voice as we left "It wasn't very exciting, was it?" & I really couldn't have agreed with him more.'[10]

The trouble was that although Margaret Rutherford was an extremely skilful comedian, Agatha hadn't intended Miss Marple to be funny. And the problem's real root was that MGM hadn't ever really wanted Agatha's skilful plot-weaving. Neither, as the 1960s wore on, did her readers. Agatha's yearly novels became less consistent in quality, indeed some of them considerably below par. But people went on buying them, in greater numbers than ever, because her personal brand had grown so strong. Agatha Christie's name now stood for quality British entertainment with a tinge of nostalgia. The content of her work became less important than the signature upon it.[11]

Nevertheless, the MGM deal creaked on. The fourth film produced was called *Murder Ahoy!* (1964). It gave Agatha a shock, because it wasn't based on one of her books, and she hadn't realised MGM's contract allowed them to use her characters in new plots of their own. In MGM's screenplay, Miss Marple gets sent on a ship. 'Excitement storms the high seas,' ran its trailer, 'on a wacky wild voyage of homicide and hilarity as only Agatha Christie can mix with such riotous abandon.'[12] One can imagine Agatha Christie's original Miss Marple pursing her lips at the very notion.

Agatha was filled with dismay, describing the script as a 'farrago of nonsense'. She vociferously insisted she hadn't been aware that

MGM have the right to write these scripts of their own featuring my characters. That, neither I nor Rosalind seem to have known [. . .] I feel really sick and ashamed of what I did when I signed up with MGM. It was my fault. One does things for money and one is wrong to do so – since one parts with one's literary integrity [. . .] I held out until seventy but I fell in the end.[13]

Gone were the days when Agatha had enjoyed collaborating with theatrical folk. She told Bachmann of her 'deep resentment' at what she saw as his 'high-handed action'.[14] She was even more disturbed when *Murder on the Orient Express* was suggested as a further MGM venture: she worried they'd turn it 'into a rollicking farce with Miss Marple injected into it and probably acting the engine driver.'[15] Bachmann, for his part, had come to think of Agatha as 'an old lady without the first instinct for making film'.[16] And indeed Agatha was quite openly suspicious of a medium where, in the words of her grandson, 'she could not control the finished article'.[17]

Rosalind, playing her part in what was now the family business, felt she could have done more to prevent her mother's pain. 'You may say,' she admitted privately to Cork, 'that it is all good money, but I do feel . . . we have really let my mother down very badly over this whole deal.'[18] Thus was born in Rosalind a deep sense of suspicion towards film and television. Scarred by the experience with MGM, she'd prove herself extremely reluctant to give her blessing to any other project she felt might belittle or demean her mother's work.

As far as MGM were concerned, Agatha had become a loose cannon. For once, she said too much rather than too little to *The Sunday Times*. 'I kept off films for years,' she told its journalist,

> because I thought they'd give me too many heartaches. Then I sold the rights to MGM . . . it was too awful! . . . I get an unregenerate pleasure when I think they're not being a success. They wrote their own script for the last one – nothing to do with me at all – *Murder Ahoy!* One of the silliest things you ever saw. It got very bad reviews, I'm delighted to say.[19]

Jack Seddon, speaking on behalf of the movie industry, agreed that 'as Miss Christie says, the screen Miss Marple is nothing like her own creation.' But there was good reason for that:

She wasn't intended to be. The Miss Marple of the books struck me as snobbish, unkind, and cold, with a stealthy, almost reptilian eye . . . That Miss Christie 'would never advise anyone to go and see them' comes a little late, as millions already have, no doubt to the great financial benefit of the principal parties.[20]

You can understand the frustration felt by both sides.

What had brought Agatha to this impasse? Clearly, she had no real need to go on working into her seventies. But equally clearly, the compulsion to write had not left her. This was partly for the pleasure of creation. And partly because her financial affairs were in fact in a mess.

People now liked to believe the Duchess of Death was enormously wealthy. When Agatha's play *Go Back for Murder* got a cool reception in 1960, her team were suspicious that rumours about her recent MGM deal had coloured the critics' response. 'I don't care how rich Miss Christie is,' ranted the *Daily Mail*'s reviewer, 'this stinks!'

It was particularly inappropriate for a female writer, it seems, to be loaded. Hubert Gregg, for example, claimed his work on Agatha's smash hit plays had come 'near to damaging my career as a director beyond the point of no returns'. And yet his skills, he complained, had been 'responsible for pouring several million pounds of subsequent sterling into her pinny'.[21] Oh, how his use of that word 'pinny' gives him away! Not only was she annoyingly rich, she was annoyingly female too.

But pinning down Agatha's own attitude towards money is a hard thing to do. One journalist found that 'like a queen, she has not the faintest idea of her income: "I only know it comes in large blocks and that then there is a dry space".'[22] That, though, was part of her absent-minded, Ariadne-Oliver-like public image. It is true that Agatha was much more businesslike than meets the eye, and definitely liked earning and spending money. However, she had no sense of business strategy. In 1949, for example, she went off to Baghdad for five months, leaving Cork with 'Power of Attorney and instructions not to trouble her about any business matter!'[23] This kind of behaviour did not lead to timely decisions. 'Did you ask me to answer anything?' she wrote from Iraq, 'If so, I can't remember.'[24]

Her fecklessness about money probably came from growing up in a family with inherited wealth. We saw that right back in the 1920s, when she blew £500 on a new car. It seems obvious, in retrospect, that she should have set some aside for tax. But because Agatha was so ambivalent about calling herself a professional writer, she struggled to act professionally about money.

Sorting out her tax was a painful process that took decades, and it often made her *feel* hard up. This was entirely in her mind: objectively she was extremely wealthy. But the supposed unfairness of tax, which grew into a personal obsession, was one of the reasons Agatha sometimes said she 'had' to go on writing into her seventies.

The pressure to keep producing – almost regardless of quality – also grew ever greater because of the number of people whose employment depended upon it. She'd created a whole industry. There was her agent, the worldwide network of sub-agents, and, of course, her publishers, which in Britain meant Collins.

1945 had seen a step-change in the success of Agatha's books. Cork got Collins to double Agatha's advances, and in return they pushed the books harder to generate better sales. This worked brilliantly: Cork boasted that 'sales have actually gone up to three times what they were'.[25] The growth continued. In 1959, UNESCO announced that the Bible had been translated into 171 languages, Shakespeare into 90, and Agatha Christie into 103.[26]

But all this income had to be taxed, and there was also the festering business of those unpaid American taxes from before the war. Despite expensive lawyers, a settlement proved elusive. Agatha couldn't keep up: 'business was worrying . . . contracts to sign, tax complications – a whole welter of stuff one didn't understand.'

In 1948, a settlement was finally reached on her US tax, but the next row was about how much interest was owed.[27] When the Americans eventually released her money, the British authorities then wanted to claim massive back tax upon it, no one knew how much. The stress this caused made 1948 a barren year for Agatha's writing, and her accountant found her 'in a very perturbed state of mind. In fact she told me that she is quite unable to concentrate.'[28] Indeed, that September Cork raised the alarming prospect that there was 'little likelihood of Mrs Mallowan avoiding bankruptcy'.[29]

During the struggle to get the US and UK authorities to agree with each other, Cork was confronted with all sorts of bureaucratic ineptitude. He received one letter from a new tax inspector who said he understood 'that Agatha Christie is to all intents and purposes a pen-name' and that 'it would appear that the tax district of the husband is the one that is required.'[30] It wasn't until 1954 that the British tax authorities finally agreed to her US tax settlement – and then those back taxes would need to be paid.

Despite her worries, though, the daughter of Frederick Miller was constitutionally incapable of living more cheaply. 'I shall go on enjoying myself,' she told Cork, 'and have a slap-up bankruptcy!'[31] She had that happy knack of putting difficulties right out of mind. 'How's everything?' she'd write from Baghdad. 'Play still surviving? Can you put a pound on Shegreen for me in the Grand National?'[32]

Agatha's books and plays were now earning so much money that Cork felt he should look to the world of showbusiness, where individuals earning large, erratic sums were seeking creative tax advice. The finances of the rock stars and footballers of the 1960s reveal some of the mistakes Agatha did not make: shady advisors, dodgy investments, fortunes lost.

Tax in post-war Britain was really quite progressive: by the 1960s, the rate on income over £15,000 a year stood at 88.75 per cent. It was becoming common for high earners to become tax exiles, from musicians like the Rolling Stones to other authors like John le Carré. Agatha's son-in-law Anthony suggested she should follow suit, but she does not appear to have taken the suggestion seriously.[33]

In 1951, Cork proposed a new way of managing Agatha Christie, not so much as an individual, but as a business. In order to reduce

Agatha's tax bill, a trust was set up to settle the proceeds of the novel *They Do It with Mirrors* and the play *The Mousetrap* upon Mathew. Ian Fleming was on to this too, obtaining a limited company to hold his literary rights, and putting film rights into trust for his son right from the start, well before there was anything significant about James Bond's success.[34]

Next came the idea of setting up a company, Agatha Christie Limited, which would employ Agatha, pay her a salary, and avoid her having to pay personal super-tax. In June 1955, Agatha Christie Limited was formed to own her new books. Its directors were Agatha herself, Rosalind and Edmund Cork. Other authors in the same league, Enid Blyton and John le Carré, would do the same thing.

Agatha herself felt slightly mystified about it all. 'I presume it's ethical?' she asked. 'So difficult to know nowadays.'[35] Left to herself, she may not even have bothered. A more astute author might also have questioned whether Cork was the right person to set up these complicated arrangements. John le Carré, for example, was notorious for chopping and changing his agents and publishers in chase of a better deal. But for Agatha, loyalty, laissez-faire and her Edwardian lady's attitude towards money meant she stuck with Cork and Collins for a lifetime, and didn't ask too many questions either. The company is 'undertaken for your benefit,' she told Rosalind and Anthony, 'not mine, since I gather that my means of livelihood (and luxury living!) are more or less unchanged . . . If you both think the possible worry and fuss is worthwhile go ahead. I personally am not going to even take much interest.'[36]

This hands-off approach was a little disingenuous, but love and money were clearly complicating the relationships within the family. There were jokes that might not have been jokes. 'As an employed wage slave I feel fine,' teased Agatha, 'but not at all like work.'[37] 'I am glad that Agatha Christie Limited is gathering some money,' wrote Rosalind to Cork, 'and sincerely hope it won't all be paid to our Wage-Slave! . . . wasn't the idea that she should get a <u>small</u> wage?!'[38] Agatha's salary, though, had to be big enough for her taxable 'expenses' (including 'the company's' Rolls-Royce) to be deducted from it. It was a fine balance. In 1958, when Cork proposed Agatha's salary be raised to £7,500, Rosalind replied that, 'I think, of course, it is a very bad idea indeed.'[39]

Meanwhile, the Christie Copyrights Trust was set up so the income from most of Agatha's backlist could be gifted away to avoid death duties. Money went to relatives, to Max's nephews and to Charlotte Fisher. Charitable donations ranged from the large (the Agatha Christie Trust for Children) to the small (a stained-glass window for the church near Greenway.) The British School of Archaeology in Iraq were regular recipients, as was the charity Harrison Homes, which looked after old ladies. But even the forming of the company *still* hadn't solved Agatha's tax problems. In 1957 the Inland Revenue, having approved the creation of Agatha Christie Limited, changed its mind, and no final settlement was reached until 1964.

On into Agatha's seventies, the earnings still mounted up. In 1961 UNESCO officially named her as the world's best-selling author, and in the same year William Collins claimed the slogan a 'Christie for Christmas' was 'good for an extra 26,000 copies'. 'Women were beginning to pop up in the business,' says Agatha's grandson, who'd ultimately take over Agatha Christie Limited, 'but she was certainly the most successful person in the writing and entertainment industry who proved that women could be equal to men. Whenever I read about some female achievement today, I think that this, in part, is Nima's inheritance.'[40]

In 1968 Agatha received yet another huge tax bill, and it seemed a good idea to shift the problem onto someone else. So, that year, 51 per cent of Agatha Christie Limited was sold to Booker Books.[41] This was a subsidiary of a huge company, Booker MacConnell, and is best known to readers for founding the Booker Prize. Four years earlier, Booker had similarly bought the estate of Ian Fleming. In return for the shares in Agatha Christie Limited, Booker paid off her tax. The decades-long saga seemed finally to be resolved, and tax planning meant the next generation was taken care of extremely generously. On 19 January 1976, the *Financial Times* would publish an article called 'The Mystery of the Christie Fortune'. It sought to explain the widespread amazement that Agatha's estate at her death seemed so small, at just over £100,000.

But the upshot of all this was that Agatha felt disenfranchised and short of cash. She grew grumpy when she couldn't keep up with the deals being done. Having told Cork for years not to bother her with business, she'd sometimes make unexpected demands. 'Will you send me my accounts,' she demanded in 1966, 'what has actually come in, I <u>don't</u> know – so that I don't know how or <u>why</u> I am spending and I find this worrying.'[42] As the Sixties turned into the Seventies, the maintenance of Agatha's houses became patchy, and visitors were surprised to find them run-down. But she still had a remarkable ability to go on enjoying her life and wealth: collecting silver, travelling for pleasure, indulging Max.

The best-selling novelist in the world did like money. She liked earning it, spending it, and she had a strong sense of her own self-worth. Ultimately, though, Agatha retained her gender and her upbringing's uneasy relationships with her cash. The mysterious 'Christie Fortune' was a bit of a mystery to its owner as well.

37

A Queer Lot

On 15 September 1960, Agatha celebrated her birthday at Greenway. Looking absolutely like the matriarch of a dynasty, she sat in a chair garlanded with flowers and surrounded by a group of people she called her family. She had a wonderful time. 'Rich hot lobster for dinner!' she crowed, 'hardly felt my age!!!'[1]

It pleases me to think of seventy-year-old Agatha enjoying her summers at Greenway, this beautiful house full of luxury. But the house and the life Agatha lived there also strike me as a kind of elaborate piece of performance art, which is not the least of the achievements of her old age.

'I consider I <u>made</u> it beautiful,' she said of her beloved house, 'or rather, displayed its beauty.'[2] A woman, muses a man in Agatha's novel *The Sittaford Mystery*, can 'alter the whole character of a room – and without doing anything very outstanding that you could put your finger on.'[3]

In staging her life as the lady of the manor, Agatha was acting out a role just as so many of her characters did. And her hyperawareness of this fact – that all of us are really acting – is essential to her art. It's the thing that makes her perspective a little bit similar to that of a queer writer.

She'd been a reluctant celebrity for decades, but in the 1960s this grew more onerous than ever. Two photographers had attempted to snap her on a beach holiday, Agatha wrote, in 1960. She'd been in a 'particularly ungainly attitude' at the time, giving them 'practically a close-up of a big behind'.[4] In 1967, a journalist in Slovenia sounds positively creepy. Agatha had chosen a remote hotel for privacy, but the writer Janez Čuček 'pretended to be a normal customer and persuaded the receptionist to give me the room next door to hers . . . I simply stepped across from my balcony.' Agatha, exasperated, told him 'she'd never wanted to be famous,' while Max wanted to call the police.[5]

But Agatha had grown more philosophical about this sort of thing. When she learned that reporter Ritchie Calder was going to write about his experiences during her disappearance of 1926, she was surprisingly relaxed. 'What does it matter after all this time?' she reassured Cork,

> One of the advantages of being seventy is that you really don't care
> any longer what anyone says about you. It's a thing that can't be
> helped – just slightly annoying.[6]

After her death, Calder would go so far as to claim he'd confronted Agatha at the hotel in Harrogate, where she'd answered to the name of 'Mrs Christie', and told him she was suffering from amnesia.[7] He later admitted he'd made the story up.[8] But over the years Calder's misreporting had helped create a powerful myth that Agatha could do nothing to counter: the myth that she was a liar.

Despite the fact she'd had just the one child, Agatha's seventieth birthday party shows how she still managed to create a large, complicated family of which she was the centre. This, after all, was how she'd always lived, bringing trusted people into the charmed circle of her friendship, from the 'Queer Women' of her nursing days, to the Wattses, to the friends of 1926 like Carlo who'd helped her through her separation. In the early days of her marriage, returning alone from her honeymoon, she'd told Max she was once more 'safe in the arms of my adopted family'. By this she meant not only Rosalind, but also Carlo, her cook Florence Potter, and certainly her dog Peter: 'P is my child, as you know!'[9]

Someone visiting Greenway found Agatha's large, and largely non-biological, family a confusing affair:

> It was rather a ramifying family. I never worked out who was who, but there was certainly a considerable number of them about the place. Not to mention dogs. Dogs and young people, they surrounded her. When I went to lunch, there would quite likely be sixteen people at the table and a lot of them young people in whom she kept an interest. Like well-brought up children, they treated her with politeness but not with any special awe.[10]

Even if everyone maintained the illusion that she was just an ordinary grandmother, Agatha's closest family were her business partners too. Peter Saunders describes what it was like to be auditioned by the family to see if entry to the circle was to be granted. During an introductory lunch, Anthony

> tried to ease things by talking on every subject under the sun . . . Agatha's daughter, Rosalind, frankly frightened me . . . I felt at the time she was keeping a careful watch on me in case I slipped my hand into Agatha's handbag and knocked off her purse.[11]

The life at Greenway was not super-luxurious, but it definitely wasn't bohemian. 'Gracious living' was how one member of staff described it. Pretension was absent, but this was a country house, not a suburban villa in Torquay. Guests were 'royally entertained,' recalls Max's nephew John, getting 'tea in bed, in their bedroom, at eight o'clock,' and 'people could even leave their shoes outside their bedroom and get them polished.'[12] Family dinners, with Agatha carving the meat, could take up to two and a half hours, and 'they also had those finger bowls with bits of lemon in, things you very rarely hear of these days.'[13] There were guests for weekends, proper old-fashioned house parties. Menus might include roast pigeon and cherry tart on Friday night, salmon and mayonnaise on Saturday night, and a Sunday lunch of roast beef.[14] 'There's nothing like having a dozen lobsters lying around when you haven't got to pay for it,' recalled Dixie Griggs, who used to cook.[15] Greenway ritual was rich and satisfying. Everything the Millers had lost, financially and socially, Agatha had regained.

Despite the 'gracious living', though, Agatha was anything but a snob. Adaptations of her novels for the screen often show a traditional, timeless version of the 'big house' in a British village, the rich man in his mansion and the poor man at his gate. In her books, though, Agatha had always shown a country house as a place for the comings and goings of modern life. Even Gossington Hall, the big house of St Mary Mead, changes hands twice within Miss Marple's experience: once when her friends the Bantrys buy it, again when they sell it to a movie star.[16]

Life in a country house also made Max a member of something like high society. Knighted in 1968, he'd overcome the outsider status given to him by his foreign parents. His mother had died rather suddenly in 1951, while he and Agatha were away in Baghdad: 'My darling Mother,' he wrote in the last of a lifetime's many letters, 'just a few lines to tell you that I think of you every day.'[17]

In 1961, while in Tehran, Max had a stroke. Although he recovered, he was physically diminished, coming 'to look twice his age, and pretty feeble'.[18] He now seemed the same age as Agatha: 'left hand and arm dragging and a bit helpless'.[19] He had a second stroke in 1967, also while travelling in Iran. 'Waiting and wondering is Hell,' Agatha wrote, while arrangements were made for a doctor to bring him home.[20]

1961 was also the year Barbara Parker returned from Iraq, to work alongside Max as a lecturer at the Institute of Archaeology. From this date, archaeological gossip would circulate rumours that they were more than friends. It was definitely a close professional partnership, although one in which Max held the upper hand: archaeologist Ellen McAdam describes Barbara as 'lacking in self-confidence' and 'constantly apologising for herself'.[21] But however much some archaeologists insist that this was also a physical relationship, there's no evidence beyond hearsay. Even if it was, it wouldn't have been a conventional heterosexual romance. The Woolleys had taught Max to believe that shared intellectual endeavours were just as important.

Greenway was also full of the children Agatha and Max hadn't had. They'd considered adopting, before deciding against: 'I think I and Max are too old.'[22] But no formal deed of adoption was necessary to join Agatha's family. Max's nephews visited, and the offspring of friends. Emma Shackle, daughter of a friend from Baghdad, recalled how 'when things went wrong', it was Agatha who 'drove me down to Greenway in her mini and was the only person who understood.'[23] They were a 'mother and father to me,' says Max's research assistant, Georgina Herrmann.[24]

And, of course, Rosalind, Anthony and Mathew were frequently present. These summers, explains Mathew, were 'a reward in part for the completion of another Christie for Christmas'.[25] In 1962, he decided that despite the family feud he wanted to meet his grandfather Archie, who was living near Godalming. Seventy-three years old, with greying hair, but still an 'upstanding good-looking fellow', Archie was suffering from bronchitis.[26] 'I saw him quite often,' Rosalind recalled, 'and we always liked and understood one another.'[27] Archie had been thinking about mortality, and had even written his daughter a letter on the subject. Realising that 'death often comes unexpectedly', he'd reread then torn up Rosalind's letters to prevent anyone else ever seeing them. Some of the letters, Archie told her, 'were very good, with new ideas and some were quite affectionate! . . . lots of love from Old Dad.'[28] The restraint, the lack of gush, the preservation of privacy suited them both.

But before the plan of introducing Mathew to his grandfather could be executed, Archie died at his home, Juniper Hill, Godalming, Surrey, on 20 December 1962. It had all been left too late.

Rosalind later spoke of her regret about the way her father had become the villain in the story of Agatha Christie: 'I hate the image of him as someone cold and unfeeling.'[29]

But this was her mother's own doing, because when Agatha's autobiography came to be published, that's how she chose to present him. Agatha was never able to forgive and forget. And this affected Rosalind too. Although she liked seeing her father, she felt her mother 'just couldn't seem to accept anything more intimate between us'.[30] So a certain amount of distance was maintained. Rosalind didn't even meet her half-brother Beau, Archie and Nancy's son, until their father's funeral. 'To me,' says Agatha's grandson Mathew, 'it's a tragedy that things that happened before I was born erected barriers between members of the family.'[31] 1926, that toxic year of trauma and media, haunted this particular family for so many years.

The year following Archie's death, 1963, his brother Campbell died. In events that harked back to their father's mental problems, he 'was found dead in the gas-filled kitchen of his home'.[32] Despite keeping Archie at arm's-length, Agatha *had* stayed in touch with Campbell, who'd gone on to become a successful playwright. She'd adopted him into her self-made family. Her nephew Jack Watts also remained constantly on the scene, and the family at Greenway grew again after 1967 when Mathew got married to Angela Maples, whom he'd met at Oxford.[33] 'We are delighted about Mathew,' wrote his grandmother, 'she is a <u>very</u> nice girl.' Having graduated from Oxford, Mathew had gone to work for frequent Greenway guest Allen Lane. Mathew's marriage meant a shuffling of the generations: he and Angela moved into Pwllywrach, the Prichard home in Wales, while Rosalind and Anthony occupied Ferry Cottage, Greenway, the better to look after the house and Agatha herself.

This expanding cast of characters performed the routines of a Greenway summer, during which Agatha happily pretended she wasn't a writer. 'You never see her working,' said one Greenway regular, 'she was the perfect hostess, always there, always joining in.' She never 'got up and said "I must go and write now" and shut herself away'.[34] But writing she nevertheless was. As Agatha's friend A.L. Rowse put it, she was 'a compulsive writer: writing was her life. Or one of her two lives – for outwardly she had a full and normal social life, family, two marriages, friends, hospitality, entertainments, housekeeping (which she was very good at), shopping (which she very much enjoyed.)'[35] Publisher Philip Ziegler, a guest at Greenway on several occasions, also noticed that she couldn't quite keep herself away from the typewriter. 'Absolutely nothing,' he thought, 'was going to stop her indulging in a certain amount of work.'[36]

As the years passed, though, it grew harder to find the staff Greenway needed. In the 1950s George Gowler, a former hospital chef, answered an advert for a butler. He was interviewed by Agatha in London and did surprisingly well considering his lack of butler-ing experience. An actor friend gave him a tailcoat, and then he was off to his new life in Devon. At Paddington station on the way, he purchased a little booklet called *How to Be a Butler.*[37]

Gowler installed himself in the house with his wife and grand-mother. He enjoyed talking to Agatha when she came into the kitchen to make mayonnaise.[38] Sometimes Agatha's family would crowd round Gowler's television, the only one in the house, to watch the racing or the golf. Unlike at Edwardian Ashfield, the front and backstage areas of the house were as one.

Gowler loved performing his role, banging the gong for dinner and performing magic tricks for guests. He felt cherished: 'you see I didn't think of Agatha as my employer, she was a friend, we seemed to be a family, all knitted together . . . in my opinion she was equiv-alent to the Queen's Mother.' Gowler, a born performer, turned professional in later life, and made a living from talking about his time as 'Agatha Christie's butler.' In this role he even got to travel on the *Orient Express,* where 'there was lots of filming and banquets beyond belief.'[39]

Gowler and his layers seem all of a piece with the theatrical performance of domestic service that's depicted in so many of Agatha's books. As early as *The Murder of Roger Ackroyd,* a parlour-maid is outed as a family member in disguise. Archie had been scep-tical when a young Agatha claimed she could easily have 'passed' for a maid, but she was proved perfectly correct: Mathew's nurse had taken her for a cook in the wartime years. Madge had gone one step further, actually pretending to be a parlourmaid at Abney when 'real' servants could no longer be found. The idea of shifting shape, after all, is what had always drawn Agatha to the theatre. 'I don't think, you know, that there is anything that takes you so much away from real things and happenings as the acting world,' she told Max, 'what a queer lot they all are!'[40]

The idea that a family, too, is something in flux, something more complicated than the conventional heterosexual pairing producing two children, reminds me of another 'Christie trick'. It's an old one, but one that turns up frequently in the novels of the 1960s: families that are not immediately apparent to the eye. Often in Agatha's books, a long-lost family member resurfaces in a new role. In *The Mirror Crack'd from Side to Side* (1962) it almost gets out of hand. Not only does the murderer's adoptive daughter pop up, but also a husband whom she'd completely forgotten she'd married.

As well as blurring the boundaries of the family, Agatha since the war had also grown increasingly comfortable about using sexuality in her plotting, in particular with her use of what critic Faye Stewart calls 'lavender herrings'.[41] These are characters whose homosexuality might appear to indicate guilt. The thoroughly nasty Lord Edgware has a hinted-at relationship with his butler in *Lord Edgware Dies* and the macabre Mr Ellsworthy with his 'womanish mouth', his 'mincing walk' and his antique shop in *Murder Is Easy* have absolutely no redeeming features. But the negative aura is entirely misleading: both characters are innocent.

Agatha's homosexual characters grew both more prominent and more sympathetic as her career wore on. In *The Mousetrap*, the sexuality of the homosexual and lesbian characters, Christopher Wren and Miss Casewell, is not overtly discussed. This allowed the censor to nod the play through, simply with the comment that the characters are 'a queer lot'.[42] But while Christopher Wren is a caricature of camp – with the original script describing his 'pansy voice' – he's charming and amusing.[43]

Christopher is still a step away though, from the sympathetically drawn lesbian couple in *A Murder Is Announced* of 1950: Miss Hinchcliffe with her 'man-like crop', her 'manly stance', and her gruff grief for her late partner, Miss Murgatroyd.[44]

In her later work Agatha extended this tolerance of difference even further. *The Clocks* (1963), for example, shows various able-bodied characters underestimating the blind woman Millicent Pebmarsh. Poirot, of course, is correct in taking her seriously. He adopts the social model of disability, which assumes the disabled person could do anything at all if only the world were designed to facilitate it, rather than the more common medical model of disability, which concentrates on the things a disabled person can't do.[45] Highly unusual as an attitude to be found in commercial fiction in 1963, it demonstrates the sort of unconventional thinking the people who think of Agatha purely as a conservative writer have failed to see.

Because it's so easy to visit beautiful Greenway today under the management of the National Trust, and because it's so carefully presented to give a sense of its glory days in the 1960s, it's also easy to assume that Greenway represents Agatha's most important mode of living.

But there's one final argument in favour of the idea that this was a place of performance. What passes most people by is the fact that Agatha didn't actually live there. Greenway, despite its splendour, was 'just' a holiday house. 'It wasn't real life,' Mathew says.[46]

Real life, and real work, took place somewhere entirely different. We'll get there, but not before celebrating the greatest achievement of Agatha's later years: Miss Marple.

38

Lady Detectives

Max once tried to explain why his wife wasn't a feminist. 'It was unnecessary,' he said, 'for her ever to have been interested in Women's Lib.'[1] It makes sense. For the most part Agatha was able to get what she wanted from life, while still laying claim to that vital Victorian quality of remaining 'ladylike'.

Part of this meant being openly anti-feminist. 'Men have much better brains than women, don't you think?' she'd say.[2] But Agatha *could* be described as a 'covert' feminist. She was someone whose actions – and whose fictional characters – spoke louder than her words.

Perhaps the most significant message in Agatha's work, besides the belief that good will triumph over evil, is that the underdog can win. Poirot's character shows that a funny little vain man can triumph against the odds. And later on, in her lady detective characters, Agatha showed that older people, and especially older women, have more to offer the world than meets the eye. 'Women,' says Jane Marple – as her creator could not – 'must stick together.'[3]

When Miss Marple made her first extended appearance in *The Murder at the Vicarage* of 1930, Dorothy L. Sayers got the point of her at once. 'Dear old Tabbies,' she wrote to Agatha, 'are the only possible right kind of female detective . . . I think this is the best you've done.'[4]

We've already learned that Miss Marple developed in a series of stages, each of them a time of turbulence and painful growth for her creator. Her earliest origins lay with Agatha's Victorian Auntie-Grannie. Miss Marple, Agatha said, was 'the sort of old lady who would have been rather like some of my grandmother's Ealing cronies.' Miss Marple's 'biographer', the literary critic Peter Keating, notes that after Agatha's psychotherapy in the 1920s, and then again during the difficult wartime years, Miss Marple adopts something of the role of a psychoanalyst. But after the war, like Agatha herself, Miss Marple retreated from her engagement with individuals. Instead, she becomes a commentator on the changes in society.

This means the puzzle aspect becomes less important in the later Miss Marples. For that very reason some readers prefer Poirot. But this is to completely miss the pleasure of Miss Marple's observant eye. And if your interest is Agatha Christie, as opposed to her writing, then we can deduce Miss Marple meant far more to her than the Belgian detective did.

For one thing, there were parts of Poirot that simply no longer worked for stories set, as Agatha's nearly always were, in the present day. He gets 'more unreal as time goes by,' she admitted in 1966. 'A private detective who takes cases just doesn't exist these days . . . the problem doesn't arise with Miss Marple.'[5]

Yet Agatha guarded Miss Marple's privacy in the same way that she guarded her own, rarely revealing details of Jane Marple's past life. She did once let slip that Miss Marple – like Agatha herself – was an experienced nurse, having had 'a good deal to do with' sick people. From 1930 onward, Miss Marple remains about sixty-five until Agatha catches up with her. After that, they age in tandem. And just like her creator, Miss Marple used domesticity – in Marple's case, a love of gardening – to distract unwelcome attention away from her formidable brain.[6]

Miss Marple once explained that when it came to solving crime, 'it's easier for gentlemen, of course.'[7] But her gender would open up new realms of detection. Female detectives are more sensitive to clues hidden in female bodies and the disguises they wear. Assistant detective Bridget in *Murder Is Easy*, for example, is the one to realise that murder victim Amy the housemaid would never have painted her hat scarlet, because it would have looked awful with her red hair. Likewise, in *The Body in the Library*, Miss Marple detects that the blonde victim's hair colour wasn't natural. With her compassionate observation of the young woman at the heart of the case, Miss Marple was demonstrating her lifelong sympathy for girls. She trains up orphaned girls to find employment as housemaids. She forces a male hairdresser to marry the woman he's made pregnant. She makes a small contribution to the wider work of the single women of her generation. 'Going back over the last 50 years,' wrote the principal of Somerville College in 1953, 'try to think of them without all the work, paid or unpaid, of single women.' In transforming nursing, education and childcare, 'they have addressed the meetings and they have addressed the envelopes.'[8]

The later Miss Marple has something of the social worker about her. Indeed, a mature Miss Marple novel, argues Peter Keating, is not so much a mystery as a novel about 'the condition of England'. The failing home for juvenile delinquents in *They Do It with Mirrors*, the corrupt businessman's dysfunctional household in *A Pocket Full of Rye*, and the selfish owner of the country estate in *4.50 from Paddington*: all express Agatha's view of a Britain that has gone wrong, but in which a single old lady can still be a force for good.

Or at least, Miss Marple is a force for good, as 'good' now seemed to exist to Agatha herself: a wealthy and successful woman, socially conservative, born in 1890, who believed in capital punishment. In her autobiography, she proposes – hatefully – that a possible alternative to the death sentence might be the transportation of the malefactor to 'some vast land of emptiness peopled only with primitive human beings.' And as the Sixties progress, Miss Marple, and her creator, grow positively terrifying in the severity of their judgements.

In *A Pocket Full of Rye*, for example, Miss Marple becomes vengeful, furious, potent. She is angry about the wickedness that's been wrought upon the murdered housemaid. And although a doddery old lady is far 'unlike the popular idea of an avenging fury . . . that was perhaps exactly what she was now.'

Miss Marple makes her final appearance in the context of her home village, St Mary Mead, in *The Mirror Crack'd from Side to Side*. Here, the Sixties have arrived. Although Agatha was now seventy-two, she was still alert to change. The village now has a supermarket instead of a grocer. Its inhabitants eat cereal instead of bacon for breakfast, and there's a new 'Development' on the village's edge. But while St Mary Mead has changed, it hasn't decayed. 'The new world was the same as the old,' thinks Miss Marple, 'the clothes were different, the voices were different, but the human beings were the same as they always had been.'

Agatha's later books have occasional passages of reminiscence that in an earlier work would have been omitted because they fail to drive the plot forward. In *Nemesis*, for example, Miss Marple muses at length at the confusing changes made to the layout of *The Times*. This was purely for the pleasure of capturing an experience with which the author was all too familiar. But even Miss Marple never quite stopped trying to keep up. 'One can never go back,' she thinks, in *At Bertram's Hotel*, 'the essence of life is going forward.' Published in 1965, the book twice echoes Harold Macmillan's phrase 'the wind of change', from his celebrated speech of 1960 on the inevitability of independence coming to the former British colonies in Africa.[9]

An increasingly frail Miss Marple in *The Mirror Crack'd* seemed to be saying goodbye to readers, and certainly we were saying goodbye to St Mary Mead. But Agatha would write Miss Marple into three more books: *A Caribbean Mystery* (1964), *At Bertram's Hotel*, a riff on 1960s crime and celebrity culture, and then her final outing in *Nemesis* (1971). In a notebook she was using in 1965, Agatha recorded an idea she called 'National Trust Tour of Gardens'. It would become the story in which Miss Marple joins a doomed coach tour of English historic houses.[10]

In the last stages of Miss Marple's life, once she's detached from St Mary Mead, she develops more and more common ground with her creator: she travels to Barbados, as Agatha did in 1956; she stays in a luxurious hotel (something Agatha had long enjoyed) and finally, in *Nemesis*, she becomes rich. And the title of this final book, taken from Greek myth, rightly suggests that Miss Marple has also become superhuman, a modern equivalent of the ancient goddess Nemesis, pre-patriarchal, inexorable.[11]

And, it has to be admitted, almost inhuman. This aspect of Miss Marple had long existed. Here she is back in 1950, in *A Murder Is Announced*, when another character notices the 'grimness of her lips and the severe frosty light in those usually gentle blue eyes. Grimness, an inexorable determination.' Now, in *Nemesis*, Miss Marple deals with other mythic figures: three sisters, who stand for the three Fates, and a crime involving same-sex desire. Late Miss Marple no longer cares about human justice and human law. She has become, in the words of the Home Secretary in the novel, 'the most frightening woman I ever met'.

Her own beliefs about good and evil, right and wrong, motivated Agatha's work ever more clearly in her later life. Unconscious motives, the 'psychological' approach of the 1930s, no longer interested her. Inspector Craddock sounds authorial in 1950 when he says he's 'pretty sick of the psychological jargon that's used so glibly about everything nowadays.'[12] Agatha had come to feel that the lax, forgiving and 'psychological' approach to wrongdoing taken by Britain's post-war society was misguided. And Miss Marple feels the same.

Despite Agatha's urge to remain up-to-date, this message resonated with her readers, who were also beginning to feel out of step with the rhetoric of a more permissive society. This silent majority weren't wearing miniskirts themselves, and rather disapproved of the minority who were. They liked the idea that their 'Christies for Christmas' were really modern morality tales (a phrase Max used to describe Agatha's work) or 'fairy stories for grown-up children'.[13]

The idea that these were children's stories for grown-ups is supported by the titles from nursery rhymes Agatha often used in the post-war years – *Mrs McGinty's Dead* (1952), *A Pocket Full of Rye* (1952), *Hickory Dickory Dock* (1955) – all hinting at the 'evil lurking within the world of childhood'.[14] 'I adore nursery rhymes, don't you?' says a character in *The Mousetrap*. 'Always so tragic and *macabre*.'[15]

One of the criticisms of Agatha Christie has always been the narrowness of her world, the limited range of people who get to take part in it. But Gillian Gill argues quite the reverse. To her, the tight focus of Agatha's vision is the very thing that creates the powerful darkness of her work.

Like childhood, St Mary Mead is a place where evil ought not to exist. Miss Marple operates in the kind of environment familiar to comfortably-off, middle-class people. 'Instead of placing violence outside the privileged world of the rich and respectable,' Gill explains, 'among people whom "we" do not know, Christie places it in our midst.'[16] Even a chocolate-box English village contains evil. 'She had no urge to *talk*' about unnatural sex, rape, incest, perversions of all kinds, Miss Marple says, but still, 'she knew them.'[17]

Although Miss Marple stories are often described as cosy crime, this is a bold, dark, troubling view of the world.

Miss Marple, and her creator, hold no illusions. They believe that evil may be found *everywhere*. In any relationship. In any one of us.

39

To Know When to Go

' To know when to go – that was one of the great necessities of
life. To go before one's powers began to fail, one's sure grip
to loosen, before one felt the faint staleness.'

That was Headmistress Miss Bulstrode, in Agatha's *Cat Among the
Pigeons* (1959), pondering on the future of her successful girls' school.
Agatha's publishing team were asking the same question. 'Don't
quote me to Agatha but this isn't the strongest story she ever wrote,
is it?' wrote her American agent in 1960.[1]

Many diehard Christie fans love Agatha's later books, seeing in
them a bizarre richness and depth. In the 1960s, though, as Agatha
became ever better known through film and TV, the screen adaptations of her earlier books were making her into something she'd
never been before: a heritage brand. The quality of each new book
began to matter less. People would buy it just because it had her
name on it. Agatha was well aware of this. 'Probably I could write
the same book again and again,' she admitted, 'and nobody would
notice.'[2] She began to try less hard.

She attempted to stay fresh and to depict Sixties life in *Third Girl*
(1966), with its references to hallucinogenic drugs and the rackety
doings of young people in rented flats, but it wasn't convincing as
detective fiction.[3] And then she took an even bigger leap in 1967
with *Endless Night*.

Rather extraordinarily, she wrote this book from the viewpoint
of a young, male, working-class psychopath. 'People shook their

heads,' Agatha recalled, 'as much as to say, "What is a county lady like that doing with such a character? She'll make a terrible mess of it!" Well I don't think I did . . . I listen to my cleaning woman talking, and to her relatives. I've always loved shops and buses and cafes. And I keep my ears open. That's the secret.'[4] *Endless Night* was produced in just six weeks, Agatha's last compulsive writing spell. 'It's rather different from anything I've done before,' she explained in a pre-publication interview, 'more serious, a tragedy really.' Indeed, Collins were nervous about how it would be received.

But they needn't have worried. While it had a different tone, in one important way *Endless Night* was very familiar. The central device of having the criminal narrate the story was exactly the same one used forty years previously in *Roger Ackroyd*. Brilliantly, people were still taken in. The *Guardian* thought it contained 'the most devastating' surprise that 'this surpriseful author has ever brought off.' 'She fooled me this time too,' admitted the reviewer in the *Sun*.

Agatha was also still producing her 'thrillers', culminating in 1970's *Passenger to Frankfurt*. This remarkable work reads today as utterly bonkers. And yet, with a big promotional push linked to her eightieth birthday, it spent more than six months in the bestseller lists.[5]

Her notebook for the work includes a list of disturbing things that might be worked into the evil organisation her hero must confront: 'Terrorist activity. American universities. Black Power etc. all this gives accounts of the rise & love of Violence – training for Sadism – etc in the last 50 or 60 years – all possibly taking in the idealism of youth.'[6]

Agatha ended up choosing a plot in which Hitler secretly survives the Second World War by hiding in a lunatic asylum, and produces a son to continue his evil work. Despite its ropey plot, the book does at least have a strong atmosphere, and one that appealed to her readers. Frightened by modernity, they saw the student protests erupting in their cities as uncontrollable violence. A true devotee has described *Passenger to Frankfurt* as 'a *Pilgrim's Progress* of the modern world . . . a serious picture of the world as she saw it, using the means of the thriller, just as Verdi made use of the operatic language he knew best when he came to compose his Requiem Mass.'[7] But if this was the world of 1970 as Agatha saw it, it was a depressing place.

Meanwhile, the people producing Agatha's books had a growing problem. Behind the scenes, Dorothy Olding had taken over from Harold Ober after his death in 1959. A grand, old-New-York lady, Olding dressed like a character from *Mad Men*, smoked through a cigarette holder, and took no prisoners. She was left bewildered by her first reading of *Passenger to Frankfurt*: 'I was bitterly disappointed in the book. It seemed to me a bad imitation of a spy story and a damned weak one at that.'[8] The *New York Times* agreed with her. 'Everyone is entitled to write a bad novel,' ran its review, 'but somebody should interpose himself and discourage its publication.'[9]

But despite expert opinion, Agatha's readers clearly still wanted to read this sort of thing. After its huge commercial success, Cork had to backtrack: 'How right you were about *Passenger to Frankfurt*,' he admitted to Agatha, 'I thought certain things should be done to it, but they were not, and it proved to be by far your most successful book.'[10]

Except in the handful of her outstanding works, Agatha had never been entirely conscientious about tying up loose ends. Poirot, for example, lives at Whitehaven Mansions, except when he lives at Whitehouse Mansions. In *Sleeping Murder*, a clerk, a receptionist and a train passenger are all accidentally given the same name of Narracott – which is *also* the name of a chambermaid, a boatman and a policeman, in three completely different books.[11]

But now little lapses grew ever easier to spot. Olding was left with questions about *At Bertram's Hotel*. How did Miss Marple know that one character was the daughter of another? Was she 'just so bright that she deduced it?'[12] Yet you can see the difficulties in passing on such views, when even Agatha's own daughter hardly dared. In 1971, Agatha insisted on having a final play, *Fiddler's Five*, staged in Bristol. Rosalind begged her mother not to try to transfer it from Bristol to the harsher scrutiny it would face in London, and Cork was nervous too: 'we must face the fact that we will get a hostile press.'[13]

But Agatha grew angry and defensive. 'I can't see why you are so opposed,' she told Rosalind, bitterly, 'I don't suppose you or Mathew or the Harrison Homes and the rest of those who benefit in the company will really refuse their cut of the takings.' This was a long-running argument about Rosalind's pessimism, and Agatha lashed out with real venom. 'If you'd succeeded in making me stick to books – there would probably have been no *Mousetrap*, no *Witness for the Prosecution*, no *Spider's Web* . . . If one doesn't take a few risks in life one might as well be dead.'[14]

Rosalind's fears were well-grounded, though, for *Fiddler's Five* featured people getting away with not paying their taxes. 'Your fans do admire your work and indeed you yourself to a quite frightening degree,' she tried to explain to her mother. 'I don't think this play is worthy of <u>you</u> – you are in this play letting people get away with crime . . . & even in fun I don't think it is funny.'[15]

Edmund Cork also came in for various epistolary rants. 'FIRST,' ran one six-page stinker, 'I've got to have more strict control over the idiotic and <u>very</u> annoying things that my publisher and others seem to take upon themselves to do . . . I'm not just a performing dog for you all – I'm the <u>writer</u> & it's misery to be ashamed of oneself.'[16] The letter reads like the fulminations of an aging King Lear.

But in recent years a sadder explanation has been put forward for the decline in Agatha's later work. Analysis of the language she uses suggests that perhaps she was beginning to suffer from the onset of Alzheimer's disease. Agatha's syntax had never been complex: it's one of the reasons her works translate so effectively into other languages, and date so little. Yet now it became simpler still.

Elephants Can Remember (1972) was the last outing for Agatha's Mrs Ariadne Oliver. The very title suggests the subject of memory was weighing upon its 81-year-old author's mind. Language researchers at the University of Toronto have calculated that the novel is 31 per cent less rich in vocabulary than *Destination Unknown*, written when she was sixty-three. And analysis by the same team also discovered that only 0.27 per cent of Agatha's youthful work *The Mysterious Affair at Styles* is made up of 'indefinite' words like 'thing', 'something' and 'anything', whereas in *Postern of Fate*, written when she was eighty-three, the percentage rises to 1.23 per cent.[17] Ian Lancashire, one of the authors of the study, points out that *Elephants Can Remember* may also be read as a portrait of the declining mental powers of Mrs Oliver, who forgets things she ought to have known, and who has to call in Hercule Poirot for help. 'It reveals an author responding to something she feels is happening but cannot do anything about,' he says, 'it's almost as if the crime is not the double-murder-suicide, the crime is dementia.'[18]

This makes criticism of the declining quality of Agatha's work, and her own defensiveness about it, read very differently. Any impatience with an artist unwilling to bow out gracefully is replaced with sympathy, for someone who was possibly beginning to struggle with an illness.

Agatha was never diagnosed with the condition. But given the reluctance people still feel in talking about dementia, especially in its earliest stages, and given that its stigma was even greater in the 1970s, it's a theory that's both heartbreaking, and worth taking seriously.

Maybe those around her were beginning to suspect that Agatha was losing her most precious possession: her mind.

❧ PART TEN ❧

Curtain — 1970s

40

Winterbrook

In 1960, planning permission was granted for Ashfield to be demolished. In its place went up flats and their garages. There was a
proposal to finish the development off with a petrol station too.[1]

When Agatha realised what was going on, it was too late to do
anything about it. Of course, she'd given up all claim to the place
when she'd sold Ashfield, long ago. But the son of her solicitor
remembered how she'd 'wanted to buy it back', putting in 'a very
late bid'. When her offer was rejected, 'she was very, very upset'.[2]

Agatha continues the story herself:

It was a year and a half before I summoned up the resolution to drive
up Barton Road . . . there was nothing that could even stir a memory.
They were the meanest, shoddiest little houses I had ever seen . . .
and then I saw the only clue – the defiant remains of what had once
been a monkey puzzle.[3]

Agatha's fiction, so often about family and home, had been deeply
rooted in Ashfield. Its physical loss reminded her of the loss of her
mother, and the loss of her younger self. The decision to sell had
been her own. But she'd subsequently described herself as feeling
'very homeless . . . I do long for Ashfield.'[4]

And so, as Agatha completed the final scenes of her autobiography, she finished where she'd begun: in Torquay. Remembering the
past became one of her chief pleasures in later life:

Long walks are off, and, alas, bathing in the sea; fillet steaks and apples and raw blackberries (teeth difficulties) and reading fine print. But there is a great deal left . . . sitting in the sun – gently drowsy . . . and there you are again – remembering. *'I remember, I remember, the house where I was born . . .'*

More recent events and places began to matter less. At seventy-nine, Agatha made her first public statement referring to the existence of Nancy Neele. 'My husband found a young woman,' she told an interviewer. She even seemed to refer obliquely to her invention of 'Teresa Neele': 'You can't write your fate. Your fate comes to you. But you can do what you like with the characters you create.'[5] She may have been talking about her own actions in 1926, or this may have been a statement of her life's philosophy. Agatha Christie had truly been a woman who'd written her own story.

In September 1970, Collins insisted on giving her an eightieth birthday party in London. Agatha attended in a feathered hat, cat's-eye spectacles and two strands of pearls. For once she didn't mind the photos, especially the one of her long-time publisher, Billy Collins. 'What a good looking publisher I have got,' she told him.[6] The party was also a launch for her so-called eightieth book. The catchy number had been reached by some clever counting on Collins' part. The matter's confused by collections of short stories, and American editions having different titles to English ones. Back in Devon, there was a dinner where Agatha enjoyed a 'special treat – half a large cup of neat cream for ME while the rest had Champagne.'[7]

In the New Year of 1971, it was announced that the Queen was to make Agatha a Dame Commander of the British Empire. This would be the last of Agatha's many name changes. 'Dame Agatha' was almost the 'Lady Agatha' she'd fantasised about being in her first ever short story. That January, she proudly put 'D.B.E.' at the top of the page in her notebook where she was developing ideas for *Nemesis*.[8]

Even her eightieth birthday hadn't stopped her from working. And the place where much of this work happened was the real home, not Greenway, in which Agatha and Max had been living all these years. Winterbrook House, on the Thames just south of Wallingford, was purchased back in 1934 during Agatha's plutocratic period when she bought houses on a whim:

> I saw an advertisement in *The Times*. It was about a week before we were going abroad to Syria . . . a delightful, small, Queen Anne house . . . meadows sweeping right down to the river.

Despite her imminent departure abroad, Agatha snapped it up at once. One visitor was in raptures, finding the house 'a joy to see, and the roses to smell. It has always seemed to me a perfect arrangement to have a river at the bottom of the garden.'[9] Another visitor describes the comfy informality: 'wine-coloured autumn light as it came flooding in the blowsy, cosy room – too large, billowing chairs (like Agatha), the lavender colour of the slagware on the chimney-piece. She brought out piece after piece of old china for me, nothing spectacular . . . just pleasant Victorian pieces (again like Agatha herself).'[10]

It was only here, in her secret home, that Agatha could put aside the role of Dame Agatha, and retreat into her favourite role of being Max's wife. 'Max's house', was how she described Winterbrook, 'always has been.' Greenway grew gradually less important; in 1959 she gave it to Rosalind, and in 1967 Rosalind and Anthony moved in to make it their main home.[11]

At Winterbrook, Agatha kept her profile pretty low, although letters addressed just to 'Mrs Agatha Christie, Berkshire', or even 'Mrs Agatha Christie, Gran Bretaña' would inevitably find their way there.[12] Agatha's guarding of her privacy, her lack of hospitality to the nosy or needy, meant she was never fully embedded into Wallingford local life. The town's former deputy mayor describes her as 'an autocratic and rather unapproachable lady'.[13] The most famous writer in the world was living in Wallingford, and Wallingford expected her to be Lady Bountiful. But Agatha showed an admirable resistance to feeling she had to oblige. As plain Mrs Mallowan, though, she could slip into the salon on the High Street to get her hair done, watch performances by the local dramatic society, and give gifts to the little boy who delivered Winterbrook's fish.[14] She and Max also attended a quiet country church in the village of Cholsey nearby.

A reason for spending more time at Winterbrook was Max's move, in 1962, to All Souls' College in nearby Oxford. He was to help with the new Oxford edition of Herodotus. The appointment meant a lot to him: 'I felt that I had through the efforts of my life-work, recovered from the lack of academic distinction in my youth.'[15] These cerebral life goals were notably different from the values of the leisured Edwardian Millers with which Agatha had been brought up. 'I have felt happiest,' Max admitted, 'when submitted to an absolutely rigid discipline. It stops me from thinking.'[16] It was international, intellectual Max who persuaded Agatha to vote (against her inclination) in favour of membership of the EU in the referendum of 1975.

During his career Max had trained many younger archaeologists, 'six of whom had gone on to become Directors of British Schools of Archaeology'.[17] But he was not universally liked. Kinder colleagues put his irascibility down to the medication he took following his strokes, but he was assiduous in maintaining many an archaeological feud. After Kathleen Kenyon's death, the woman with whom she lived burned Max's letters on the grounds that they were 'so nasty' she didn't want other archaeologists to see them.[18]

Meanwhile, in the last pages of the family photo albums kept for more than eighty years, Agatha meets new grandchildren, sits smiling in a room crammed with books, hyacinths and greetings cards, or lolls in a sunchair. She attends chilly-looking picnics on Dartmoor, or snuggles in her fur coat. She walks with difficulty, on Max's arm, or with a stick. She is surrounded by adoring dogs. She often wears a red hat. In one photo, just like the poem about eccentric and self-confident older ladies, she even wears a purple outfit to go with it.[19]

But Winterbrook in the 1970s was falling slowly into decay. The creation of the 'Christie Empire', as Cork called it, with its complicated tax arrangements, meant that cash for day-to-day purposes was in strangely short supply. Winterbrook's wiring became dangerous and wasn't repaired, and Cork found himself roped into helping with maintenance work. In 1971 Agatha described 'a lot of wind and rain and somewhere water is running or dripping . . . there must be SOS on Monday to a plumber *and* an electrician.'[20] 'What bliss 3 good servants and a small house would be nowadays,' she sighed.[21]

In June 1971, Agatha broke her hip, and made a stay at the Nuffield Orthopaedic Centre before a welcome return to her own bed.[22] 'Things were critical for a day or two,' Cork told colleagues, 'but I am delighted to tell you that she has made a miraculous recovery.'[23] Soon she was 'taking the first halting steps between parallel bars'.[24] The querulous demands now vanished from her correspondence. 'Dearest Rosalind,' she wrote, 'it was wonderful to escape from Hospital and get HOME! You arranged that room beautifully . . . Dear Rosalind it was so good of you to come up & to do all you have.'[25]

After her fall, Agatha began to plan for the end. In 1972 she sent Cork a collection of poems for him to publish if he felt fit. 1973's book was *Postern of Fate*, the final appearance of an elderly Tommy and Tuppence. The house it featured was full of echoes of Agatha's last great preoccupation: Ashfield. But as fiction it was repetitive and flawed. 'Pretty ghastly, isn't it?' Olding thought. 'Much worse than the last two . . . Poor dear, I wish there were a way for somebody to tell her that this shouldn't be published – for her sake.'[26] Yet again, though, it became a bestseller.

And rather poignantly, Agatha's very last notebooks still contain ideas for yet another novel. It was to feature an entirely new idea, about two students who murder a boy purely as an experiment. As critic John Curran notes, it was 'her powers of development' that were waning, 'not her powers of imagination'.[27]

In 1974, Agatha had a heart attack, and was prescribed a medicine that caused her to lose a great deal of weight. Tony Snowdon came to Winterbrook to photograph her, producing a set of striking and tender images of a very old and very tiny lady. He asked Agatha how she'd like to be remembered, and her modest reply – of course – was simply as 'a rather good writer of detective stories'.[28]

That autumn she was still getting out and about, and there was one final important public appearance still to come. In 1972, perhaps surprisingly, Agatha had accepted an invitation once again to try films. This time the suggestion came from a man with his finger in many twentieth-century pies, Lord Mountbatten. He approached Agatha to help his son-in-law, John Brabourne, and Brabourne's co-producer Richard Goodwin, who wanted to dramatise *Murder on the Orient Express*. 'None of us feel,' he wrote, 'that the films so far made do real justice to the "Agatha Christie" spirit.'[29]

The time was ripe for a fresh attempt at cinema. Things had changed since the 1960s when MGM took liberties with Agatha's books.[30] This new set of producers considered *Murder on the Orient Express* as a classic piece of storytelling, rather like Dickens or Austen, something to be respected and preserved. Goodwin, for one, was motivated to do the film after seeing his ten-year-old daughter devouring the novel.

Once Sidney Lumet was attached to the project as director and once Albert Finney and Sean Connery had accepted parts, all the best actors were – in Brabourne's words – 'queuing up to be in the picture'.[31] They included Ingrid Bergman, Lauren Bacall, Vanessa Redgrave and John Gielgud. Goodwin puts the success of the film down to the casting of all these 'old stars who'd come through the studio system. Firstly, they were terribly disciplined. Secondly, they were just wonderful.' The producers met their author on only a handful of occasions, and 'she didn't say much,' says Goodwin. 'But somehow everyone knew what she wanted – she had a kind of aura.'[32]

The budget rose to a scary £4.5 million, the most expensive film in its producers' experience. Agatha had learned the hard way that she might not like the film. But this time she was pleased with what she saw.[33] *Murder on the Orient Express* became what was then the most successful British film ever at the box office. It topped the charts in America, and also had an electric effect on book sales.[34] After its rapturous reception across the Atlantic, the film had a charity premiere in London in November 1974, with not only the Queen present, but also the Queen of Crime. 'It must have been hard for her,' said Goodwin of Agatha's attendance in a wheelchair, but 'she knew she needed to do it.'[35]

After the premiere there was a banquet at Claridges. At the end of the evening, Max retained in his mind's eye the image of Mountbatten escorting his wife out of the dining room at midnight, and Agatha's 'raising her arm in farewell'.[36]

It was a final farewell, to London, and to a life's work. In 1974, a collection of stories, *Poirot's Early Cases*, had been published instead of a book, and in 1975 that book written decades earlier, *Curtain: Poirot's Last Case*, appeared. The *Guardian*'s reviewer paid it a touching compliment. For 'the egotistic Poirot, hero of some 40 books,' the review ran, 'it is a dazzlingly theatrical finish. "Goodbye, cher ami," runs his final message to the hapless Hastings. "They were good days." For addicts, everywhere, they were among the best.'[37] Poirot's obituary also appeared in the *New York Times*.

Very frail, now, in the summer of 1975, Agatha started to sleep downstairs at Winterbrook. A nurse came in at night to look after her, and Max and also Barbara Parker were always on hand.[38] Making preparations for what was to come, Agatha wrote down the quotation from Edmund Spenser she wanted on her memorial:

Put on my Slate: Sleep after Toyle, Port after Stormie Seas. Ease after Warre, Death after Life, Doth greatly please. Bach Air in D from 3rd Suite played at my funeral please. Also Nimrud [sic] from the Elgar Variations.

Then autumn at Winterbrook turned into a last winter, and on 12 January 1976, Agatha finally died. It happened, Max said, 'as I wheeled her out in her chair after luncheon to the drawing-room . . . Death came gently and peacefully, a merciful release and I thank God that she was spared suffering.'[39]

Max phoned the local doctor to say 'she's gone,' and added a warning: 'Don't say a word.'[40] But word got out nonetheless. Vast numbers of journalists began to descend on quiet Wallingford, to cover the ending of both an era and a remarkable life.

Later in January 1976, Agatha was buried at the church of St Mary's in Cholsey near Winterbrook. Her family asked that the funeral remain private.[41] But inevitably, said her grandson, it 'was a media event (how that would have horrified Nima) with cameras peeping everywhere.'[42] Max had to answer 500 letters of condolence, letters that showed him he hadn't fully 'realised how widely she was loved as well as admired'.[43]

Agatha was buried in her wedding ring, and Max, of course, was still there to escort her to the grave. She left him a poem about love surviving death:

I died – but not my love for you.
That lives for aye – though dumb,
Remember this
If I should leave you in the days to come.[44]

During the last years of her life, Agatha had often reflected on just how well her impetuous marriage had turned out. Her sister had 'implored' her not to marry Max. But oh, Agatha thought, 'I'm thankful I didn't listen to her! Forty years of happiness I should have missed.'[45]

What secrets did this marriage contain? 'You are clever with women,' Agatha once told Max. 'It's a pity we are a monogamous country – you could keep 2 or 3 wives & happy!!!'[46] It's long been speculated that Max in later life had affairs, and Barbara Parker's name is the one most often mentioned. It's a staple of Christie novels that the female employees of professional men should fall in love with them – 'an occupational disease of secretaries' is how one detective puts it.[47] Anthony Hicks is reported as saying that 'Max and Barbara would lock themselves in the room to work on the

Nimrud papers and she'd leave the shoes outside the door . . . the shoes . . . were some kind of signal.'[48] A friend of Max's arriving to visit him shortly after Agatha's death was surprised to find Max's devoted assistant massaging her boss's feet.[49]

To judge by the late-twentieth century ideal of marriage as true romantic love and lifelong sexual fidelity, perhaps there was something to criticise here. But that's such a limiting view of matrimony. Agatha's second marriage had many aspects that were most unusual for the year of 1930 in which it began. As a divorced single parent, she unexpectedly found herself a much younger partner who looked after her until her dying day. It was a lifelong intellectual conversation between two questing minds, with companionship at its heart. 'No one else,' Max explained, 'could have been for me the perfect companion that you are. It happened that you and I just fitted together: now and again two souls meet that fit, not because they are alike, but because they are counterparts.'[50] 'She possessed so many of the things that I lack,' he thought, 'a saintly humility . . . her inner spirit lived in near sympathy with Christ.'[51] This was a companionate marriage that proved remarkably endurable and successful.

And it reminds us that our own conventions about relationships do not represent the only way to live. 'Have a good time, darling,' Agatha had once said, 'and do <u>anything</u> that you want to and you need – just so long as I am held in your heart in deep friendship and affection.'[52] She didn't need to know exactly what he was up to. It's only our modern, romantic idea that marriage should provide all of life's intensity that makes it an issue.

And Max certainly kept his side of the bargain they'd made. In 1945, he told her from Libya how her photograph had accompanied him for the entire three years of their separation. 'Even when I slept in the desert at night,' he wrote, 'I used to put it out on the side of my camp bed so that I could see you in the morning.' His wife, he thought, 'will always have a lovely face and a lovely smile to me even when she is as I hope she will be, 90 years old!'[53] He was true to his word. 'Max looks after me nobly at night,' wrote Agatha, as ninety drew near, 'commode absolute heaven.'[54]

As long ago as 1936, Max had written Agatha a love letter. 'Sometimes,' he said,

> but not so very often two people find real love together as we do . . . we know that what we have cannot perish . . . for me you will remain beautiful and precious with the passing of years.[55]

After her death, a photo of Mathew, and that same letter, folded up small, were found in Agatha's purse.

She had carried it with her for thirty-nine years.

But Max, it turned out, simply couldn't bear to live alone. Just over a year after Agatha's death, in March 1977, he was writing to Rosalind to announce a second marriage. Of course, it was to Barbara. 'No one will ever take the place of my dear Agatha,' he said, 'but I think she would have approved for she used to tell me to marry in case anything happened to her . . . it is lonely now, and will not be so with Barbara who has always been a devoted friend.'[56] In September 1977, after Max had been a widower for a year and seven months, he and Barbara married quietly at Kensington Register Office.

Barbara Parker's role in this story, it seems to me, is to stand for all the archaeological wives who made the tea, organised the logistics, typed the manuscripts, and kept the wheels of twentieth-century archaeology turning. And even when Max finally made her his wife, it wouldn't last long. Less than a year later, Max was at Greenway when he experienced 'acute myocardial failure' and Barbara was present at her husband's death.[57] She buried him next to Agatha in the churchyard of St Mary's.

Barbara inherited the London house in Cresswell Place, and vacated Winterbrook in favour of a smaller house in Wallingford. From there she travelled to spend her days at the Oriental Institute in Oxford.[58]

So Max and Agatha were reunited. She'd planned that they should lie together like this since the first weeks of their engagement in 1930, writing that she'd like to be both buried beside him, and then, one distant day, dug up again: 'by some nice young archaeologist (!) of the future . . . it would be such fun to be of some <u>use</u> after you were dead.'[59]

Standing at her graveside in the grassy, windy, Oxfordshire churchyard, as so many people do, it's nice to think that yes, indeed, Agatha is still of some very considerable 'use' after death.

Still giving a huge number of people a huge amount of pleasure.

41

After the Funeral

On the night of Agatha Christie's death, the lights were dimmed in two West End theatres to mark her passing. The casts of both *Murder at the Vicarage* and *The Mousetrap* paid their respects from the stage, and 'the audience stood in silent tribute'.[1]

Agatha was also mourned in the world of archaeology, not least at the British School in Iraq she'd supported for so long. Her presence lived on at the school's building in Baghdad in the form of her portable toilet. Designed to be taken into the field, this item was a tea chest with a brass-hinged mahogany seat attached. There are rival stories about what happened to it. One version is that it was 'inadvertently burnt by an intoxicated member of the excavation team on Guy Fawkes night sometime in the late 1970s'.[2] But Ellen McAdam remembers it being taken onsite for an archaeological investigation carried out in advance of the building of the Hemrin Dam. When the archaeologists reopened their rented house for a new season's work, 'the cry went up "Agatha's got termites!" And had to be burned.'[3]

The school itself would eventually lose its government funding before reinventing itself as the British Institute for the Study of Iraq, a charity with the aim of supporting Iraqi rather than British archaeologists, and focussing more on 'helping people and their heritage and less on putting large holes in archaeological sites'.[4] In 2011, the British Museum purchased many of the ivory carvings from Max and Agatha's excavations at Nimrud. They've become all the more precious since some of the other ivories were crushed underfoot during the ransacking of Baghdad Museum in 2003. But other traces of Max and Agatha's life in West Asia remain. A beautiful 2021 documentary by German film-maker Sabine Scharnagl recorded how a family living near Max's excavation at Chagar Bazar in Syria were worried that IS might take their village, and knew that if this happened their books would be destroyed. So their Agatha Christies have a safe and secret hiding place in a water tank.[5]

In the wider world, there was incredulity when the contents of Agatha's will emerged. Everyone was 'astonished at the low value of her estate,' said her solicitor.[6] However, her company's earnings in 1975 were close to £1,000,000. The success of the film of *Murder on the Orient Express* shifted three million paperback copies of the novel.[7] Agatha's will left bequests to family, friends, godchildren and employees, and showed a most characteristic concern with knick-knacks. A codicil of 1975, added just a few months before her death, redistributed various treasured items: a stone Buddha to Anthony, a green Venetian glass fish to Mathew.[8]

For Rosalind, Edmund Cork, and the rest of the 'Christie Empire', life and the work of licensing and looking after Agatha's literary estate went on. A survey in 1983 revealed that of the twenty-eight plays by women performed in Britain's repertory theatres that year, Agatha had written twenty-two of them.[9] In 1988, Cork died at the age of ninety-four. From 1994, when Peter Saunders retired, the author's royalties for *The Mousetrap* were given to charities to support the arts; Saunders himself died in 2003 at ninety-one. In 1998, Chorion PLC, the company that already owned Enid Blyton's works, took over Booker McConnell's stake in Agatha Christie Limited, later being replaced by Acorn Media.[10]

Mathew remained happily in occupation of Pwllywrach. A visiting journalist in 1978 described it as an 'art-filled gray stone manor', and found Mathew and Angela's three children playing with their pony, their black retriever, 'a terrier named Piddles and three cats'.[11] Meanwhile Rosalind and Anthony at Greenway worked hard to maintain the house and gardens. One visitor, Henrietta McCall, who was there to research Max's papers, describes her feeling that they 'never had pots of cash'. She was woken in the night by rainwater coming in through her bedroom ceiling.[12]

Something clearly had to be done. In 2000, Rosalind, Anthony and Mathew jointly decided to give Greenway to the National Trust. 'It was not easy to make the decision,' Mathew explained, but the family hoped the Trust would 'preserve and enhance' the beauty of a magical place.[13] It was the garden, rather than the house, that initially attracted the National Trust, and the grounds were quickly opened to visitors. But the conservation charity was not universally welcomed on the banks of the Dart. There was local outcry at the prospect of visitors driving along the narrow lanes. 'It must be terribly painful when one makes a gesture like yours that everyone immediately jumps up and down in protest,' sympathised the local MP in a letter to Rosalind.[14] So plans were made to bring many visitors by ferry along the river.

Once the gardens had become a visitor destination, the house itself was closed for a conservation project. The outer wall of Max's bedroom was leaning outwards, only remaining intact because – appropriately – his long built-in bookcase was holding it together.[15] Decades of occupation meant 'Greenway was very cluttered in a splendid way.' Rosalind's desk was 'a great slagheap of letters, bills – so spectacular that some artist asked if he could paint it.'[16] Volunteers sat in Portakabins cataloguing the 20,000 objects in Greenway's collection.

There wasn't room to display all these accumulated possessions, so in 2006 a sale was held in Exeter to raise money for the conservation project. Eager fans snapped up lots such as some Greenway House writing paper, which was offered at a guide price of £150, but which sold for £740.[17] The luckiest purchaser paid £100 for a locked 'old travelling trunk', probably one of those used for Agatha's childhood exile in France when the Millers' funds were running low. Four years later, its new owner finally got it open, to discover inside it a diamond ring that had belonged to Clara.[18]

In 2004, the 85-year-old Rosalind died, followed a few months later by her husband. She'd been devoted to her mother's memory, frightening off anyone who tried to tarnish it. Like a member of the Royal Family, born into her job, Rosalind could never relinquish her sense of duty to an institution. 'She didn't trust any of us to get it right,' says her grandson James, who today manages his great-grandmother's literary legacy.[19] Having told her life's story, I feel deeply sorry for Rosalind. It seems to me that for her mother's legend to live, some part of Rosalind's life as an independent person had to die.

Agatha in her lifetime had insisted on the privacy of her papers, and claimed that she'd destroy correspondence and diaries 'without regret'.[20] But when the end came, she actually left behind a huge stash of letters and papers, which are today in the care of the Christie Archive Trust and which enabled the writing of this book.

She also left her autobiography, published in 1977 after her death. Rosalind was involved in editing the final text, and allowed the inclusion of the short chapter about the painful events of 1926. Something, after all, would have to be said. And as the keeper of her mother's flame, Rosalind was still trying to counter the view that Agatha was a manipulative minx who'd staged the 'disappearance'.

In later life, Agatha had grown able to treat the matter almost lightly. 1962's *The Mirror Crack'd from Side to Side*, for example, contains a little joke about a lady who can't recognise her own relatives: Miss Marple thinks this may be 'shrewdness rather than memory loss'. Rosalind, on the other hand, felt she could never relax her guard, and after the autobiography, she maintained a strict policy of silence about the 'disappearance'. During his grandmother's lifetime, Mathew had 'never exchanged a word on it' with her, and 'it's not something that has ever been discussed in the family.'[21] 'I always felt slightly resentful my mother didn't show me the famous letters concerning the disappearance,' he says.[22] The events of 1926 still cast a shadow on people's lives nearly a century later.

But this silence created a vacuum in which various theories could take root. When the journalist Gwen Robyns had her request to write an authorised biography refused, she apparently took her revenge. 'I am of the opinion,' she wrote in her book of 1978, that when Agatha Christie disappeared, she 'knew exactly what she was doing . . . she decided to teach her husband a lesson.'[23] The next year a feature film, *Agatha*, went even further. In it, a character based upon the real Agatha attempted both to murder Nancy Neele and to kill herself. The film, Rosalind said, was 'altogether against our wishes and is likely to cause us great distress.'[24]

Eventually Rosalind decided a controlled glimpse of her mother's archive might help reshape the narrative. In 1984, she allowed author Janet Morgan to publish a biography of Agatha Christie that was thorough, fair and scrupulous. Morgan described her own initial impression of Christie as 'strange, manipulative, fertile in thinking of ways to murder and trick,' but a closer acquaintance with the evidence changed her mind. She concluded that the author was a consummate professional, and a kind and happy person. So much is indisputable. But I think there's something more that Morgan and the family at the time didn't fully acknowledge. In 2022 it's okay in a way that it wasn't, in the 1980s, to accept that a woman might have been kind and hardworking, but *also* 'strange, manipulative, fertile in thinking of ways to murder and trick.' That's not a disparagement. It's an acknowledgment of a woman's complexity.

And even in spite of Morgan's book, the myth persisted that Agatha was a bad person. There've been scores of writers, and presumably their readers, who still haven't believed Agatha when she tells us she was ill. Biographer Jared Cade in 1998 thought she disappeared because 'she had wished to spite' Archie.[25] Here's journalist Ritchie Calder's son, writing in 2004, and stating in terms of absolute fact what we know to be an untruth: that his father had 'tracked Agatha Christie down in a hotel in Harrogate after she went missing so that her cheating husband would be accused of her murder.'[26]

It means that despite all Agatha's achievements, there's a lingering sense of unfinished business about her life, that mental illness has been conflated with mendacity, that lies are believed instead of truth.

With society's growing willingness to talk about mental health, perhaps the tide will turn. It's already done so when it comes to assessing Christie's status as an artist. When Laura Thompson wrote the second authorised biography in 2007, it contained a tender and passionate celebration of Agatha's work. But Thompson was still pushing uphill, making the case for Christie as a serious novelist in a time when she was commonly dismissed as trashy.

Within the last fifteen years, though, the definition of what constitutes 'culture' and what's worthy of study has exploded. Academics started asking why someone so widely read was so little studied, and Christie now appears regularly in syllabuses and theses.

Part of the reluctance to take her seriously was, ironically, the very success of the television adaptations of her work. In 1989 David Suchet first appeared as ITV's Hercule Poirot, a part he'd play until 2013. Joan Hickson was Miss Marple for a generation on the BBC between 1984 and 1992, followed by Geraldine McEwan and then Julia McKenzie as ITV's Miss Marples between 2004 and 2013. These programmes put Christie into a box in people's minds labelled 'heritage nostalgia', undemanding and comforting.

These British television adaptations of the 1990s and 2000s usually set Agatha's stories in an unspecified year floating about somewhere in the earlier twentieth century, and they were so widely watched around the world that they became a powerful part of Britain's tourist brand. But they also had the effect of making Agatha's work seem blander and more homogenous than it really is. Here's the *Chicago Tribune* in 1991: 'the fictional world that Christie created – with its antique-filled drawing room, manicured gardens and orderly, goreless murders that rarely left so much as a stain on the Aubusson rug – seems increasingly quaint.'[27] Not if you read the actual books.

This changed dramatically when the BBC engaged Sarah Phelps to write a new, darker series of Christie retellings, which got off to a flying start in 2015 with a brutal, gripping *And Then There Were None*. There was nothing nostalgic about Phelps' writing, which placed each story carefully back into the historical context of the year in which it was written. The left-wing bent of the writing displeases some Christie fans, but even Phelps's critics admit she respects the source material in a way earlier adaptors did not.

This change in the way Christie's represented on screen is linked to what critics and scholars have been saying about her. The roster of people who don't enjoy Agatha Christie is impressive. Edmund Wilson, Raymond Chandler, Bernard Levin and Robert Graves have all, at one time or another, criticised her style, her characters, her readability.

It took two female scholars to begin the reappraisal. Gillian Gill, publishing in 1990, refused to take Christie at face value. I love the way Gill began to feel through the veils towards the elusive genius who lay behind. For a start, she pointed out that Agatha wasn't a single person. Over a lifetime, the woman we're talking about was constantly reinventing herself. Agatha Miller became Mrs Archibald Christie, Agatha Christie, Teresa Neele, Mrs Mallowan and Mary Westmacott, then a beloved grand-mother called Nima who ended up as Dame Agatha. And Gill also began to dismantle Agatha's notorious sense of privacy. It had been both a wonderful and a terrible thing. It allowed her to live her life as she wished, yet it destroyed her reputation.[28] If the writer herself was unwilling to speak of her work and take it seriously, why should anyone else?

But rather than taking Christie's denigration of her writing at face value, we should look at the work itself. This is exactly what Alison Light did, in her influential study *Forever England: Femininity, Literature and Conservatism Between the Wars* (1991). She deserves much of the credit for repositioning Christie, not as a conformist, but 'an iconoclast . . . a writer dealing in family secrets, reworking the conventional forms of Victorian transgression – the inheritance drama, mistaken identities, hidden madness.'[29]

Agatha may never have been able to take herself seriously. Finally, though, other people started to do it for her.

*   *   *

Agatha's legacy is clearly her work, but I think there's another legacy too that's hiding in plain sight. Not only was Agatha Christie the most successful novelist of the twentieth century. She was also someone who redefined the rules for her social class and gender.

It's so easy to overlook this because Agatha took such pains to deny that she was a bona fide novelist at all. 'I do not quite feel as though I am an author,' she'd still say, in her eighties. It was only her daughter, perhaps the person who believed most in 'Agatha Christie', who would say: 'But you *are* an author, Mother. You are quite definitely an author.'

Rosalind, close on thirty years younger, had a different notion of what an author ought to be like. It was her very own mother who'd broadened the definition. No longer was an author a grand old man with a beard.

Agatha experienced so many of the twentieth century's great changes, for good and for ill: a hasty wartime marriage, a working life in the hospital, a family fear of 'madness', divorce, mental illness, psychotherapy, bereavement in the Second World War, and professional success in the entertainment industry on an unprecedented global scale.

But while the century shaped Agatha, it did not *make* her. With her willpower and independence and industry, she made herself. To restate Margaret Lockwood in 1954: 'Agatha has the gift of doing what all women want to do. She achieves something . . . in her heart every woman . . . would like to do these things . . . all we can do is dream.'[30]

Agatha never felt able to describe the ambition to achieve that doubtless burned within her, and would always have chosen a much more humble definition of the scope of her life. Her book about archaeology begins with a warning. 'This is not a profound book,' she says,

there will be no beautiful descriptions of scenery, no treating of economic problems, no racial reflections, no history. It is, in fact, small beer – a very little book, full of everyday doings and happenings.[31]

After the dramas of 1926, Agatha's daily life may also read as small beer, full of everyday doings and happenings.

But small though her ambition was, she left a profound influence on the culture of the twentieth century.

Sources

Archive Sources

The Bodley Head Ltd Archive, Reading University Library (BHL)
British Museum (BM)
Christie Archive Trust (CAT)
Exeter University Library, Department of Special Collections, Hughes Massie Archive (EUL)
The National Archives (TNA)
National Trust archive at Greenway, Devon (NT)
Personal collection of Georgina Herrmann (GH)
Surrey History Centre (SHC)
Archive of the Institute of Archaeology at University College London Library (UCLL)
Harrogate Library

Select Printed Sources

Mark Aldridge, *Agatha Christie on Screen* (2016)
Jane Arnold, 'Detecting Social History: Jews in the work of Agatha Christie', *Jewish Social Studies,* vol. 49, no. 3–4 (Summer–Autumn, 1987) pp. 275–282
Rachel Aviv, 'How A Young Woman Lost Her Identity', *New Yorker* (26 March 2018)

Earl F. Bargainnier, *The Gentle Art of Murder* (1980)

Robert Barnard, *A Talent to Deceive* (1979; 1987 edition)

Marcelle Bernstein, 'Hercule Poirot is 130', *Observer* (14 December 1969)

James Carl Bernthal, 'A Queer Approach to Agatha Christie', PhD thesis, University of Exeter (2015)

– 'If Not Yourself, Who Would You Be?': Writing the Female Body in Agatha Christie's Second World War Fiction', *Women: A Cultural Review* (vol. 26, 2015) pp. 40–56

– ed., *The Ageless Agatha, Essays on the Mystery and the Legacy* (2016)

– *Queering Agatha* (2017)

Vera Brittain, *Testament of Youth* (1933)

Erica Brown and Mary Grover, eds., *Middlebrow Literary Cultures: The Battle of the Brows, 1920–1960* (2012)

Jared Cade, *Agatha Christie and the Eleven Missing Days* (1998; 2011 edition)

Ritchie Calder, 'Agatha and I', *New Statesman* (30 January 1976) pp. 128–9

Stuart Campbell, 'Arpachiyah' in Trümpler, ed., (1999; 2001 edition) pp. 89–103

Lydia Carr, *Tessa Verney Wheeler: Women and Archaeology Before World War Two* (2012)

Agatha Christie, *An Autobiography* (1977; 2011 edition)

Sarah Cole, *Modernism, Male Friendship, and the First World War* (2003)

Artemis Cooper, *Cairo in the War, 1939–45* (1989; 2013 edition)

Donald Elms Core, *Functional Nervous Disorders* (1922)

John Curran, *Agatha Christie's Secret Notebooks* (2009; 2010 edition)

– *Agatha Christie, Murder in the Making: More Stories and Secrets from Her Notebooks* (2011)

Elizabeth Darling, *Wells Coates* (2012)

Miriam C. Davis, *Dame Kathleen Kenyon* (2008)

Leyla Daybelge and Magnus Englund, *Isokon and the Bauhaus in Britain* (2019)

Nigel Dennis, 'Genteel Queen of Crime', *Life* (May 1956)

Arthur Conan Doyle, *Letters to the Press* (1986)

Andrew Eames, *The 8.55 to Baghdad* (2004; 2005 edition)

Martin Edwards, ed., *Ask a Policemen, by Members of the Detection Club* (1933; 2013 edition)

Brian Fagan, *Return to Babylon* (1979)

Alison S. Fell and Christine E. Hallett, eds., *First World War Nursing: New Perspectives* (2013)

Martin Fido, *The World of Agatha Christie* (1999)

Gillian Franks, article in the *Aberdeen Press and Journal* (23 September 1970) p. 5

Gillian Gill, *Agatha Christie: The Woman and Her Mysteries* (1990)

Julius Green, *Curtain Up – Agatha Christie: A Life in Theatre* (2015; 2018 edition)

Hubert Gregg, *Agatha Christie and All That Mousetrap* (1980)

Richard Hack, *Duchess of Death* (2009)

Christine E. Hallett, *Nurse Writers of the Great War* (2016)

Kathryn Harkup, *A Is For Arsenic: The Poisons of Agatha Christie* (2015)

Wilfred Harris, *Nerve Injuries and Shock* (1915)

Peter Hart, *Fire and Movement: The British Expeditionary Force and the Campaign of 1914* (2014)

Bret Hawthorne, *Agatha Christie's Devon* (2009)

Emily Hornby, *A Nile Journal* (1908)

Janet H. Howarth, *Women in Britain* (2019)

Dorothy B. Hughes, 'The Christie Nobody Knew', in Harold Bloom et al, *Modern Critical Views: Agatha Christie* (1992; 2002 edition)

Nicola Humble, *The Feminine Middlebrow Novel, 1920s to 1950s: Class, Domesticity and Bohemianism* (2001)

Maroula Joannou, *The History of British Women's Writing, 1920–1945* (2012; 2015 edition)

H.R.F. Keating, ed., *Agatha Christie: First Lady of Crime* (1977)

Peter Keating, *Agatha Christie and Shrewd Miss Marple* (2017)

Viola Klein and Alva Myrdal, *Women's Two Roles* (1956)

Marty S. Knepper, 'The Curtain Falls: Agatha Christie's Last Novels', *Clues,* vol. 23, issue 5 (2005) pp. 69–84

Ian Lancashire and Graeme Hirst, 'Vocabulary Changes in Agatha Christie's Mysteries as an Indication of Dementia: A Case Study', *19th Annual Rotman Research Institute Conference, Cognitive Aging: Research and Practice* (2009)

Alison Light, *Forever England: Femininity, Literature and Conservatism between the Wars* (1991; 2013)

– *Mrs Woolf and the Servants* (2007)

Hilary Macaskill, *Agatha Christie at Home* (2009; 2014 edition)

Merja Makinen, *Agatha Christie: Investigating Femininity* (2006)

M.E.L. Mallowan *Twenty-Five Years of Mesopotamian Discovery* (1959)

– *Mallowan's Memoirs* (1977; 2021 edition)

M.E.L. Mallowan and J. Cruikshank Rose, 'Excavations at Tall Arpachiyah, 1933', *Iraq,* vol. 2, no. 1 (1935) pp. 1–178

Henrietta McCall, *The Life of Max Mallowan* (2001)

Katie Meheux, '"An Awfully Nice Job". Kathleen Kenyon as Secretary and Acting Director of the University of London Institute of Archaeology, 1935–1948', *Archaeology International,* vol. 21, no. 1 (2018) pp. 122–140

Billie Melman, *Empires of Antiquities: Modernity and the Rediscovery of the Ancient Near East, 1914–1950* (2020)

Richard Metcalfe, *Hydropathy in England* (1906)

Janet Morgan, *Agatha Christie: A Biography* (1984; 2017 edition)

John Howard Morrow, *The Great War In The Air: Military Aviation from 1909 to 1921* (1993)

Juliet Nicolson, *The Great Silence, 1918–1920: Living in the Shadow of the Great War* (2009; 2010 edition)

Andrew Norman, *Agatha Christie: The Disappearing Novelist* (2014)

Joan Oates, 'Agatha Christie, Nimrud and Baghdad', in Trümpler, ed. (1999; 2001 edition) pp. 205–228

Richard Ollard, ed., *The Diaries of A.L. Rowse* (2003)

Charles Osborne, *The Life and Crimes of Agatha Christie* (1982; 2000 edition)

– 'Appearance and Disappearance', in Harold Bloom et al, *Modern Critical Views: Agatha Christie* (1992; 2002 edition) pp. 108–9

Mathew Prichard, ed., *Agatha Christie: The Grand Tour* (2012)

Gordon C. Ramsey, *Agatha Christie: Mistress of Mystery* (1967)

Eleanor Robson, 'Old habits die hard: Writing the excavation and dispersal history of Nimrud', *Museum History Journal* (vol. 10, 2017) pp. 217–232

Gwen Robyns, *The Mystery of Agatha Christie* (1978; 1979 edition)

A.L. Rowse, *Memories and Glimpses* (1980; 1986 edition)

Dennis Sanders and Len Lovallo, *The Agatha Christie Companion* (1984)

Peter Saunders, *The Mousetrap Man* (1972)

Mary Shepperston, 'The Turbulent Life of the British School of Archaeology in Iraq', *Guardian* (17 July 2018)

Dorothy Sheridan, ed., *Wartime Women: A Mass-Observation Anthology* (2000)

Adrian Shire, ed., *Belsize 2000: A Living Suburb* (2000)

Michael Smith, *Bletchley Park and the Code-Breakers of Station X* (2013; 2016 edition)

Tom Stern, 'Traces of Agatha Christie in Syria and Turkey' in Trümpler (1999; 2001 edition) pp. 287–302

Faye Stewart, 'Of Red Herrings and Lavender: Reading Crime and Identity in Queer Detective Fiction', *Clues: A Journal of Detection,* vol. 27.2 (2009) pp. 33–44

Judy Suh, 'Agatha Christie in the American Century', *Studies in Popular Culture,* vol. 39 (Fall 2016) pp. 61–80

Julian Symons, *Bloody Murder* (1972; 1974 edition)

– 'Foreword: A Portrait of Agatha Christie', in Harold Bloom et al, *Modern Critical Views: Agatha Christie* (1992; 2002 edition)

Marguerite Tarrant, 'Mathew Prichard', *People* (10 April 1978)

James Tatum, *The Mourner's Song: War and Remembrance from the Iliad to Vietnam* (2003)

Laura Thompson, *Agatha Christie: An English Mystery* (2007; 2008 edition)

Charlotte Trümpler, ed., *Agatha Christie and Archaeology* (1999; 2001 edition)

Lynn Underwood, ed., *Agatha Christie, Official Centenary Edition* (1990)

H.V.F. Winstone, *Woolley of Ur* (1990)

Lucy Worsley, *A Very British Murder* (2013)

Peter Wright, 'In the Shadow of Hercule: The War Service of Archibald Christie', *Cross & Cockade International,* vol. 41/3 (2010) pp. 161–4

Francis Wyndham, 'The Algebra of Agatha Christie', *The Sunday Times* (26 February 1966)

Web Sources

David Burnett's blog, williamhallburnett.uk

Juliette Desplatt, 'Decolonising Archaeology in Iraq?' The National Archive Blog (27 June 1917) https://blog.nationalarchives.gov.uk/decolonising-archaeology-iraq

Carine Harmand, 'Sparking the imagination: the rediscovery of Assyria's great lost city', https://blog.britishmuseum.org/sparking-the-imagination-the-rediscovery-of-assyrias-great-lost-city

Peter Harrington, dealer, catalogue for the sale of inscribed books from the library of Charlotte 'Carlo' Fisher, https://www.peter-harrington.co.uk/blog/wp-content/uploads/2016/09/Christie.pdf

Matt Houlbrook, 'How the "Roaring Twenties" myth obscures the making of modern Britain', https://www.historyextra.com

Kyra Kaercher, 'Adventure Calls: The Life of a Woman Adventurer', Penn Museum blog (29 February 2016) https://www.penn.museum/blog/museum/adventure-calls-the-life-of-a-woman-adventurer

Archives of the Red Cross, online at museumandarchives.redcross.org.uk

Eleanor Robson, 'Remnants of Empire: Views of Kalhu in 1950', oracc.museum.upenn.edu (2016)

Unpublished Secondary Sources

Tim Barmby and Peter Dalton, 'The Riddle of the Sands: Incentives and Labour Contracts on Archaeological Digs in Northern Syria in the 1930s', University of Aberdeen Business School, discussion paper (2006)

Tina Hodgkinson, 'Disability and Ableism', a paper presented at the Agatha Christie conference at Solent University, Southampton (5–6 September 2019)

Ann Laver, 'Agatha Christie's Surrey', research paper, copy available at SHC (2013)

Janet Likeman, 'Nursing at University College, London, 1862–1948', PhD thesis, University of London (2002)

Hélène Maloigne, '"Striking the Imagination through the Eye": Relating the Archaeology of Mesopotamia to the British Public, 1920–1939', PhD thesis, University College London (2020)

Henrietta McCall, 'Deadlier Than The Male: The Mysterious Life of Katharine Woolley (1888–1945)'

Margaret C. Terrill, 'Popular (Non) Fiction: The Private Detective in Modern Britain', MA thesis, Dedman College, Southern Methodist University (2016)

Christopher Charles Yiannitsaros, 'Deadly Domesticity: Agatha Christie's "Middlebrow" Gothic, 1930–1970', PhD thesis, University of Warwick (2016)

Acknowledgements

F or permission to quote from copyright material I thank the
following: the Trustees of the Christie Archive Trust (Mathew
and James Prichard, Nigel Wollen and John Mallowan), Mathew
Prichard personally for the unpublished letters and poems of Agatha
Christie, The Trustees of the British Museum, The Imperial War
Museum, Harold Ober Associates, the estate of Dorothy L. Sayers,
Anthony Steen, The estate of Adelaide Phillpotts, Exeter University
Library, Special Collections, Georgina Herrmann, Nicholas and
Caroline Christie, and Professor Sue Hamilton as Director of the
UCL Institute of Archaeology. The works of Agatha Christie are
quoted courtesy of HarperCollins Publishers, @ Agatha Christie
(1921, 1922, 1923, 1924, 1925, 1930, 1931, 1932, 1933, 1934, 1935,
1936, 1939, 1941, 1942, 1944, 1945, 1946, 1947, 1950, 1952, 1955,
1956, 1962, 1964, 1967, 1968, 1975, 1976).

I've found previous writers on Christie to be a very generous lot.
For their stimulating conservations I thank Mark Aldridge, Kemper
Donovan, Julius Green, Alison Light, Henrietta McCall, Tony
Medawar, Janet Morgan, and, of course, J.C. Bernthal, whose appli-
cation of queer theory to Christie's work inspired the approach of
this book. I'd also like to acknowledge the expertise to be found in
Laura Thompson's beautiful book, *Agatha Christie: An English
Mystery* (2007), and in Jared Cade's *Agatha Christie And The Eleven
Missing Days* (1998). Judy Dewey, Mark Aldridge, Tony Medawar,
Kemper Donovan and J.C. Bernthal all kindly read the manuscript

and made detailed corrections and improvements. I'm also immensely grateful for support – whether practical, intellectual or emotional – from Colleen A. Brady, Simon Bradley, Juliet Carey, Paul Collins, Rosalind Crone, John Curran, John Curtis, Ophelia Field, Paul Finn, Gillian Gill, Daisy and Richard Goodwin, Annie Gray, Edgar Jones, Christine Hallett, Georgina Herrmann, Katherine Ibbett, Josh Levine, Jane Levi, Tracey Loughran, John Mallowan, Ellen McAdam, Katie Meheux, Pastor Michael Mortimer, Eleanor Robson, Caroline Shenton, Judy Suh, Alexandra Wilson, and Philip Ziegler. Thanks go to Kevin Plant at Wrexham Archives, to the trustees of the Royal Welch Fusiliers Museum Trust, and to Belinda Smith, Laura Murray and Laura Cooper of the National Trust. I'm also grateful for access to the research of the late National Trust volunteer Patrick Dipper. I'm indebted to Dr Phil Wickham of the Bill Douglas Cinema Museum and Anna Harding in Special Collections at the University of Exeter, to Avril McKean at Harrogate Library, and to Malcolm Neesam, local historian of Harrogate and to Claire Hilton of the Royal College of Psychiatrists. I'd like to pay special tribute to Kemper Donovan and the late Catherine Brobeck's wonderful podcast, *All About Agatha,* and to Hélène Maloigne, for her expert help with research into archaeology. I thank my BBC colleagues Rachel Jardine, Edmund Moriarty and Eleanor Scoones for their work and their friendship. At Hodder, I love working with Rupert Lancaster, Ciara Mongey, Vero Norton, Alice Morley and Juliet Brightmore, and I'm grateful to copyeditor Jacqui Lewis. At Pegasus, my sincere gratitude goes to Claiborne Hancock, Jessica Case and team. This was my final collaboration with my much-missed literary agent Felicity Bryan, and I'm deeply grateful to Catherine Clarke and everyone else at Felicity Bryan Associates, as well as to Tracey MacLeod and her colleagues at KBJ Management. But my biggest debts of all are to the generous and hospitable people without whom this book would not have been possible: James, Mathew and Lucy Prichard, aided by Joe Keogh, and to my friends and family, especially Enid Worsley and Jim Emerson and, of course, Mark Hines.

Notes

Preface

1. Godfrey Winn, 'The Real Agatha Christie', *Daily Mail* (12 September 1970)
2. Agatha Christie, *An Autobiography* (1977; 2011 edition) p. 517. All further quotations in the text without endnotes are from the same source.
3. See in particular Gillian Gill, *Agatha Christie: The Woman and Her Mysteries* (1990)

The House Where I Was Born

1. *Torquay Times & South Devon Advertiser* (19 September 1890) p. 1; *Morning Post* (18 September 1890)
2. Richard Hack, *Duchess of Death* (2009) p. 6
3. Police missing persons description 1926; Ramsey (1967) p. 22; her passport
4. CAT photograph album
5. CAT the Miller family's book 'Confessions, An Album to Record Thoughts Feelings' (27 October 1903)
6. Mathew Prichard, personal conversation (29 September 2020)
7. CAT 'Confessions' (15 October 1897)
8. *Daily Mail* (January 1938)
9. CAT Adelaide Ross (née Phillpotts) to Agatha (15 March 1966)
10. Gillian Gill, *Agatha Christie: The Woman and Her Mysteries* (1990) pp. 5-6
11. I'm grateful for the dedicated and detailed research of Colleen A. Brady
12. CAT unpublished typescript of 'The House of Beauty'
13. *Endless Night* (1967); see also Laura Thompson, *Agatha Christie: An English Mystery* (2007; 2008 edition) p. 7

Insanity in the Family

1. 'The H.B. Claflin Company', *New York Times* (20 April 1890); Colleen A. Brady
2. I examined the dress while it was unpacked for conservation at Greenway, May 2021
3. CAT no. 30, letter to Whitelaw Reid, American ambassador to London (2 April 1909)

4. Ian Rowden, 'When Agatha Christie kept the cricket score', *Torquay Times* (24 September 1974)

5. Advert for sale of leasehold, *The Times* (9 October 1880)

6. Miss Gwen Petty quoted in Gwen Robyns, *The Mystery of Agatha Christie* (1978; 1979 edition) p. 36

7. CAT 'Confessions' (1 May 1871)

8. CAT Garrison of Dublin, Certificate of Baptism (14 March 1854)

9. This is all due to the tremendous geneaological sleuthing of Colleen A. Brady

10. CAT typescript of 'The House of Beauty'

11. CAT 'Album' of family poetry written in the hand of Clara Miller

12. Max Mallowan, *Mallowan's Memoirs* (1977; 2021 edition) p. 196

The Thing in the House

1. *Torquay Times and South Devon Advertiser* (6 January 1893) p. 7

2. NT 121991, book in Clara Miller's hand of 'receipts for Agatha'

3. Quoted in Robyns (1978; 1979 edition) pp. 49–50

4. NT 122993, 122998, 123010, 122953, 122976, 123024 bills for Ashfield

5. *Daily Mail* (7 December 1926)

6. CAT 'Confessions' (1870)

7. *The Mirror Crack'd from Side to Side* (1962)

8. *By the Pricking of My Thumbs* (1968)

9. Francis Wyndham, 'The Algebra of Agatha Christie', *The Sunday Times* (26 February 1966)

10. Marcelle Bernstein, 'Hercule Poirot is 130', *Observer* (14 December 1969)

11. *Sleeping Murder* (1976)

12. Mallowan (1977; 2021 edition) p. 195

13. *Giant's Bread* (1930)

14. Alison Light, *Forever England: Femininity, Literature and Conservatism between the Wars* (1991; 2013) p. 94

15. CAT typescript of 'The House of Beauty'

Ruined

1. *An Autobiography*, p. 103

2. 'A.B. Townsend Tries Suicide', *New York Times* (15 March 1901) p. 1

3. *New-York Daily Tribune* (10 January 1896) p. 7

4. https://www.findagrave.com/memorial/196044102/margaret-frary-watts

5. CAT unpublished typescript 'Then and Now' (1949)

6. CAT 'Confessions' (n.d.)

7. CAT notebook of Monty (1924)

8. CAT Frederick to Clara (24 October 1901)

9. CAT Agatha to Frederick (undated, probably 1901)

10. *An Autobiography*, p. 111; items in CAT

11. Hack (2009) p. 28

12. *Law Reports – East Africa Protectorate*, vol. 4, p. 135; *An Autobiography*, p. 382

13. http://www.nationalarchives.gov.uk/pathways/census/living/making/women htm; http://www.nationalarchives.gov.uk/pathways/census/events/polecon3.htm

14. *An Autobiography,* p. 113

Waiting for The Man

1. Barbara Cartland quoted in Juliet Nicolson, *The Great Silence: 1918–1920* (2009; 2010 edition) pp. 3–4
2. http://www.nationalarchives.gov.uk/pathways/census/living/making/women.htm
3. CAT 'Confessions' (14 October 897)
4. CAT Madge to Agatha (26 February, n.y.)
5. James Burnett, *Delicate, Backward, Puny and Stunted Children* (1895) pp. 90–91
6. Gillian Franks, *Aberdeen Press and Journal* (23 September 1970) p. 5
7. Wyndham (1966)
8. *Murder Is Easy* (1939)

Best Victorian Lavatory

1. CAT unpublished typescript, 'Then and Now' (1949)
2. CAT 'Confessions' (19 April 1954)
3. 1901 England census
4. Clare Hartwell, Matthew Hyde and Nikolaus Pevsner, *Cheshire: The Buildings of England* (2011) p. 207
5. Jared Cade, *Agatha Christie and the Eleven Missing Days* (1998; 2011 edition) p. 32
6. *An Autobiography,* p. 139; Cade (1998; 2011 edition) p. 34

The Gezireh Palace Hotel

1. The trip has previously been dated to 1910, but the SS *Heliopolis* stopped serving Cairo at the start of 1909. For this and other reasons, Colleen A. Brady dates it to 1908.
2. Artemis Cooper, *Cairo in the War, 1939–45* (1989; 2013 edition) pp. 489, 511
3. Karl Baedeker (firm), *Egypt and the Sudân, Handbook for Travellers* (1908) p. 74
4. CAT red leather photo album of Agatha's youth
5. According to her passport
6. CAT unpublished typescript 'Then and Now' (1949)
7. *Dead Man's Folly* (1956)
8. Bernstein (1969)
9. David Burnett's blog williamhallburnett.uk (14 September 2017)
10. CAT unpublished typescript *Snow upon The Desert,* pp. 31, 4–5, 36
11. CAT Eden Phillpotts to Agatha (6 February 1909)

Enter Archibald

1. Quoted in Robyns (1978; 1979 edition) p. 49
2. Julius Green, *Curtain Up – Agatha Christie: A Life in Theatre* (2015; 2018 edition) pp. 45–6
3. *The Secret of Chimneys* (1925)
4. Robert Barnard, *A Talent to Deceive* (1979; 1987 edition) pp. 31–2
5. *Murder on the Orient Express* (1934)

6. Quoted in Robyns (1978; 1979 edition) p. 66
7. SHC *Admissions to Brookwood and Holloway Mental Hospitals* (1867–1900) entry for Archibald Christie (patient number 1744)
8. CAT copy of a handwritten notebook listing the events of Archie Christie's life
9. *Exeter and Plymouth Gazette* (2 January 1913) p. 5
10. CAT copy of a handwritten notebook listing the events of Archie Christie's life
11. *Western Daily Mercury* (28 December 1912) p. 4
12. https://www.thegazette.co.uk/London/issue/28725/page/3914

Torquay Town Hall

1. https://www.rafmuseum.org.uk/research/online-exhibitions/rfc_centenary/the-rfc/the-central-flying-school.aspx
2. CAT Archie to Agatha (n.d., 1913) 'Monday 10pm Royal Flying Corps Netheravon'
3. CAT Archie to Agatha (n.d., 1913) 'Sunday Royal Flying Corps Netheravon'
4. CAT Archie to Agatha (n.d., 1913) 'Wednesday RFC'
5. CAT copy of Archibald Christie's flying logbook (1913)
6. CAT Archie to Agatha (n.d., 1913?) 'Sunday Royal Flying Corps'
7. CAT Archie to Agatha (n.d., 1913) 'Wednesday RFC'
8. CAT Archie to Agatha (n.d., 1913) 'Wednesday, Royal Flying Corps Netheravon'
9. TNA AIR 76/86/79
10. Peter Wright, 'In the Shadow of Hercule: The War Service of Archibald Christie', *Cross & Cockade International,* vol. 41/3 (2010) pp. 161–4, 162
11. John Howard Morrow, *The Great War In The Air: Military Aviation from 1909 to 1921* (1993) p. xv
12. CAT Archie to Agatha (n.d., 1914) 'Sunday Royal Flying Corps'
13. *Unfinished Portrait* (1934)
14. CAT photograph (studio Lafayette) of Archibald Christie (no. 53218a)
15. *Giant's Bread* (1930)
16. Imperial War Museum audio interview (16 /October 1974) accession number 493
17. Franks (1970) p. 5
18. Imperial War Museum audio interview (16 /October 1974) accession number 493
19. Vera Brittain, *Testament of Youth,* (1933) p. 210
20. Brittain (1933) pp. 213; 211
21. Christine E. Hallett, *Nurse Writers of the Great War* (2016) p. 190
22. Alison S. Fell and Christine E. Hallett, eds., *First World War Nursing: New Perspectives* (2013)
23. *Giant's Bread* (1930)
24. John Curran, *Agatha Christie's Secret Notebooks* (2009; 2010 edition) p. 309
25. Agatha Miller's Red Cross service card, museumandarchives.redcross.org.uk/objects/28068
26. Clementina Black, *Married Women's Work* (1915) p. 1
27. British Private Thomas Baker in 'Voice of the First World War: Home on Leave', Imperial War Museum podcast, https://www.iwm.org.uk/history/voices-of-the-first-world-war-home-on-leave
28. Imperial War Museum audio interview (16 /October 1974) accession number 493
29. CAT album called 'What we did in the Great War', a spoof magazine, 'Hints on Etiquette'

30. ibid., 'M.E's Dream of Queer Women'
31. Miss Marion Eileen Morris service card, vad.redcross.org.uk
32. CAT album called 'What we did in the Great War', a spoof magazine, 'Police Court News, Coroners Inquest at Torquay'

Love and Death

1. CAT copy of Archibald Christie's war journal
2. *London Gazette* (20 October 1914)
3. Patrick Bishop, *Fighter Boys* (2003) p. 10
4. Quoted in Bishop (2003) p. 12
5. TNA AIR1/742/204/2/50 (25 May 1915) quoted in Peter Wright, 'In the Shadow of Hercule: The War Service of Archibald Christie', *Cross & Cockade International*, vol. 41/3 (2010) pp. 161–4, p. 163
6. *The Murder on the Links* (1923)
7. CAT copy of Archibald Christie's war journal
8. *Giant's Bread* (1930)
9. https://www.nationalarchives.gov.uk/first-world-war/home-front-stories/love-and-war/
10. CAT typescript 'THE A.A. ALPHABET for 1915'
11. CAT Archie's 'Character of Miss A.M.C. Miller' (9 July 1916)
12. Janet H. Howarth, *Women in Britain* (2019) p. xxxiv
13. Gill (1990) p. 56; *A Caribbean Mystery* (1964)
14. Quoted in Nicolson (2009; 2010 edition) p. 123
15. Marie Stopes, *Married Love* (1918) Chapter 5, p. 7
16. CAT Archie to Agatha (21 December 1915)
17. ibid.
18. CAT Archie to Agatha (n.d., '26th' 1916?)
19. Wright (2010) p. 163
20. CAT Archie to Agatha (4 April 1917)
21. *Unfinished Portrait* (1934)

Enter Poirot

1. Quoted in Anthony Thwaite, ed., *Further Requirements, Philip Larkin* (2001; 2013 edition) p. 57
2. 'In a Dispensary', reproduced in *Star Over Bethlehem and other stories* (2014 edition) p. 207
3. CAT notebook 40; Janet Morgan, *Agatha Christie: A Biography* (1984; 2017 edition) p. 70
4. Lynn Underwood, ed., Agatha Christie, Official Centenary Edition (1990) p. 18
5. Kathryn Harkup, *A Is For Arsenic: The Poisons of Agatha Christie* (2015) pp. 291–307, p. 71
6. *An Autobiography,* p. 211
7. See Gill (1990) pp. 55–61 and Light (1991; 2013) pp. 66–7 for compelling readings of *Styles*
8. *Unfinished Portrait* (1934)
9. Rupert Brooke quoted in Peter Hart, *Fire and Movement: The British Expeditionary Force and the Campaign of 1914* (2014) p. 256

10. *Curtain* (1975)
11. Arthur Conan Doyle, *A Study in Scarlet* (1887; 1974 edition) p. 43
12. *The Murder on the Links* (1923)

The Moorland Hotel

1. Nigel Dennis, 'Genteel Queen of Crime', *Life* (May 1956) p. 102
2. Advert for the Moorland Hotel (1916) in Bret Hawthorne, *Agatha Christie's Devon* (2009) p. 71
3. Charles Osborne, *The Life and Crimes of Agatha Christie* (1982; 2000 edition) p. viii
4. Eden Phillpotts, *My Devon Year* (1916) p. 192
5. Bernstein (1969)
6. Gill (1990) p. 46
7. Gill (1990) pp. 47–57

Enter London

1. Nicola Humble, *The Feminine Middlebrow Novel, 1920s to 1950s* (2001) p. 111
2. Nicolson (2009; 2010 edition) p. 7
3. Humble (2001) p. 125
4. Alison Light, *Mrs Woolf and the Servants* (2007) p. 132
5. Quoted in Nicolson (2009; 2010 edition) p. 37
6. The Labour Research Department, *Wages Prices and Profits* (1922) pp. 54, 63, 87
7. George Orwell, *The Road to Wigan Pier* (1937; 2021 edition) p. 84
8. Howarth (2019) p. xiv
9. Howarth (2019) p. l
10. *Unfinished Portrait* (1934)
11. Suzie Grogan, *Shell Shocked Britain: The First World War's Legacy for Britain's Mental Health* (2014) pp. 99–136

Enter Rosalind

1. CAT 'Confessions' (27 October 1903)
2. *Evil under the Sun* (1941)
3. *Unfinished Portrait* (1934)
4. *Unfinished Portrait* (1934)
5. See Thompson (2007; 2008 edition) p. 123–5
6. CAT Agatha to Max (20 February 1944)
7. *The Body in the Library* (1942)
8. Humble (2001) p. 116
9. Nicolson (2009; 2010 edition) p. 183
10. Philip Gibbs quoted in Sarah Cole, *Modernism, Male Friendship, and the First World War* (2003) p. 206
11. *Unfinished Portrait* (1934)

The British Mission

1. CAT Eden Phillpotts to Agatha (6 February 1909)

2. Quoted in Underwood (1990) p. 34

3. Peter D. McDonald, 'Lane, John', *Oxford Dictionary of National Biography* (2004)

4. BHL reader's reports for *Styles* (one dated 7 October 1919)

5. James Carl Bernthal, 'A Queer Approach to Agatha Christie', PhD thesis, University of Exeter (2015) p. 29

6. *The Man in the Brown Suit* (1924)

7. *Pall Mall Gazette* (20 January 1922)

8. Matt Houlbrook, 'How the "Roaring Twenties" myth obscures the making of modern Britain', https://www.historyextra.com/period/20th-century/roaring-twenties-myth-britain-british-history-1920s-interwar-why-important

9. Light (1991; 2013 edition) p. 90

10. *The Times* (21 January 1922)

11. Quoted in Mathew Prichard, ed., *Agatha Christie: The Grand Tour* (2012) p. 31

12. Hilary Macaskill, *Agatha Christie at Home* (2009; 2014 edition) p. 24

13. Quoted in Prichard, ed., (2012) pp. 223, 156

14. ibid., pp. 98, 90

15. ibid., p. 344

Thrillers

1. John Curran, 'An introduction' to *The Mysterious Affair at Styles* (1921; 2016 edition) p. 1

2. *Times Literary Supplement* (2 March 1921); Hack (2008) p. 75

3. Dennis Sanders and Len Lovallo, *The Agatha Christie Companion* (1984) p. 10

4. Harkup (2015) p. 15

5. Quoted in Underwood (1990) p. 34

6. BHL Agatha to Basil Willets (19 October 1920)

7. *Pall Mall Gazette* (20 January 1922)

8. Adrian Bingham, 'Cultural Hierarchies and the Interwar British Press' in Erica Brown and Mary Grover, eds., *Middlebrow Literary Cultures: The Battle of the Brows, 1920–1960* (2012) pp. 55–68

9. Maroula Joannou, *The History of British Women's Writing, 1920–1945* (2012; 2015 edition) pp. 1; 3

10. *The Murder at the Vicarage* (1930)

11. EUL MS 99/1/1956/1 Agatha to Cork (8 January 1956)

12. Virginia Woolf, 'Middlebrow' (1932) in *The Death of the Moth and Other Essays* (1942) p. 119; Christopher Charles Yiannitsaros, 'Deadly Domesticity: Agatha Christie's 'Middlebrow' Gothic, 1930–1970', PhD thesis, University of Warwick (2016) p. 30

13. Joannou (2012; 2015 edition) p. 15

14. Merja Makinen, *Agatha Christie: Investigating Femininity* (2006) p. 30; *The Secret Adversary* (1922)

15. Bernthal (2015) pp. 26–7

16. *Daily Mail* (19 May 1923)

17. BHL Agatha to Basil Willett (17 September 1920); Archie to The Bodley Head (3 October 1921); Agatha to Basil Willett (6 December 1921)

18. Quoted in Robyns (1978; 1979 edition) p. 77

19. BHL Agatha to Basil Willetts (4 November 1923)

20. Cade (1998; 2011 edition) p. 66
21. ibid., p. 53; Hack (2009) p. 84
22. Margaret Forster, *Daphne du Maurier* (1993) p. 235
23. *The Secret of Chimneys* (1925); Gill (1990) pp. 81–2
24. Bernstein (1969)
25. Osborne (1982; 2000 edition) p. 43
26. *Why Didn't They Ask Evans?* (1934)
27. Gill (1990) p. 90
28. Barnard (1979; 1987 edition) p. 17

Sunningdale

1. Reproduced in Trümpler (1999; 2001 edition) p. 390
2. Bernard Darwin, *The Sunningdale Golf Club* (1924) pp. 8, 12
3. Quoted in Andrew Lycett, *Ian Fleming: The Man Who Created James Bond* (1995) p. 387
4. *The Secret of Chimneys* (1925)
5. Margaret Rhondda, *Leisured Woman* (1928) quoted in Howarth (2019) p. 41
6. CAT typescript 'THE A.A. ALPHABET for 1915'
7. I'm grateful to Christine Hallett for these points
8. Cade (1998; 2011 edition) p. 57
9. CAT Agatha to Max (5 November 1930)
10. CAT Madge to Jimmy Miller (n.d., 1924)
11. *The Secret of Chimneys* (1925); *The Secret Adversary* (1922)
12. CAT typescript of the play *Ten Years*
13. Green (2015; 2018 edition) p. 50
14. *The Sittaford Mystery* (1931)
15. CAT notebook of Monty (1924)
16. *Western Times* (2 April 1931)
17. *Western Morning News* (22 July 1926) p. 2
18. CAT notebook of Monty (1924); Thompson (2007; 2008 edition) pp. 54–5
19. Nicolson (2009; 2010 edition) pp. 133–4
20. *Giant's Bread* (1930)
21. CAT notebook of Monty (1924)
22. *Western Times* (2 April 1931) p. 1
23. *Torquay Times and South Devon Advertiser* (28 May 1987) p. 3

The Mysterious Affair at Styles

1. *Daily Sketch* quoted in Sanders and Lovallo (1984) p. 35
2. Wyndham (1966)
3. Quoted in Ramsey (1967) p 37
4. *Daily Mail* (27 May 1926)
5. *Westminster Gazette* (6 June 1925) p. 10; *The Times* (17 May 1927)
6. *Daily Express* (10 December 1926)
7. Rosalind Hicks in *The Times* (8 September 1990) p. 65
8. *Daily Mail* (7 December 1926)
9. https://www.peterharrington.co.uk/blog/wp-content/uploads/2016/09/Christie.
   pdf

10. A letter from Charlotte Fisher to Rosalind, paraphrased in Morgan (1984; 2017 edition) pp. 130–134

11. *Westminster Gazette* (8 December 1926) p. 1

12. Morgan (1984; 2017 edition) p. 128

13. 'Mr London' in the *Daily Graphic* quoted in *Portsmouth Evening News* (20 August 1926)

14. *Montrose, Arbroath and Brechin Review* (6 March 1925) p. 3

15. *Dundee Courier* (17 December 1926)

16. CAT Archie to Agatha (n.d., 1913) 'Wednesday, Royal Flying Corps Netheravon'

17. CAT Agatha to Max (6 May 1944)

18. *Murder Is Easy* (1939)

19. Yiannitsaros (2016) p. 11

20. *Daily Mail* (10 December 1926)

21. *The Times* (3, 4 December 1926)

Disappearance

1. *Daily Mail* (10 December 1926)

2. *Daily Mail* (7 December 1926)

3. *Daily Mail* (7 December 1926)

4. Bernard Krönig in *Goodwin's Weekly* (1915) vol. 16, p. 11

5. *Daily Mail* (7 December 1926)

6. *Daily Mail* (10 December 1926)

7. *Daily Mail* (11 December 1926)

8. *Daily Mail* (7 December 1926)

9. *Daily Mail* (9 December 1926)

10. *Daily Mail* (11 December 1926)

11. *Daily Mail* (16 February 1928)

12. *Daily Mail* (9 December 1926)

13. *Daily Mail* (16 February 1928)

14. *Daily Mail* (6 December 1926)

15. *Daily Mail* (9 December 1926)

16. *Daily Mail* (7 December 1926)

17. 'She must leave this house', *Daily Mail* (15 December 1926); Morgan (1984; 2017 edition) p. 155

18. *Daily Express* (15 December 1926)

19. Morgan (1984; 2017 edition) p. 155

20. *Daily Mail* (7 December 1926)

21. *Daily Mail* (16 February 1928)

22. *Daily Mail* (9 December 1926)

23. *Daily Mail* (11 December 1926)

24. *Surrey Advertiser* (11 December 1926) pp. 6–7

25. *Daily Mail* (16 February 1928)

26. *Daily Mail* (6 December 1926)

27. *Daily Mail* (11 December 1926)

28. *Unfinished Portrait* (1934)

29. *The Hollow* (1946)

30. Mallowan (1977; 2021 edition) p. 201

31. *Daily Mail* (16 February 1928)

32. *Daily Mail* (6 December; 9 December 1926)

33. TNA HO 45/25904

34. *Daily Express* (7 December 1926)

35. TNA HO 45/25904

36. Andrew Norman, *Agatha Christie, The Disappearing Novelist* (2014) p. 107

37. *Daily Express* (16 May 1932)

38. *Surrey Advertiser* (18 December 1926) p. 6

39. *Daily Mail* (11 December 1926)

40. Ritchie Calder, 'Agatha and I', *New Statesman* (30 January 1976) p. 128

41. *Daily Express* (11 December 1926)

The Harrogate Hydropathic Hotel

1. Rachel Aviv, 'How A Young Woman Lost Her Identity', *New Yorker* (26 March 2018)

2. ibid.

3. Hubert Gregg, *Agatha Christie and All That Mousetrap* (1980) p. 36

4. *Daily Mail* (16 February 1928)

5. *Daily Mail* (15 December 1926)

6. *Daily Mail* (16 February 1928)

7. *Daily Mail* (17 December 1926)

8. According to *The Times,* quoted in Norman (2014) p. 43

9. *Daily Mail* (16 February 1928)

10. Bernstein (1969)

11. *Daily Mail* (16 February 1928)

12. I am indebted to Tracey Loughran and Christine Hallett for their help

13. I am indebted to David Luck of the Bethlem Royal Hospital for his help

14. Mrs da Silva in the *Daily Mail* (7 December 1926)

15. *Daily Mail* (15 December 1926)

16. Richard Metcalfe, *Hydropathy in England* (1906) p. 214

17. *Daily Mail* (15 December 1926)

18. Cade (1998; 2011 edition) p. 137

19. *Daily Mail* (15 December 1926)

20. The evidence of Rosie Asher is quoted at length in Cade (1998; 2011 edition) p. 126

21. *Daily Mail* (16 December 1926)

22. *Daily Express* (15 December 1926)

23. TNA HO 45/25904

24. *The Times* (7 December 1926)

25. *Daily Mail* (7 December 1926)

26. *Daily Mail* (7 December 1926)

27. *Surrey Advertiser* (18 December 1926) p. 6

28. *Daily Mail* (15 December 1926)

29. Ritchie Calder quoted in Robyns (1978; 1979 edition) p. 105

30. *Daily Mail* (11 December 1926)

31. *Daily Sketch* quoted in Cade (1998; 2011 edition) p. 93

32. *Daily Mail* (15 December 1926)

33. Cade (1998; 2011 edition) p. 125
34. *New York Times* (6 December 1926)
35. Cade (1998; 2011 edition) pp. 124–5
36. *Daily Mail* (15 December 1926)
37. *Daily Express* (10 December 1926)
38. *Daily Mail* (17 December 1926)
39. *Daily News* (7 December 1926) p. 7
40. *Westminster Gazette* (7 December 1926) p. 1
41. Mrs da Silva in *Daily Mail* (7 December 1926)
42. *Daily Mail* (8 December 1926)
43. Wilfred Harris, *Nerve Injuries and Shock* (1915) p. 108
44. I am indebted to Tracey Loughran for this point
45. *Daily Mail* (8 December 1926)
46. *Daily Mail* (15 December 1926)
47. *Daily Express* (15 December 1926)
48. *Westminster Gazette* (8 December 1926) p. 1; TNA HO 45/25904
49. *Daily Telegraph* (15 December 1926) p. 11
50. Agatha Christie, 'The Disappearance of Mr Davenheim' quoted in 'Why people disappear', *Daily Mail* (7 December 1926)
51. *Daily Express* (16 May 1932)
52. *Daily Mail* (8 December 1926)
53. *Daily Mail* (8 December 1926)
54. *The Times* (8 December 1926)
55. *The Times* (8 December 1926)
56. *Daily Mail* (14 December 1926)
57. *Daily Express* (9 December 1926)
58. *Daily Express* (9 December 1926)
59. *Daily Mail* (9 December 1926)
60. *Daily Express* (9 December 1926)
61. *Armstrong's Illustrated Harrogate Hand-book* (1900) p. 38
62. *Daily Mail* (16 February 1928)
63. *Daily Express* (9 December 1926)
64. *Daily Mail* (16 February 1928)
65. Quoted in Cade (1998; 2011 edition) p. 126
66. *The Times* (11 December 1926) p. 1
67. *Daily Express* (13 December 1926)
68. *Westminster Gazette* (9 December 1926) p. 1
69. *Daily Mail* (16 February 1928)
70. *Daily Mail* (16 December 1926)
71. *Daily Mail* (16 December 1926)
72. Ritchie Calder (1976)
73. Robyns (1978; 1979 edition) p. 101
74. *Daily Mail* (9 December 1926)
75. Cade (1998; 2011 edition) p. 126
76. *Daily Mail* (10 December 1926)
77. *Daily Mail* (10 December 1926)
78. *Baltimore Sun* (12 December 1926)
79. *Evening News* quoted in Thompson (2007; 2008 edition) p. 228

80. *Daily Mail* (11 December 1926)
81. Cade (1998; 2011 edition) p. 126
82. *Daily Telegraph* (11 December 1926) p. 5
83. *Daily Telegraph* (15 December 1926) p. 11
84. *The Times* (13 December 1926)
85. *Daily Mail* (10 December 1926)
86. *Daily Mail* (13 December 1926)
87. John Michael Gibson and Richard Lancelyn Green eds., *Arthur Conan Doyle, Letters to the Press* (1986) p. 322
88. *Daily Express* (13 December 1926)
89. Edgar Wallace, 'My Theory of Mrs Christie', *Daily Mail* (11 December 1926)
90. Harris (1915) p. 108
91. *Daily Telegraph* (13 December 1926) p. 9
92. *Daily Mail* (11 December 1926)
93. *Daily Mail* (14 December 1926)
94. Cade (1998; 2011 edition) p. 131
95. Hack (2009) p. 98
96. Production notes for the 1979 film *Agatha,* copy at the Bill Douglas Cinema Museum, Exeter, p. 6
97. Cade (1998; 2011 edition) pp. 118–9
98. *The Times* (14 December 1926)
99. *Daily Mail* (14 December 1926)

Reappearance

1. *Daily Express* (15 December 1926)
2. *Daily Mail* (15 December 1926)
3. *The Times* (15 December 1926)
4. *Daily Express* (15 December 1926)
5. *Daily Mail* (15 December 1926)
6. *Daily Mail* (15 December 1926)
7. *Daily Mail* (15 December 1926)
8. *Daily Mail* (16 December 1926)
9. *Daily Mail* (15 December 1926)
10. *Yorkshire Post* (15 December 1926) p. 10
11. *Daily Mail* (15 December 1926)
12. Gibson and Green, eds., (1986)
13. *Daily Express* (16 December 1926)
14. *Daily Mail* (16 December 1926)
15. *New York Times* (16 December 1926); *Manchester Guardian* (16 December 1926)
16. *Daily Express* (16 December 1926)
17. *Daily Mail* (16 December 1926)
18. *Daily Mail* (17 December 1926)
19. *New York Times* (16 December 1926)
20. *Daily Mail* (15 December 1926)
21. *Daily Mail* (16 December 1926)
22. *Daily Mail* (17 December 1926)
23. George Rothwell Brown, 'Post-scripts', *Washington Post* (16 December 1926)

24. *Surrey Advertiser* (18 December 1926) p. 6
25. *Daily Mail* (17 December 1926)
26. *Daily Telegraph* (11 February 1927) p. 6
27. TNA HO 45/25904
28. *Westminster Gazette* (17 December 1926) p. 2
29. *New York Times* (17 December 1926)
30. *Daily Express* (17 December 1926)
31. *Daily Mail* (17 December 1926)
32. *The Times* (17 December 1926)
33. Rosalind Hicks in *The Times* (8 September 1990) p. 65
34. Donald Elms Core, *Functional Nervous Disorders* (1922) p. 349
35. *Daily Mail* (16 February 1928)
36. Morgan (1984; 2017 edition) p. 148
37. *Giant's Bread* (1930)
38. William Brown, *Suggestion and Mental Analysis* (1922) pp. 22, 41; Grogan (2014) pp. 99–101
39. I am indebted to Tracey Loughran and especially to Rachel Jardine for advice on 1920s psychotherapy
40. Harris (1915) pp. 109–108
41. *Daily Mail* (16 February 1928)
42. Harris (1915) p. 109; p. 108
43. Core (1922) p. 357
44. CAT Agatha to Max (undated, May 1930)
45. *The Times*, law report (10 February 1928)
46. *Daily Mail* (16 February 1928)
47. Lawrence Stone, *The Road to Divorce, 1530–1987* (1990) p. 396
48. Robyns (1978; 1979 edition) p. 129
49. *The Times*, 'Decree Nisi for a Novelist' (21 April 1928)
50. *Unfinished Portrait* (1934)
51. TNA J 77/2492/7646 divorce court file
52. Document kept 'in a writing case along with Archie's letters', quoted in Morgan (1984; 2017 edition) p. 165, not found at CAT
53. Mallowan (1977; 2021 edition) p. 195
54. See John Baxendale and John Shapcott's contributions to Erica Brown and Mary Grover, eds., *Middlebrow Literary Cultures: The Battle of the Brows, 1920–1960* (2012)
55. Osborne (1982; 2000 edition) p. 57
56. Elizabeth Walter, 'The Case of the Escalating Sales' in H.R.F. Keating, ed., *Agatha Christie: First Lady of Crime* (1977) pp. 13–24, p. 15
57. A.L. Rowse, *Memories and Glimpses* (1980, 1986 edition) p. 78

Mesopotamia

1. CAT typescript of poem, 'A Choice'
2. CAT Agatha to Max (undated, probably November 1930)
3. *Come, Tell Me How You Live* (1946) p. 12
4. Andrew Eames, *The 8.55 to Baghdad*, London (2004; 2005 edition) p. 274
5. Hélène Maloigne, '"Striking the Imagination through the Eye": Relating the Archaeology of Mesopotamia to the British Public, 1920–1939', PhD thesis, University College London (2020) p. 43

6. *Murder on the Orient Express* (1934)
7. Trümpler (1999; 2001 edition) p. 330
8. Mallowan (1977; 2021 edition) p. 34
9. *Come, Tell Me How You Live* (1946, 2015 edition) p. 49
10. *The Secret of Chimneys* (1925)
11. Judy Suh, 'Agatha Christie in the American Century', *Studies in Popular Culture*, vol. 39 (Fall 2016) p. 71
12. Maloigne (2020) p. 12
13. Mallowan (1977; 2021 edition) p. 35
14. It's often incorrectly said he used a pistol. The research of Henrietta McCall in the National Archives for her detailed biographical study of Katharine Woolley, 'More Deadly Than The Male: The Mysterious Life of Katharine Woolley (1888–1945)', puts the record straight
15. Quoted in Kaercher (2016); H.V.F. Winstone, *Woolley of Ur* (1990) pp. 137–9
16. Quoted in Winstone (1990) p. 143
17. Winstone (1990) p. 147
18. Mallowan (1977; 2021 edition) pp. 36, 208

Enter Max

1. NT 123598 Leonard Woolley to Max Mallowan (2 August 1927)
2. 'The World This Weekend' (11 September 1977) BBC Archive
3. For a full biography, see Henrietta McCall, *The Life of Max Mallowan* (2001)
4. Mallowan (1977; 2021 edition) p. 36
5. Mallowan (1977; 2021 edition) p. 29
6. NT 123593 Marguerite Mallowan to Max Mallowan (2 December 1926)
7. Mallowan (1977; 2021 edition) p. 14
8. NT 123612.1 Marguerite Mallowan to Frederick Mallowan (27 December 1929)
9. Mallowan (1977; 2021 edition) p. 19
10. NT 123591 Max Mallowan to Marguerite Mallowan (16 February 1919)
11. NT 123665 Marguerite Mallowan to Max Mallowan (23 November 1926)
12. Mallowan (1977; 2021 edition) p. 28
13. Mallowan (1977; 2021 edition) p. 36
14. McCall (2001) pp. 41–3
15. CAT Agatha to Max (undated, 1930)
16. CAT Max to Agatha (23 November 1930)
17. CAT Agatha to Max (undated, 1930)
18. CAT Agatha to Max (undated, 1930)

I Think I Will Marry You

1. CAT Agatha to Max (undated, May 1930)
2. CAT Max to Agatha (14 May 1930)
3. CAT Agatha to Max (undated, 1930)
4. CAT Agatha to Max (11 December 1930)
5. CAT Agatha to Max (23 October 1931)
6. CAT Agatha to Max, from Ashfield (21 May 1930)
7. *Murder in Mesopotamia* (1936)

8. CAT Max to Agatha (1 September 1930)
9. CAT Max to Agatha (13 May 1930)
10. CAT Agatha to Max (undated, probably November 1930)
11. CAT Agatha to Max (21 May 1930)
12. CAT Max to Agatha (14 May 1930)
13. CAT Max to Agatha (19 May 1930)
14. CAT Agatha to Max (undated, May 1930)
15. CAT Max to Agatha (15 May 1930)
16. CAT Max to Agatha (6 September 1930)
17. CAT Agatha to Max (undated, May 1930)
18. CAT Agatha to Max (undated, probably November 1930)
19. CAT Agatha to Max (undated, 1930)
20. CAT Max to Agatha (25 February 1945)
21. CAT Agatha to Rosalind (undated, July 1971)
22. CAT Agatha to Max (undated, July 1930)
23. CAT Max to Agatha (31 July 1930)
24. CAT Agatha to Max (undated, probably autumn 1930)
25. CAT Agatha to Max (21 May 1930)
26. CAT Max to Agatha (18 July 1930)
27. CAT Max to Agatha (31 July 1930)
28. CAT Max to Agatha (14 May 1930)
29. CAT Max to Agatha (26 August 1930)
30. NT 123612.1 Marguerite Mallowan to Frederick Mallowan (27 December 1929)
31. CAT Agatha to Max (undated, 1930)
32. CAT Max to Agatha (1 September 1930)
33. CAT Max to Agatha (29 July 1930)
34. CAT Max to Agatha (4 September 1930)
35. *Towards Zero* (1944)
36. CAT Max to Agatha (27 August 1930)
37. CAT Agatha to Max (undated, August 1930)
38. CAT Max to Agatha (1 September 1930)
39. CAT Max to Agatha (17 August 1930)
40. *Daily Express* (17 September 1930)
41. CAT notebook 40
42. CAT Agatha to Max (undated, October 1930)
43. CAT Max to Agatha (8 November 1930)
44. CAT Agatha to Max (undated, autumn 1930)
45. CAT Max to Agatha (15 December 1930)
46. CAT Agatha to Max (10 October 1931)
47. CAT Agatha to Max (31 December 1931)
48. CAT Agatha to Max (24 December 1930)

Eight Houses

1. Light (1991; 2013 edition) p. 94
2. Wyndham (1966); Yiannitsaros (2016) p. 41
3. *Death on the Nile* (1937)

4. Yiannitsaros (2016) p. 13

5. *The Secret Adversary* (1922)

6. Agatha Christie, 'Detective Writers in England', republished in Martin Edwards, ed., *Ask A Policeman* (1933; 2013 edition) pp. xiii–xx, p. xx

7. Humble (2001) p. 124

8. Dennis (1956) p. 88

9. Light (1991; 2013 edition) p. 94

10. *Star* quoted in Thompson (2007; 2008 edition) p. 284

11. CAT Agatha to Max (26 November 1930)

12. Dorothy L. Sayers quoted in Edwards, ed. (1933; 2013 edition) p. v

13. CAT Agatha to Max (undated, November 1930); (undated, possibly 5 December 1930)

14. Quoted in Thompson (2007; 2008 edition) p. 506

15. Quoted in Mark Aldridge, *Agatha Christie on Screen* (2016) pp. 59–62

16. CAT Dorothy L. Sayers to Agatha (17 December 1930)

17. CAT Rosalind to Agatha (7 February 1931)

18. NT Rosalind Christie, Benenden School Report (summer term, 1935)

19. CAT Agatha to Max (5 November 1930)

20. CAT Agatha to Max (26 November 1930)

21. CAT Agatha to Max (13 October 1931)

22. CAT Agatha to Max (23 October 1931)

23. CAT Agatha to Max (10 October 1931)

24. CAT Max to Agatha (25 October 1931)

25. CAT Max to Agatha (27 September 1942)

26. *An Autobiography* wrongly says 48, see Emily Cole, ed., *Lived in London, Blue Plaques and the Stories Behind Them* (2009) p. 211

27. Gill (1990) p. 10

28. M.E.L. Mallowan, *Twenty-Five Years of Mesopotamian Discovery* (1959) p. 1

29. BM Archives CE32/42/6, letter of Sidney Smith (3 May 1932)

30. BM Archives CE32/42/25/1 (21 November 1932)

31. Reproduced in Michael Gilbert, 'A Very English Lady' in Keating, ed. (1977) p. 64

32. Mallowan (1977; 2021 edition) p. 302

33. Stuart Campbell, 'Arpachiyah' in Trümpler (1999; 2001 edition) pp. 89–103

34. Trümpler (1999; 2001 edition) p. 167

35. NT 123770.2 undated shopping list for an expedition in Agatha's hand

36. Dr Juliette Desplatt, 'Decolonising Archaeology in Iraq?' The National Archive Blog (27 June 2017) https://blog.nationalarchives.gov.uk/decolonising-archaeology-iraq

37. NT 123609 Max to *Mentor* magazine, New York (29 September 1929)

38. Richard Ollard, ed., *The Diaries of A.L. Rowse* (2003) p. 437

39. Tim Barmby and Peter Dalton, 'The Riddle of the Sands, Incentives and Labour Contracts on Archaeological Digs in Northern Syria in the 1930s', University of Aberdeen Business School (2006)

40. Tom Stern, 'Traces of Agatha Christie in Syria and Turkey' in Trümpler (1999; 2001 edition) pp. 287–302; pp. 300–301

41. *The Secret of Chimneys* (1925)

42. *Come, Tell Me How You Live* (1946; 2015 edition) p. 7

43. McCall (2001) p. 124
44. Mallowan (1977; 2021 edition) p. 48
45. CAT Rosalind to Agatha (27 January 1936)
46. CAT Rosalind to Max (undated, 'Thursday', probably May 1936)
47. CAT Rosalind to Agatha (25 May 1936)
48. CAT Agatha to Rosalind (30 January 1937)
49. CAT Agatha to Max (9 April 1944)
50. Macaskill (2009; 2014 edition) p. 50
51. Colleen Smith interview in *Torquay Herald Express* (1990) quoted in Macaskill (2009; 2014 edition) p. 50
52. NT 122918.2 'Survey of the Greenway Estate' (1937)
53. *Country Life* (27 August 1938) p. xviii
54. NT 122918.22, receipt for purchase (28 October 1938)
55. *Come, Tell Me How You Live* (1946; 2015 edition) p. 242

The Golden Age

1. *Hercule Poirot's Christmas* (1938)
2. EUL MS 99/1/1942 Agatha to Cork (21 February 1942)
3. Wyndham (1966)
4. Elizabeth Walter, 'The Case of the Escalating Sales' in Keating, ed. (1977) pp. 13–24, p. 15
5. *Observer* (29 April 1928)
6. Green (2015; 2018 edition) p. 8
7. *Murder in Mesopotamia* (1936)
8. *Cards on the Table* (1936)
9. *Dead Man's Folly* (1956); Curran (2009; 2010 edition) p. 87
10. Cade (1998; 2011 edition) p. 165; Keating (2017) p. 677
11. 'Meet Britain's Famous "Mrs Sherlock Holmes"', *Sydney Morning Herald* (1 April 1954)
12. *New York Times* (30 November 1930)
13. CAT Agatha to Max (17 December 1931)
14. Trümpler, ed. (1999; 2001 edition) p. 281
15. Bernstein (1969)
16. Trümpler (1999; 2001 edition) p. 15
17. *Death on the Nile* (1937)
18. Quoted in Osborne (1982; 2000 edition) p. 129
19. *Murder in Mesopotamia* (1936)
20. Quoted in Trümpler (1999; 2001 edition) p. 419
21. *All About Agatha* podcast, 'A Very Special Episode: Interview with Jamie Bernthal' (2020)
22. Light (1991; 2013 edition) p. 92
23. Curran (2009; 2010 edition) p. 167
24. *And Then There Were None* (1939)
25. *New York Times* (25 February 1940)

Beneath the Bombs

1. Morgan (1984; 2017 edition) p. 233
2. Janet Likeman, 'Nursing at University College, London, 1862–1948', PhD thesis (2002) p. 246
3. Morgan (1984; 2017 edition) p. 233
4. Jack Pritchard, *View from a Long Chair, The Memoirs of Jack Pritchard* (1984) p. 19
5. Robyns (1978; 1979 edition) p. 156
6. EUL MS 99/1/1940 Harold Ober to Edmund Cork (14 June 1940)
7. Mallowan (1977; 2021 edition) p. 167
8. TNA HO 396/58/188A, 189
9. Judy Suh's forthcoming article 'Rerouting Wartime Paranoia in Agatha Christie's *N or M?*'; *N or M?*, p. 95
10. CAT Max to Rosalind (3 July 1940)
11. EUL MS 99/1/1940 Agatha to Cork (31 July 1940)
12. Edwards, ed., (1933; 2013 edition) pp. xiii–xx
13. EUL MS 99/1/1940 Agatha to Cork (5 June 1940)
14. EUL MS 99/1/1940 Agatha to Cork (31 July 1940)
15. NT 122921, National Registration Identity Card
16. EUL MS 99/1/1942 Agatha to Cork (2 June 1942)
17. EUL MS 99/1/1940 Agatha to Cork (22 July 1940)
18. EUL MS 99/1/1940 Agatha to Cork (14 September 1940)
19. EUL MS 99/1/1940 Cork to Agatha (10 September 1940)
20. EUL MS 99/1/1940 Agatha to Cork (18 April 1940)
21. Recollections of Doreen Vautour collected by the National Trust
22. EUL MS 99/1/1940 Agatha to Cork (22 July 1940)
23. EUL MS 99/1/1940 Cork to Agatha (29 August 1940)
24. Forster (1993) p. 174
25. EUL MS 99/1/1940 Cork to Ober (19 December 1940)
26. EUL MS 99/1/1940 Agatha to Cork (6 November 1940)
27. Quoted in Janet Morgan (1984; 2017 edition) p. 247
28. http://bombsight.org/explore/greater-london/camden/gospel-oak
29. Leyla Daybelge and Magnus Englund, *Isokon and the Bauhaus in Britain* (2019) pp. 164–6
30. Adrian Shire, ed., *Belsize 2000: A Living Suburb* (2000) p. 96
31. Shire, ed., (2000) p. 91
32. Elizabeth Darling, *Wells Coates* (2012) p. 72; Light (2007) p. 181
33. CAT Agatha to Max (2 March 1944)
34. EUL MS 99/1/1940 Agatha to Cork (22 October 1940)
35. Quoted in James Tatum, *The Mourner's Song* (2003) p. 152
36. Dorothy Sheridan, ed., *Wartime Women: A Mass-Observation Anthology* (2000) p. 72
37. Michael Smith, *Bletchley Park* (2013; 2016 edition) p. 32
38. Harold Davis, 'Dame Agatha Christie', *Pharmaceutical Journal,* vol. 216, no. 5853 (25 January 1976) pp. 64–5, p. 65
39. Celia Fremlin, 'The Christie Everyone Knew' in Keating, ed., (1977) p. 118
40. EUL MS 99/1/1940 Robert F. de Graff to Agatha Christie (19 February 1940)
41. Dennis (1956) pp. 97–8
42. J.C. Bernthal, 'If Not Yourself, Who Would You Be?': Writing the Female Body

in Agatha Christie's Second World War Fiction', *Women: A Cultural Review* (vol. 26, 2015) pp. 40–56

43. Keating (2017), especially Chapter 7

A Daughter's a Daughter

1. *Western Mail* (13 June 1940) p. 6; information from the trustees of the Royal Welch Fusiliers Museum Trust
2. 'Mr Hubert Prichard, majority celebrations at Colwinstone', *Western Mail* (28 April 1928)
3. EUL MS 99/1/1940 Agatha to Cork (11 June 1940)
4. CAT 'Confessions' (19 April 1954)
5. NT Rosalind Christie, Benenden School Report (Christmas term, 1934)
6. CAT Agatha to Max (29 November 1942)
7. Anne de Courcy, *Debs at War, How Wartime Changed Their Lives, 1939–45* (2005) p. ix
8. CAT Agatha to Max (31 August 1942)
9. CAT Max to Rosalind (15 September 1942)
10. *Come, Tell Me How You Live* (1946; 2015 edition) p. 13
11. CAT Max to Agatha (29 July 1930)
12. Eames (2004; 2005 edition) pp. 247–8
13. NT 119087.57.7, annotated draft article on Greenway's garden, by Audrey Le Lievre, published in *Hortus* (Spring, 1993)
14. CAT Agatha to Max (26 August 1943)
15. CAT Agatha to Max (15 December 1942)
16. Cooper (1989; 2013 edition) p. 103
17. EUL MS 99/1/1942 Cork to Agatha (21 September 1942)
18. CAT Agatha to Max (22 November 1942)
19. CAT Max to Agatha (15 June 1942)
20. CAT Agatha to Max (27 October 1942)
21. CAT Max to Rosalind (7 December 1941)
22. CAT Max to Rosalind (15 September 1942)
23. CAT Agatha to Max (31 August 1942)
24. EUL MS 99/1/1942 Agatha to Cork (4 October 1942)
25. CAT Max to Agatha (20 September 1942)
26. CAT Max to Agatha (16 October 1943)
27. *Coventry Evening Telegraph* (22 April 1942)
28. EUL MS 99/1/1941 Cork to Ober (3, 31 January 1941)
29. CAT Agatha to Max (15 May 1943)
30. CAT Agatha to Max (27 October 1942)
31. CAT Agatha to Max (17 October 1942)
32. CAT Max to Agatha (20 September 1942)
33. CAT Max to Agatha (12 January 1943)
34. CAT Max to Agatha (20 September 1942)
35. CAT Agatha to Max (7 March 1945)
36. CAT Agatha to Max (6 May 1944)
37. CAT Max to Rosalind (17 June 1943)
38. CAT Max to Rosalind (15 October 1943)

39. CAT Agatha to Max (19 May 1943)
40. CAT Agatha to Max (8 August 1943)
41. GH Agatha to Georgina Herrmann (8 February, late 1960s)
42. CAT Agatha to Max (22 September 1943)
43. CAT Max to Agatha (16 October 1943)
44. CAT Max to Rosalind (15 October 1943)
45. Quoted in Thompson (2007; 2008 edition) p. 341

Life Is Rather Complicated

1. CAT Agatha to Max (12 October 1943)
2. CAT Agatha to Max (20 October 1943)
3. CAT Agatha to Max (16 December 1943)
4. *Sparkling Cyanide* (1945)
5. CAT Agatha to Max (26 August 1943); CAT Agatha to Max (undated, 1945)
6. CAT Max to Agatha (22 March 1943)
7. CAT Max to Agatha (3 March 1943)
8. CAT Agatha to Max (20 February 1944)
9. CAT Agatha to Max (1 October 1943)
10. CAT Agatha to Max (30 October 1943)
11. CAT Agatha to Max (20 October 1943)
12. CAT Agatha to Max (27 March 1943)
13. CAT Agatha to Max (22 November 1942)
14. CAT Agatha to Max (12 March 1943)
15. CAT Agatha to Max (19 May 1943)
16. CAT Agatha to Max (12 March 1943)
17. CAT Stephen Glanville to Agatha (18 November 1943)
18. CAT Stephen Glanville to Agatha (9 March 1943)
19. CAT Agatha to Max (22 November 1942)
20. CAT Max to Agatha (16 October 1943)
21. Curran (2009; 2010 edition) p. 167
22. Trümpler (1999; 2001 edition) pp. 351; 362–5
23. Mallowan (1977; 2021 edition) p. 172
24. Thompson (2007; 2008 edition) p. 331
25. Trümpler (1999; 2001 edition) p. 28
26. Rosalind Hicks in *The Times* (8 September 1990) p. 65
27. Mallowan (1977; 2021 edition) p. 173
28. CAT Agatha to Max (9 January 1944)
29. CAT Agatha to Max (2 August 1944)
30. CAT Agatha to Max (9 April 1944)
31. Claire Langhamer, *The English In Love: The Intimate Story of an Emotional Revolution* (2013)
32. *Five Little Pigs* (1942)
33. Howarth (2019) p. xxxiv
34. CAT Agatha to Max (1 July 1944)
35. CAT Agatha to Max (9 January 1944)
36. CAT Agatha to Max (2 March 1944)
37. CAT Agatha to Max (9 June 1944)

38. CAT Agatha to Max (23 July 1944)
39. CAT Agatha to Max (28 April 1944)
40. Mathew Prichard in Underwood, ed., (1990) p. 65
41. CAT Agatha to Max (25 May 1944)
42. EUL MS 99/1/1947/1 Agatha to Cork (11 January 1947)
43. CAT Agatha to Max (25 August 1944)
44. CAT Agatha to Max (31 August 1944)
45. CAT Agatha to Max (13 October 1944)
46. CAT Agatha to Max (31 August 1944)
47. CAT Agatha to Max (6 October 1944)
48. McCall (2001) p. 148
49. EUL MS 99/1/1951 Agatha to Cork (14 February 1951)
50. CAT Agatha to Max (2 November 1944)
51. EUL MS 99/1/1944 Cork to Ober (22 February 1944)
52. EUL MS 99/1/1944 Agatha to Cork (19 December 1944)
53. CAT Agatha to Max (16 December 1944)
54. Norman (2014) p. 91

By Mary Westmacott

1. EUL MS 99/1/1942 Agatha to Cork (21 February 1942)
2. EUL MS 99/1/1944 Agatha to Cork (11 October 1944)
3. CAT Max to Agatha (12 January 1943)
4. CAT Agatha to Max (14 April 1943)
5. CAT Agatha to Max (20 February 1944)
6. Quoted in Cade (1998; 2011 edition) pp. 276–7
7. Mallowan (1977; 2021 edition) p. 195
8. Curran (2011) p. 191
9. *The Hollow* (1946)
10. EUL MS 99/1/1940 Agatha to Sydney Horler, copy (16 November 1940)
11. Wyndham (1966)
12. *An Autobiography*, p. 499
13. *Absent in the Spring* (1944)
14. Green (2015; 2018 edition) p. 430
15. Quoted in Green (2015; 2018 edition) p. 431
16. Martin Fido, *The World of Agatha Christie* (1999) p. 94
17. Jeffrey Feinmann, *The Mysterious World of Agatha Christie* (1975)
18. Dorothy B. Hughes, 'The Christie Nobody Knew', in Bloom et al, (1992; 2002 edition) p. 20
19. Rosalind Hicks in Underwood, ed. (1990) p. 51
20. EUL MS 99/1/1947/1 Agatha to Cork (10 April 1947)
21. EUL MS 99/1/1949 Agatha to Cork (13 March 1949)
22. EUL MS 99/1/1970/2 Agatha to Yasuo Suto (undated, 1970)
23. EUL MS 99/1/1952 Cork to Ober (18 January 1952)
24. Gill (1990) p. 151
25. *Giant's Bread* (1930)

A Big Expensive Dream

1. CAT Agatha to Max (1 July 1944)
2. *A Daughter's a Daughter* (1952)
3. *The Hollow* (1946)
4. ons.gov.uk, annual percentage of employed women in the UK
5. Viola Klein and Alva Myrdal, *Women's Two Roles* (1956) pp. 1–28
6. NT 123881 former Coast Guard to Agatha (16 September 1970)
7. NT 123882 former Coast Guard to Agatha (10 October 1970)
8. Recollections of Tessa Tattershall collected by the National Trust
9. NT 122918.3 R.J. Knapton & Son, builders and contractors, to Agatha (28 July 1945)
10. EUL MS 99/1/1951 Agatha to Mrs MacPherson (undated)
11. EUL MS 99/1/1952 Cork to Agatha (25 April 1952); Macaskill (2009; 2014 edition) p. 51
12. EUL MS 99/1/1958/2 Hughes Massie Agency employee to Dorothy Olding (12 December 1958); 99/1/1962/1 Hughes Massie Agency employee to Harold Ober Associates employee (21 February 1962)
13. *Sunday Dispatch* (30 August 1959) p. 8
14. NT 123690 Inventory and Valuation of Greenway (12 October 1942) p. 21
15. Bernstein (1969)
16. Morgan (1984; 2017 edition) p. 200
17. EUL MS 99/1/1950 Agatha to Cork (17 August 1950)
18. GH Agatha to Georgina Herrmann (12 June, late 1960s)
19. Morgan (1984; 2017 edition) p. 245
20. Saunders (1972) p. 109
21. Mathew Prichard in Underwood (1990) p. 66
22. Saunders (1972) p. 116
23. *Sparkling Cyanide* (1945)
24. *The Times* (8 November 1949)
25. CAT Rosalind to Agatha (23 October 1949)
26. Mallowan (1977; 2021 edition) p. 202
27. CAT Rosalind to Agatha (23 October 1949)
28. Mathew Prichard, personal conversation (27 July 2021)
29. Mallowan (1977; 2021 edition) p. 202
30. Quoted in Robyns (1978; 1979 edition) p. 294
31. CAT Agatha to Rosalind (undated)

They Came to Baghdad

1. CAT Agatha to Max (undated, January or February 1944)
2. UCLL letter from the Director of the Institute of Archaeology to the Academic Registrar (3 February 1947)
3. McCall (2001) p. 155
4. EUL MS 99/1/1950 Cork to Agatha (2 March 1950)
5. CAT Max to Rosalind (5 May 1947)
6. Matthew Sturgis, 'The century makers: 1931', *Telegraph* (5 July 2003)
7. Quoted in Robyns (1978; 1979 edition) p. 148

8. CAT Max to Rosalind (5 May 1947)

9. Eleanor Robson, 'Remnants of empire: views of Kalhu in 1950', oracc.museum. upenn.edu (2016)

10. M.E.L. Mallowan, 'The Excavations at Nimrud (Kalhu), 1951', *Iraq* 14, no. 1 (1952) pp. 1–23; 1

11. Quoted in McCall (2001) pp. 158–9

12. CAT Agatha to Rosalind (7 January, n.y.)

13. McCall (2001) pp. 194; 162

14. Georgina Herrmann, personal conversation (18 January 2022)

15. Quoted in Curran (2011) p. 264

16. CAT Max to Agatha (17 February 1943)

17. Suh (2016) pp. 63–66

18. Mallowan (1977; 2021 edition) p. 248

19. Trümpler (1999; 2001 edition) p. 52

20. Mallowan (1977; 2021 edition) p. 248

21. Oates, in Trümpler, ed. (1999; 2001 edition) p. 215

22. Donald Wiseman in Underwood, ed. (1990) p. 62

23. Mallowan (1977; 2010 edition) p. 290

24. EUL MS 99/1/1953/1 Cork to Harold Ober (6 February 1953)

25. Donald Wiseman in Underwood, ed. (1990) p. 62

26. Joan Oates quoted in Thompson (2007; 2008 edition) p. 420

27. Dr Paul Collins, personal conversation (27 April 2021)

28. Robson (2016)

29. Donald Wiseman in Underwood, ed. (1990) p. 62

30. Joan Oates quoted in Thompson (2007; 2008 edition) p. 420

31. Donald Wiseman in Underwood, ed. (1990) p. 62

32. Joan Oates, 'Agatha Christie, Nimrud and Baghdad', in Trümpler, ed. (1999; 2001 edition) pp. 205–228; p. 211

33. Donald Wiseman in Underwood, ed. (1990) p. 61

34. Mallowan (1977; 2010 edition) p. 290

35. Quoted in McCall (2001) p. 174

36. Mallowan (1977; 2021 edition) pp. 237, 233

37. McCall (2001) p. 176

38. Quoted in Thompson (2007; 2008 edition) p. 417

39. Trümpler (1999; 2001 edition) p. 161

40. https://www.bbc.co.uk/news/world-middle-east-37992394

41. Eames (2004; 2005 edition) p. 330; the dig house is destroyed in second 58 of the video at https://www.bbc.co.uk/news/world-middle-east-37992394

42. Eleanor Robson, 'Old habits die hard: Writing the excavation and dispersal history of Nimrud', *Museum History Journal* (vol. 10, 2017) pp. 217–232, footnote 52

43. Sabine Scharnagl, *Agatha Christie in the Middle East*, a documentary premiered at the International Agatha Christie Festival, Torquay Museum (12 September 2021)

Christie-Land after the War

1. *A Murder Is Announced* (1950)

2. Humble (2001) pp. 103, 107

3. Dennis (1956) p. 98

4. John Mallowan, personal conversation (8 January 2022)

5. Osborne (1982; 2000 edition) p. 272

6. Morgan (1984; 2017 edition) p. 270

7. EUL MS 99/1/1962/1 Olding to Cork (25 April 1962)

8. EUL MS 99/1/1964/2 Sara Jane Beal to Dodd, Mead (23 April 1964)

9. EUL MS 99/1/1964/2 employee of Hughes Massie to Sarajane Beal (9 June 1964)

10. Arnold (1987) p. 279

11. EUL MS 99/1/1949 James Wise to Raymond Bond (21 January 1949)

12. EUL MS 99/1/1947/1 Ober to Cork (6 February 1947)

13. Gill (1990) p. 161

14. *An Autobiography*, p. 192

15. EUL MS 99/1/1953/1 Cork to Ober (25 February 1953)

16. Quoted by Frelin in Keating, ed., (1977) pp. 13–24, p. 19; Osborne (1982; 2000 edition) p. 277

17. 'Agatha's last mystery – her fortune', *Chicago Tribune* (26 January 1976)

18. Wyndham (1966)

19. Agatha talk on BBC Radio Light Programme (13 February 1955)

20. EUL MS 99/1/1949 Agatha to Cork (13 March 1949)

21. Curran (2011) p. 24

22. Curran (2009; 2010 edition) p. 44

23. ibid., pp. 99–101

24. ibid., p. 74

25. Rowse (1980; 1986 edition) p. 74

26. CAT Agatha to Max (10 October 1931)

27. CAT Agatha to Max (13, 16 and 26 October 1931)

28. Curran (2011) p. 139

29. ibid., pp. 25, 335

30. Notebook 36 quoted in Curran (2011) p. 355

31. Mathew Prichard in Underwood (1990) p. 66

32. Rosalind Hicks in *The Times* (8 September 1990) p. 65

33. EUL MS 99/1/1947/1 Agatha to Cork (7 February 1947)

34. EUL MS 99/1/1952 (undated draft blurb)

35. Robyns (1978; 1979 edition) p. 25

Second Row in the Stalls

1. *Daily Mail* (14 April 1958). In *An Autobiography,* Agatha confuses the party for the 1,000th performance with the party for the 10th anniversary in 1962. It's understandable: Peter Saunders did love parties.

2. Peter Saunders, *The Mousetrap Man* (1972) pp. 7–8

3. *Daily Mail* (14 April 1958)

4. CAT Agatha to Max (31 January 1945)

5. Saunders (1972) p. 9

6. *Daily Mail* (14 April 1958)

7. John Bull, ed., *The Dictionary of Literary Biography volume on British and Irish Dramatists Since World War II* (2001) pp. 281, 98

8. Green (2015; 2018 edition) p. 1

9. CAT 'Confessions' (15 October 1897); Green (2015; 2018 edition) p. 7
10. *Daily Express* (16 May 1928)
11. EUL MS 99/1/1940 Agatha to Edmund Cork (15 January 1940)
12. Agatha talk on BBC Radio Light Programme (13 February 1955)
13. Light (1991; 2013 edition) pp. 96–7
14. EUL MS 99/1/1942 Agatha to Cork (17 September 1942)
15. Green (2015; 2018 edition) p. 165
16. CAT Agatha to Max (17 November 1943)
17. Peter Haining in Underwood, ed. (1990) p. 71
18. Aldridge (2016) p. 308 clarifies the usual version of this story
19. Saunders (1972) p. 106
20. Gregg (1980) pp. 50–1, 19, 32, 37, opposite p. 80; quoted in Green (2015; 2018 edition) p. 266
21. Green (2015; 2018 edition) pp. 305, 320
22. Saunders (1972) p. 141
23. EUL MS 99/1/1952 Agatha to Cork (3 February 1952)
24. *Daily Express* quoted in Green (2015; 2018 edition) p. 367
25. Saunders (1972) p. 143
26. Lucy Bailey, director of *Witness for the Prosecution,* quoted in the *Guardian* (28 November 2018)
27. Quoted in Green (2015; 2018 edition) p. 318
28. CAT Agatha to Max (3 January 1945)
29. Quoted in Hack (2009) p. 215

A Charming Grandmother

1. Dennis (1956) pp. 88–9
2. EUL MS 99/1/1966/2 letter from Cork (31 January 1966)
3. EUL MS 99/1/1957/1 Cork to Rosalind (22 February 1957)
4. EUL MS 99/1/1940 Agatha to Edmund Cork (15 January 1940)
5. EUL MS 99/1/1960/1 Agatha to Cork (6 June 1960)
6. Philip Ziegler, personal conversation (16 November 2021)
7. Wyndham (1966)
8. EUL MS 99/1/1971/1 Cork to Mrs Arthur F. Chuttle (22 June 1971)
9. Philip Ziegler, personal conversation (16 November 2021)
10. Joseph G. Harrison, 'Agatha Christie's life – less interesting than her novels', *Christian Science Monitor* (1 December 1977)
11. Quoted in Robyns (1978; 1979 edition) p. 31
12. CAT Agatha to Max (23 October 1931)
13. Gill (1990) p. 212
14. EUL MS 99/1/1957/1 Cork to Rosalind (27 June 1957)
15. EUL MS 99/1/1950 Agatha to Cork (8 September 1950)
16. EUL MS 99/1/1953/1 Agatha to Cork (12 February 1953)
17. Quoted in Robyns (1978; 1979 edition) p. 190
18. Robyns (1978; 1979 edition) p. 270
19. CAT copy of a letter from Cork to Olding (6 October 1966) (original not found in EUL)
20. Rowse (1980; 1986 edition) pp. 84, 73

21. Quoted in Robyns (1978; 1979 edition) p. 192

22. Gregg (1980) p. 161

23. Margaret Lockwood interviewed in *Reynolds News* (17 January 1954) quoted in Green (2015; 2018 edition) p. 403

24. Quoted in Thompson (2007; 2008 edition) p. 483

25. Mallowan (1977; 2021 edition) p. 201

26. Susan Pedersen and Joanna Biggs, 'No, I'm not getting married!' *London Review of Books Conversations* podcast (9 June 2020)

The Mystery of the Christie Fortune

1. Aldridge (2016) pp. 27–8

2. ibid., pp. 82–91

3. EUL MS 99/1/1955/1 Cork to Ober (8 September 1955)

4. Green (2015; 2018 edition) pp. 391–2

5. EUL MS 99/1/1960/1 Agatha to Cork (20 January 1960)

6. *Daily Mail* (12 March 1960)

7. EUL MS 99/1/1960/3 Cork to Rosalind (26 February 1960)

8. EUL MS 99/1/1961/1 Agatha to Cork (18 August 1961)

9. EUL MS/99/1/1961/3 Cork to Rosalind (11 January 1961)

10. EUL MS 99/1/1961/1 Agatha to Cork (17 September 1961)

11. Aldridge (2016) p. 150

12. Quoted in Aldridge (2016) p. 150

13. EUL MS 99/1/1964/1 Agatha to Pat Cork (18 March 1964)

14. EUL MS 99/1/1964/2 Agatha to Larry Bachmann (11 April 1964)

15. Quoted in Underwood (1990) p. 40

16. Quoted in Hack (2009) p. 213

17. Mathew Prichard in Underwood, ed. (1990) p. 68

18. EUL MS 99/1/1964/5 Rosalind to Cork (25 March 1964)

19. Wyndham (1966)

20. Peter Seddon letter to *The Sunday Times* (17 November 1974) with thanks to Mark Aldridge

21. Gregg (1980) p. 16

22. Dennis (1956) pp. 88–9

23. EUL MS 99/1/1949 Cork to Ober (20 January 1949)

24. EUL MS 99/1/1951 Agatha to Cork (16 April 1951)

25. EUL MS 99/1/1945 Cork to Ober (15 June 1945)

26. Osborne (1982; 2000 edition) p. 296

27. EUL MS 99/1/1947/1 'liability for income tax . . . 1930–1944'

28. EUL MS 99/1/1948 Norman Dixon to Cork (17 September 1948)

29. EUL MS 99/1/1948 Cork or Ober (30 September 1948)

30. EUL MS 99/1/1950 Inspector of Taxes to Hughes Massie (27 January 1950)

31. EUL MS 99/1/1948 Agatha to Cork (30 August 1948)

32. EUL MS 99/1/1950 Agatha to Cork (16 February 1950)

33. Adam Sisman, *John le Carré* (2015) pp. 271–2; EUL MS 99/1/1953/2 Hicks to Cork (19 December 1954)

34. Lycett (1995) p. 277

35. EUL MS 99/1/1955/1 Agatha to Cork (19 February 1955)

36. CAT Agatha to Rosalind and Anthony (20 February 1956)
37. EUL MS 99/1/1956/1 Agatha to Cork (8 January 1956)
38. EUL MS 99/1/1956/3 Rosalind to Cork (2 June 1956)
39. EUL MS 99/1/1958/2 Rosalind to Cork (5 December 1958)
40. Mathew Prichard, personal conversation (5 January 2022)
41. Janet Morgan, 'Christie Dame Agatha Mary Clarissa', *Oxford Dictionary of National Biography* (2017) summarises this neatly
42. EUL MS 99/1/1966/2 Agatha to Cork (29 March 1966)

A Queer Lot

1. EUL MS 99/1/1960/1 Agatha to Cork (16 September 1960)
2. CAT Agatha to Max from Greenway (27 October 1942)
3. *The Sittaford Mystery* (1931)
4. EUL MS 99/1/1960/1 Agatha to Cork (11 January 1960)
5. Eames (2004; 2005 edition) pp. 86–7
6. EUL MS 99/1/1962/2 Agatha to Cork (undated, but September 1960) (filed in the wrong folder)
7. Ritchie Calder (1976)
8. He said as much in the unpublished first draft of his memoirs, Janet Morgan, personal conversation (3 January 2022)
9. CAT Agatha to Max (undated, probably autumn 1930)
10. Edmund Crispin quoted in Keating, ed., (1977) p. 45
11. Saunders (1972) p. 109
12. Sabine Scharnagl's documentary *Agatha Christie in the Middle East* (2021)
13. CAT 'In the Service of a Great Lady, the Queen of Crime', typescript by George Gowler, pp. 5, 16
14. NT 121991, list slipped into book in Clara Miller's book of 'receipts for Agatha'
15. Recollections of Dixie Griggs collected by the National Trust
16. Light (1991; 2013 edition) pp. 79–82
17. McCall (2001) p. 165
18. EUL MS 99/1/1961/1 Cork to Olding (29 August 1961)
19. Ollard, ed., (2003) p. 438
20. EUL MS 99/1/1968/2 Agatha to Cork (18 October 1968)
21. Ellen McAdam, personal conversation (8 April 2021)
22. CAT Agatha to Rosalind and Anthony (20 February 1956)
23. Programme for the Agatha Christie conference at Solent University, Southampton (5–6 September 2019) Emma Shackle's abstract, p. 9
24. Georgina Herrmann, personal conversation (18 January 2022)
25. Mathew Prichard in Underwood, ed. (1990) p. 65
26. Rowse (1980; 1986 edition) p. 77
27. Rosalind Hicks in *The Times* (8 September 1990) p. 66
28. CAT Archie to Rosalind (24 October 1958)
29. Quoted in Cade (1998; 2011 edition) p. 257
30. Rosalind Hicks quoted in Thompson (2007; 2008 edition) pp. 410–11
31. Mathew Prichard, personal conversation (5 January 1922)
32. 'Maj-Gen Campbell Christie', *The Times* (22 June 1963)
33. Marguerite Tarrant, 'Mathew Prichard', *People* (10 April 1978)

34. Underwood (1990) p. 42
35. Rowse (1980; 1986 edition) p. 89
36. Philip Ziegler, personal conversation (16 November 2021)
37. CAT 'In the Service of a Great Lady, the Queen of Crime', typescript by George Gowler, p. 4
38. George Gowler quoted in 'Devon cream', *Daily Telegraph* (7 October 1993)
39. CAT 'In the Service of a Great Lady, the Queen of Crime', typescript by George Gowler, pp. 16–22
40. Morgan (1984; 2017 edition) p. 239; EUL MS 991/1/1945 Agatha to Cork (18 January 1945)
41. Faye Stewart, 'Of red herrings and lavender: reading crime and identity in queer detective fiction', *Clues: A Journal of Detection,* vol. 27.2 (2009) pp. 33–44
42. Green (2015; 2018 edition) p. 306
43. Curran (2009; 2010 edition) p. 179
44. *A Murder Is Announced* (1950)
45. Tina Hodgkinson, 'Disability and Ableism', a paper presented at the Agatha Christie conference at Solent University, Southampton (5–6 September 2019)
46. Mathew Prichard in conversation (28 July 2021)

Lady Detectives

1. Mallowan (1977; 2021 edition) p. 227
2. Wyndham (1966)
3. 'The Affair at the Bungalow' in *The Thirteen Problems* (1932) p. 261
4. CAT Dorothy L. Sayers to Agatha (17 December 1930)
5. Wyndham (1966)
6. Keating (2017) pp. 327, 425
7. *The Body in the Library* (1942)
8. Margery Fry, *The Single Woman* (1953) pp. 31–3, quoted in Howarth (2019) p. 154
9. Keating (2017)
10. CAT notebook 27
11. Gill (1990) p. 201
12. *A Murder Is Announced* (1950)
13. Gill (1990) p. 208
14. Thompson (2007; 2008 edition) p. 373
15. *The Mousetrap* (1954) p. 19
16. Gill (1990) p. 203
17. *A Caribbean Mystery* (1964)

To Know When to Go

1. EUL MS 99/1/1960/1 Olding to Cork (6 July 1960)
2. Wyndham (1966)
3. Curran (2011) p. 350
4. Franks (1970) p. 5
5. Curran (2011) p. 375
6. CAT notebook 3, 'Notes on Passenger to Frankfurt', p. 30
7. Osborne (1982; 2000 edition) pp. 340, 42

8. EUL MS 99/1/1970/2 Olding to Cork (30 June 1970)

9. *New York Times* (13 December 1970)

10. EUL MS 99/1/1971/1 Cork to Agatha (2 August 1971)

11. Macaskill (2009; 2014 edition) p. 73

12. EUL MS 99/1/1965/2 Olding to Hughes Massie employee (29 March 1965)

13. EUL MS 99/1/1971/1 Cork to Agatha (2 August 1971)

14. CAT Agatha to Rosalind (July 1971)

15. CAT Rosalind to Agatha (20 July 1971)

16. EUL MS 99/1/1966/2 Agatha to Cork (31 December 1966)

17. Ian Lancashire and Graeme Hirst, 'Vocabulary Changes in Agatha Christie's Mysteries as an Indication of Dementia: A Case Study', *19th Annual Rotman Research Institute Conference, Cognitive Aging: Research and Practice* (2009)

18. Ian Lancashire quoted in Alison Flood, 'Study Claims Agatha Christie had Alzheimers', *Guardian* (3 April 2009)

Winterbrook

1. 'Scheme for Torquay flats gets approval', *Herald Express* (1 October 1960); 'An appeal against planning refusal', *Torbay Express and South Devon Echo* (3 November 1962)

2. Macaskill (2009; 2014 edition) p. 42

3. *An Autobiography,* p. 531

4. CAT Agatha to Max (24 December 1943)

5. Bernstein (1969)

6. CAT Agatha to Billy Collins (28 October 1970)

7. Morgan (1984; 2017 edition) p. 365

8. CAT notebook 28, 14 pages from the back

9. NT 123654 Reginald Campbell Thompson to Max Mallowan (14 June, n.y. probably 1934)

10. Ollard, ed. (2003) p. 437

11. NT 119087.57.7, typescript history of Greenway

12. CAT, just a couple of examples among reams of fan mail

13. Michael Mortimer, personal conversation (12 January 2022)

14. The archives of Wallingford Museum contain much more information about Agatha's life in the town, thanks to its curator Judy Dewey.

15. Mallowan (1977; 2021 edition) p. 293

16. CAT Max to Rosalind (15 October 1943)

17. McCall (2001) p. 191

18. Davis (2008) p. 136

19. CAT family photograph album

20. Morgan (1984; 2017 edition) p. 368

21. EUL MS 99/1/1966/2 Agatha to Cork (29 March 1966)

22. *Sun* (16 June 1971)

23. EUL MS 99/1/1971/1 Cork to Ober's agency (21 June 1971)

24. EUL MS 99/1/1971/1 Max to Cork (24 June 1971)

25. CAT Agatha to Rosalind (summer 1971)

26. EUL MS 99/1/1973/1 Olding to Cork (27 July 1973)

27. Curran (2011) p. 407

28. Quoted in Curran (2009; 2010 edition) p. 68
29. CAT Mountbatten of Burma to Agatha (8 November 1972)
30. Aldridge (2016) p. 174
31. Underwood (1990) p. 41
32. Richard Goodwin, personal conversation (22 May 2021)
33. Underwood (1990) p. 41
34. *The Times* (11 February 1975)
35. Richard Goodwin, personal conversation (22 May 2021)
36. Mallowan (1977; 2021 edition) p. 215
37. *Guardian* (9 October 1975)
38. EUL MS 99/1/1975/1 Max to Cork (31 July 1975)
39. Mallowan (1977; 2020 edition) p. 311; GH Max to Georgina Herrmann (29 January 1976)
40. Morgan (1984; 2017 edition) p. 376
41. 'Agatha Christie buried after closed funeral', *Hartford Courant* (17 January 1976)
42. Mathew Prichard in Underwood, ed. (1990) p. 69
43. GH Max to Georgina Herrmann (29 January 1976)
44. 'Remembrance', reproduced in Agatha's *Star Over Bethlehem and other stories* (2014 edition) p. 191
45. CAT Agatha to Rosalind (undated, July 1971)
46. CAT Agatha to Max (undated, 1930)
47. *The Mirror Crack'd from Side to Side* (1962)
48. Henrietta McCall, personal conversation (7 May 2021)
49. Cade (1998; 2011 edition) p. 280; McCall (2001) p. 193
50. Max to Agatha (22 December 1943)
51. GH Max to Georgina Herrmann (29 January 1976)
52. CAT Agatha to Max (20 October 1943)
53. CAT Max to Agatha (25 February 1945)
54. CAT Agatha to Rosalind (summer 1971)
55. CAT Max to Agatha (9 September 1936)
56. Quoted in Thompson (2007; 2008 edition) p. 453
57. NT Max Mallowan certified copy of an entry pursuant to the Births and Deaths Registration Act 1953
58. McCall (2001) p. 196
59. CAT Agatha to Max (21 May 1930)

After the Funeral

1. Nicholas de Jongh, 'Agatha Christie remains unsolved', *Guardian* (13 January 1976)
2. Mary Shepperston, 'The Turbulent Life of the British School of Archaeology in Iraq', *Guardian* (17 July 2018)
3. Ellen McAdam, personal conservation (8 April 2021)
4. Shepperston (2018)
5. Sabine Scharnagl's documentary, *Agatha Christie in the Middle East* (2021)
6. 'Prolific Author's Fortune Gone', *Los Angeles Times* (2 May 1976)
7. Osborne (1982; 2000 edition) p. 368
8. Robyns (1978; 1979 edition) p. 271
9. Green (2015; 2018 edition) p. 15

10. *The Times* (4 June 1998)
11. Tarrant (1978)
12. Henrietta McCall, personal conversation (7 May 2021)
13. Macaskill (2009; 2014 edition) p. 107
14. NT 119087.1 Anthony Steen MP to Rosalind Hicks (12 January 2000)
15. Hawthorne (2009) p. 18
16. Quoted in Macaskill (2009; 2014 edition) p. 125
17. Bearnes Hampton & Littlewood auction report (12 September 2006)
18. https://www.irishtimes.com/life-and-style/homes-and-property/fine-art-antiques/agatha-christie-and-the-mystery-diamonds-1.1898074
19. James Prichard, personal conversation (4 May 2021)
20. CAT Agatha to Dorothy Claybourne (21 October 1970)
21. Tarrant (1978); *Liverpool Echo* (13 March 1990) p 8
22. Mathew Prichard, personal conversation (5 January 2022)
23. Robyns (1978; 1979 edition) p. 120
24. Letter to *The Times* (14 October 1977)
25. Cade (1998; 2011 edition) p. 131
26. Angus Calder, *Gods, Men and Mongrels* (2004) p. 2
27. Beth Gillin, 'Dame Agatha herself is still a big mystery', *Chicago Tribune* (11 January 1991)
28. Gill (1990) p. 2
29. Light (1991; 2013 edition) p. 61
30. Margaret Lockwood quoted in Green (2015; 2018 edition) p. 403
31. *Come, Tell Me How You Live* (1946) p. 2

Index

Abney Hall, Cheadle (Staffordshire)
family home of the Watts' family
33–5
AC refuses to go to 101
AC retreats to after Harrogate episode
159–60, 162, 163
AC writes letters to Max from 189
Rosalind meets Hugh de Burgh
Prichard at 233
requisitioned by the military 239
sold by Jack Watts 301
Rosalind takes on domestic duties
post-war at 321
Ackerley, R.J. 200–1
Acorn Media 349
Agatha Christie Limited 312, 313, 349
Agatha Christie Trust for Children 313
Agatha (film, 1979) 154, 352
Air Raid Precautions Auxiliary Reserve
(St John Ambulance Brigade) 224
Albury, Surrey 129
Aldershot Motor Cycling Club 154
Aldridge, Mark 305
All Souls' College, Oxford 340
Allingham, Margery 89, 101, 299
Amis, Kingsley 280
anti-Semitism 81, 102–3, 283–5
Arbuthnot, Mr and Mrs 225–6
archaeology, archaeologists
AC's involvement in 176–81, 203, 270,
272–9, 313, 348–9
Max's work in 185, 192, 195, 203, 270,
270–9, 272, 318, 340

Barbara Parker's work in 246, 272, 273,
318
Steven Glanville's knowledge of 246,
247
Arpachiyah, Iraq 203–5
Ashburnnasirpal II 274
Asher, Rosie (hotel chambermaid) 140,
147–8, 154
Ashfield house, Torquay 40, 46, 57, 70,
127, 341
life at 3, 5–6, 10, 13–14, 16–19, 23, 58,
70
bought by Clara 6, 10
rented out 21
birth of Rosalind at 84–5
AC's financial help for 101
AC retreats to 118
Rosalind recuperates at 186
Max proposes to AC at 187
sale of 207–8
redevelopment of 337
Ashmolean Museum, Oxford 179, 185
Astor, Caroline Schermerhorn 21
Athens 195
Atomic Energy Reseach Establishment,
Harwell 282–3
Attenborough, Richard 289
'Auntie-Grannie' *see* Miller, Margaret
West
Austral Trust Ltd. 107
Auxiliary Territorial Service (ATS) 232

Bacall, Lauren 342

Baghdad 175, 179, 195, 272, 309–10, 311, 319, 348

Baghdad Museum 349

Baker, Thomas 57

Baltimore Sun 150

Barnard, Robert 103

Bastin, Elizabeth 223

BBC radio 200–1, 293–4

BBC television 353

Beirut 209

Belcher, Major Ernest 90–1, 92, 93, 120, 254

Bell, Gertrude 176, 179

Benenden School, Kent 201, 233–4

Bennett, Arnold 168

Bergman, Ingrid 342

Bernthal, J.C. 215, 230–1

Best, Jack 131

Beverley, Yorkshire 126, 127

Billington, Michael 295

Blackburn Times 39

Bletchley Park, Bedfordshire 229

Blyton, Enid 312

The Bodley Head (publishers) 88–9, 94, 99, 100, 101

Boehmer, Clara (AC's cousin) 11

Boehmer, Clara Margaret *see* Miller, Clara Margaret Boehmer

Boehmer, Friedrich (AC's maternal grandfather) 10

Boehmer, Polly (AC's maternal grandmother) 10–11, 38, 85

Booker Books 313

Booker McConnell 313, 349

Brabourne, John 342

Bracken, Brendan 236–7

Brisley, Bert (gardener at Greenway) 266

British Empire Exhibition (1924) 90, 91–4

British Foreign Office 205

British Institute for the Study of Iraq 348

British and Irish Dramatists Since World War II (dictionary) 290

British Museum 185, 186, 189, 202–3, 227, 246, 247, 271, 348–9

British School of Archaeology, Iraq 203, 272, 273, 275, 313, 348

Brittain, Vera 55

Brixham Home Guard 223

Brixham Horticultural Society Show 266

Broadford Hotel, Skye 194

Brookwood Mental Institution, Surrey 45

Brown, William 163–4

Cade, Jared 153, 352

Café Royal, London 200

Cairo 36–8, 235–6, 244

Calder, Ritchie 133, 142, 149, 316, 352

Caledonia School, Bexhill 173, 201

Callicott, William Henry 13

Canary Islands 165

'Carlo' *see* Fisher, Charlotte 'Carlotta' or 'Carlo'

Carnie, Ethel 39

Cartland, Barbara 29

Cataract Hotel, Aswan (Egypt) 215

Chagar Bazaar, Syria 349

Chandler, Raymond 354

characters in novels, plays and films
  characters in novels, plays and films
  Alfred Inglethorpe (*The Mysterious Affair at Styles*) 75

  Amy (*Murder Is Easy*) 325–6

  Andrew Pennington (*Death on the Nile*) 20

  Anthony (*The Secret of Chimneys*) 102

  Ariadne Oliver (detective) 212, 333–4

  Arlena Stuart (*Evil under the Sun*) 231

  Bridget (*Murder Is Easy*) 325–6

  Bundle (*The Secret of Chimneys*) 178

  Captain Hastings (Poirot stories) 69, 75, 86, 99, 343

  Carmichael (*They Came to Baghdad*) 273

  Celia (*Unfinished Portrait*) 118, 167, 254

  Christine Revel (*The Secret of Chimneys*) 101

  Christopher Wren (*The Mousetrap*) 322

  Colonel Arbuthnot (*Murder on the Orient Express*) 43, 176–7

  Colonel and Mrs Bantry (*The Body in the Library*) 231

  Colonel Race (*Sparkling Cyanide*) 267

  Cynthia (*The Mysterious Affair at Styles*) 68

  Dermot (*Unfinished Portrait*) 118

Dolly and Arthur Bantry (friends of Miss Marple) 318

Dorcas (*The Mysterious Affair at Styles*) 86

Dr Leidner (*Murder in Mesopotamia*) 215

Elsa Greer (*Five Little Pigs*) 249

Evelyn (*The Mysterious Affair at Styles*) 75

Frankie Derwent (*Why Didn't They Ask Evans?*) 102

Gerda (*The Hollow*) 255

Gopal Ram (*Hickory Dickory Dock*) 285

Harley Quin (detective) 211

Hercule Poirot 71–2, 74, 99, 103, 112, 145, 162, 197, 211, 212, 215, 224, 230, 249, 253, 255, 284, 287, 291–2, 323, 325, 331, 332, 353

Herman Isaacstein (*The Secret of Chimneys*) 102–3

Inspector Craddock 328

Inspector Kemp (*Sparkling Cyanide*) 267

Joan (*Absent in the Spring*) 256

Lady Horbury (*Death in the Clouds*) 112

Lady Tressilian (*Towards Zero*) 43

Laura (*A Daughter's a Daughter*) (1952) 256–7

Leonard (*The Murder at the Vicarage*) 97

Linnet (*Death on the Nile*) 197

Lombard (*And Then There Were None*) 292

Lord Edgware (*Lord Edgware Dies*) 43, 287, 322

Lucy Eyelesbarrow (*4.50 from Paddington*) 80

Major Bletchley (*N or M?*) 229

Midge (*The Hollow*) 130

Millicent Pebmarsh (*The Clocks*) 323

Miss Casewell (*The Mousetrap*) 322

Miss Gilchrist (*After the Funeral*) 282

Miss Hinchcliffe (*A Murder Is Announced*) 322

Miss (Jane) Marple 15, 17, 64, 212–13, 224, 231, 253, 258, 281, 293, 306–8, 318, 324–9, 332, 351, 353

Miss Marple 323

Miss Murgatroyd (*A Murder Is Announced*) 322

Mitzi (*A Murder Is Announced*) 283

Mr Akibombo (*Hickory Dickory Dock*) 285

Mr Satterthwaite (detective) 211

Mrs Inglethorpe (*The Mysterious Affair at Styles*) 69, 75

Mrs Tucker (*Dead Man's Folly*) 37–8

Narracott (*Sleeping Murder*) 332

Nurse Leatheran (*Murder in Mesopotamia*) 215

Parker Pyne (detective) 211–12

Philip Lombard (*And Then There Were None*) 216

Rosalind (*Sparkling Cyanide*) 244

Tommy and Tuppence 98–9, 137, 223, 341

Vera (*And Then There Were None*) 292

Vernon (*Giant's Bread*) 164, 259

Victoria (*They Came to Baghdad*) 273

Virginia (*The Secret of Chimneys*) 102

Charlecote House, Warwickshire 47

Cheltenham Ladies' College 30

Chicago Tribune 353

Chorion PLC 349

Christie, Agatha (formerly Prichard née Miller)

anecdotes, clichés and misconceptions xiii–xvi

birth, family background and childhood 3–7, 8–12

character and description 4–5, 6–7, 33, 35, 36, 37, 63–4, 107, 148, 174, 190, 206, 297, 299–300, 338, 340

life at Ashfield and Craven Gardens 13–19

as homemaker 15, 80–1, 118, 197–200, 202–3, 205, 208–9

belief in horror, evil and the Gun Man 17–19, 119, 198, 324, 328, 329

family finances and death of her father 20–5

education 29–32

courtships, proposals and engagements 42–4, 46–7, 186

meets and marries Archibald Christie 44, 46–7, 51–3, 62–6

decides to write a murder-mystery 68–72, 73–5

holidays at home and abroad 73, 165–6, 174–81, 202, 285, 287

married life in London with Archie 79–83

attitude towards politics and the British Empire 82, 92, 178

interviews, photographs and press coverage 90, 99, 107, 166, 174, 194, 272, 297–9, 308, 315–16, 338, 340, 341–2

joins Archie on a nine-month Grand Tour 90–4, 234

increasing professionalism of 95–103

breakdown of her marriage to Archie 101, 109, 110–11, 117–22, 123, 124, 125, 148, 166

grief at her mother's death 117–18, 135

health and mental state 117, 118–19, 123–4, 135, 138–9, 163, 195, 222, 231, 236, 238, 243–4, 252

events leading up to her disappearance 123–32

love of food, shopping and the good life 123, 149, 159, 199, 204, 245, 266–7, 268, 300, 311, 317–18, 320–1

media coverage of her disappearance 128–9, 133, 134, 137, 141, 142, 143–4, 145, 146–7, 148, 149–52, 153, 155

investigation and speculation concerning her disappearance 134–5, 136–40, 141–2, 143–7, 150–5

decides to become 'Mrs Teresa Neele of South Africa' 138–41

given sanctuary at Abney Hall by her sister Madge 156–60

negative publicity, speculation and portrayals 160–1, 235, 293, 297–8, 316

agrees to psychiatric treatment 162–5, 252

divorce from Archie 166–8

becomes an 'author-as-celebrity' 168–9

lasting impact of 1926 disappearance 169, 252, 297, 298

forms lasting friendship with Katharine Woolley 174–81

first encounter with archaeology and archaeologists 176–81

meets and marries Max Mallowan 182–3, 185–7, 188–96

correspondence with Max 186, 188–90, 191, 192, 193–4, 195–6, 200, 214, 236, 237–9, 241, 243–4, 245, 253, 299

agrees to take part in radio series 200–1

financial situation and tax demands 211, 222, 224, 226, 238–9, 252, 266, 270–1, 309–14

celebrates post-menopausal state 236

delighted at Max turning forty 240

delighted at birth of her grandson Mathew 241, 243

mistaken as the cook in Campden Street flat 243, 321

friendship with Stephen Glanville 244–9, 292

and death of Hubert Prichard 251

joins Max at Nimrud 272–9

passion for modern life 282–3

anti-Semitic and stereotypical views 283–5

method of work, plotting and keeping of notebooks 285–8, 322

awards and honours 297, 338

distaste for fame and publicity 298–300, 315–16

dismayed at use, in films, of her characters only 307–8

enjoys summers spent at Greenway 315–23

and development of Miss Marple 324–9

liking for nursery rhymes 328

declining years and possible onset of Alzheimers 330–4

celebrates her 80th birthday in London 338

final years and death at Winterbrook 339–47

legacy and reappraisal of 348–55

as playwright 110-11, 289–95, 300-1;, see also theatrical productions

social season in Egypt 36–8

writes her first full-length novel 38–41

works as a VAD and in the dispensary during the First World War 53–7, 67–8 produces spoof hospital magazine 58–9

pregnancy and birth of Rosalind 65, 84–6

use of poisons and opiates in her writings 68, 70, 95–6, 112

relationship with her sister Madge 109

suicidal thoughts 125, 126, 128–31, 137, 138, 166

writes distressing letter to Carlo 125, 126–7, 138

possibly suffers from dissociative fugue rather than 'memory loss' or 'nervous breakdown' 134–40, 144

writes backup letter to Campbell Christie 137–8, 145–6, 152

stays at the Hydropathic Hotel in Harrogate 139–40, 142–3, 144, 147–9, 151, 154–5

visits Iraq 174–8, 182–3

relationship with Max 188–9, 196, 236, 237, 240, 244, 246, 249, 299

writing spaces 199, 201

spends part of every year with Max in West Asia 201–6

suffers a miscarriage 202, 241

relationship with Rosalind 206–7, 210, 233–5

as a professional and successful writer 210–17, 288, 305–14

wartime publications 221–31, 236

works in hospital pharmacies during Second World War 221, 224–5, 229–30, 252, 255–6

stores manuscripts in bank vault for Rosalind and Max 224

profound sadness at leaving Greenway 238, 239

teases Max on his girlfriends and wives 244

writing as 'Mary Westmacott' 253–9

returns to Greenway after the war 264–9

post-war life and novels 280–5

tolerance of difference 322–3

upset at redevelopment of Ashfield 337

Christie, Archibald 'Archie'(AC's 1st husband)

birth, education and family background 44–5

character and description 44, 45, 81, 87, 117, 120–1, 186

meets and marries AC 44, 46–7, 51–3, 62–6

joins the Royal Flying Corps 51–3

sent to France 53, 60–1, 65–6

married life in London 79, 81, 82–3

returns from the War a hero 79

health of 83, 93

reaction to AC's pregnancy 84

unable to settle into life post-War 87

goes on nine-month British Empire exhibition mission 90–4

dislikes being AC's secretary 99

breakdown of his marriage to AC 101, 109, 110–11, 117–22, 123, 124, 125, 148, 166

supports AC in her writing career 101

life at Sunningdale 107–9

relationship with Nancy Neele 132–3

and AC's disappearance 133, 141, 142, 149–51, 154

takes AC to Abney Hall from Harrogate 156–60, 162

divorce from AC 166–8

marries Nancy Neele 173

meets and marries Max Mallowan 182–7

awards and honours 297

and death of Nancy Neele 301

correspondence and relationship with Rosalind 319

death of 319, 320

Christie, Archibald Snr (AC's father-in-law) 44–5

Christie Archive Trust 351

Christie, Beau (Archie's son) 173, 320

Christie, Campbell (AC's brother-in-law) 137–8, 145–6, 152, 320

Christie Copyrights Trust 313

Christie, Ellen Ruth Coates 'Peg' (AC's mother-in-law)

in India 44

and her husband's mental illness 45

believes Archie is too young to marry 47

relationship with AC 109

notices AC isn't wearing her wedding
ring 124

reaction to AC's disappearance 130, 132

Christie residences

Addison Mansions, Olympia 86–7

Campden Street, Kensington 199–200,
228, 243

Craven Gardens, Ealing 15–16

Cresswell Place, Chelsea 166, 173,
186–7, 199, 228

flat in Sunningdale, Berkshire 107–9,
113

Green Lodge, Sheffield Terrace
(Kensington) 203, 228

Kensington High Street 163

Lawn Road Flats (Isokon Building),
Belsize Park 221–2, 227–8, 229,
253–4, 255, 259, 263

Mayfair and St James's 209

Northwick Terrace, St John's Wood
79–83

The Styles, Sunningdale 115–18, 121–2,
123, 125–6, 133, 141, 148, 149, 166

Swan Court, Chelsea 271

Winterbrook, Wallingford
(Oxfordshire) 205, 228, 271, 339–42,
343–4

see also Ashfield House, Torquay;
Greenway, Devon

Christie, Rosalind see Hicks, Rosalind
(formerly Prichard née Christie)

Christie tricks

dislikes describing people or places 102

drawing room reveals 74

families not immediately apparent to
the eye 322

hidden couple 75

incorporating life into art 283

insertion of details from a real-life
crime 214

misleading implications 216

planting of clues 74, 215

recycling of plots 286–7

use of appearance to make an
assumption 102, 237

use of contemporary news story in a
plot 282–3

use of real places 264, 283

use of stereotypes 283–5

Churchill, Winston 175

Claflin, Mellon & Company 8, 20, 47

Clalridge's hotel 343

class 43, 97–8, 176, 189, 281

Clifton College, Bristol 45

Colville, Geoffrey 300

Compagnie Internationale des Wagons-
Lits 175

Connery, Sean 342

Continental Hotel, Cairo 236

Corbett, Miss (hotel entertainment
hostess) 143, 144

Core, Dr Donald Elms 163, 165

Cork, Edmund

appointed as AC's literary agent 100

fails to notice AC's state of mind 124

deals with AC's finances 222, 226, 252,
310–14, 341

asked by AC to make sure family
would have money in case of her
'sudden demise!' 224

explosion disrupts office life 225

informed of Rosalind's wedding 233

badgered by AC to have some articles
commissioned by the Saturday
Evening Post 236

moves 'Mary Westmacott' to
Heinemann 258

reaction to The Burden 259

engaged in AC's life at Greenway 266

helps Max get his magnum opus
published 278

defends AC in use of real events and
anti-Semitism 283–4

and staging of AC's plays 292

and AC's reluctance to promote herself
298

refutes belief that AC said
archaeologists make the best
husbands 298

concerned at AC's weight 299

prioritises film rights 306

given Power of Attorney by AC
309–10

persuades Collins to double AC's
advances 310

and AC's philosophical attitude towards comments 316
receives various epistolary rants 333
death of 349
Cotes, Peter 295
Country Life 208
Courcy, Anne de 234
Coward, Noël 292
Cowie, Miss (Harrogate librarian) 143
Crime Club News 217
Crispin, Edmund 268
Cross, Ernest 128–9
Čuček, Janez 316
Curran, John 285, 341

da Silva, Joyce 123, 124, 143
Daily Chronicle 146
Daily Express 144, 146–7, 173, 194, 291, 295
Daily Mail 99, 128, 137, 141, 142, 143–4, 145, 147, 149–50, 152, 153, 159, 160–1, 290, 298, 309
Daily News 143
Daily Sketch 142
Daily Telegraph 145, 151, 301
Damascus 175
Dane, Clemence 110
Delaney, Shelagh, *A Taste of Honey* 301
Detection Club 200
Dickens, Monica 257
Directorate of Allied and Foreign Liaison 227, 235
Doyle, Arthur Conan 69
Sherlock Holmes character 68, 71–2, 98
A Study in Scarlet 71–2
and AC's disappearance 152, 159
Du Maurier, Daphne 101, 226

Egypt 36–8, 215, 235–6
Eliot, T.S., *The Waste Land* 97
Enigma machine 229
Evening News 100, 150–1
Evening Standard 155

Ferry Cottage, Greenway (Devon) 223, 266, 320
Fido, Martin 257

Fields, Gracie 306
film productions 318, 330
And Then There Were None (1945) 292
Murder She Said (1961) 306–7
Murder Ahoy! (1964) 307
Murder on the Orient Express (1974) 308, 342–3, 349
Financial Times 314
Finney, Albert 342
First World War 47, 53–7, 60–1, 79–80, 83, 109, 112, 135, 184, 253
Fisher, Charlotte 'Carlotta' or 'Carlo' 119
friendship with Agatha 116–17, 234, 252, 316
finds Agatha missing from The Styles 122
enjoys dancing 124, 125
receives distressing letter from Agatha 126, 127, 138, 141
informs Archie of Agatha's disappearance 133
believes AC is alive 141
learns that Agatha has been found 154, 156, 158
takes Rosalind to Abney Hall 162
looks after AC's home in Chelsea 173
enables AC and Max Mallowan to marry in Scotland 193, 194
Ackerley's correspondence with 200
retires to Eastbourne 285
gifted money by AC 313
Fisher, Mary 116, 193, 194
Fleming, Ian 312
Flynn's Weekly 100
Forster, E.M., *A Room with a View* 37, 39
Fowles, John 280
Freud, Sigmund 164–5
Froude, Charlotte 14
Fuchs, Klaus 282

Garrod, Dorothy 179
General Strike (1926) 109
Gezireh Palace Hotel, Cairo 37, 39
Gielgud, John 342
Gill, Gillian 203, 299, 329, 354
Glanville, Ethel 245
Glanville, Stephen
as respected Egyptologist 227, 246

wartime work 227, 245
character and description 244–5
friendship with AC 245–9, 292
marriage and family 245, 249
as inspiration for two of AC's novels 246–9
takes a mistress, Margaret 248
Goddard, Superintendent Charles 133, 141–2, 146–7, 158
Good Housekeeping 98, 198
Goodwin, Richard 342
Gothenburg Trade and Shipping Journal 298
Gowler, George (butler at Greenway) 321
Grand Hotel, Torquay 17
Grand Magazine 100
Graves, Robert 354
Great War *see* First World War
Green, Anna Katharine, *The Leavenworth Case* 68, 74
Green, Julius 110, 291, 295
Greene, Graham 224, 228
Greenway, Dartmouth (Devon)
packed with possessions 14
bought by AC 208
Max and AC spend the 'Phoney War' period at 222–3
rented out during Second World War 225–6
AC hopes Rosalind will help her with 234
planting trees at 236
taken over by the Admiralty 238, 239
depicted in AC's fiction 264, 283
derequisitioned and renovated 264–9
taken over by the National Trust 265, 323
ritual of reading AC's latest book out loud 287–8
AC's birthday celebrations at 315
family and friends at 315–23
grows less important to AC 339
sale in 2006 of some of the contents 350
Gregg, Hubert 293, 300, 309
Griggs, Dixie 318
Guardian newspaper 100, 331
Guernsey, C.I. 21

Guildford, Surrey 131
Guyer, Miss Mary 31

Hack, Richard 153
Hallett, Christine 55
Hamilton, Robert 272, 273, 277
Hammersmith Palais 89
Hammett, Dashiell 281
Hamoudi, Hoja 179
Happy Hydro Boys (band group) 154
Harben, Philip 228
Harkup, Kathryn 68
Harris, Wilfred 144, 153, 165
Harrison Homes charity 313
Harrogate Hydropathic Hotel 138–40, 142–5, 148–9, 151, 154, 156–9, 316
Harrogate Royal Baths 138, 139, 147
Harrow School 22
Heinemann (publishers) 258
Helmsley, William 45
Hentschel, Irene 292
Herrmann, Georgina 319
Heyer, Georgette 299
Hicks, Anthony 268, 270, 312, 317, 319, 320, 349–50
Hicks, Rosalind (formerly Prichard née Christie)
birth of 65, 84–6
left with AC's sister Madge for nine months 92–3, 234
soft-focus photograph of 99
childhood 107, 109
character and description 109, 207, 233–4, 250
importance of 'Carlo' to 116
visits Peg near Dorking 124
memories of her reunion with AC at Abney Hall 162, 234
relationship with her father, Archie 166, 319–20
education 173, 201
ill with pneumonia 186
cautiously approves of AC's marriage to Max Mallowan 191–2
relationship with AC 206–7, 210, 233–5, 243, 333
sent to Paris and Munich 206–7
as debutante 207

lives at Greenway 223, 225

meets and marries Hubert de Burgh Prichard 232–3, 235

relationship with her step-father, Max 235, 237–8, 240, 241, 251

pregnancy and birth of her son Mathew 240–1

comment on *Death Comes as the End* 247

grief at death of Hubert 250–1

comment on the Westmacott novels 258

marries Anthony Hicks 267–8

given advice on health insurance 299

appointed director of Agatha Christie Limited 312

moves into Ferry Cottage 320

unhappy at AC's final play *Fiddler's Five* 332–3

decides to give Greenway to the National Trust 349–50

helps in licensing and looking after AC's estate 349

death of 351

agrees to controlled glimpse of AC's archive 352

states unequivocally that AC is an author 355

Hickson, Joan 293, 353

Hitler, Adolf 263, 331

Hodder & Stoughton 75

Holland House, Kensington 203

Holloway Sanitorium, Surrey 45

Honolulu 93

Horizon magazine 227

How to Be a Butler (booklet) 321

Howard, Esmé 184–5, 190, 193

Howarth, Janet 82

Hughes, Dorothy B. 258

Hughes Massie (literary agent) 100

Hull, E.M., *The Sheik* 178

Humble, Nicola 80–1, 281

Hurtmore Cottage, Godalming 132, 133

Hussein, Muzahim Mahmoud 274

Iles, Francis 285

Illustrated London News 179, 185, 205, 277

Imperial Chemical Industries (ICI) 272

Imperial and Foreign Investment Corporation 81

Imperial Hotel, Torquay 17

Inland Revenue 99, 313

Institute of Archaeology, University of London 270, 271, 318

Iraq 175–8, 195, 202–5, 270–1, 310

Iraq Petroleum Company 271–2, 276

Islamic State (IS) 278, 349

Isokon Building (Belsize Park) 227–8

ITV 353

James, Madge 132, 133, 148

James, Sam 132, 133, 148

Jersey, C.I. 10

Jessie (nursemaid at Addison Gardens) 86

Joannou, Maroula 98

Jordan, Dr Julius 204

Joyce, James, *Ulysses* 97, 98

Keating, Peter 212, 231, 325, 326

Kelly, Katherleen 223

Kenward, Superintendent William 126, 131–2, 133, 141–2, 145–6, 152, 153, 154, 158–9

Kenyon, Kathleen 270, 340

Kerner, Annette 'Mrs Sherlock Holmes' 213

Kirwan, Stella 285

Knox, Alfred Dillwyn 'Dilly' 229

Lancet 163

Lancing College, Sussex 184

Lane, Allen 271, 320

Lane, John 88–9, 94, 100

Langhammer, Claire 248

Larkin, Philip 67, 280

Laughton, Charles 291–2

Lavin, Frank (gardener at Greenway) 266

Layard, Sir Henry 271
    Nineveh and Its Remains 278

Le Carré, John 312

Lemming, Bob (musician) 154

Leroux, Gaston, *The Mystery of the Yellow Room* 68

Levin, Bernard 354

Lewis, Susan 14

Libya 240

Light, Alison 98, 198, 216, 292
    *Forever England: Femininity, Literature
    and Conservatism Between the Wars*
    354
Lilly (cook at The Styles) 125, 126
Lindbergh, Charles 214
Lloyd George, David 80
Lockwood, Margaret 300–1, 355
London Gazette 79
Lucy (maid at Addison Gardens) 86
Lucy, Marguerite 284
Lucy, Reggie 44, 46–7
Lumet, Sidney 342

McAdam, Ellen 318, 348
McAllister, Edward 129
MacDowell, Inspector 157
McEwan, Geraldine 353
McKenzie, Julia 353
Macmillan, Harold 327
MacPherson, Mrs 265–6
Makinen, Merja 217
Mallowan, Frederick (AC's father-in-law)
    183, 184, 189, 193, 223, 238
Mallowan, John (AC's nephew) 282, 317,
    319
Mallowan, Marguerite (AC's mother-in-
    law) 183–4, 193, 223, 238
Mallowan, Max (AC's 2nd husband)
    character and description 182, 189, 275,
        340
    meets and marries AC 182–3, 185–7,
        188–96
    birth, family background and
        education 183–4
    career in archaeology 184, 185, 186,
        192, 201–6, 271–9
    correspondence with AC 186, 188–90,
        191, 192, 193–4, 195–6, 200, 214,
        236, 237–9, 241, 243–4, 245, 253,
        287, 297, 299
    relationship with and marriage to AC
        188–9, 196, 236, 237, 240, 244,
        344–7
    depicted in AC's novels 215
    early War employment 223, 224
    wartime suspicions concerning his
        family 223

joins the RAF's Intelligence Branch
        226–7
    posted to Egypt and Libya 235–6,
        237–8, 240, 244
    relationship with Rosalind 235, 237–8,
        240, 241
    plants trees at Greenway 236
    asks AC about her financial affairs
        238–9
    concerns over Stephen Glanville's
        relationship with AC 246, 247
    comment on Anthony Hicks 268
    appointed Professor of Western Asiatic
        archaeology 270–1
    works at Nimrud in Iraq 270–1
    given a knighthood 318
    suffers a stroke 318
    tries to explain why AC wasn't a
        feminist 324
    and AC's final years and death at
        Winterbrook 339–40, 343–4
    takes up a position at All Souls'
        College, Oxford 340
    death of 346–7
    marries Barbara Parker 346
    Nimrud and Its Remains (1966) 278
Mallowan, Nan (AC's sister-in-law) 258,
    301
Maples, Angela *see* Prichard, Angela
    Maples
marriage and motherhood 85–6, 91, 92–3,
    110–11, 206–7, 234–5, 248
Marsh, Ngaio 89, 299
Marston, Sir Charles 203
Mary, Queen 293–4, 300
Mass Observation 229, 230
Metropolitan Museum, New York 275
MGM 308–9, 342
Miller, Agatha *see* Christie, Agatha
Miller, Clara Margaret Boehmer (AC's
    mother)
    character and influence 3–4, 6–7, 10,
        12, 70
    buys Ashfield 6, 10
    marriage to Frederick Miller 9, 10,
        11–12
    sent to live with Auntie-Grannie 11
    family finances and death of her

husband 20–4, 47
attitude towards education and
    marriage 29, 30–2
takes Agatha to Cairo for three months
    36–8
sends Agatha to house parties in search
    of a husband 42–3
at the birth of Rosalind 84–5
supports Agatha's decision to
    accompany Archie on his British
    Empire mission 92
death of 117
diamond ring found in old travelling
    trunk 350
Miller, Frederick Alvah (AC's father) 4
birth and family background 8–9
addicted to shopping 9, 14
character of 9
marriage to Clara Boehmer 9, 10,
    11–12
finds the gardener's body hanging from
    a rope 13
financial situation, illness and death
    20–3, 33
trains in the hospital pharmacy 57–9
Miller, Louis Montant 'Monty' (AC's
    brother)
birth of 10
character and description 21–2, 23
remains in Africa after the Boer War
    23, 111
education 30
problems with opiates 111–13
death of 113
Miller, Margaret Frary 'Madge' see Watts,
    Margaret Frary 'Madge' Miller
Miller, Margaret West ('Auntie-Grannie')
    69
relationship to Agatha 4
marries Nathaniel Miller 9
Madge named after 10
character of 15
life in Ealing 15–16
lives at Ashfield 58
at birth of Rosalind 85
as origin of Miss Marple 258, 325
Miller, Martha (or Minerva) (AC's
    paternal grandmother) 8

Miller, Nathaniel Alvah (AC's paternal
    grandfather) 8, 9, 20
Ministry of Information 224
Mitchell, Dorothy 223
Moorland Hotel, Haytor (Dartmoor) 73–4
Morgan, Janet 119, 163, 352
Morris, Eileen 58
Mortimer, Robert Cecil 252
Mountbatten, Lord Louis 342, 343

Nasser, Kheiriddin 279
National Trust 265, 323, 327, 350
Nazi Party 204
Neagle, Anna 289
Neele, Nancy 161, 320
press coverage of 120, 148
relationship with Archie Christie 120,
    132–3, 142, 166
depicted in the 1979 film Agatha 154,
    352
sent on a round-the-world cruise 162
marries Archie Christie 173
death of 301
AC's first public statement on 338
Netheravon, Wiltshire 51–2
New College, Oxford 184
New Statesman 98
New Woman 30–1, 36
New York 21
New York Times 160, 216, 332, 343
New Yorker 134
Newlands Corner, Surrey 125, 127–31,
    137, 142, 145
Nimrud (Kalhu), Iraq 270–1, 348–9
Nineveh 201
North, Dorothy 244
North, Susan 207
Novel Magazine 100
Nuffield Orthopaedic Centre 341

Oates, Joan 274, 275, 276
Ober, Harold 222, 278, 332
Observer newspaper 211
Olding, Dorothy 332, 341
Omar Khayyám 39
O'Neill, Dennis 283
opiates 57, 58–9, 68, 70, 95–6, 111, 112,
    330

Orient Express 174, 176, 321
Orwell, George 81–2
Outwitting Our Nerves (J.A. Jackson &
    H.M. Salisbury, 1921) 164

Paris 21, 32
Parker, Barbara 272–3, 278, 318, 343, 346
Penguin publishers 278, 288
Perkins, Edith 223
Peshawar 44
Peter (AC's dog) 117, 222, 316
Pharmaceutical Journal 95
Phelps, Sarah 353–4
Phillpotts, Eden 40–1, 73, 88, 99
Plunkett, Elizabeth 81
Poe, Edgar Allan 74
Pontecorvo, Bruno 282
Potter, Florence (cook at Ashfield) 207–8,
    316
Prichard, Angela Maples 320, 349
Prichard, Hubert de Burgh (AC's
    son-in-law)
  birth, family background and military
    career 232–3
  character and description 232
  meets and marries Rosalind Christie
    233, 235
  reaction to birth of his son Matthew
    241
  takes part in Normandy landings
    249–50
  death of 250–1
Prichard, Mathew Caradoc Thomas (AC's
    grandson)
  birth of 241
  relationship with AC 243, 256
  calls AC 'Nima' 250
  recalls life and rituals at Greenway 267,
    319
  likes his new stepfather 268
  and ritual of AC reading from her latest
    book 287–8
  trust set up from proceeds of a novel
    and play 312
  fails to meet his grandfather, Archie
    319
  marries Angela Maples 320
  moves to Pwllywrach 320, 349

  and death of AC 344
  AC's bequest of a Venetian glass fish to
    349
  agrees to give Greenway to the
    National Trust 350
Prichard, Rosalind *see* Hicks, Rosalind
    (formerly Prichard née Christie)
Priestley, J.B. 168
Prince of Wales Theatre, London 291
Pritchard, Jack 227
Pritchard, Molly 227
publications
  reviews and serialisations 95
  4.50 from Paddington (1957) 35, 80, 326
  The ABC Murders (1935) 203, 216, 247,
    284
  Absent in the Spring (1944) 255–6, 258,
    259
  'The Adventure of the Cheap Flat'
    (1923) 197
  After the Funeral (1953) 34
  And Then There Were None (1939)
    216–17
  At Bertram's Hotel (1965) 327, 332
  An Autobiography (1977) 3, 5–6, 119,
    121, 130–1, 204, 255, 278, 288,
    298–9, 337, 337–8, 351
  The Big Four (1927) 168
  The Body in the Library (1942) 17, 230,
    231, 326
  The Burden (1956) 259
  By the Pricking of My Thumb (1968) 287
  Cards on the Table (1936) 212
  A Caribbean Mystery (1964) 327
  Cat Among the Pigeons (1959) 330
  The Clocks (1963) 323
  Come, Tell Me How You Live (1946)
    207
  Crooked House (1949) 282, 286
  Curtain: Poirot's Last Case (1975) 224,
    343
  A Daughter's a Daughter (1952) 256–7
  Dead Man's Folly (1956) xii, 37–8, 283
  Death in the Clouds (1935) 112, 214, 215
  Death Comes as the End (1945) 246–8,
    249
  Death on the Nile (1937) 20, 197, 203,
    214, 215

Destination Unknown (1954) 282–3, 333–4

'The Disappearance of Mr Davenheim' 145

Elephants Can Remember (1972) 333

Endless Night (1967) 287

Endless Night (1967) 330–1

Evil under the Sun (1941) 16, 224, 231

Five Little Pigs (1942) 211, 230, 249, 255, 283, 288

Giant's Bread (1930) 54, 112, 164, 255, 259

Hickory Dickory Dock (1955) 285, 328

The Hollow (1946) 130, 255, 264, 283–4, 285

'The House of Beauty' 17

The Labours of Hercules (1947) 112

Lord Edgware Dies (1933) 43, 201–2, 322

The Man in the Brown Suit (1924) 92, 100, 254

The Mirror Crack'd from Side to Side (1962) 96, 283, 322, 327, 351

The Moving Finger (1943) 85, 230, 231

Mrs McGinty's Dead (1952) 328

The Murder at the Vicarage (1930) 97, 212, 213, 324

A Murder Is Announced (1950) 281, 283, 322, 328

Murder Is Easy (1939) 237, 282, 322, 325–6

The Murder on the Links (1923) 94, 99, 151, 162

Murder in Mesopotamia (1936) 112, 179, 189, 215–16

Murder on the Orient Express (1934) 43, 176–7, 203, 214

The Murder of Roger Ackroyd (1926) 103, 114–15, 116–17, 168, 177, 213, 230, 253, 286–7, 321, 331

The Mysterious Affair at Styles (1921) 68–71, 73–5, 88–9, 95, 96, 99, 334

The Mystery of the Blue Train (1928) 124, 168, 210, 284

N or M? (1941) 223, 224, 229, 230

Nemesis (1971) 327–8, 338

One, Two, Buckle My Shoe (1940) 225

Ordeal by Innocence (1958) 282, 284

Passenger to Frankfurt (1970) 331–2

Peril at End House (1932) 17

A Pocket Full of Rye (1952) 275, 288, 326, 328

Poirot Investigates (1924) 100

Poirot's Early Cases (1974) 343

Postern of Fate (1973) 341

The Rose and the Yew Tree (1947) 257, 258, 284

The Secret Adversary (1922) 91, 94, 98–9, 198

The Secret of Chimneys (1925) 101–3, 110, 178

The Seven Dials Mystery (1929) 168–9

The Sittaford Mystery (1931) 111, 197, 287, 315

Sleeping Murder (c.1942) 224, 231, 332

Sparkling Cyanide (1945) 244, 267

'The Sunningdale Mystery' 108

Taken at the Flood (1948) 280

They Came to Baghdad (1951) 273

They Do It with Mirrors (1952) 35, 312, 326

Third Girl (1966) 330

Three Act Tragedy (1935) 210–11

Towards Zero (1944) 43, 230

Unfinished Portrait (1934) 13, 167, 202, 254

Pugin, A.W.N. 34

Pwyllywrach manor house, Glamorgan (South Wales) 232, 235, 243, 250, 320, 349

'Queen Mary' (Max's lavender blue lorry) 204

Queer Women 58, 63, 72, 132, 316

racism 112, 206, 216

radio plays
And Then There Were None (1947) 292
Three Blind Mice (1947) 294

Ratcliffe, Jane 14

Reagan, Ronald 305–6

Red Cross 53

Redgrave, Vanessa 342

Representation of the People Act (1928) 167

Rhodes 202, 287

Robinson, Misses Olive and Gwen of Dartmouth (dressmakers) 300
Robson, Eleanor 271–2, 276, 278–9
Robyns, Gwen 153, 351–2
Roedean School, Brighton 30
Rowe, Jane 13, 14
Rowse, A.L. 320
Royal Air Force 61, 79, 81, 226–7, 272
Royal Field Artillery 45
Royal Flying Corps 45, 46, 51–3, 61
Royal Institution's Christmas lectures 246
Royal Magazine 100
Royal Military Academy, Woolwich 45
Rutherford, Margaret 306–7

St Cuthbert's, Edinburgh 194
St Mary's church, Cholsey 344
Sassoon, Siegfried 87
Saturday Evening Post 236
Saunders, Peter 289–90, 293, 294, 317, 349
Savoy Hotel, London 289, 290
Sayers, Dorothy L. 89, 101, 103, 152, 201, 299, 324
Scharnagl, Sabine 349
Second World War 221–31, 232, 235–6, 239–40, 241, 249, 263, 265, 273
servants 42
    average salary of a housemaid 24
    at Abney Hall 34, 321
    in fiction 37–8, 43, 70, 71, 326
    attitudes towards 70, 71, 86–7
    AC fantasises at being a parlourmaid 80
    at Addison Mansions 86
    at The Styles 124, 125, 126, 146, 152
    chambermaid at the Hydropathic Hotel 140, 142, 151
    theatrical impersonation by Madge 239
    AC mistaken as cook at Campden Street flat 243, 321
    at Greenway 321
    AC's wish for at Winterbrook 341
sex, sexuality
    AC notice's her sister Madge's sexual magnetism 30
    AC's attitude towards 36, 39, 64–5, 190, 193, 196, 202, 345
    illness associated with 45
    and living sexless lives 58
    in AC's fiction 75, 193, 211, 248, 257, 322, 328
    and the Woolleys 180
    and homosexuality 184–5, 301, 322, 328, 329
Shackle, Emma 319
Shebani (Monty's Black servant) 111
The Sketch 100, 107
Skye 193–4
Smart Set 108
Snowdon, Tony 341–2
South Africa 92
Spenser, Edmund 343
SS *Heliopolis* 36
SS *Kildonan Castle* 92
Stark, Freya 176, 180
Stern, Tom 206
Stewart, Faye 322
Stopes, Marie, *Married Love* 64–5
Stoppard, Tom 290–1
Story-Teller 100
Suchet, David 353
The Sunday Times 95, 258, 285
Surrey Advertiser 129, 141
Syria 205

Tappin, Bob (musician) 154
Tatler 232
Tattersall, Tessa 265
Taylor, Mr W. (hotel manager) 140, 144
Taylor, Mrs 144, 158
Tehran 318
television adaptations 330
    And Then There Were None (1949) 292
    And Then There Were None (2015) 353–4
    for CBS and NBC 305–6
    Hercule Poirot series 353
Tell Brak, Syria 206
Tey, Josephine 299
theatrical productions 349
    Alibi (reworking of *The Murder of Roger Ackroyd* but not by AC) (1928) 211, 291–2
    And Then There Were None (1943) 241, 243, 246, 292–3
    Appointment with Death (1945) 293

Black Coffee (1930) 200, 211
A Daughter's a Daughter (not performed) 257
Go Back for Murder (1960) 309
The Hollow (1951) 293
The Lie 110, 111
The Mousetrap (1952) 268, 283, 289–90, 293–4, 295–6, 300, 312, 322, 328, 348, 349
Murder at the Vicarage (1949) 348
Peril at End House (not adapted by AC) (1940) 295
Spider's Web (1954) 300–1
Ten Years 110–11
Three Blind Mice (radio play) (1947) 294
Verdict (1958) 301
Witness for the Prosecution (1953) 294–5, 296
Thompson, Laura 353
Thompson, Reginald Campbell 201
Tierney, Gene 283
The Times 79–80, 91, 95, 112, 146, 148, 151, 157, 327
The Times Literary Supplement 95
Torbay Hospital, Torquay 54, 224–5
Torquay 10, 16–17
Torquay Pavilion Theatre 46
Torquay Times 113
Trenchard, Hugh 60–1

Ugbrooke House, Devon 44
UNESCO 278, 310, 313
University College Hospital, Gower Street (London) 221, 229–30, 252, 255–6
unpublished works
  'The A.A. Alphabet for 1915' (verse) 63
  Eugenia and Eugenics 43
  'In a Dispensary' (verse) 67
  Snow upon The Desert 38–40
Upp, Hannah 134
Ur 175–9, 186, 195
US Coast Guard 265
US Copyright Agency 258

Vanity Fair magazine 30, 38
Vautour, Doreen 226
Vogue magazine 98

Voluntary Aid Detachment (VAD) 53–6

Waldorf Hotel, New York 21
Wallace, Edgar 153
Washington Post 161
Watts, Sir James 34
Watts, James (AC's brother-in-law) 33–5, 159, 160
Watts, James 'Jack' (AC's nephew) 190, 257, 301, 320
Watts, Margaret 'Madge' Miller (AC's elder sister)
  named after Auntie-Granny 10
  as talented actress and author 18, 30, 38, 110, 239
  received by Caroline Astor in New York 21
  marriage 23, 30, 33–4, 35
  education 30
  looks after Rosalind whilst AC is on British Empire mission 92–3
  relationship with AC 109
  The Claimant 110
  helps Monty to buy a property on Dartmoor 111–12
  provides refuge for AC after she is found in Harrogate 159–60, 162
  insists AC receive psychiatric treatment 163
  uncertain about AC's marriage to Max Mallowan 191, 193
  introduces Hubert de Burgh Prichard to Rosalind 233
  wartime life at Abney Hall 239–40
  copes with loss of servants post-war 281, 321
  death of 301
Waugh, Evelyn 285
  Brideshead Revisited 184, 185
Wembley Exhibition (1924) 90
West, Margaret *see* Miller, Margaret West
Westmacott, Mary (aka Agatha Christie) 40, 253–9
Westminster Gazette 145, 148
Wheeler, Sir Mortimer 299
Whipple, Dorothy 257
Whiteley, Albert (musician) 154
William Collins, Sons (publishers) 100,

101, 115, 169, 210, 217, 257, 258, 273, 298, 312, 338

Wilson, Edmund 247, 354

Wodehouse, P.G., *The Inimitable Jeeves* 101

Woman and Home magazine 198

Woods, Mrs 79, 80

Woolf, Virginia 81, 97–8, 203, 276

Woolley, Charles Leonard 178, 179, 180, 185, 192

Woolley, Katharine (formerly Keeling née Menke)
  forms lifetime friendship with AC 176–81

character and description 179–81, 185

early life and marriages 179

as troubled character in *Murder in Mesopotamia* 179, 181

relationship with Max Mallowan 185–6

mildly surprised at Max Mallowan and AC's marriage 192

Adventure Calls (1929) 181

Ziegler, Philip 298, 321

Picture Acknowledgements

Many of the photographs are reproduced with the kind permission of the estate of Agatha Christie. © Christie Archive Trust 2022.

Additional sources:
Alamy Stock Photo: 12 below/Picturelux/The Hollywood Archive, 14 below left/Pictorial Press Ltd, text Part Seven/Interphoto, text Part Eight/Trinity Mirror/Mirrorpix, text Part Ten/Keystone Press.
AP/Shutterstock: text Part Six. Bridgeman Images: text Part Five. © The Trustees of the British Museum: 10 above left and centre right. Courtesy of Caroline Christie: 8 below right. Mary Evans Picture Library:
14 centre right/image courtesy Ronald Grant Archive.
Popperfoto/Getty Images: 14 above left, 15 centre right. © Photograph by Snowdon/Trunk Archive: 16. Lucy Worsley: 8 above right, 15 above left.